INTRODUCT
TO
MAGIC

VOLUME III

"Those who look to Julius Evola's work for guidance have often wondered what practices Evola himself used to get in contact with Tradition. The answer lies in *Introduction to Magic,* which represents the records left behind by the UR Group, the mysterious occult order that was the medium through which Evola first experienced the reality of Tradition and grasped its essence. Many of the themes and concepts which were to recur in Evola's later work are already present in these documents. The great importance Evola attached to these volumes is attested by the belief of Evola's biographer that the original manuscripts were the only belongings he took with him when he was forced to flee Rome in 1944. The fact that this work is finally available in its entirety to Anglophone readers, masterfully translated by Joscelyn Godwin, is therefore a great service to genuine spiritual seekers everywhere."

JOHN MORGAN, FORMER EDITOR IN CHIEF
OF ARKTOS MEDIA

"I am impressed by this fine translation of some of my old mentor Julius Evola's works. I find that 'Aristocracy and the Initiatic Ideal' conveys very well the baron's own beliefs and sentiments as to what it means today to be a true aristocrat among the ruins. Exceedingly insightful comments, as one would indeed expect. A truly excellent publication."

FATHER FRANK GELLI, AUTHOR OF
JULIUS EVOLA: THE SUFI OF ROME

INTRODUCTION
TO
MAGIC

VOLUME III

Realizations of the
Absolute Individual

JULIUS EVOLA
AND THE UR GROUP

TRANSLATED BY JOSCELYN GODWIN

Inner Traditions
Rochester, Vermont

Inner Traditions
One Park Street
Rochester, Vermont 05767
www.InnerTraditions.com

Certified Sourcing
www.sfiprogram.org
SFI-00854

Text stock is SFI certified

Originally published in Italian under the title *Introduzione alla Magia,
Volume Terzo* by Edizioni Mediterranee, Via Flaminia 109-00196 Rome
First U.S. edition published in 2021 by Inner Traditions

Cataloging-in-Publication Data for this title is available from the Library of Congress

ISBN 978-1-62055-719-8 (print)
ISBN 978-1-62055-720-4 (ebook)

Printed and bound in the United States by Lake Book Manufacturing, Inc.
The text stock is SFI certified. The Sustainable Forestry Initiative® program
promotes sustainable forest management.

10 9 8 7 6 5 4 3 2 1

Text design and layout by Debbie Glogover
This book was typeset in Garamond Premier Pro with Gill Sans and Weiss used as
display typefaces

Contents

PART III

PART IV

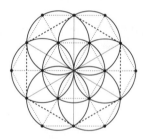

Introduction to
the Third Volume

This third volume continues and concludes the exposition of traditional, esoteric, and magical doctrines that was begun in the two preceding ones.

It offers further details and directions concerning practice, orientation, experimentation, and doctrine, and further texts, either translated or reproduced. It reports the views of known and qualified exponents of our disciplines, which we explain in relation to other fields of spirituality or knowledge, such as mysticism, "depth psychology," and metaphysics. We also continue to treat symbolism, and to recall some of the past expressions of Tradition, from Hyperborean prehistory up to the Roman and medieval eras.

This volume also contains a wider variety of practical instructions. Besides enriching the general perspective, they are aimed at the interests and dispositions of individual readers. But they maintain the essential unity of our instructive method, which is that of an active, lucid, and "magical" approach to the suprasensible[1] and the transcendent.

---

1. [Italian *soprasensibile*. As with *sopranaturale,* here rendered as "supranatural" rather than "supernatural," I avoid the tendency, both in Italian and English, to use the prefix *super* merely as an intensifier, rather than with its correct meaning of "above." —*Trans.*]

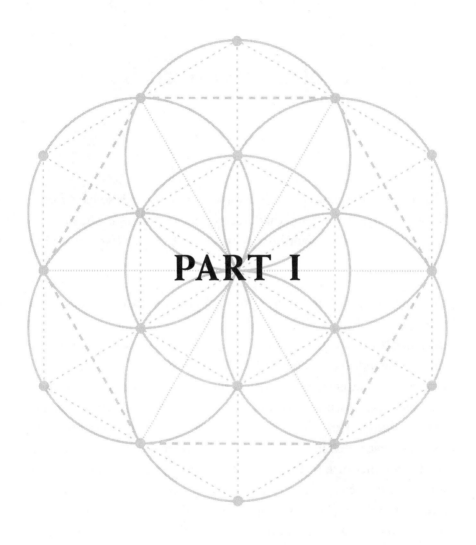

PART I

Paths of the Western Spirit

There have been few epochs like today's, in which it is so hard for the West to find an orientation that exactly suits its tradition. The situation is mainly due to an extraordinary option to which the West has limited itself.

On the one hand, we see in today's West a world of achievements that have developed under the signs of clear vision (science) and precise action (technology)—but a world devoid of light. Its law is that of an uncentered movement, its limit is matter and the call of matter. On the other hand, there arises an impulse toward something higher—but an impulse that emerges in various forms of escapism and regression. Consequently, when the West affirms the active and realistic principle of its tradition, there is no spirit there; and when it aspires to the spirit, that principle is no longer present, giving way to its opposite. This takes the form either of humanitarian, christianizing, democratic, and universalist tendencies, or else of the neospiritualist currents often associated with irrationalism, the religion of the life force, or theories of the unconscious: a confused world in stark contradiction to the virile spirit of the West.

This state of affairs has given rise to a sort of dilemma. The first step is to understand it. But salvation could only come from eliminating that option altogether.

The spiritualist reaction to the materialism of the modern world certainly has its virtue, but not in its blanket rejection of some very disparate things, ignoring the fundamental principles that stand at the basis of the Western experience, despite their currently degraded and materialistic forms. The modern, realistic world is intensely Western in spirit. Admittedly, it has produced the Ahrimanic regime of the machine, of finance, of quantification, of the steel and concrete metropolis, devoid of any contact with transcendence and extinguishing any sense of the invisible and living forces of things. Yet throughout all this the Western soul has maintained a "style," whose value is discernable if one can look beyond the purely material plane and its forms of realization.

It is the attitude of *science,* as experimental, positive, and methodical knowledge—instead of any instinctive intuitionism, any irrationalism, any tendency toward the indeterminate and the "mystical."

It is the attitude of *technology,* as the exact knowledge of obligatory laws in the service of action, whereby given certain causes, certain effects follow that are predictable and determined without the intrusion of irrational and emotional elements.

Last it is the value of the *personality,* capable of an active initiative, aimed at autonomy.

An impulse is at work in these Western endeavors, albeit in very variable aspects and degrees, following these fundamental directions. The mistake has been in confusing them with the materialism of many of the results to which they have given rise. Thus, every reaction to materialism and every desire to overcome it has since been accompanied by a denial of the Western spirit, a gradual evasion of the Western law of realism, action, and personality. Hence today's neospiritualism, even when it preserves something authentically spiritual, should always be considered as a *danger* and a degenerative element with respect to the deepest core of our tradition.

The forms of this spiritualism have developed considerably after the First and Second World Wars. There are the movements that adapt poorly understood Eastern doctrines to the worst Western prejudices; there is the morbid interest in problems of the subconscious (psychoanalysis), and worse yet, in mediumism and "parapsychology"; there is the path of "return" to the most decrepit Christianity, due to an inner alienation and capitulation; and the various aspects of a new cult of

"Life," more or less pantheistic and promiscuous. No matter how much these forms may differ from one another, they all have the same significance, reflecting a climate of escapism, impatience, and exhaustion. It is the soul of the West that is tottering and crumbling. It can only be glimpsed in the world shut off from below: behind the lords of mathematics, chaining or unchaining the forces of matter; the finance and industry that gives laws to nations and governments; the machines in which every day a purblind heroism hurls itself through sky and ocean.

The lack of any impulse whereby the living values on this plane can escape, reaffirm themselves, and integrate themselves into a higher order—the lack of such an impulse in the modern West is its bondage, the cause of its petrification and decadence. The Western tradition will not revive until a new civilization, no longer bewitched by material reality, asserts a style of clarity, of absolute action and true personality, beyond the "spiritualist" miasma and all those other forms of escapism and dissolution. And because of the analogy of such a style with the special significance we have given to the terms "magic" and the "magical vision of the world," we can say this: it is through a *magical epoch* that the West will eventually be able to cut the knot of the "dark age"—the Kali Yuga, the Age of Iron. It will be no mere alteration: in an epoch of active realism, transcendent and intensely individual, the new traditional form that the West will make its own will arise from the spirit of its most ancient tradition: from the ancient Arctic-Atlantic spirit, the light that descended from North to South, then passed from West to East, everywhere bearing the signs of a cosmic symbolism beside the legacy of heroic, active, and conquering races.

We can name specific themes: beyond the world of the One, its articulation in a plurality of gods and heroes, on upward and downward paths; "mortal immortals, immortal mortals," in Heraclitean and Hermetic terms; an end to nostalgia, to pacifism and passivity, to looking up to the "Mothers"; an end to all cloudy intoxication, rejection of all confused ecstasy and subpersonal demonism; a sense of *being* and *advancing,* gazing straight ahead like one forging new paths and new passes, or who draws and defends new frontiers to his domain, where others fail or fall short. In a magical epoch, such meanings are reaffirmed through the very contact with the suprasensible. And for the West, we are basically speaking of themes recurring in one form or another throughout its history: of the spirit of world conquest by white Europe, and further back, through the epics of chivalry and crusade to the purest forms of its spirit: Roman and Aryo-Mediterranean, Doric-Achaean and Homeric; and earlier still, to the echoes of the primordial white seafarers and conquerors—those of the "strange great ships," of the signs of the Ax and the "solar Man with uplifted arms"—coming down from their Arctic homelands to the centers of the first traditional civilization of the West.

The problem is in seeing how far contacts can be renewed in this direction. Among the great shadows, on the shaky ground and beneath the Ahrimanic glare of the modern world, this must be the reference point for freeing the West without denaturing it. Beyond both materialistic activism and the "spiritualist" peril, this must be the direction for the corrective and life-giving action of those called to spiritual leadership, for the "defense of the West."

ABRAXA

The Cloud and the Stone

The symbols of our Science, which is also an Art, contain not only possibilities of intellectual realization but also elements of *actions*—secret paths of power by means of the mental Fire awakened in the sacred Work.

In the medieval writings of this tradition, you will have found recurrent themes such as FIRE AROUND THE BLACK STONE or CLOUD WHICH ARISES FROM IT.

You may smile at those who imagine common chemical operations here—combustions and vapors emitted by the heating of certain *dead* substances—if you know that the "Stone" is the animal body, the "Cloud" the subtle body, and the "Fire" something difficult to understand by one who has never kindled it. But even if you already know this, be assured that you are still a long way from the ritual realization of the *power* of the formula.

I will now instruct you on this.

First and foremost, you must *know* the separate elements through preparation, "confection," and in practice: they are the *black Stone* and the *Fire.* As for the third, which is the *Cloud,* the very act of the Ritual is intended to give you the experience of it.

You know that our laboratory is the body: this "vessel," eight spans tall, comprises the elements, the origin of the elements, their life and their resolution on either upward or downward paths, according to the Action and the Ritual.

Like one who unravels something that was intertwined, and once its parts are separated, distinguishes, knows, and replaces them piece by piece—just so, with the subtle spagyric art, while enclosed in your form, amalgamated with your substance, frozen in magical equilibrium, you will separate and extract from your "compound" the elements needed for the operation.

(KNOWLEDGE OF THE STONE)

This has already been mentioned to you more than once. Supine position, strictly horizontal, immobile: like someone who has been knocked to the ground by a mortal blow, in symbolic-magical analogy to the condition of radical passivity that precedes the *living resurrection.*

Immobilization of thought. Extinction of the specialized sensations of the various organs, functions, and sensory centers.[1]

Having reached the state of "silence"—undifferentiated calm, interiority reposing in itself—acting in a subtle and gentle way, you cause a somehow *imponderable* sensation of your immobile body to emerge.

Hold onto the state that ensues: imprint it exactly on your consciousness.

Then add Saturn to Mercury—in other words, *with an instantaneous mental act, realize the image-sensation of yourself as a* SKELETON: reduce yourself to naked bones, empty, fleshless, lifeless. And remain firm and fearless in your mind.

The transfomation is: *blacker than black, mortal* ice, petrification of minerality.

It is the *lapis niger* [black stone]. Take possession of it.

If apparitions arise—kill them: detaching your attention from them

---

1. With reservations similar to what Abraxa will say about "concentration," one should not expect that if certain actions can be described in a few lines, their realization will be equally rapid. It may be necessary to persist *for hours* in immobility, with tenacious and calm *patience:* in a state of mind like someone in a situation from which he is powerless to exit, resigned and quietly waiting for thought to exhaust itself and cease, and with it every reaction and sensation of the physical body. (Note by UR)

and holding it firm in silent identification; centered, profound, hieratic in the resultant state.

(KNOWLEDGE OF THE FIRE)

Bring yourself back to the "silence." But now with an intensely vitalized attitude, with a warm, fervid attention that runs through the body, that is felt and collected in the body. Not conscious concentration, but an *intense, ardent* concentration.

As though completely absorbed with vibrant enthusiasm in some work or thought, in which "your whole soul is plunged"—but here with no thought, no object,[2] or if you prefer: with its sole object being this absorption itself, this growing attention, intensive deepening, will-life-ardor, which without losing active concentration thrusts into ever deeper strata of the substance made from the general sensation of the body.

All this, in immobility. As you know, there should be no "strain": if you touched the coarse, physical fabric of the body, stopping the energies, all would be in vain. In this desire of holding and conjoining with oneself—like water immersed in water—think of an enfolding, a cooking, nourishing, hatching—an "enveloping, feverish heat" (I would even say *passionate*) is the indication that a text has already given you.[3]

If you can work thus, you will notice at a certain moment and in a distinct form *a special state of warmth diffused through the body,* no ordinary warmth but a strange, living, and *vibrant* one.

Uniting yourself directly with it—now that you are able—*increase it.*

Then let the perception of the body fall away, concentrating only on the state. Close and fix it.

Thus, you have the second element.

---

2. Alternatively, begin by taking an object, image, or thought which one considers suitable for arousing and vitalizing the relevant state. Then abstract yourself from the object, to concentrate and operate solely on the state itself. (Note by UR)

3. The *Turba Philosophorum*, a Hermetic text translated in *Introduction to Magic,* vol. II, essay VIII.3. The expression is found on page 278. (Note by UR)

(THE RITUAL SYNTHESIS)

Always keep in mind what I have told you about the magic of the image (*Introduction to Magic,* vol. I, 266–72): it asks you to learn how to amalgamate an image with a state—to *project* an image that is at the same time *the presence of a state.*[4] Otherwise the creative spark for any Hermetic operation will be lacking.

I have told you about the preparation of the Stone and the Fire. Through tenacious and *long* practice, you know that "all haste is from the Devil"—just as the uncertain and difficult attempt becomes with practice an ability, an automatism instantly obedient to the will—thus too your spirit must have in its power the states corresponding to these two symbols: like a precise memory or a notion once acquired and understood which you can recall at will. *It is a matter of linking these states with the effective images of Stone and Fire*—but do not proceed to the operative synthesis before you are entirely secure in possession of what I have now told you.

If you also want to operate with ritual arrangements, remember what you were told concerning the work with the Mirror (*Introduction to Magic,* vol. I, 72–78). Send yourself back into the "Silence." Once released, remain there. Calm. No worry, no thought anticipating what you are to do. Suddenly, like a scene illuminated by a flash of lightning and returning to the dark, the mind will REALIZE the vision: *Stone—Fire that strikes the Stone—white Cloud that frees itself and ascends.*[5]

If the projection is *accurate* in its direction, sufficient in its energy, and *animated* (the states of visualizing Fire and Stone that you have prepared and mastered must burn *intensely*), then the complete detachment may occur, *the transference into the magical body.*

---

4. To understand what is involved, think of certain images of things strongly experienced, which cannot be evoked without being straightway seized by a corresponding emotion. (Note by UR)

5. Beside the method of "projection" indicated by Abraxa, we may mention another method that is not instantaneous but uses a "magnetic," prolonged, and progressive contemplation of the image. (Note by UR)

This is a powerful ritual. It is not free of dangers for someone wanting in firmness of mind, rapidity in the restraint and destruction of every instinctive and instant reaction of the psychic entity. In case of difficulty in regaining control of the physical body, recall what I have told you about doubling (*Introduction to Magic,* vol. I, 218–27).

The ritual is powerful, but the soul of this power, its key, lever, and unique instrument of awakening, is *concentration.*

I say it again, to avoid misunderstandings about what has been communicated in these pages. Some may be deluding themselves about the presumed virtues of some neat formula or "secret" when thought is habitually wandering, absentminded, flitting, abstracted, or discontinuous. *Before undertaking any work, you must be able to achieve* ABSOLUTE CONCENTRATION. That means: I think the object, I think of the object, I think about the object, I live the object, neither "I" nor any other exists, but the object *stands* steady, unique, isolated at the center of the mental fire: just as the arrow once shot and deeply embedded moves no more—like the solid rock unmoved by the gusts of wind—*thus the single object subsists in the "void" of the mind.*

It matters not whether this takes you months or years. If you lack the strength, or if this condition seems too hard for you, consider what other excellent things in human life you can direct your action to, besides Magic.

(SATURNIAN FIRE)

Many means are known for lighting the Hermetic and philosophic Fire. Reviewing what I and others have said previously, you will be able to find elements of instruction, and choose from them. The following law will furnish you with one more:

Each time a wish is translated into a physical movement, an apparition of the Fire is produced in the substance of the subtle body.

Depending on how far you have come, you will see how you can make use of this knowledge.

The Fires or Sulfurs that you can master by this means are of a very precious quality. They are the so-called *Sulfurs of Saturn,* also known as *metallic.*

The present essay by Abraxa can be recommended to those who may have organized a "chain," as an instrument to be substituted in a later phase for that of simple silence in the individual discipline. On this, see Introduction to Magic, *vol. II, 42–52.*

I.3

BRENO

Modern Initiation and Eastern Initiation

1. In these notes I will treat briefly the following problem: Does a *specifically Western initiation* exist, distinct from Eastern initiation? If so, what is the difference? And does it affect the path? Or is the *goal* different, too?

The importance of the problem is due to the many Eastern teachings of an initiatic nature (yoga, etc.) that have become widespread in the West. Those who not only know of them but intend to put them into practice often ask whether such methods can bear fruit in today's Western world, and whether they have the same results.

It is not hard to see that the problem hinges on whether the constitution of today's Westerner, with regard to initiatic methods, is the same as that of the Easterner for whom they were intended. If the answer is no, there are only two solutions: either the Westerner must bring himself into the condition of the Easterner, or he must investigate the possibility of a different method, suitable to the Westerner, which would be none other than *Western initiation*.

2. There is no doubt that both now and in the past East and West have had a different orientation, not only as civilizations but also in their assumptions about experiencing suprasensible reality. This, however, does not prevent the contents from being the same from a higher point

of view; for in its supreme achievement, initiation allows no divergence; it transcends differences of race, civilization, and tradition. At that level it makes no sense to speak of a "Western initiation" as something specific. The adepts of every land and every tradition form a single chain— the chain of the "Living"—using the same words, possessing the same wisdom.

It is on the technical level that one may, and even must, speak of differences. But on this level it is necessary to refer to a more general antithesis: that which divides ancient man (whether of East or West) from modern man. *As far as initiation is concerned, the constitutions of ancient Western man and Eastern man are not noticeably different; but there is a difference between modern man and ancient man in general.* And the terms East and West only enter into this distinction inasmuch as Western man today specifically incarnates the "modern" type, whereas even in our day, the Eastern man often preserves more or less of the structure of ancient man.

3. We now recall what I have said about the types of consciousness that correspond to the three seats of the human body (*Introduction to Magic*, vol. II, 360–66). When the consciousness of the higher seat dominates, conscious and logical thought results; one has the distinct and objective experience of physical reality that is common to everyone today, and there is an accentuation of the sense of what could be called the physical, individual I. But historically, all this has a relatively recent origin.

Comparative philosophy tells that the first efforts of logical and speculative reflection appeared almost simultaneously in the West (Greece), in India, and in China, no earlier than the sixth century BC.[1] Around the same epoch there arose on the one hand a physical conception of nature in place of a symbolic conception of it, and, on the other, the first stirrings of individualism, anti-traditionalism, and the critical spirit. In the East, these tendencies had a limited development or were absorbed and framed by forms of the more ancient spirit, whereas in the West they found fertile ground, and gradually went on to construct

---

1. P. Masson-Oursel, *La philosophie comparée* (Paris, 1923), 84–85.

what we may call the modern European spirit. In this way modern man now sees and perceives in an utterly different mode from ancient man, without even wanting to do so. We are dealing, in fact, with a condition based on his occult constitution: *a new consciousness fixed in the higher seat is opposed to a consciousness that mainly belonged to the "median man."* The latter consciousness was still open or half-open to receive communications, points of non-difference, contacts; hence the fringes of a psychic perception, taking the form of "reflections" unburdened by the yoke of cerebral control, together with a special sensation of the body and its functions that was simultaneously physical and "subtle."

These are the implicit presuppositions of most Eastern techniques. The fluctuation that has recently arisen between the state of the higher seat and that of the median seat tends to be resolved by Eastern initiation in favor of the latter. It can speak of the "I" as a shell to be broken, because it has a barely veiled sensation of the true "I," which it is ridiculous to call "mine": the supramental Self that is the true center and light. Thus, there is less danger that by "opening up," one might dissolve and lose oneself. It is also significant that in the Eastern texts it is very rare to find references to what Western mystics called the "dark night of the soul" and the Hermetists the "black work." It is as though for that human type, this change of state, essential to every form of initiation, does not assume the character of a profound crisis.

4. The situation is different with the average modern Western man. First, there is the case of one who has thoroughly adopted the mode of being connected to the upper seat. It will be difficult for him to take advantage of Eastern-type practices; used to feeling himself rigidly as "I," with a logical mind, critical sense, and clear but crudely physical perception, he will find a sort of barrier in himself, preventing him from *realizing* certain teachings or from creating the necessary inner conditions on which many Eastern techniques work. As he advances a little, he finds his *sleep* disturbed—an unconscious sleep, or with dreams caused by subjective residues and organic repercussions—sleep being the natural state that mostly occurs today when the psychisms of the higher seat cease and the center of one's being moves into the

median seat. This is why ancient traditions in which sleep figured as a condition favoring suprasensible knowledge[2] seem incomprehensible or fantastic today. There is an essential difference between what happens to ancient and to modern man when they fall asleep, because the habitual point of support of consciousness differs between them.

But we must also consider the case of those modern men who are only incompletely thus, such that the consciousness of the upper seat is not altogether stabilized. Ancient or Eastern methods may often work for them and produce a transference, accompanied by consciousness, to the median seat. Yet the result will often be *disintegrating* and *involutive* regarding everything that is their principle, "I," clarity, discriminative faculty, and sense of reality. Instead of reaching the light, they are in danger of falling into semi-mediumistic and visionary states and being subject to the phenomena of a chaotic and uncontrolled psychism.

A noted writer on esoteric matters has emphasized the fact that most cultivated, active, and clear-minded people today feel an instinctive revulsion for everything to do with suprasensible reality, whereas this order of things chiefly attracts people of weak critical capacity, with a minimum faculty of judgment and true awareness, and quite often women. This author has indicated a *positive,* constitutional reason for this. The aversion of the former type is only an unconscious defense against a danger darkly sensed by their "physical I." In the latter, this "I" does not have a strong enough sense of self-preservation to react and resist it.

5. During the intermediate period before modern civilization, two tendencies predominated in the West: the *devotional* and the *magical.* This also had its reasons. Both tendencies allowed for relations with the suprasensible world, while still allowing one to preserve the sense of one's own personality.

---

2. Heraclitus said that in sleep "man kindles a light for himself in the night" (frag. 26) and shares in the activities going on in the universe (frag. 75). In Pindar (frag. 131) and in Aeschylus (frag. 104 and 105) the same teaching recurs: the "eye of the soul" which opens in the night is opposed to that of the body, to which daytime vision belongs.

The relation between creator and created, basic to all devotion, implies a dualism that, while reconciling the devotee with the divine, allows him the sense of being a distinct principle and restrains him from venturing on the dangerous path toward the formless. We may conclude that the reasons for Catholicism's violent negation of all pantheism and extreme mysticism are not so much doctrinal as practical and pragmatic, even when those who held such an attitude were ignorant of the fact.

Also in magic (here meaning the ceremonial kind), the operator, by assuming a relationship of command, can maintain himself before the forces that he evokes and which project themselves, in his experience, in beings and forms that take on an objective appearance. Thus, the possibility remains of affirmation and non-identification.

However, both cases—devotion and ceremonial magic—still deal with intermediate forms. For protecting the person, both paths have set a limit to realization, thereby often compromising by exteriorization and dualism the transparency of the suprasensible experience. As time went on, even these forms have been left behind.

6. The problem therefore remains of Western initiation, or rather the initiatic method suited to Western man as a modern man. Technically, the instruction *visita interiora terrae* (visit the interior of the earth), that is, the assumption of the median seat, is the fundamental procedure in every case. *But the transfer, today, should not occur before a "quintessence" has been extracted from the consciousness of the upper seat,* or a principle that contains all its properties in a "subtle" form, so that one can maintain it while approaching the condition of the median seat. The fundamental difference between ancient or Eastern practice and that which suits modern man is that in the former, it was a matter of denuding the Gold, whereas in the latter it must be *fabricated.* We have described what usually happens to a normal man of today if this descent occurs while the quintessence is lacking: he either falls into the "mystical" forms of the confused visionary, or upon attaining the "light of nature" the personality is not sustained; it loosens and disintegrates, and he falls into a state of passive, ecstatic contemplation.

However, when this quintessence is present, the consciousness of the median seat undergoes a transformation upon contact with it. Just as one drop of a chemical reagent can suddenly make an opaque solution clear and limpid, here a light is produced that clears the "median region" of all cloudiness and permits a lucid, sharp, and certain vision of spiritual reality, comparable to what today's science has won over physical nature and mathematical entities. "Our Gold" in fact contains the most potent exorcism against the demons and phantasms of the median seat.[3] Moreover, the final stage of the experience also acquires a special significance thereby: the suprasensible intellectual essences, instead of being suspended in the aether of pure contemplation, become *energized*—one might even say *electricized*. This is the effect of the power of the "mind" principle, the quintessence extracted from the very elements offered by the modern spirit when it is clear, active, and individuated.

7. On this basis it is understandable why certain methods of initiation are too "dry" to be recommended to the man of today: those which suddenly suspend all the faculties of the upper seat, and "open up." This is an adventure that a differently constituted human type might undertake, because his consciousness had sufficiently firm support in other seats. But already in the Mediterranean mysteries there were hierophants and assistants present to "support" the initiate's consciousness at the moment when the ground vanished from under his feet. Without a doubt, the difficulty of detachment and the danger of the sudden wrench are greater today, while the possibility of such assistance is almost entirely absent, and virtually no organized initiatic centers exist.

For this reason, a modern man should use a method whose point of departure is instead the faculty of wakefulness in the upper center, to be maintained as the basis for the sense of self, and submitted to a certain work of liberation. This work is long, demanding unbroken constancy and control and a gradual illumination; yet it is a work that

---

3. One could describe this as a *destruction of the Unconscious,* as opposed to superstitiously setting it up as an entity in itself, to be "scientifically" explored, which is the error of modern psychoanalysis. (Note by UR)

anyone can do for himself, for the most part, given that for a long time he will not encounter obscure zones where it is uncertain whether or not his feet will find firm ground. Another important characteristic of this method is that due to its strong basis, once contact is achieved, *the forms of higher consciousness can be made to act permanently within waking consciousness*—they are not limited to separate experiences, nor in principle do they require abnormal states of the human being. Every other method, in contrast, brings the danger of reducing the whole experience to fleeting glimpses unable to provide *mastery,* and whose effect on many people is probably little different from that of certain drugs.

With reference to the theory of the occult "centers" of the body, some are of the opinion that the Western method differs from the Eastern in that the latter awakens the lower centers before the higher ones, whereas the former takes the opposite course. This is quite erroneous. In either case it is first a matter of descending; then one *exits* from the base; then re-ascends (compare the theory of septenaries in *Introduction to Magic,* vol. II, 28). The real difference, as stated above, is whether consciousness of the higher or the median seat is taken as the principle and basis of the whole process. Given that the structurally "non-modern" man naturally gravitated more or less toward the latter, to which the subtle state corresponds, it is possible that practices for the *direct* awakening of the basal energy of the lower seat (the Hindu *kundalini,* the ancient Egyptian *uraeus*) would yield a result for him. This becomes very difficult for the majority of modern Westerners, who must first traverse the median seat. The same applies to the practices with breathing. Abraxa, in the instructions for sexual magic (*Introduction to Magic,* vol. II, 335–47), has rightly said that it is impossible to "touch" the energy of which the reproductive is only a low-grade manifestation, unless one is already able to attain a form of active ecstasy and to maintain it. Compare also the methods of Taoist alchemy (*Introduction to Magic,* vol. II, 379–94).

8. As for the essence of the method most advisable to the modern Westerner, it consists in ensuring that the energies and faculties that are linked in normal life to organic processes, and refer almost

exclusively to the "physical I," come step by step to detach and free themselves. For a method of this kind we find no lack of tools in the Eastern traditions. For example, one of the fundamental disciplines is to systematically create a "thought of thought," that is, a continuous, uniform, constant awareness of all common thoughts, mental modifications, and perceptions. The elements of this discipline of conscious thought are expounded in the clearest way in the Buddhist canon— the reader may here consult the extracts contained in *Introduction to Magic*, vol. I, 173–80. He may also review what Leo has written about the separation of a subtle counterpart in every perception or feeling in the fully waking state (*Introduction to Magic*, vol. I, 60–63). As for the "will," the significances of "liberated action" often mentioned by Ea can serve as a basis. However, we do not intend to enter into technical details here, but only to define the *notion* of the most suitable initiatic method for the modern Westerner. We can add a simile. Imagine the physical body as a sheath containing the form of the inner, spiritual man. To enable contact with the inner light, one might imagine a detachment occurring by the inner man *exiting* from the physical sheath. But one can also conceive of a detachment taking place through *rotating* the inner man around his axis, so that the center is not displaced (that of the inner man remaining the same as that of the physical body). This would be the actual effect of the method we have been speaking of: the counterpart of a perfect continuity of active, waking consciousness even in the suprasensible states, and of the transposition of such states into the habitual experience of things and of beings.

Nevertheless, this should not lead one to believe that initiation can be a purely human affair or a construction of the individual. Although it may happen almost insensibly, at a certain moment other forces must come into action and substitute themselves for those with which one has proceeded in the preparation. But in practice the sense of an autonomous procedure persists: unlike the abandonment of the person who expects phenomena, revelations, or salvations, there is the action of preparing a *magnet*, which through natural law will attract the energies as needed for further development. Thus, on this path, even in experiences of a higher order, the initiate will always have the power of *fixing* the volatile. As was said, in these contacts, far from losing himself in ecstatic identifications, he will have the power to *penetrate* and *energize* the forces with which he unites himself. In a word, it is a "magical" contact, in which the initiate has a decisively masculine role.

I.4

HAVISMAT

The Zone of Shadow[1]

In traditional orthodoxy, light tends to signify the domain of truth, while darkness is normally the symbol of ignorance. For the common man the relationship is exactly the opposite: the kingdom of light is that in which his material life unfolds, while darkness is the domain of truth, inaccessible to him. In Dante's terms, this is the point of view of the "living—of the life that hastens toward death," of those who die instead of living, ignorant of what true life is and what possibilities of infinite developments it offers to him who can rise to them.

But what interests us here is that, no matter whether one takes the point of view of truth or of ignorance, there is an intermediate zone between what man knows or thinks he knows, and what he does not know: a zone that we will call provisionally the *zone of shadow*. We prefer this term to those used by psychologists and "spiritualists," both of whom hold to a unilateral point of view, hence erroneous and unacceptable.

From this zone comes the great majority of actions and reactions, slow or sudden, that emerge without warning in the everyday life of individuals and peoples, causing inexplicable crises and constituting the domain of the *unforeseeable:* a much-used term, especially in long periods of crisis, in which one neither knows nor sees how the world may turn out in the near future. No sensible person resorts to *chance* to

---

1. [This article, by Guido De Giorgio (1890–1957), was added to the 1971 edition of *Introduzione alla Magia. —Trans.*]

explain what escapes normal observation: whether one admits an order and an ordering principle in the world, or believes that events are determined by so-called natural laws, there is no place for chance; that only exists in the fantasies of what we might call "accidentalists," that is, the systematically shortsighted.

Let us say right away that this zone of shadow is an extremely orderly world, whose actions and reactions happen as a reflection of what men do in their ordinary life, and whose repercussions they are unconscious of, wrapped as they are in semi-obscurity. The Romans—to mention those more or less known to all—were fully aware of this intermediary world, and sought to imprint every action of their lives with a character of attunement or conciliation toward the forces that erupt unexpectedly, sometimes appearing as a veritable fatality.

The moderns seem to ignore this, preferring to relegate all that escapes their materialistic and superficial vision of things to the domain of the unforeseeable. This zone is a vast reservoir from which arise currents, impulses, instantaneous crashes, and insidious surges that literally *undermine* the existence of men and peoples. The forces that currently seek to damage all that still bears the seal of Tradition draw most of their energy from the zone of shadow, to maintain and reinforce the current disorder.

To anyone who wishes to pursue ideas of this kind, we will say that this zone of shadow *never forgives,* nor can it forgive, because it does not obey any moral law: only a precise order that works with an accuracy far more scrupulous than that of natural laws. Acting on men and peoples who are ignorant of it, it bursts out unpredictably, as it were, in inextricable complexes, whose chaotic character only shocks the ignorant and the unwary.

It is the duty of all guardians of the sacred science to point out the dangers of these anti-traditional forces, which take advantage of the serpentine currents of the zone of shadow to prevent the world, during the travail and deviation of these last centuries, from recovering that attitude, that order of power and truth, without which it will be condemned to plunge fatally into the darkest anarchy.

1.5

EA

Poetry and Initiatic Realization[1]

Those who know how closely the "rhythmic" and "imagistic" elements are connected to the primary forms of subtle consciousness can understand how certain transcendent experiences can be better expressed through *poetry* than through ordinary abstract thought.

It is true that *music,* even more than poetry, is made from rhythm. But the rhythmical world of music is still too directly and prevalently addressed to the sub-intellectual elements of sensitivity and emotionality. In contrast, poetic rhythm requires a more subtle and intellectual organ to grasp it: it requires an activity that forms part of the conscious mind.

We know that in India even the wisdom teachings were cast in the form of rhythmic poetry, while the Sanskrit language itself has a characteristic rhythmical element. The latter still persists in Greek, but gradually fades away in modern languages. Poetic rhythm can restore it, so long as it is not mere acoustic virtuosity, but modulates itself according to internal states that are inherently rhythmical.

To be sure, the rhythmic element in poetry is not limited to metrical cadences, consonances, strophes, and so forth. Another rhythm may arise from certain relations between verbal values—and this has the

---

1. [In translating this essay I have only attempted a literal, line-by-line translation of Onofri's verses, and included the original excerpts for those who can appreciate them. Il Marchese Mina di Sospiro kindly helped with the elucidation of some passages. All ellipses are in the original. —*Trans.*]

same superiority to the former as poetry itself with respect to music. There is a subtle art of associating certain words that no one would think of juxtaposing on the basis of their usual correspondence with the world of the senses. Those who are not disconcerted by such associations but can actively accept them may be led to intuitions that already have a certain illuminating character—precisely because the mind has had to act independently of the meanings that come from the sense-world. Situations of this kind are frequent in modern poetry, especially symbolist and analogistic—for example, Rimbaud, Mallarmé, Maeterlinck, Stefan George, Eliot, Auden—even if they arise instinctively and by chance, without any conscious relationship to esotericism.

In contrast, a deliberate attempt, combined with a certain occult knowledge, has appeared in Italy with Arturo Onofri.

For this reason, Onofri's poetry is unique of its kind, and criticism—whether positive or negative—that comes from a necessarily profane and literary point of view is far from seeing what is most original in it. From our point of view, on the other hand, we must mention various "irregularities" in the elements of "occult science" influenced by the Anthroposophy that Onofri accepts. (We could not possibly agree with the doctrinal positions outlined in his book *Nuovo Rinascimento come arte dell'Io* [New Renaissance as Art of the I], Bari: Laterza, 1925.) We must admit that the thrills of objective sensations are often lost in simple lyricism, and that a disagreeably didactic tone pervades his expressions. All the same, there remain many elements of value in themselves, corresponding not to mere "images" created by the poet's subjective fancy but to genuine inner experiences, known and recognizable by all who are sufficiently versed in our disciplines. Moreover, Onofri's poetry renders these elements in verbal rhythms that have a very evocative quality.

We have chosen here some of the most characteristic passages among those which can be considered as enlightened transcriptions of experiences and teachings already familiar to our readers.[2]

---

2. We give here all the sources of passages quoted in the present article: A. Onofri, *Trombe d'Argento* (Lanciano: Carabba, 1924), 69, 89, 94, 122, 134, 146, 138; *Terrestrità del Sole* (Florence: Vallecchi, 1925), 7, 14, 18, 24, 71, 87, 130; *Vincere il Drago* (Turin: Ribet, 1928), 9, 12, 29, 30, 48, 59, 63, 73, 75, 83, 84, 88, 94, 118, 153, 170, 154, 145, 148, 172.

... *un tragico silenzio*
(quello che vige oltre pianeti e sole)
ottunde la stanchezza che mi duole
come un corpo distaccato a cui presenzio ...
Un mutismo irreale, antecedente
alla natività di tutti i mondi,
scava abissi impossibili, i cui fondi
precipitosi, intimano alla mente
　　　un nulla smisurato.

(. . . a tragic silence
(that which reigns beyond planets and suns)
dulls the fatigue that pains me
like a detached body in which I am present ...
An unreal muteness,
preceding the birth of all the worlds,
digs impossible abysses,
whose precipitous depths suggest to the mind
　　　a measureless nothing.)

The next passage relates to a subsequent phase of "solution" or "liquefaction," of resurrection of the "black stone" (the "black diamond") in the first sacred visions:

Una scorrevole estasi di caldo
trapassa la mia polpa irrigidita,
e al calore fluente dalle dita
sembra che il mondo sgeli, a spaldo a spaldo.
Tutto il buio del cuore, duro e saldo
come un nero diamante, apre un'uscita
alla densità sua, dispessita
in fiamme d'ametista e di smeraldo.

(A flowing ecstasy of heat
runs through my stiffened flesh,
and at the fluid warmth from the fingers

the world seems to thaw, layer by layer.
All the heart's darkness, hard and solid
as a black diamond, opens an exit
for its density, scattered
in flames of amethyst and emerald.)

It is the loosening of the "bond of the heart," the opening of the "median seat." The reference to the heart is uniform in both Eastern and Western traditions. The *serpent* that in certain symbolisms curls around it, corresponds in the Nordic-Atlantic cosmic symbology to the *ice* and *darkness* of the winter season, after which at the winter solstice the "Light of the Earth" returns. The mystics, too, often speak of the "illumination in the heart." As for the "subtilization" that follows it, the "breeze of vivifying air" that revives consciousness, and the ensuing possibility of "luminiously perceiving one's own body," the Upanishads mention it, as does Gichtel in the West (*Theosophia Practica*, III, 36; IV, 8; V, 51–52, 65; VI, 44: see *Introduction to Magic*, vol. II, 17–34). Here are two relevant passages:

O musica di limpidi pianeti
che nel sangue dell'Io sdemoniato
articoli i tuoi cosmici segreti:
nella tua chiarità, che ci riscatta
dalla tenebra morta del passato,
la densità ritorna rarefatta.

(O music of limpid planets,
which in the blood of the exorcised I
voices your cosmic secrets:
in your clarity, which delivers us
from the deathly darkness of the past,
density returns rarefied.)

Dal più deserto azzurro
balénan-mio-corpo rutilando
le tue curve cantanti
e gli occhi di silenzio del futuro . . .

Ed ecco il tuo strale sonoro in mezzo al petto,
ecco i timpani d'oro in queste tempie,
ecco le corde-in-fremiti dei reni.

(From the most void azure
there flash through my body, resplendent,
your singing curves
and the silent eyes of the future . . .
And behold your sounding arrow in the center of the breast,
behold the golden drums in these temples,
behold the trembling strings of the loins.)

The *azure,* as resolution of the "ice" and the "black blacker than blackness," as well as the impressions recorded by the various organs, are strictly objective elements. As the vision begins:

Di notte, quando l'intimo slancio dell'albero si
*   emancipa dalla sua scorza di secoli,*
e nell'azzurro, finalmente nero, disegna in limpide
*   formule di luce*
la direzione esatta al nostro sforzo, verso i suoi paradisi
*   feroci—*
ci lampeggiano intorno, in silenzio, i fragori e i cicloni
*   della visione reale,*
che non può chiamarsi nemmeno "domani," essendo
*   essa sola . . .*

(At night, when the tree's inner surge escapes its age-old bark,
and in the blue, finally black, draws in limpid forms
    of light
the exact direction of our effort, toward its wild
    paradises—
there flash around us, in silence, the din and cyclones
    of the real vision,
which cannot even be called "tomorrow," being itself
    alone . . .)

The reference to the "tree" may relate to a theme of meditation used as analogical support for entering another form of consciousness that, as we will explain, is related to the vegetal world. The vision develops:

> *. . . il notturno sangue, rallentato*
> *nel suo sonno lucente, a un tratto esulta . . .*
> *L'Uomo, che veglia le sue membra stese*
> *n'ode in ampiezza cosmica l'occulta*
> *gloria d'angioli, in lui fatta palese.*

> (. . . the nocturnal blood, slowed
> in its lucid sleep, suddenly surges up . . .
> The Man, who watches over his outstretched limbs,
> hears in cosmic fullness the hidden
> glory of the angels, manifested in him.)

And also:

> *. . . s'allentano i legami ostinati del cuore*
> *e si profila nel buio delle mie notti un paese di luci e di*
> *   musiche*
> *un paese ove incontro me stesso come un essere nuovo . . .*
> *Nell'improvviso barlume del sangue*
> *io respiro le scene autorevoli, come d'un altro,*
> *le gesta mondiali di un nume di ferreo vigore e di tutta*
> *   certezza.*

> (. . . the obstinate bonds of the heart are eased
> and in the darkness of my nights appears a land of lights
>   and music,
> a land wherein I meet myself like a new being . . .
> In the sudden glow of the blood
> I breathe the imposing scenes, as if they were another's,
> the worldwide gestures of a god of iron strength and utter
>   certitude.)

And yet again:

> *Esseri d'oro affiorano improvvisi*
> *giú da nubi svuotate d'ogni buio;*
> *ripùllulano in gesta musicali*
> *dentro il mio vegetale respirarli.*
> *Sonagliere di lampi, e coloriti*
> *crudeli, come dèi d'epoche morte,*
> *fanno sbandieramento di battaglia*
> *suì mio riposo diventato sguardo.*

> (Golden beings suddenly bloom
> beneath clouds free of all darkness;
> they swarm again with musical gestures
> within my vegetal breathing of them.
> Jingling flashes and painful colors,
> like gods of dead epochs,
> unfurl their banners
> over my sleep that has become watching.)

It is precisely the "memory of the blood" that is awakened and becomes a vision of primordial states. The "vegetal" attribute given to breathing in this state of consciousness is technically exact and linked to the state of sleep. Sleep and the median seat correspond in effect to the vegetal world, antecedent to the demonism of animal forms of consciousness, and which appears in initiatic reintegration as the *Tree* or *Wood of Life*. The physical, animal I is crucified upon it ("passion" and "mortification"), and in Rosicrucian symbolism, there bloom the roses of the "spiritual blood."

In the "god of iron strength" we glimpse a reference to a deeper state, which "adjoins" the mineral or Saturnian element, the true seat of the "Gold," naked power, which in man appears and acts as "I." The next passage, at any rate, must refer to this:

> *Con la piú cruda scarica di gelo*
> *ho toccato lo schema del possibile . . .*

È il punto nullo, ove converge il corpo
fuor d'ogni suo disegno abituale,
nato pianeti e sfere di potenza . . .
È l'attimo turchino, senza scopi,
di lá d'ogni durata . . .
È l'esser nulla, essendo Io solamente.
Folgore d'un crearsi onnimondiale
tu dormivi negli umidi recessi
del mio vegliare addormentatamente:
ma il tuo risveglio è forza di quïete
come una sparsa musica
rappresa in un tacersi.

(With the cruelest discharge of ice
I have reached the outline of the possible . . .
It is the null point, where the body converges
beyond any of its usual designs,
born planets and spheres of power . . .
It is the turquoise instant, purposeless,
beyond all duration . . .
It is being nothing, being I alone.
Lightning-stroke of a universal self-creation
you sleep there in the damp recesses
of my drowsy vigil:
but your awakening is the force of quietude
like a scattered music
congealed in a silence.)

"Quietude," in the sense of calm stablility subsisting without conflict: *pax* (peace) in the initiatic and what may be called the *regal* sense of the term. And the "silence" is like that Silence, which is the "Gold," wherein is concentrated the "word" or rhythm, which is "silver." From this point there proceed realizations that actualize certain occult relationships with the natures of the mineral world. Here are the "Creators":

Esseri tutta potenza sopraggiungono sopra di noi:
sono Esseri-cielo che pensano ferro e diamante dentro i
    macigni sepolti,
e saviamente spezzano ghirlande di fiacchi abbracci . . .
A stento s'accorda il loro frenetico giungere col ritmo del
    nostro petto
ché fiamme al galoppo sono il loro corpo dall'ampie
    criniere di vento . . .
Sfolgoranti potenze, da voi sgorga la forma perfetta del
    cristallo . . .
Alla vostra veglia frenetica spetta il nome che ognuno
    di noi già dice a sé stesso in anticipo.
Ed ivi ogni belva riceve quell'inaudito coro di pianeti
    ch'è il suo elastico slancio tessuto di sogni, in profilo
    di corpo.

(All-powerful beings exist above us:
they are heavenly beings who think iron and diamond
    inside the buried boulders,
and discreetly break wreaths of sluggish embraces . . .
Their frenetic arrival scarcely accords with the
    rhythm of our breast
for galloping flames are their body, with its thick
    mane of wind . . .
Fulgurating powers, you disgorge the perfect form of
    the crystal . . .
To your frenetic awakening belongs the name that
    each of us has already spoken to himself.
And there every beast receives that unheard chorus of
    planets, which is its elastic impulse woven from
    dreams, in bodily profile.)

The last phrase is a remarkable intuitive synthesis of the occult
essence of the animal world. It will not be "hermetic" for anyone who
can relate it to something that he himself has experienced. For the

others, it would be of little use to explain it. Another allusion, to "sacred forms, wandering animals" says much less.

> *che a fior del suolo adombrano, dai cieli,*
> *movimenti e stature siderali*

> (which on the surface of the ground shadow the
> motions and sidereal formations of the heavens)

The "name, which each of us has already spoken to himself," referring to a "drowsy vigil," is the "I": its truth, as already stated, is its absolute power "in iron strength and utter certitude" which awakes at the mineral or earthly level. Once again we recall the Hermetic maxim: "Its power is perfect if it is converted into earth." Moreover, we have referred elsewhere to the bony system, which is the seat of minerality in man and the limit of that *syncope* of the absolute force, from which the mortal body has originated. It is in fact felt as a halt and a cessation:

> *. . . il fuoco spento*
> *di antichi dèi nel corpo minerale,*
> *ove l'uomo è feticcio*
> *irreale e terriccio.*

> (. . . the spent fire
> of ancient gods in the mineral body
> where man is unreal
> fetish and compost.)

Suggestions of their resurrection are often given, especially in two passages, the second of which belongs to a poem entitled *Il macigno ritorna luce* (The Rock Returns Light).

> *Sussulti d'armonie cosmiche, in croce*
> *d'ossa stanno inchiodati a vecchi istinti*
> *d'inerzia, quali antichi esseri estinti*
> *che sono organi e sangue, ma che in voce*

rivivranno, e in corale
d'un uomo universale.

(Tremors of cosmic harmonies are nailed
on a cross of bones of old instincts
of inertia, like ancient extinct beings
which are organs and blood, but which
will revive in voice, and in chorus
of a universal man.)

Il dolore incristallito della terra pesa dentro di noi,
     quale scheletro vivo.
È l'antichissimo fuoco gelato di tutti i nostri sentieri
     quaggiú.
Figlio del sole, che dormi dentro la ressa delle tue ossa,
ti desterà la potenza di fuoco d'un volere mondiale
     rinato in te uomo,
Quello che vai presentendo, come un sogno, nel macigno
     pulsante del sangue.

(The crystallized pain of the earth weighs within us,
     like a living skeleton.
It is the primordial frozen fire of all our paths here
     below.
Son of the sun, who sleeps within the throng of your
     bones,
the fiery power of a global will, reborn in you, man,
     will awaken you,
That which you are anticipating, like a dream, in the
     pulsing rock of the blood.)

This power of the Fire—the *Ur* of the Mediterranean magical tradition anciently associated with the Bull, then later with the Ram (in relation to the zodiacal sign which, due to the precession of the equinoxes, rules the point of the annual return of the solar force)—is also called *slancio agita-numi* (god-stirring impulse).

Riècco i millenari impedimenti
accerchianti il mio sangue agita-numi
che misurò in sillabe stellari
ombre di deità piú che reali.

(Here again are the millennial obstacles
encircling my god-stirring blood
which measured in stellar syllables
shades of more than real deities.)

It is also conceived as the motive principle in the pure state, the motion that sleeps in motions, and, in us, principally in that of the blood:

La volontà che scuote il nimbo rosso
del sangue, in un alterno e sonnolento
polso, onde muove il moto in cui son mosso,
è la stessa che vuole alberi al vento.

(The will that shakes the red nimbus
of the blood, in an alternating and sleepy
pulse, whence moves the movement in which I am
      moved,
is the same that wills trees in the wind.)

Among the mineral correspondences, the following is especially forceful:

Nell'utero dei mondi hanno, le brame
nostre, virtú d'indurimenti atroci:
ossa-diamante e crudi ferro e rame
che sognano di sciogliersi . . .

(In the womb of the worlds, our desires
have qualities of terrible hardness:
diamond bones, and raw iron and copper
that dream of melting . . .)

The outbreak, when

> *l'oceanica angoscia d'esser mondi*
> *suona nel polso del mio sangue . . .*

> (the oceanic pain of being worlds
> resounds in the pulse of my blood . . .)

and when the

> *impeto insensuale a dismisura*
> *verso eccelsi splendori onniveggenti*
> *fa di noi l'entità che disoscura*
> *le tenebre del corpo in firmamenti*

> (senseless and excessive impetus
> toward exalted all-seeing heights
> makes of us the entity that dispels
> the darknesses of the body in firmaments)

is that of the Creative Word, the primordial deed whereupon

> *allora soltanto sei tu, libera e solo te stessa,*
> *quando fulminea crei le tue distruttrici presenze.*

> (only then you are, free and yourself alone,
> when lightning-fast you create your destructive
> presences.)

They are both destructions and illuminations, laying bare the being-forces hidden behind the simple reflexes resulting from the human perception of things. Here is one of these experiences:

> *Ecco il ritmo frenetico del sangue*
> *quando gli azzurri tuonano a distesa*
> *e qualsiasi colore si fa fiamma*
> *nell'urlo delle tempie.*

Ecco il cuor mio nella selvaggia ebbrezza
di svincolare in esseri le forme
disincantate a vortice di danza . . .
E fra l'altre manie del mezzogiorno,
ecco me, congelato in stella fissa,
ch'esaspero l'antica aria di piaghe
metalliche, sull'erba di corallo.

(Here is the frenetic rhythm of the blood
when the azure thunders ceaselessly
and every color becomes flame
in the roar of the temples.
Here is my heart in the savage intoxication
of disentangling the forms in beings
disenchanted in the swirl of the dance . . .
And among the other noontide madnesses,
here am I, frozen in a fixed star,
which exasperates the ancient air of
metallic grief, on the coral grass.)

Giving grass the attribute of coral, along with some other associations that may seem like futurist extravagances, actually corresponds objectively to a special psychic perception. The same can be said of the reference to the temples of the head. The "frenetic rhythm of the blood" in the visionary state can sometimes have a physical correlation: in some traditions, even of Christian saints, there is talk of heat and a fever-like state. In our own environment, incidentally, we have observed special forms of consciousness accompanied by temperatures of over 40 degrees celsius [= 104°F], and by interesting phenomena.

"Frozen in a fixed star," juxtaposed to the Dionysiac element of the vision, is not a mere figure of speech: its symbolic-magical value is known in the initiatic traditions.

A transformation correspondingly takes place in the human forms of the faculties. From speech there arise *"immagini sonanti di una potenza libera che vola"* ("sounding images of a freely flying power"), by means of

moti, che in noi lampeggiano dai suoni
dell'aria, che l'orecchio al sangue imprime,
rattenuti in motivi d'ascoltarsi.

(motions, which flash in us from the sounds
of the air, which the ear imprints on the blood,
held back in motives for listening.)

And for thinking connected to the brain:

> . . . *i pensieri, che un rigore acuto*
> *ammutisce entro schemi àlgidi e cupi,*
> *fremono già nel lampo rattenuto*
> *che ne farà miracolosi sciupi*
>   *di colori e di suoni*
>   *sbocciano in visioni.*

> (. . . the thoughts, which a sharp rigor
> silences among dark and frozen shapes,
> already quivering in the slowed flash
> which makes of them miraculous masses
>   of colors and sounds,
>   bloom in visions.)

"Bloom" is actually the technical term (*sphota*) used in Indo-Tibetan esotericism. We have already mentioned the corresponding esotericism of the "flower" in the West. Extraordinary sensations appear from external things:

> *Il profilo corporeo di un pensiero*
> *che scese fuoco d'angelo inveduto*
> *apre le braccia in albero . . .*
> *L'aroma che si leva su dai suoli*
> *simile ad incenso in nuvola propizia,*
> *è il tatto d'uno spirito, che inizia*
> *nuove energie di lave e di petroli.*

(The bodily profile of a thought
which descends like unseen angelic fire
opens its arms like a tree . . .
The aroma which arises from the soils
like incense in a benign cloud,
is the touch of a spirit, which launches
new energies from lavas and petrolea.)

The will of spirits which *raise* thoughts like birds:

Sono pensieri di dèi, che a strati a strati
s'infusero allo scheletro terrestre
e risorgono in voli su dai prati
scattando come frecce da balestre.

(They are the thoughts of gods, which layer by layer
infused themselves in the earthly skeleton
and resurge in flights over the fields
shooting like bolts from a crossbow.)

These are perceptions no longer felt in the physical body, but in other locations, toward which the blood, turned to light, opens the way for them to be lived as *meanings*.

Osanna al corpo portentoso, aperto
agli influssi plurali: infimi, eccelsi!
Purgato d'invadenze, alacre in ogni
scia di veleni, è diafana purezza
di nutrimenti e filtri: è il lampeggiante
riconoscersi in queste atroci forme
di vizi e di paralisi d'oggetti.

(Hosanna to the marvelous body, open
to multiple influxes: low, high!
Purged from infections, alert to any
trace of poison, it is diaphanous purity

of nourishments and philters: it instantly
sees itself in these terrible forms
of vices and paralyses of objects.)

This surely refers to what was said in the commentary on Milarepa (*Introduction to Magic*, vol. II, 216–28) about the value of food for the yogi. Here too the idea of "paralysis" gives an effective sense of the knowledge of things from the point of view of physical reality. Some macrocosmic correspondences:

> *Nella testa e negli omeri è la forza*
> *che in angeli potenti pensa terra,*
> *come nel petto è sangue e ritmo il Sole . . .*
> *E l'alta volontà, che stelle serra,*
> *al ventre e nelle gambe arde e si smorza.*

(In the head and the shoulders is the strength
Which in potent angels thinks earth,
Just as in the breast there is blood and rhythm
  of the Sun . . .
and the high will, which follows the stars
flares up and dies down in the belly and legs.)

On the return from realizations during the nocturnal state, we have the following passage:

> *. . . qualcuno stanotte m'ha scosso.*
> *Ad occhi socchiusi, nel buio, come pian piano tornando*
> *alla terra da altezze celesti,*
> *mi sentivo discendere e svegliare.*
> *Ed esseri-luce uscivano intanto da me, dileguando*
> *Finché ho ritrovato me stesso, occhi aperti, nel letto.*

(. . . someone disturbed me last night.
With eyes half-closed, in the dark, as I was gradually
  returning to earth from celestial heights,

I felt myself descend and waken.
And meanwhile light-beings came out of me,
    vanishing
until I found myself, open-eyed, in bed.)

When one comes to detach the I from its human condition, one stablilizes this absolutely active relationship, through which the former sense of self as a given individual resembles a *single* word, as compared to the free faculty of speech which can also pronounce a whole series of *other* words. Then follows what our sciences call *individuum individuans,* and the East calls *kārana-sharīra* = causal body—of which we have already spoken (*Introduction to Magic,* vol. I, 196–202). Onofri's final poems contain various references to it, which also help one to understand the *plural* nature of this I, or state of the I: "*L'arco, il cui dardo è ciascuno degli uomini sparsi nel mondo*" ("The bow, whose arrow is every man shot into the world")—"*L'uomodio, che sarà l'intera umanità*" ("The man-god, who will be the whole of humanity")—and also:

> . . . *noi, sparsi al mondo a torme a torme,*
> *vivremo la parola una e infinita*
> *che in corpi innumerevoli aurea dorme.*
> *Ritrova, nel tuo divenire-*
> *te-stesso, quell'Io glorioso*
>   *che ha il proprio crearsi*
>   *ma in uomini sparsi.*

> (. . . we, scattered in the world in our hordes,
> will live the one and infinite word
> which sleeps golden in innumerable bodies.
> Find, in your self-becoming,
> this glorious I
>   which has its own self-creation
>   but is scattered among men.)

Being absolutely oneself leads to being one who is beyond any "selfhood"—to the absolute individual. Onofri, not yet free from the influence of certain Christian views, put more emphasis on "us," the "human" or "communal" aspect in such realizations, rather than on the higher aspect relating to an active and transcendent unity—one might even say the "god-stirring" and "men-stirring" aspect—that is more consonant with the initiatic-magical tradition. But that touches on a different subject from the one treated here. It does not lessen the value of whatever in this poetry reveals an authentic experience, and which, beside its intrinsic interest, may offer useful suggestions about more than one esoteric theme already treated in these pages.

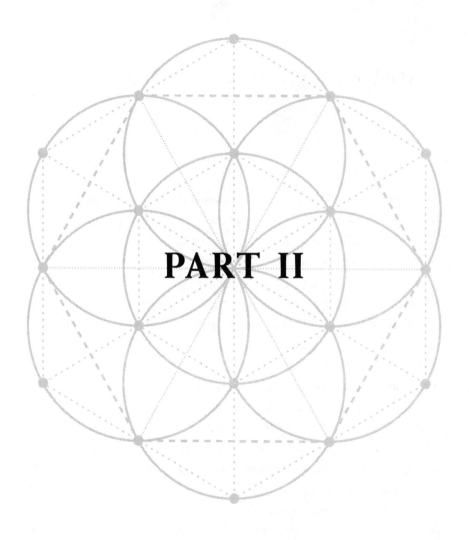

PART II

EA

Aristocracy and the Initiatic Ideal

Among the typical confusions of today's various "spiritualist" groups is their disclaiming of the eminently aristocratic character of everything pertaining to initiatic science.

Seen from the outside it is a blatant absurdity that shows the mental level of today's spiritualist currents, especially the Theosophical ones. While they pretend to be proclaiming and revaluing the teachings of the ancient Wisdom, they indulge in democratic and humanitarian views, professing the gospel of more or less universal equality, if not a sort of "social service," and applying this to a progressivism and evolutionism even in cosmic terms. Anthroposophy, too, beside its initiatic pretensions and the excesses of what it claims to be clairvoyance, has given as the watchword for the immediate tasks of "evolution" the Christianizing motive of "love." But contradiction and absurdity are at their most blatant in modern Freemasonry. This organization, to which some still attribute the initiatic character that it has long lacked, and which is structured internally by a complex hierarchical system of degrees and honors (though often only artificial ones), is the selfsame organization that from the start has embraced the "immortal principles" of the French Revolution and of liberalism, presenting itself with rare exceptions as a sort of laic and militant religion of world democracy.

Against all this, we must state outright that the only principles that an initiatic knowledge, rightly understood, can establish and justify are those of difference, higher authority, hierarchy, and aristocracy.

Whereas today's counterfeits of esoteric wisdom draw their membership from the fringes of culture, political life, and official science, one should not forget that in every normal and traditional civilization that wisdom held an eminently *central* position. It was the heritage and privilege of royal and priestly castes, the legitimate holders of supreme power, who exercised a formative and orienting influence on every facet of life in the subordinate social strata. Esotericism and adeptship are by definition as antidemocratic as one could possibly imagine.

We move on to a second point, the main one to which we want to draw attention. Keeping in mind that esoteric science is simultaneously a regal and a priestly art, Éliphas Lévi asks with good reason of anyone wanting to approach it: Do you feel a kingly nature within yourself? A priestly one? Such a question is not meant to demoralize, but indicates that one must at least have clear ideas about a basic human qualification. This is especially true in our time, when the type of the adept is lumped together with the often suspect type of the "occultist," and of creatures like mediums, spiritualists, sensitives, and diviners who do not even attain the level of a sane and normal man. A certain natural aristocratic qualification, as the mark of a human type that is not just normal but superior, is the general premise for any participation in an initiatic order, which for that reason was restricted to an elite, and always will be.

At the same time, among those who have attained a certain level there is the "Hermetic," Rosicrucian, or Taoist type of initiate, whose true nature is imperceptible and who from the outside may be mistaken for an ordinary man. Yet there is also the superior form of expression that materialized in what was once the *aristòcrate,* and it formed the foundation of the spiritual significance that originally belonged to every true nobility.

The idea that the aristocracies emerged and established themselves through a sort of Darwinian "natural selection" and through domination of the strongest, even if of the Nietzschean "superman" type, stems from misunderstanding or ignorance. The origins of almost all ancient aristocracies and of royalty itself were *sacral,* having some definite reference to the initiatic order itself. Especially within the framework of a heroic-warrior tradition (see *Introduzione alla Magia,* vol. II, cap. XI[1]), it was essentially the aristocracy that exercised that mediating function and demonstrated higher human possibilities: a function that in the religious-sapiential traditions was represented by the figure of the priest and the ascetic. Moreover, in Western chivalry and partly also in feudalism, the nobility often displayed that inner and spiritual dimension, given the existence of a chivalric initiation and of hidden veins that nourished its most typical organizations. A special study of the heraldry and emblematics of ancient noble lineages might uncover references to an effective esoteric symbolism, even if these elements often only survive as mute witnesses, yet no less significant for that. Giambattista Vico himself suspected as much.

The aristocratic way of being is typified by a superiority that is virile, free, and personalized. It corresponds to the demand—which had typical expressions in the classical world—that what is lived internally as spirituality should manifest outwardly in an equilibrium of body, soul, and will; in a tradition of honor, high bearing, and severity in attitude, even in the details of dress; in a general style of thinking, feeling, and reacting. Even though from the outside it may seem like mere formality and stereotypical rules (into which nobility may often have fallen), that style can be traced to its original value as the instrument of an inner discipline: to what we might call a *ritual* value.

On the inward side, the traditional aristocratic type possesses a special "ascesis," a sense of superiority to the mere appetite for life; a predominance of *ethos* over *pathos;* an inner simplicity and disdain for the crude immediacy of urges, emotions, and sensations. Therein lies the secret of a serenity that is not indifference but regal superiority, the capacity of an alert and keen mind no less than of firm and decisive action, typical of the noble type. The absence of the impulses

---

1. [In the 1971 edition, "vol. II, cap. IX," but in the 1955 edition, "v. II, c. XI." In either case, there is no obvious point of reference. However, in numbers 11–12 of the *UR* journal from 1928 there is an essay on "La donna e le modalità dell'iniziazione" (Woman and the Modes of Initiation), much longer than the commentary on "Woman and Initiation" in *Introduction to Magic,* vol. II, 395–98, which does address this matter, and which is cited elsewhere in the 1929 version of the present essay. —*Trans.*]

that drive men to the banquet of life as though they were starving; the self-possession that is not a preoccupation but a simplification, as of an ever-present second nature; the composure and conscious equilibrium that is both "style" and "rule"—all this, while forming part of the ideal aristocrat or gentleman, is also found in the description of figures like the Greek sage, the Buddhist ascetic, or the Perfect Man of the Far East. Inner superiority, rather than simple force, gives rise naturally to the dignity, capacity, and rights of the true leaders, who can arouse in others a spontaneous recognition and a pride in following and serving them.

What distinguishes the aristocratic quality from that of an ascetic in the common Christian sense is the fact that its effective superiority, as described, does not imply renunciation nor despise appearances, but takes concrete form in a worldly expression, making it the principle of a regular process of refinement and selection. Nobility includes aspects of good taste, tact, generosity, and regality, which were traditionally due to its superiority to immediate interests and the crude demands of naturalistic life, rather than to possessing greater material wealth. And if from the moralistic point of view it was sometimes accused of corruption, it should be understood thus: one should not confuse the privilege of someone who can permit himself certain things only because he also has the power to abstain from them, with the licentiousness of one who is a slave to vice and excess; for if there were ever two contraries, it is these.

Another point needs emphasizing. If the aristocrat becomes master of himself; if he is prepared to count life and happiness as something less than honor, faith, and tradition; if he is capable of forbearance and active sacrifice—this comes from a direct intuition of the blood, which makes him realize that all this is *good,* that to will all this is *good* and makes one superior and *noble.* To *feel* these specific values spontaneously is the very sign of *nobility.* Not to feel them but to need supports and external justifications defines the common man. Thus, the aristocratic code is sufficient unto itself, based on an innate style and on a different nature from that of the majority of humans.

Naturally, we must recognize the role that heredity also plays here. Just as there is a physical and biological heredity, there is also a psychic and spiritual one, which in traditional societies justified the principle of exclusion and caste that seems so intolerable to the demagogy and individualism of our day. Just as an animal does not become domesticated at a stroke, thus aristocratic tradition only won its effective and objective value through the slow and steady acquisition, conservation, and preservation of subtle dispositions on the basis of an influence from above, passed down from one generation to another. Hence bearing an illustrious name and its heraldic arms also meant possessing, as a psychophysical and subtle preformation, the virtual heredity of special forms of interest, sensibility, and instinct. Given this, the individual found himself in a privileged position for aspiring to a level and an achievement that would have cost others, dependent only on their own resources, a life of toil, striving, and even violence to their own nature. And because of this essential refinement, which is even imprinted on the facial and bodily features and attitudes, it is largely true that "Lords" are born and not made. The principle is equally true that the mixture of castes, when these really answer to their function in traditional civilizations, is a crime, because it thoughtlessly breaks an occult and precious continuity, which is of the blood and also beyond the blood.

Certainly, that which has already been destroyed, due to multiple factors, cannot by its very nature be rebuilt from scratch. Today one can only count on fragments and on the timely emergence in one person or another of heredities, actualized in different ways from what was normal in other civilizations, where they were largely based on blood alone.

In any case, given the unfavorable conditions of our times we should be under no illusions, because this esoteric teaching is as true as ever: that spirituality has nothing to do either with simple "culture" or with beliefs and "theories," or with vague aspirations—in short with nothing peripheral to the existential core of each person. Spirituality means an effective superiority woven into the very rhythm of the blood. An equally well-known teaching is that the only things of initiatic value are those efforts and realizations which succeed in molding and transforming a deep stratum that should be considered, not metaphorically but objectively, as bound up with the blood: thus with inborn tendencies, atavistic forces, obscure organic energies, and with the subconscious of the I. We know that in a teaching such as Hinduism, it is often said that the final goal of yoga can only be attained as the end of an effort that in previous existences has prepared a suitable body and a complex of subtle dispositions. Even if this is only taken as a popular way of expression, the basic idea is still valid and connects with what we have been saying about the tradition of aristocracy. Hence one may understand why in some civilizations access to the Mysteries and initiation was reserved for the higher castes. Remember that the qualities recognized in the aristocratic type are the same as those of the outward type of the initiate, especially as the "regal" tradition conceived of it. The purity of aristocratic blood, understood in a strict and *real* sense, with the dispositions linked to it, is the best "support" for an initiatic realization, already containing that "quintessence" that, when higher influence intervenes, yields the best fruit.

These principles always presuppose a complete and traditional type of civilization.[2] Yet even in the present state of affairs, despite the democratic and humanitarian ideas of modern "spiritualism" that we have criticized, this close relation between the aristocratic quality and everything initiatic must still exist. This holds good both in the upward direction, because initiation can never be a concern of the masses or of a majority, and implies a distinctive quality even on the organic level, and in the downward direction, because as though coming full circle, the figure of the aristocrat is the one that best suits the expression and exteriorization of the quality awoken, or reawoken, by the "Royal Art."

---

2. The possible objection raised even in that type of civilization by an apparent injustice (because someone born into a given caste—in the present case, being born "noble"—found himself in a certain privileged position even with respect to spirituality) is resolved like the difficulty aroused by any kind of difference within the modern and democratic concept of "justice." Besides the fact that difference is the very law of *reality* (since two beings who were genuinely equal in every respect would no longer be two, but a single being), there is the general view that birth does not happen by chance, but is defined by a prenatal determination or choice, and by laws of correspondence and sympathy. This view, as we know, substitutes in the true esoteric teaching for the myth of heredity created by preceding earthly existences.

A final point that perhaps merits attention is that the aristocratic ideal, described above as chiefly linked to a tradition of the warrior type, is essentially incompatible with the views of the religion that has come to predominate in the West.

Whereas this ideal rests on the necessity and the spiritual value of difference and inequality among men, the presupposition of Christianity is a religious consecration of the contrary principle of equality and brotherhood. The aristocrat, on the basis of his experience of superiority toward himself and a heroic disdain for existence, knows neither the rights nor the respect for "man" that Christianity has introduced in the West and which has grown into a veritable superstition. The law of the nobleman is honor, justice, the healthy pride of one who holds high his own tradition and is armed with the calm awareness of his own virtue. All that has a notoriously "luciferic" odor for Christianity, whose values are more of feeling oneself as a "sinner," humility, repentance, charity, forgiveness, and prayer. The Gospel principle of returning good for evil is not for aristocrats: they may pardon and be generous, but only to a vanquished enemy, not to one still standing in all the force of his injustice. Nor is love an aristocratic principle, in the sense of a need to embrace, commune with, and take care of those who may not even want or deserve it. Relations between aristocratic equals have nothing communistic or fraternal about them: they are facts of loyalty, recognition, mutual respect, with each keeping his own dignity distinct. For this reason there is nothing in the hierarchy of the warrior caste resembling a "mystic" bond, an incorporeal and impersonal dependency. Bonds are formed in the open, by free relations between free forces—taking the term "force" in the broadest sense, of which the physical represents only a particular and inferior case.

From all this it is evident that if a true aristocratic tradition could be reconstituted, it would also open a way for the West to rediscover itself, discarding the influences of a spirituality and a morality that are, after all, alien to it, and then to seek out those influences that truly suit it: those that are not only compatible with initiatic values, but which for that reason can represent its most natural expression.

One hardly need mention the state of degeneration in which the remnant of European nobility finds itself today, compared to its original tradition.[3] Things seem to have reached a point where reconstructive action can no longer find a basis in it. Besides, the whole trend of modern civilization is against a return to normality, which would begin precisely with the restoration and recognition of aristocratic values. In practice, what we have been saying mainly concerns the form of an ideal achievement that is in a sense individual, when contingent circumstances or a special inner attitude do not lead to the inscrutable "Hermetic" type of esotericist. But the recovery of contact with a higher order of influences might also lead to the resurgence of a physical and spiritual race that has virtually disappeared.

---

3. We should point out that Europe's surviving nobility derives from an aristocracy which, unlike that of its origins and of other civilizations, was predominantly one of warriors in an already secular sense. Due to the character of Christianity, no tradition of blood and caste exists as counterpart to a tradition of the spirit, because of the rule of celibacy imposed on the clergy.

BŘEZINA

Canticle of the Fire[1]

O Mystery of the Fire. Liberator.
Radiant symbol of the Omnipresent.
Superb breath of strength. Embrace transformed into Light.
You who rise upward.
Illusion of the colors collapsed into a single blaze.
Tongues of fire flaming above the heads of the Saints.
Gardens of flames hidden in the depths of things and blooming
*   with the glory of the passings from the visible to the invisible.*
In your avenues, behold: the souls of the Strong go with their own
*   love and like a song of love is for them the whispering of your*
*   smiles, O Flames, friends of the new wind.*
In you, the Victors light their torches for the dusks of times to come,
and in your midst the sorrow of the multitude wanders, gathering
*   with abrupt gestures your bloody and vibrant flowers,*
from whose crown it then tears, with bare hands, all the ardent
*   leaves, like rose petals,*
to throw them, changed into light and perfumes,
onto the path of the soul.

---

1. Translated by B. Vendis from the Czechoslovakian text *Větri od Pólů* (Prague: Mànes, 1926). [The original book by Otakar Březina (1868–1929) was published in 1897. This is translated from the Italian. —*Trans.*]

About an "Arithmetical Oracle" and the Backstage of Consciousness

Many years ago, a person whom we later came to know was a boy, vacationing in a region not far from Rome (Bagnaia, near Viterbo). While there, he happened to help an old man whom he found injured in a country lane: a man who had the reputation among the local peasants of a strange and even suspicious character, and who had lived alone for many years in a sort of hut off the beaten track.

After this meeting, a spontaneous friendship arose between the two. When the time came for the boy to return to the capital, the old man made him a gift of a handwritten notebook, telling him it was *"a small part of a big affair"* that might one day be useful to him. But he made the boy swear that, come what may, he would not communicate the whole contents to anyone else.

For years the notebook, with its seemingly incomprehensible writing, was left forgotten in a drawer, until the boy, now grown up, made friends with a person who was interested in occultism. One day he told this person of the strange friendship and the mysterious gift received so many years ago, and was urged to take a serious look at what it was about. Thus, the encoded notebook was brought out of oblivion and studied. We ourselves were informed of the matter.

This is what it was about. It gave a series of rules, based on a cipher for translating the letters of the alphabet into corresponding numbers.

These were combined through complicated arithmetical procedures, sometimes ordered by the structure of certain geometrical figures, so as to yield a series of numbers that were retranslated into letters. At the same time it gave, as a "key," a number, which indicated that every "nth" letter of the series (every third, fourth, etc.), should be set apart, because together those letters will constitute a phrase with its own meaning. This whole method was applied to an initial phrase that summed up a certain question, which the phrase finally obtained was supposed to answer.

What is striking about all this is the *absolutely mechanical and impersonal method.* The person concerned plays no part in it. It is a series of operations that are what they are, without any dependence on choice, interpretation, or intuition on the operator's part. Once you have formulated the question, everything that happens is given. One need only apply the method, and anyone who knows the rules will arrive at the same result, providing no mistakes are made in the calculation. If necessary, since sometimes the operations can take four or five hours, one can use a calculating machine or entrust some of them to another person.

Thus, unlike crystal-gazing, visions in the mirror, cartomancy, "spiritualist" table-tapping, and so forth, the method is not an expedient for focusing the attention and enabling transition to another state of consciousness: here the method is the center of it all. The interesting thing is that through this method the letters and syllables of the question *produce* another phrase by themselves, which almost always has the value of an answer, and which in any case is formulated in complete words.

As for the significance of these answers, we do not have the information for confidently evaluating them. The person who received the mysterious notebook and his friend have made many experiments, asking advice about practical matters, information, predictions (they maintain that experience has often confirmed the responses); also on doctrinal matters, in connection with which it is often declared that both the teaching and the method itself originate from the "Three Sages." But even apart from the precision and value of the answers, the case is no less interesting for anyone who reflects on it and draws the due inferences.

It opens a new window on the subconscious and the "infraconscious," on the occult psychisms that slip through the web of our mental processes, especially at the obscure moment of their formation. The possibility of a method such as we have described would be inexplicable, unless one admits that the question potentially contains an answer, via connections that escape us; and admits, therefore, that in the act of presentation, and especially the formulation in certain words made from certain letters, something acts that cannot be reduced to conscious thought, and through unknown laws determines what is needed for the impersonal and automatic process of the mathematical method to yield at least a meaningful phrase.

Second, the existence of such a method thus confirms there is a science (recalling the *Ars combinatoria* of Ramon Llull and the arithmosophic methods used by some kabbalistic interpreters) relating to the deep and occult laws of language, and particularly to those laws that secretly link certain subtle elements to certain letters or syllables in the expression. Only under this assumption is it possible to formulate a precise and objective rule for the extraction of what already exists invisibly from letter to letter in a phrase. Hence the case we have described should serve, above all, to make one suspect a backstage of which science and philology know nothing, but which nevertheless "someone" has discovered.

Hence, too, the suspicion with which one should regard the so-called interior world, in relation to what has already been discussed by Iagla.[1] Here is another way to convince us of the relativity and incompleteness of that "waking consciousness" in which people feel so safe. Underground roots lead to its forms, and behind the scenes invisible elements pull the threads of many a "conscious" thought process without anyone suspecting it. *Our case shows that the brief moment of concentration in which a question is formulated is in fact a kind of interruption of the continuity of consciousness, enough for a group of infraconscious elements to emerge, and through precise laws to embody themselves in the conceptual and verbal expression.*

---

1. "Subterranean Logic," *Introduction to Magic,* vol. II, 53–58.

If one seeks to know the nature of these elements, one should first consider a class that is personal, in the strictest sense of the word. For example, if the question bears on something that preoccupies us, whether or not we admit it, the act of formulation will often arouse a constellation of more or less definite feelings of doubt, hope, or fear. This will guide the subconscious process so as to include in the question itself an answer reflecting what is desired or feared, or at least what is formulated in the subconscious. We notice the same thing in the case of some false predictions of the future, when the seer, instead of objectively transcending time, merely makes contact with the psyche of the questioner; then the "prediction" is only the telepathic reading or visualization of what lies hidden there, relating precisely to what it expects or desires for the future.

Beside this individual domain of the subconscious, there is a collective one where the opinions, beliefs, or dominant feelings of an epoch are at work. These too are influences that can act behind the scenes and cause various mental complexes. For example, the pretended "revelations" that in some modern "spiritualist" circles have been taken as gospel truth and made the basis of extraordinary theories can often be explained by these collective influences, which like the former ones have an irrational and infraconscious nature.[2]

However, one should not think of phenomena of this kind as limited to the collective, sub-individual field, manifesting in beliefs and prejudices. It is much more interesting and important to confirm the presence of similar influences at the basis of many ideas that are supposedly acquired and verified in the fields of culture and even science.

---

2. The answers of the arithmetic oracle sometimes seem to come from real, intelligent beings; an illusion similar to that found in certain mediumistic phenomena or in automatic writing. As one example, we wanted to test the objective divinatory power of the method. We asked it what word was at the beginning of a certain line of a given page of a closed book. The reply was another question: "What for?" Something similar was found in other answers. Either a "second personality" or an extra-individual "influence" must have been involved in the act of formulation, which seemed to express itself in a whole series of answers obtained through the mathematical method, and which claimed to come from the "Three Sages" mentioned above.

For example, someone who could focus a mental "spectroscope" on the criteria, the evidence, and the ways of seeing that are sanctified in modern culture concerning historical events, personalities or epochs, certain ancient sciences or traditions, and certain non-Western doctrines, would make very disconcerting discoveries. He would find falsifications and one-sided interpretations that cannot be considered as chance or conscious, but which give the feeling of a precise *intention* and a kind of *plan*. It is in fact a matter of forces that are anything but irrational, and through infraconscious processes come to determine what happens in the seat of judgment and conviction of specific personalities, so that certain things will be seen and others not, and the collective psyche adopts a corresponding orientation. The examination of so-called public opinion from this point of view would bring to light things that people today are far from suspecting.

Third, there may be elements of *genuine* knowledge incorporated in the infraconscious psychisms, which are part of the integral being of man, if only in latent form with respect to the known content of the mind, and acquired in a different way from that of the common sources of cognition.

If this is the case, either the arithmetical method or some other method of "divination" should be considered as an indirect means for bringing such knowledge to consciousness.

Last, we draw attention to the case of influences of a higher character, linked neither to "intentions" nor to collective currents, nor to individual semi-conscious complexes or "wandering influences" somehow inserting themselves. Here one should refer to what was said (*Introduction to Magic*, vol. II, 163[3]) about the higher meanings that may lie latent in many myths, legends, fables, elements of folklore, and also

---

3. [This is the corresponding page in the English edition. The original reference is "vol. II, cap. VI, 158," or in the 1955 edition "vol. II, cap. VI, 174," although the page in question is in the fifth, not the sixth issue. There appears to be nothing relevant in that location. The French edition (Julius Evola, *Tous les écrits . . . signés Arvo—Agarda—Iagla*, [Milan: Archè, 1986], 126n.) suggests correspondences in the *Introduction to Magic* articles "On the Hyperborean Tradition" (vol. II, essay XI.3) and "The 'Primitives' and Magical Science" (vol. III, essay X.3). —*Trans.*]

in the etymological structure of names of persons, divinities, places, and so on. We said there that finding such higher meanings does not always indicate a conscious intention and the equally conscious possession of a genuine esoteric consciousness on the part of individuals or groups; but that is not to say that it all comes down to imposing gratuitous and irrelevant interpretations. Both points of view miss what is really in question.

It is quite simplistic, even materialistic, to believe that mythology, fable, certain stories and names contained in sacred scriptures, and so forth, always go back to "initiates" who created it all as a diguise of superior knowledge for popular use. On the contrary, subtle influences may act in the form of instinct within certain people's poetic and religious fantasy, while they are far from suspecting that there is *also* an objective sapiential content in what they believe they have created. For this reason, different interpretations of this kind of literature neither exclude nor contradict each other: a literal meaning may coexist with a symbolic one; a poetic meaning with a religious, physical, or metaphysical one. To believe that only one interpretation is correct, usually invoking the author's "intention," is wrong because it ignores the multiplicity of conscious, subconscious, individual, and supraindividual elements that concur in any process of the human psyche, and especially in some individuals and in special circumstances.[4]

It was really to draw attention to all these matters that we have written here about the "numerical oracle," *a small part of a big affair.* These remarks should indicate the direction of the first steps of an occult work. It is a matter of detecting the subtle and "hermetic" element due to an occult wisdom and influence, which circulates in the texture of what man believes to be most intimate and most his own, evading the gross senses and definite mental states like water running through the fingers. However little we have advanced in this direction by awakening a form of sensitivity and subtle control, we will have taken one step, whose importance cannot be overestimated, along the path of emancipation and power.

---

4. On this subject it may be helpful to refer to what Abraxa has written about the "Solutions of Rhythm and Liberation" in *Introduction to Magic,* vol. II, 108–14.

POSTSCRIPT

The case of this mathematical oracle should provide an example of how easily legends and "spiritualist" currents are created. We have come to learn that the affair that came to our attention in 1928, and which we valued merely as an interesting curiosity, gave rise on the strength of its responses to a sort of movement or group in Paris christening itself the "Polaires." As for the old man of Viterbo who transmitted the ciphered notebook, he was made out to be an initiate of Tibet, and to have subsequently returned thither . . . (Note by UR)

Experiences

The Crown of Light

The eyes, as commonly spoken of, are not the only eyes. To be exact, one should speak of many more than two eyes, or even better, of a unique "eye" as spiritual awareness that can move to various "centers," realizing in each one its "organ" and a "mode" of vision, each with distinct aspects and characteristics.

This at least is what my own experience has taught me. I must add, however, that at present I can only speak with certainty about three of these centers of vision. They can be related respectively to the crown of the head, the center of the forehead, and the region of the heart. Students of the subject will know that these are the locations that Hindu doctrine assigns to the *sahasrāra-cakra,* the *ājñā-cakra,* and the *anāhata-cakra.*

I repeat that each of these "centers" gives its own particular vision, as different from one another as are the senses of the physical body. That said, I will try to explain how I came to knowledge of them and how it manifested to me, limiting myself for now to the first.

To start with, I must mention that the practices to be briefly described here followed others that had already led me to certain phenomena that I have referred to in these pages (see *Introduction to Magic,* vol. I, 141–43). I believe this preface is necessary, because I may have brought to the present practices a spiritual condition that was responsible for their success, and lacking which they might possibly have come to nothing.

So, sitting comfortably facing the sun, and having a keen sense of its presence as a spiritual being, I looked at it for a little with half-closed eyes, then closed them and continued to look from beneath my eyelids.

I was led to repeat this many times, until suddenly the way the sun appeared to me changed completely. It was enlivened by the most pure and refulgent colors, first as flashes, then with roughly shaped edges, then with slow haloes of green, purple, violet, and so forth, that revolved around the central light.

I emphasize the sensation that there was something alive about these colors; a sensation I'm afraid I cannot communicate, together with a corresponding sensation of "deadness" in regard to all the other common colors, however radiant they might be.

I continued with these experiments, prolonging them as long as I could without over-tiring myself. Repeating them day after day, I came to be able to stare at the sun for a long time without blinking. I add that rhythmical breathing and the concentration of the subtle breath-energy at the crown of the head helped to make the experiment work better, but I don't believe that this is an essential condition.

At the beginning the exercise is not pleasant, because headaches soon develop, as well as a constant ache in the pupils that can last for weeks. But I advise anyone who wants to follow my practice not to be alarmed by this. I can state that in my case my vision does not suffer from it in the least, and that the headaches only happen when the experiment goes on too long. The ache in the pupils is bearable, and will also end with habitual practice, *and above all with recognizing what it is in us that enters into play here,* so as to be able to regulate it deliberately. *Physical vision is in reality a simple support, and one passes into other states of consciousness.*

Once I had reached something like a deep meditation, a moment came in which the chaos of colors that arose, moving lazily around the star, formed little by little into a concentric order, losing the intensity of their shades until they all ended in a solemn, golden luminosity, which momentarily attained a splendor such that the sun's very light, that ordinary light which shines on everything, seemed to me pallid in comparison.

Proceeding further, personalized figures began to appear in these circular orders, in groups like garlands; but at a certain moment the vision took on the most rapidly expanding motion, then vanished completely. I did not even see the sun anymore.

My inner state was one of inability to formulate the slightest thought or to recall a single word. *And at this point, everything knowingly stands suspended in the spiritual condition of "silence" and the most utter "immobility."*

Sight, that sight of the physical eyes that only looks ahead, is entirely suspended. And now a new sensation "glides" in. At the crown of the head an eye of clarity is felt opening very gradually, at first forming itself around the vision of a crown of light faintly gilded; a crown that keeps expanding in ever-larger circles, ever deeper and more potent, rather like sound waves.[1]

Now the garlands of figures return, moving in a slow, circular motion, composing scenes that transform with extreme slowness and majestic solemnity, against a bright background of molten gold.

Sometimes the experience takes on quite a different character. The coronal center becomes a center that projects fulminating lines that sometimes, with unimaginable precision, describe figures of staggering complexity, sometimes tracing what seem like grandiose alchemical or magical symbols. Each of the latter imprints the spirit with an indelible and profound sensation, which is also like a knowledge that one is as yet unable to grasp.

I must connect these experiences with a truly novel language in which the masterpieces of painting have come to speak to me: Raphael, Leonardo, Michelangelo, Correggio. It seemed that I had only now

---

1. In the "Mithraic Ritual" of the *Great Magical Papyrus of Paris,* translated in vol. I, the same two successive phases may be found, although the operation is not one of contemplative identification but of theurgical-ceremonial action. First the doors open and the world of the gods inside them appears; then the solar rays converge on the theurgist, who becomes their center (*Introduction to Magic,* vol. I, 107–8).

understood them, and only now discovered an arcane sense hidden in them, which transfigured them.

I knew with direct and irrefutable evidence that the forms, colors, scenes, and figures immediately visible in these works of art were only *symbols;* they were only shadows cast on the light. Through them, and blazing up in them, were the states of transcendent and solar contemplation that were welling up in me from the depths; and I felt that the foreshadowing of those states—rather than anything man-made—was the true substance of everything grand and sublime made by the creators of all eras. I repeat that this is no theory: it is a proof that has presented itself to me directly, suddenly, together with astonishment at the fact that I had not noticed it until that moment.

In any case, returning to ordinary human life, beside the indelible memory of these contemplations, one carries within oneself an almost unbearable surge of creative energy, a new will for accomplishment, a wealth and rapidity of images, that bears no comparison.

One also carries the direct sensation that what the physical eyes show us in the world are nothing but fragmentary arrangements, sporadic apparitions of a wholeness. Sight, once returned to the limits of the bodily prison, fights against it like a bird trapped in the dark. Between the eyebrows it *feels* a quantity of things that it cannot yet manage to *see.* It longs to release itself; longs to return to the light, to the golden crown of light enthroned at the body's summit. None can ever take away this crown from him who has once known it; nor is there a sovereign on earth who could wear a more beautiful one.

II.5

GERHARD DORN

Clavis Philosophiae Chemisticae
(The Key of Alchemical Philosophy)

Edited by Tikaipôs

The literary and alchemical activity of Gerhard Dorn or Dornaeus, who lived in Strasbourg, Basel, and Frankfurt-am-Main, lasted from 1563 (*Diction. Chem. Theophrasti*) until 1583 (*De Natura Lucis*). *Clavis Totius Philosophiae Alchemicae* (Leiden, 1567) was his first true and original treatise on the subject, and the following extracts are taken from the first part of it. There followed *Lapis Metaphysicus* (Basel, 1569) and *Astronomia, Chymia, Anatomia Viva* (Basel, 1577). It seems that he might have written nothing about Magic, under the usual pretext of Alchemy or Medicine, had he not been drawn to defend his admired master Paracelsus (1493–1541) against the many posthumous and even learned attacks. Dorn was brief enough, and relatively clear enough in this, his first writing, which like the whole work is divided into three parts: Theory, Practice, and Applications. Thereafter—perhaps condemned by the Hermetists—he too became obscure, diffuse, and digressive, except when repeating frequent and long passages from his first work. Evidently the latter soon became impossible to find, through retention by his followers and destruction by his many adversaries. Nothing would remain of it today without Zetzner's *Theatrum Chemicum* and Manget's *Bibliotheca Chemica.*[1]

These passages are extracted from the first part of Dorn's treatise (in *Theatrum Chemicum,* vol. I, 205–44), for the use of those who have already achieved through practice something physiologically and sensibly concrete, and who can gain from it a certain light to guide them through the next developments. I have underlined some phrases and added clarifications here and there. Have I finally profaned the secret? Hardly! First, the clarifications are mostly of words; second, they are not always encouraging; last, in Dorn's era the throng of the hopeful was enormous, and almost all of them panting after material gold; now the throng is small—and in Italy it is tiny, which may be the best thing about it. One can therefore be confident that this rare fragment of greater clarity introduced into such texts will only reach those who can make use of it.

THREE BOOKS ON THE CHEMICAL ART

> *Alterius non sit, qui suus esse potest.*
> (*He belongs to none other who can be his own.*)
>
> PARACELSUS

To the Reader: . . . Now I only want to warn you of this: first and foremost, you should not exceed the limits of a medicine for the human body. If instead you are looking for the metamorphosis of vulgar metals, you will only come to regret your error . . . (13)

---

1. [Tikaipôs's use of these anthologized sources reflects the state of interlibrary communication in the 1920s. The present translation of his chosen excerpts is based on Dorn's Latin original of 1567, now accessible thanks to the British Library and Google Documents. Page numbers in parentheses refer to this edition. Tikaipôs's emphases, originally printed as widely spaced letters, are here underlined to distinguish them from italicized matter. While in cases of doubt I follow Dorn's Latin, Tikaipôs is responsible for adding the commentary in brackets, the ellipses, and the capitalization of terms. —*Trans.*]

Book I: Alchemical Theory

1. *Alchemical philosophy* teaches the investigation of the <u>latent forms</u> of things, according to the truth of things and not their appearance. (14)

2. *Nature,* for the Alchemists, is an operation (*exercitatio*) of Heaven [Ether, Materia prima, universal Thelema] with the Elements[2] in the generation of all things that exist. (16)

3. *Form* is the action and power of the ethereal region upon the elementary region. By the transmutation of Elements into one another, Nature works on Matter, including Form therein like the seed in the womb: pregnant with this virtue, like a mother it produces the fetus in a specific act. This is what the Philosophers mean by saying that *Form is deduced* (extracted) *from the potency of Matter.* For Matter itself can bring to light what has been generated in it by Form. . . . (16–17)

4. *Matter* for us is the whole elementary region, which may be divided into four parts that we call Elements: Fire, Air, Water, and Earth, of which two are principal, namely Fire and Water. For Air appears to be nothing but Water <u>released by heat in the world's creation</u>, while Earth is also Water <u>condensed or rather dessicated by heat and dryness</u>.[3] . . . (17–18) Nothing is consumed by Fire: but by way of transmutation, what leaves one Element joins another. Thus, day by day <u>wise Nature</u>, by thus transmuting the elements into one another, and by form, diligently brings forth new forms, so that what has been deformed by corruption is reformed by <u>regeneration</u>; hence nature's <u>operation is circular, like the heavenly motions</u>. (20–21)

---

2. The four well-known Elements: in the macrocosm, Earth, Water, Air, and Fire; in the microcosm, *physical form* (Salt, Saturn, Lead, etc.), *lunar form* (passive Mercury, Silver, sensitive Spirit), *mercurial form* (active Mercury, Quicksilver, rational Soul), and *solar form* (ethereal Sulfur, higher Mind). Dissolve and recompound them: indeed, the name of Alchemy was not badly chosen.

3. Note that in every case Fire plays its own part, as the superior active element and the least distant from the First Principle.

5. [*Quintessence—Form*].[4] Many keen naturalists, not yet expert in the facts, raise this argument against us. . . . Natural bodies are only made from four Elements, so where is the fifth? We reply that all natural bodies are made both from the four Elements and from Form, which is indeed something, and <u>the most potent part</u>[5] of any compound. . . . Through this bond, Nature compounds all bodies. The Philosophers tell us enigmatically: "Make peace between enemies, and you will have the entire mastery," namely the alchemical. . . . (21–22)

6. *Generation* means the manifestation of what was occulted, following the occultation of the manifest. All bodies are made in three dimensions, namely manifest Height, occult Depth, and Breadth between them. The Philosophers have transmitted this occultly to us in these words: "There is no transition from extreme to extreme except through a medium" [plastic mediator]. Thus, we cannot know the occult form of any body from its manifest form, except through corruption of the manifest, by which its occult quality (*proprietas*) appears. . . . (25–26)

7. *The Ternary.* The whole Universe was constructed by the Holy Trinity in order, number, and measure through Unity. For Unity is not a number, but the pact of concord. The Binary, which is truly the first number [because primordial unity was not even thinkable as an element of numeration], the source and origin of discord, was cut off from unity by the assumption of Matter, and cannot go back to join in one except through an indissoluble bond—which is the One alone. . . . (29) As Trithemius says, let the Binary be thrown out again, and the Ternary will be reducible to the simplicity of the One . . . ; this ascent being known

---

4. *Form,* in the most Brunonian of the various senses that it would assume a few years later from Bruno himself, for example in *De la Causa, Principio e Uno* (*Opere ital.*, 2nd ed., Gentile, 192). Nonetheless, Bruno would repeatedly rail, at least materially, against the Quintessences—more Aristotelian in origin, and already employed by some against Copernicus.

5. [Italian: *la piú pura parte* ("the most pure part"); but in the original Latin: *potissima pars. —Trans.*]

only to those in whose mind is the Ternary, and who, rejecting the Binary through assumption of the Ternary, are received into the simplicity of unity. . . . (30)[6]

8. *The Earth.* Basis and container of everything, both of celestial influences and solid bodies. . . . Trismegistus says: "It ascends from Earth to Heaven, and descends again from Heaven to Earth. . . . Of that *one* the Sun is father and the Moon, mother; the Wind carried it in its belly, AND THE EARTH IS ITS NURSE." (31–32)

9. *The Minerals.* Those who strive to make gold potable seem to work in vain (as Marsilio Ficino says) unless they have first resolved Gold into its first matter, namely Quicksilver and Sulfur: the matter which is the first, proximate, and immediate of all metals. . . . (37)

Beneath the common metals, the Wise conceal the physical and philosophical medicines;[7] likewise what they prepare from vulgar metals in their transmutation is of philosophical metals, so that through equivocation the great treasure of Medicine should remain unknown to the vulgar. Sometimes even the learned Physicians who make no small profession of Philosophy can scarcely understand it. (43–44)

Book II. Alchemical Practice

1. *The praxis of the alchemists.* It is the demonstration to the senses of what the Philosopher, through sure and known philosophical reasons and through his intellect, has realized practically concerning the latent forms of natural things. But I do not think that one should rely on their writings alone, nor prefer their opinions to what experience can better teach. Often they have

---

6. Almost all the letters in which the eminent Trithemius (1462–1516), a German Benedictine, discusses Magic were collected as the appendix to his *De Septem Secundeis* (Strasbourg: Zetzner, 1613). Dorn often cites him and also dedicates to him a special chapter, *Physica Trithemii,* in the present volume of his *Theatrum,* preceded by a *Physica Trismegisti.*

7. The real and theoretical magical agents.

not gone deeply into things, and make assertions and statements concerning what they themselves hardly know. . . . (51)

2. *Alchemical laboratory.* A three-in-one furnace . . . in which three different operations can be made, <u>though with a single dissolving fire</u>. . . . (52)

3–4. *Furnaces and stoves.* [There are two woodcuts here. As every reader knows, the laboratory, furnaces, stoves, and all the rest are contained in ourselves.]

5. *The instruments.* The proper instrument of the Alchemist, as of Nature herself, is Fire.[8] The internal fire is proper to every substance, and is naturally within it, which the Alchemist must understand. . . . (64–65)

6. *The operation.* It is double, *solutio* and *congelatio.* Solution [dissolution] is calcination [fluidification] of the body; congelation is instead [and at the same time] condensation of the spirit[9] reduced to vapor. . . . In this way the earthy body is dissolved into a calx, the watery into an airy spirit, which is again congealed into a watery [or mercurial] body, <u>albeit in a single operation</u> that the vulgar call distillation and the Philosophers, more properly, <u>separation</u>.[10] . . . And <u>rectification</u> is none other than repeated distillations. . . . (66–67, 69)

Book III. Applied Alchemy

1. *Preparation of medicines.* When the empirics strive to imitate Physicists without knowledge of Physics, most cannot achieve

---

8. The Fire of *active Love,* O my reader; and this, practically, in the humid way, is the *essential;* all the rest either follows by itself, or remains more or less as literature.

9. *Spiritus,* the Spirits—from Dante's *spiritelli,* to the *spiriti vitali* of the vitalists—were concrete and material fluidities: hence reducible to fluid forms, whether more dense or more subtle.

10. Separation here is of our four—or three, or two—constituent elements: so that for the preparation of the new, higher unity each of them acquires—or reacquires—its own veritable autonomy. This is essentially *abnormal,* consequently not without more or less serious dangers. Hence the strict secrecy of Magic, so as not to reveal and bestow itself except on him who, after long waiting, trials, and disappointments, seems to inspire some confidence in his sound temper and high character.

what they hope for, because they force bodies to mix with other bodies without previous preparation, while trying to prepare them at the same time. I will not deny that the Alchemists <u>mix Bodies with Spirits in a physical way</u>, so that similar things ally to one another; after which they <u>reject the bodies</u> as unsuitable for Medicine. They do even better, separating the spirits thus mixed from one another in a most subtle way. (72–73)

2–5. *Preparation of the vitriol, aquavita, and oils, in furnaces on a slow fire.* (73–87)

6. *Virtues of the Quintessence.* It is remarkable, and incredible to the vulgar, that the Spirit of Wine,[11] extracted from its body and completely separated by a continual circular motion, should have the power of extracting any other spirits from their bodies, whether vegetal, mineral, or animal, by infusion alone. The chemical Philosophers know nothing more true, or more proven by experience, than that Active things, separated from their Passive parts, act on any Compound, dissolve it through the keenness of the active spirit, and segregate the spirit from it through *symbolization*.[12] Seeing that similar things are attracted, not impeded, by each other, the spirit wants its own nature to be freed from bodily shackles and to return to its own origin, as like joins to like. Hence it is not surprising if the *Fifth Virtue and First Essence* of the *Wine*[13] attracts the *energies* [forces, faculties] of all things infused in it, and divides them from the

---

11. The whole paragraph, hermetically speaking, has multiple meanings: subjective and objective, individual and collective, particular and universal, human and divine. I will not underline anything, because I would have to underline it all.

12. [The Italian text translates the Latin "per symbolisationem" as *per condissoluzione.* —*Trans.*]

13. By *Vinum* (Wine) is meant: in the microcosm, the *vinum vinens,* red wine, or live human blood in the living veins—and not the blood extracted and defiled in the abominations of sorcery; and in the macrocosm, the *Vinum-Unum-Vita,* or the living Substance, omnipresent, eternal, and timeless; the concrete and profound Matter-Form-Life of the *Unum-Universum.* Further on we will see another relevant Enigma concerning *Vinum.* In the microcosm all this is sometimes understood as human semen and any human fluid, and even as wine in its true and proper sense, provided that it is good.

elements by dissolving the natural bond, while through desire and action the spirits rise above the passive parts. . . . (87–88)

7–11. *Solution by itself.* Almost all the alchemists teach us to *distill* (dissolve) the metals, some with redistilled vinegar, or with strong lye; some with waters or juices taken from sharp substances (*ex acuentibus*). I, however, will now show a way of distilling any metal without mixture, but by itself, which I think none has taught hitherto, or if they I have, I do not remember reading it. Every metal that is consumed by fire will be distilled by evaporation, if put by itself in a bowl or earthenware alembic, the mouth firmly sealed with clay, placed on a <u>melting fire</u> and kept <u>for a very long time</u> in the molten state. . . . This way of dissolving metals is not to be spurned, but diligently noted:[14] while something far better[15] may occur to you here, if only you know it. (89–91)

12. *Mineral riddle.* "Visita(bis) Interiora Terrae; Rectificando, Invenies Occultum Lapidem (Veram Medicinam)"[16]—(You will) visit the interior of the Earth; by rectification, you will find the occult stone (the true medicine).[17]

"Hujus Lapidis, jam nobis manifesti, libras *sex* . . . calcinabimus." First meaning: "We will calcine *six* pounds of this [occult] Stone, now manifested to us." Second meaning, reading *six* as Latin VI = *vi* = by force or virtue: "*By virtue* of this [occult and divine] Stone, we will calcine those which are *balanced* [our Elements]. . . ." (102)

13. *Vegetal riddle.* "Unum post quinque, nihil n, post quinque millenum colloca." After five (V), put one (I), and *nihil* or *enim*

---

14. [In the Latin text of 1567, the chapter ends at this point. —*Trans.*]

15. That is, to pass from the wet to the dry way: *si sapis,* if you know how.

16. [This sentence is reproduced exactly from the Italian translation. The 1567 text reads: "Visitabis interiora terrae, reperies ibidem occultum lapidem veram medicinam." —*Trans.*]

17. It is the famous enigma whose first form—without the parts in parentheses—was by Basil Valentine. The initials of the Latin words form VITRIOL(UM), the name that Valentine also gave to the mysterious Philosophic Stone. Thus: visit the inward part of your own being; then rectify without tiring and without erring.

(which are both abbreviated as N), and after five (V) put a thousand (M). [Hence it gives VINUM, wine].[18]

"Hujus partes 16 aequales . . . destillabimus." First meaning: "Of this (*Vinum*) we will distill 16 equal parts. . . ." Second meaning, reading 16 = XVI = *Xristi vi* = "In the virtue of Christ, we will distill the equal parts of this Wine" [i.e., the lunar and the mercurial part]. (109)

14. *Animal riddle.*[19] We will deliver up the *vile but precious Gift* [the physical body] to the caduceus-bearing dragon [to the dissolving mercurial principle] to devour for its sixth part [the VI, the *vi,* the force that is *part* or gift] of it. Having eaten it, this restless serpent [the fugitive Mercury] calmly halts and goes to sleep. It is given to drink the waters trickling from two fountains, white and green [the so-called wintry or *lunar* influences, and the so-called vernal or *venereal*], until the next summer returns [the so-called *solar* influences arrive], which with its fierce heat dries up the waters, and the dead corpse [of the old Adam] appears in the depths of the sea. When thrown onto the Fire, it revives, and regaining its wings, flies up in the air, but leaving in the fire a fetus, to which it gave birth after conceiving from the *Gift*. This fetus, as it was born in Fire, is to be fed with Fire like the Salamander, until it is adolescent, when it becomes very ruddy and sanguine. Then it is to be bathed and submerged in waves more pleasant than those which mothered it, so that by its death [by immersion] the weak parts live more happily. From its now pallid body, the soul is separated with the blood: which is such a gift to us that all bodies are worthless.[20] The Philosophers have ascertained that this altogether

---

18. Ramon Llull (1232–1315) has already made much use of the term *Vinum*—sometimes white, sometimes red (lunar and mercurial, human semen and blood, and so on). But I did not know this riddle, and believe that it is certainly by Dorn. On Llull one may now consult the rather timid but conscientious volume of Lucien-Graux, *Le Docteur Illuminé* (Paris: Fayard, 1927).

19. It is certainly all by Dorn himself; and I give it complete, with some clarifications in the usual brackets.

20. [I omit Tikaipôs's footnote discussing alternative meanings, posited on later sources, because the 1567 original confirms the given interpretation. —*Trans.*]

healthy soul, infused in a sickly body, purifies it from every disease by the simplicity of its own virtue.[21] This is the most perfect of all medicines and the simplest, leaving no corruption in the human body;[22] it revives all weariness, and returns whatever is unbalanced and imperfect to the tempered state. With its unifying innocence it makes peace between mortal enemies;[23] grants life in this age, if God allows, even to the half dead, and bestows health on sick bodies. (112–14)

CONCLUSION

Everyone ignorant of this Art, even the most learned of the universities, habitually rejects it. What wonder, since they will never have heard or experienced the like? It does not follow that an art should be condemned because learned men are ignorant . . . (114–15).

We have with us, or rather within ourselves, not distant from us, whatever we seek from the outside or from others . . . (117). In every mixed or individual thing is found something other than hot, cold, dry, wet, or the element. What our art separates from all these is not the wet, the dry, the the cold, much less the hot, but a certain *aethereum,* just as Heaven [Ether and Fire] is segregated from the lower Elements. Hence the Philosophers call this Medicine Heaven, because it acts on the body as Heaven acts on lower things, and also because in respect to the body from which it is taken, it is like Heaven[24] with respect to the Elements. For the Elements in themselves are dead, and produce nothing unless they are vivified by the Soul or Spirit of the World. Likewise the Earth, which if it were not beneath the sky, however rich would yield nothing. But being placed under the open air it gives forth its plants and little beasts. There is nothing so solid in the earthly globe [and so

---

21. Many initiatic bodies, both ancient and not so ancient—Rosicrucians, Paracelsians, and so forth—were known to consist of healers, and maybe they still do.

22. Nor, of course, in the astral bodies, which are also subject to infections.

23. Such as Body and Soul.

24. This "Heaven" is evidently understood here, sooner or later, as it would later be understood by Bruno: as the sole universal Matter, or the universal Matter-Form.

much the less in the human organism] that could prevent this soul from penetrating right to its center . . . (119–21). Whoever could think that the Elements were self-generated is no more a philosopher than someone who asserts that a woman can naturally be impregnated without a man. . . . Thus that elementary Fire whose first origin is in the center of the earth . . . works with a power of dissolution on the other Elements, but the gift of generation is due to Heaven, not to the Elements, whence we may conclude that all generation takes place between Heaven and the Elements. . . . The fetus is a mixture, <u>formed from the substance of both parents, produced for its perfection</u> (122–23).

Lest we seem to be pandering to the prostitution of Nature's secrets, a little of these things will suffice for the sons of Wisdom: they will easily grasp what we intend by it. Those who laugh at our art out of ignorance should get away from here, for it is set to ruin them, since seeking they shall not find, and hearing they shall not understand. . . . The sons of Wisdom take their food not by mouth but by the spirit, that they may live more with the Mind than with the body. But they also wish one to have *Mens sana in corpore sano* (a healthy mind in a healthy body) until, freed from Nature's bonds, these three [physical Body, mercurial Spirit, and neoplatonic *Mens*], reunited in *one*, will live in eternity (124–25).

Various Commentaries

DIFFICULTIES OF BELIEF

The "difficulties of belief" concerning some things in our disciplines are often curious.

For example, if it is said that during a "magical chain" a human being was taken and transported from the city he was in and found himself in another city, you can at best expect a pitying smile. But if you tell the same person that in a certain mediumistic séance, there was a phenomenon of "apport" (a foreign object appearing in a closed environment), it would not cause a great scandal these days.

From the *objective* point of view, it would be difficult to show much difference between the two phenomena. Both are cases of dematerialization (taking the term in a positive sense) and rematerialization, with an intermediate state free from spatial conditions. If the "apport" phenomenon corresponds to a possibility that has now been positively verified, we see no reason why a substantially identical process should be less conceivable. The only difference is that instead of being brought about unconsciously and unintentionally in the trance state of a medium, it is presumed possible for it to happen deliberately, through the active ecstasy of the magus. No other assumption is required for getting one's head around the "incredible" phenomena of this kind.

These considerations may be applied to various other possibilities that have now been experimentally proven by psychical research.

Modern man seems extraordinarily defeatist toward himself. It is only reluctantly, through the evidence—if not actually the force—of "experience," that he will admit certain extranormal possibilities. But beyond that, when you invite him to see if perhaps by a certain method he might master himself and become directly cognizant of them, that is too much for him. He gets *distracted,* thinks of something else, or rants against the visionaries and hoaxers who think they can disinter *magic* in this day and age!

HE WHO "SAW" THE GODS

Among the current prejudices that most hinder the comprehension of ancient traditions, or of forms of civilization that still differ from the predominant Western one, is thinking that humans have always perceived the sense-world as they do today.

If, for example, we take the imagination, we find that for most people, in the waking state, it is nothing but a *subjective* faculty. It brings up forms belonging to the world of the I, with no relation to reality. To call something imaginary is to call it unreal or baseless: it is all the same today. This judgment then extends to everything in ancient traditions that seems to belong to such a faculty, like fairy tales, myths, and so on.

This opinion rightly applies to a certain condition of the imaginative faculty, in which it is isolated from the outer world and receives only the impulses that come from the subjective world of the I. But it is possible for the imagination to enter a different and contrary state, in which it is isolated from the subjective world and open to the objective world, just as happens with the faculties of physical perception. We have reason to believe that this was a normal state in primordial civilizations, whereas today it can only be reached through extranormal and exceptional means. In such a state, the natural forces act in the same way as they do on the sense-organs, producing a perception or representation that is valid as real knowledge. They act on the imagination to create a phantasm, vision, or image, which is equally valid. Symbolic and imagined forms arise, translating into images a contact with the forces of things.

In this way ancient man *saw* the gods, *saw* the gnomes, sylphs, undines, demons, genii, and so forth. All that was no "invention" or poetic fantasy, but a direct datum of experience, inserting itself spontaneously in the texture of what the physical senses revealed, and, as it were, extending it. We repeat that it is still possible today, if one is able to isolate oneself while still awake in what we have elsewhere called the "lunar man."[1]

Let us put this more plainly. If a man with a certain aesthetic sensitivity looks out on a stormy ocean, a relationship arises in which he feels a certain aesthetic emotion, beyond the commonplace representation of the senses. At a later time, starting from that emotion, he may be able to develop poetic and fantastic images, of a purely personal value. Objectively speaking, this is what has happened: a certain invisible action of the forces physically manifesting in the ocean has suddenly transformed and absorbed itself in a *subjective* state: the I has intervened, has taken only its emotional energy and built upon that as the poet's private affair. But to do the same thing with a physical perception would have been impossible, since the I cannot intervene in the process of sensory perception before a representation has been produced that has a real, objective character. Now, if in the previous case the I could also be provoked spontaneously to this kind of inability to intervene and appropriate, then the outside event would no longer meet the "transformer" that captures it in the form of a subjective sensation, poetic or otherwise. It would continue on its way and meet the imagination in a *pure* state, which would react by producing an image, a vision, an apparition. For example, it might be the figure of Ocean's "being." In such a case, imagination would act as a faculty of *knowledge,* as real as that which the ordinary senses provide.

We should never forget the *symbolic* character of these visions. The true state of affairs can be expressed as follows:

---

1. See the experiences described in *Introduction to Magic,* vol. II, 182–88. In the "lunar man," fantasy is active at night and produces dreams, whose procedure has exactly the same character of symbolic translation, though of contents that normally continue to belong to the subjective world of the I (stimuli, desires, repressed thoughts), or to the world of physical sensations (e.g., the noise of a falling chair that the dream translates into a cannon shot). Only rarely do they contain messages from the higher worlds.

1. World of emotions and sensations—world without form—purely private affair of the I.
2. World of "visions"—world with form—there is a content of reality, but as a symbol to be deciphered.
3. Ultimate state—again without form—because the I neutralizes the faculty of imagination, so that the impression is no longer caught as an image, and goes directly to the center: to the I itself, without intermediaries. Then it has *metaphysical* or *unitive contact,* which is *knowledge* in the integral sense of the word.

But limiting ourselves to the second degree, there is much to be learned if the moderns would only *see,* when studying the visions, legends, and myths not only of the ancients but even of their degenerate remains that are the primitive peoples.

MEN AND GODS

There are two orders of reality: men and gods. They, in space; we, on earth. They have put us down here *as their doubles,* while leaving us a certain autonomy.

They are space, whose curvature is the shore of the Infinite. The earth is for us. Here is our mission.

They have made the heavens descend to earth. They have directed evolution up to the human form. And they seem to have rested there. Now man will act, on the *seventh day.* The celestial universe is inclined toward us, universal justice and mercy converge on this strange planet of blood and mud, which is the Center of the Universe. The seven heavens turn around it. Like a mirror, it returns their seven rays, placed on seven seals. And all that is below is like that which is Above.

Our flesh is forged after the divine model. But the resemblance was not painlessly achieved. It took centuries for even a satisfactory image: many are unformed or deformed. But the reproduction sometimes succeeds. Then, among a thousand or ten thousand people, a truly divine face is to be seen. This is enough for him who can see.

Every man is the double of a god. Enclosed as by an iron ring, the Kabbalah has given a name to his guardian: THE DRAGON OF THE THRESHOLD. It runs to and fro and *eats dust* every day, every day!

It dies. But it is to be reborn, to die and be reborn. One day it becomes aware of itself. In the end—for everything down here has an end—in the end, it wakes up as a god.

(FROM *LE SYMBOLISME*)

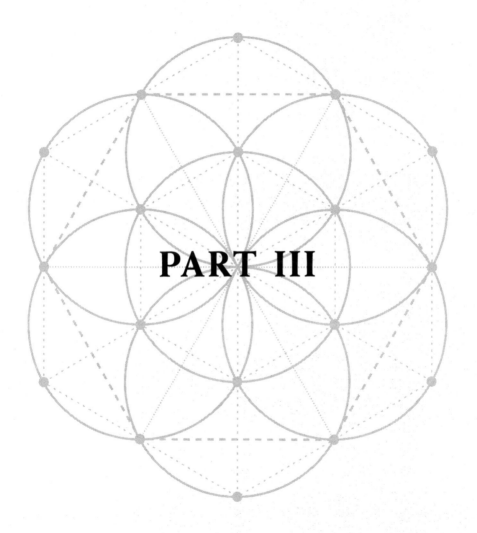

PART III

EA

The Legend of the Grail and the "Mystery" of the Empire[1]

There is an idea that constantly recurs, in one form or another, in the traditions of many peoples: that of a mighty "Lord of the World" and of a mysterious realm above any visible one, a residence serving as a pole or axis, in the higher sense; an immutable center, depicted as a terra firma in the middle of the ocean of life, a sacred and intangible country, a land of light, or a solar land.

Metaphysical meanings, symbols, and obscure memories are inextricably mixed here. A central motif is the idea of Olympian regality and the "mandate from heaven." Confucius says: "He who rules through the Virtue (of Heaven) resembles the pole star. He remains immobile while all things turn around him." The idea of the "King of the World" as *cakravartī* dominates a series of secondary themes: the *cakravartī*—King of kings—turns the wheel, the wheel of the *Regnum,* of the "Law," while he himself is unmoving. Invisible as the wind, his action has the irresistibility of natural forces. In multiple forms, and closely connected with the idea of a Nordic-Hyperborean land, there stands out the sym-

---

1. [This article, by Julius Evola, was added to the 1971 edition of *Introduzione alla Magia.* A previous version of it was published in French in *Études Traditionnelles,* nos. 239–40 (Nov.–Dec. 1939) and reproduced in Julius Evola, *Tous les écrits de Ur & Krur* [*"Introduction à la magie"*] *Krur 1929* (Milan: Archè, 1985), 291–310. —Trans.]

bolism of the seat in the center, the immutable seat, the island, the mountain peak, the city of the sun, the protected land, the white isle or splendid isle, the land of heroes. Hellenic tradition says "The sacred land is reached neither by land nor by sea." Far Eastern tradition murmurs "Only the spirit's flight can take you there." Other traditions speak of a mysterious magnetic mountain, and of the mountain to which all who have achieved perfect spiritual illumination vanish or are taken. Others again speak of a solar land, from which come those destined to take on the role of legitimate kings among leaderless peoples. This is also the *Isle of Avalon,* that is, the island of Apollo, the solar, Hyperborean god whom the Celts call Aballun. Legendary "divine" races like the Tuatha dé Danann, who came from Avalon, are also said to have come from "heaven." The Tuatha brought with them from Avalon certain mystical objects: a stone that indicates the rightful kings, a lance, a sword, a vessel that gives perpetual food, the "gift of life." They are the same objects as figure in the legend of the Grail.

These legendary motifs came down from primordial times to the Middle Ages, when they took on characteristic forms such as the traditions of Prester John's and King Arthur's realms.

"Prester John" is not a name, but a title: there is mention of a dynasty of "Prester Johns" who, like the descendants of David, held both the kingly and the priestly office. The realm of Prester John often has traits of the "primordial place" and the "earthly paradise." It is there that the Tree grows, which in some versions of the legend appears as the Tree of Life, in others as the Tree of Victory and universal dominion. There too is found the Luminous Stone, a stone that has the power to resuscitate the imperial bird, the Eagle. John subdues the peoples of Gog and Magog—the elementary forces, the demons of the collective. Various legends tell of symbolic journeys to Prester John's country or to lands of similar meaning, taken by the greatest leaders of history in order to receive a kind of supranatural sanction for their power. For his part, Prester John is said to have sent symbolic gifts to emperors such as "Frederick," which had the significance of a "divine mandate." One of the heroes supposed to have reached the legendary land was Ogier the Dane. But in Ogier's legend Prester John's realm is identified with

Avalon, hence with the Hyperborean island, the solar land, and the "white island."

It was to Avalon that King Arthur retired. Tragic events, variously described in the sources, forced him to seek refuge there. This retirement of Arthur's really means that a principle or a function became latent. According to legend, Arthur has never died, but lives on in Avalon and will come again. In the figure of King Arthur we have one of the many versions of the "polar ruler," the "king of the world." The historical element here is charged with a suprahistorical one. The old etymology already derived Arthur's name from *arkthos,* meaning "bear," which brings us back to the idea of the "center" via the astronomical symbolism of the polar constellation. The symbolism of the Round Table, of whose knightly order King Arthur is the supreme head, is both "solar" and "polar." Like Midgard, the luminous dwelling of the Ases, the "divine heroes" of the North, Arthur's palace is built at the "center of the world" (*in medio mundi constructum*). Some texts have it turning around a central point, just as the swastika revolves in the "white island" (*śvetadvīpa*) remembered by the Indo-Europeans of Asia, in the Hyperborean land whose god is the solar Vishnu; just as the Celtic-Nordic "isle of glass"—a facsimile of Avalon—turns; like the wheel of destiny of the *cakravartī,* the Aryan "King of the World." The supranatural and "magical" powers of this figure are incarnated, as it were, in Myrddhin, or Merlin, King Arthur's inseparable counselor, who is not so much a figure in his own right as the personification of the supranatural part of Arthur himself. Arthur's knights will go in quest of the Grail. They recruit their members from all lands and have as their motto: "May he who is chief be our bridge." In ancient etymology, *pontifex* signifies "bridge builder," that is, he who establishes the connection between two banks, or two worlds.

Obscure historical memories have added to this, together with geographical transpositions of temporal notions. The "island" that various traditions situate at the "ends of the earth" really stands for the primordial center in very early times. For the Greeks, the land of the sun is Thule (*Thule ultima a sole nomen habens* [furthest Thule having its name from the sun]), and Thule is equivalent to the *Airyanem-Vaējō,* the extreme northern land of the ancient Persians. Airyanem-Vaējō is the "seedbed" of the primordial Aryo-Iranian race, in which the image of the King of kings as representative of the God of Light even appeared historically. The Airyanem-Vaējō witnessed the reign of the solar Yima, the "age of Gold." But Hesiod recalls: "When this age (the age of Gold) declined, these divine men continued to live like the daimons (τοὶ μὲν δαίμονές εἰσί) and became in invisible form (ἠέρα ἐσσάμενοι) the guardians of men."[2] Then, because the "direction of history" is downward, the Golden Age was succeeded by the Silver Age, the age of the Mothers; then that of Bronze, the age of the Titans; and finally the age of Iron, the "dark age," *kali-yuga,* "twilight of the gods." Why? Many myths seem to want to connect "fall" with *hybris,* Promethean usurpation, Titanic revolt. But again Hesiod recalls that Zeus, the Olympian principle, has created within the Iron Age a generation of heroes, who are more than "titans" and have the possibility of winning a life similar to that of the gods (βίος ὥστε θεοί).[3] One symbol is Hercules, the Doric-Achaean ally of the Olympians, enemy of titans and giants.

The doctrine of the supreme center and of the ages of the world is closely connected with that of cyclic laws and periodic manifestations. If these reference points are ignored, many myths and traditional memories remain as incomprehensible fragments. "This happened once—this will happen again," says tradition. And again: "Every time the spirit declines and impiety triumphs, I manifest myself; from age to age I take on a body for the protection of the just, the destruction of the wicked, and the establishment of the law."[4] All traditions include, in various forms and more or less completely, the doctrine of the cyclical manifestations of a unique principle, which continues in a latent state during the intermediate periods. The Messiah, Last Judgment, *Regnum,* and so forth are nothing but a religiously and fantastically deformed tradition of this knowledge. The same knowledge underlies those confused legends of a

---

2. [Hesiod, *Works and Days,* lines 122, 125. Greek orthography corrected from Hesiod, *Works: Selections,* vol. I, ed. and trans. Glenn W. Most (Cambridge, Mass.: Harvard University Press / Loeb Classical Library, 2006), 96. —*Trans*].

3. [Hesiod, *Works and Days,* line 112. Corrected as above. —*Trans.*]

4. [*Bhagavad Gita,* IV, 7–8. —*Trans.*]

ruler who has never died, but retired to some inaccessible place—basically identical to the "Center"—and who will reappear on the day of the "last battle"; of a sleeping emperor who will awaken; a wounded prince who awaits the one who will heal him and restore his decayed or devastated realm to new glory. All these familiar motifs of the medieval imperial legend go far back in time. The primordial myth of the *Kalki-avatāra* already contains these ideas, significantly linked with other symbols that we have mentioned. The Kalki avatar was "born" at Shambhala—one of the names for the primordial Hyperborean center. The doctrine was transmitted to him by Paraśurāma, the "never dead" representative of the tradition of "divine heroes," the destroyer of the rebellious warrior caste. The Kalki avatar fights against the "dark age" and above all against the chiefs of its demonic forces, Koka and Vikoka. Even etymologically, these relate to Gog and Magog, the subterranean forces vanquished and enchained by Prester John, who will escape in the dark age and against which the reawakened emperor will have to fight.

• • •

The legend of the Grail must be connected to this order of ideas, for only on the basis of these traditional facts and this universal symbolism can it be understood, either from the historical or the suprahistorical point of view. Those who consider the story of the Grail solely as a Christian legend, or an expression of "pagan Celtic folklore," or the creation of high chivalric literature, will only grasp its most external, accidental, and insignificant aspects. Every attempt to trace the themes of the Grail to the spirit of a particular people is equally mistaken. For example, one may well claim that the Grail is a Nordic "mystery," but only on condition that by "Nordic" one means something far more profound and comprehensive than "German" or even "Indo-Germanic": something identical with the Hyperborean tradition itself, which is one with the primordial tradition of the present cycle. It is in fact from that tradition that all the chief motifs of the Grail legends derive.

In this respect it is very significant that, according to *Perceval li Gallois,* the books containing the Grail story were found on the "Isle of Avalon," where the "tomb of Arthur is." Other texts call the country to which Joseph of Arimathea first brought the Grail, and where certain enigmatic ancestors of Joseph lived, the "White Island" and *Insula Avalonis:* names, once again, of the primordial Nordic center. Although England often appears in this literature as the promised land of the Grail, and the one in which the essential Grail adventures take place, there are many signs that the country in question is a symbolic one. England was also called "Albion" and the "White Island"; part of it was called "Albany"; Avalon is the location of Glastonbury. Ancient Celtic-Britannic place-naming seems to have transferred to England, or to a part of it, certain memories and meanings that really refer to the primordial Nordic center, to Thule, the "solar land." This is the true country of the Grail, and the reason that the realm of the Grail is closely linked to the symbolic realm of Arthur, to the waste land—*la terre gaste*—the realm whose sovereign is wounded, in lethargy or decline. A mountainous island, an island of glass, an island that revolves (*the Isle of Turnance*[5]), a dwelling surrounded by water, an inaccessible place, an alpine peak, a solar castle, a wild mountain and a mount of salvation (*Montsalvatsche* and *Mons Salvationis*), an invisible citadel only accessible by the elect, and even for them only through deathly peril, and so on: these are the principal scenes against which the adventures of the Grail heroes unfold. They are nothing more or less than figures of the "Center," of the symbolic residence of the King of the World. The theme of the primordial land also recurs: one text calls the land of the Grail "Eden." The Lohengrin cycle and the *Sachsenkronik von Halberstadt* say expressly: "Arthur with his knights was in the Grail, which was once Paradise and has now become a place of sin."

In the chivalric literature, the Grail is actually a supernatural object with the following essential virtues: it feeds ("gift of life"); it gives light (spiritual illumination); it gives invincibility (according to Robert de Boron, he who has seen it *n'en court de bataille venchu* [never runs beaten from battle]). As for its other aspects, there are two of special importance.

---

5. [Quoted in English in the original text, as "*the isle of the tournance.*" The expression comes from Malory, *Morte d'Arthur,* bk. 17, chap. 4. —*Trans.*]

First of all, the Grail is a heavenly stone, which not only singles out the king—like the stone that the Tuatha brought with them from Avalon—but also indicates the rulers destined to become "Prester John" (according to the *Titurel*).

Secondly, the Grail is said to be the stone that fell from Lucifer's crown at the moment of his defeat (according to the *Wartburgkrieg*). As such, it symbolizes the power that Lucifer lost through his fall, and in other texts it also keeps the character of a *mysterium tremendum* (awe-inspiring mystery). Like a terrible energy, the Grail kills, shatters, or blinds the knights who approach it unworthily or without being of the elect (according to the *Grand St. Graal, Joseph d'Arimathie,* etc.). This aspect of the Grail relates to the trial of the "Siege Perilous." One person was missing from Arthur's Round Table, one place left vacant, which really belonged to the supreme head of the Order. He who sits there without being the expected hero is struck by lightning or swallowed by a sudden abyss. The Grail can only be achieved through combat—*er muos erstritten werden,* says Wolfram von Eschenbach.

The mystery of the Grail comprises two motifs. The first relates to a symbolic realm, conceived as an image of the supreme center; a realm to be restored. The Grail is no longer present there, or else it has lost its virtue. The king of the Grail is sick, wounded, decrepit, or under an enchantment, by which he seems to be alive though he has been dead for ages (according to the *Diu Krone*). The other motif is the arrival of a hero who, having seen the Grail, feels obliged to restore it; otherwise he will betray his mission, and his heroic strength will be cursed (according to Wolfram von Eschenbach). He must repair a broken sword. He must be the avenger. He must "ask the question."

What question is this? And what is the real mission of this "chosen one"? It seems to be the same as Hesiod attributes to the "heroes," or to that generation which, though born in the dark age of decadence, still has the possbility of restoring the "Golden Age." And just as Hesiod's hero must overcome and master the titanic element, so we see the Grail hero having to overcome the Luciferic danger. It is not enough for the Grail knight to be "the best and most valiant knight in the world" with a heart of steel—*ein stählernes Herz*—in every kind of adventure, natural or supranatural: he must also be "free from pride" and must "gain wisdom" (according to Wolfram and Gautier). If the Grail was lost by Lucifer, there are texts (*Grand St. Graal*, Gerbert de Montreuil, *Morte d'Arthur*) that refer specifically to Lucifer as the demonic agent in various trials against the knights of the Grail. Moreover, the old Grail king has become impotent and unable to reign, due to a fatal wound from a poisoned lance while he was in the service of Orgeluse. It is obvious enough that this Orgeluse is a female personification of the principle of "pride." However, other Grail knights such as Gawan (Gawain) are tested in Orgeluse's own castle, but they do not succumb. They win and marry—"possess"—her. The meaning of this trial is the realization of a pure force, a spiritual virility; it transposes the heroic qualification onto a plane aloof from everything chaotic and violent. "The earthly chivalry must become a heavenly chivalry," says the *Quête du Graal*. This is the condition for opening the path to the Grail, for occupying the Siege Perilous without being thunderstruck—as the titans were struck by the Olympian god.

However, the fundamental theme of the whole Grail cycle is as follows: the hero of all these trials is given a final and decisive task. Once admitted to the Grail castle, he must feel the tragedy of the wounded Grail King, paralyzed or only seemingly alive, and he must take the initiative for an action of absolute restoration. The texts express this in various enigmatic forms: the Grail hero must "ask the question." What question? It seems that the authors have chosen to remain silent. One has the impression that something prevents them from speaking, and that a banal explanation would hide the true one. But if we follow the inner logic of them all, it is not hard to understand what is really at stake: *the question to be asked is the question of the Empire*. It is not a matter of knowing—reading the texts literally—what certain objects in the Grail castle mean, but a matter of understanding the tragedy of decadence, and, having "seen" the Grail, to pose the problem of restoration. Only on that basis can the miraculous virtue of this enigmatic question become comprehensible: since the hero has not been indifferent and has "asked the question," he thereby redeems the realm. He who only seemed to be alive dies; he who was wounded is healed. In every case the hero becomes the new and true king of the Grail, succeeding the last one. A new cycle begins.

According to some texts, the dead knight who seems to summon the hero to his mission and to vengeance appears in a coffin drawn on the sea by *swans*. Now, the swan is the bird of Apollo in the land of the Hyperboreans, in the primordial Nordic land. Drawn by swans, the knights depart from the supreme center, in which Arthur is king: from Avalon.

In other sources the Grail hero is called the *knight of the two swords*. In the theological-political literature of the time, especially on the Ghibelline side, the two swords signify no less than the *double power, temporal and supranatural*. A classic text speaks of the Hyperborean land as the place whence come dynasties that, like the Heraclides, incarnate both the royal and the sacerdotal dignity. In one Grail text the sword that is reforged has a guardian, whose name is *memoria del sangue* (memory of the blood).

• • •

The inaccessible and intangible realm of the Grail is also a reality in its form, in that it is not bound to any one place, to any visible organization, or to any earthly realm. It represents a native land to which one belongs in a different way from physical birth, by having the sense of a spiritual and initiatic dignity. This land unites, in an unbreakable chain, men who may seem scattered in the world, in space, in time, in nations, to the point of appearing isolated and unknown to each other. In this sense the realm of the Grail—like that of Arthur and Prester John, like Thule, Midgard, Avalon, and so on—*is ever present*. Following its "polar" nature, it is *immobile*. Consequently, it is not sometimes closer and sometimes further from the current of history; it is rather the current of history itself, which men and their realms may approach more or less closely.

There is a certain period, that of the Ghibelline Middle Ages, that seems to represent the closest approximation to this. It offers historical and spiritual evidence that the realm of the Grail was able to emerge from occultation into visibility, and to give rise to a reality that was interior and exterior at the same time, as in the primordial civilizations. On this basis one can assert that the Grail was the crown and the "mystery" of the Medieval imperial myth, and the supreme profession of faith of high Ghibellinism. Such a profession of faith translates more into legend and myth than into the clear political will of the time. It is analogous to what happens in the individual, when what is deepest and most dangerous is expressed less through the forms of his reflective consciousness than through symbolism and a supraconscious[6] spontaneity.

The Middle Ages awaited the hero of the Grail so that the Dry Tree of the Empire should bloom again; every usurpation, conflict, or opposition should be destroyed; and a new solar order should truly reign. The realm of the Grail, which would have risen to new splendor, was the Holy Roman Empire itself. The hero of the Grail, who could have become "the master of all creatures," and he to whom "the supreme power is entrusted," is the historical Emperor—"Federicus"—if he had been the one to realize the mystery of the Grail, the Hyperborean mystery.

For an instant, history and suprahistory seem to have met: there ensued a period of high metaphysical tension, a zenith, a supreme hope—then a new collapse and dispersion.

The whole Grail literature seems to be compressed into a relatively short period: no text seems to predate the last quarter of the twelfth century, and none to postdate the first quarter of the thirteenth century. After the latter period, mention of the Grail suddenly stops, as though on command. Writing about it only resumes many years later, and then in a different spirit. It seems (as Jessie Weston says) that at a certain moment an underground current surfaced, then as suddenly vanished again. The epoch of this sudden disappearance of the first Grail tradition coincides more or less with the tragedy of the Templars. Perhaps that was the beginning of the fracture.

In Wolfram von Eschenbach, the Grail knights are called *templeise*—"templars"—although there is no temple in his story, only

---

6. [Following the French *spontanéité supra-consciente* (see note 1), rather than the Italian *spontaneità subconsciente.* —Trans.]

a court. In some texts the monk-knights of the mysterious "island" receive the sign of the Templars: a red cross on a white ground. In other sources the Grail adventures take a course like a "twilight of the gods": the hero of the Grail does fulfill the "vengeance" and restore the realm, but a heavenly voice announces that he must retire with the Grail to a mysterious island. The ship that comes to take him is the ship of the Templars: it has a white sail with a red cross.

Like scattered channels, secret organizations seem to have preserved the ancient symbols and the Grail traditions even after the fall of the ecumenical imperial civilization. The Ghibelline "Fedeli d'Amore," the troubadours of the later period, the Hermetists. Finally, we come to the Rosicrucians. There again the same myth appears: the solar citadel; the *Imperator* as "Lord of the Fourth Empire" and destroyer of every usurpation; an invisible fraternity of transcendent personalities, uniquely united by their essence and their intention; and, finally, the strange mystery of the resurrection of the King, a mystery that turns into the realization that the King to be resuscitated was already alive and awake. He who assists in this process bears the sign of the Templars: a white standard with a red cross. The Grail bird, the dove, is also present.

But a watchword seems to have been given in this case, too. Suddenly no one is talking about the Rosicrucians. Tradition tells that in the period when absolutism, rationalism, individualism, and illuminism were preparing the way for the French Revolution, and the Treaty of Westphalia sealed the definitive collapse of the autonomy of the Holy Roman Empire, the last Rosicrucians abandoned the West to retire to "India."

"India" here is a symbol, equivalent to the home of Prester John, of the King of the World. It is Avalon; it is Thule. According to the *Titurel,* dark times have come for Salva Terra, where reside the knights of Monsalvat. The Grail can no longer stay there. It is transported to "India," to the realm of Prester John, which is "near Paradise." Once the Grail knights have arrived yonder, Monsalvat and its citadel appear there, magically transported, because "none of that must remain among the sinful peoples." Parsival himself takes on the function of "Prester John."

And still today the Tibetan ascetics sometimes say of Shambhala, the sacred city of the North—reached by the "northern road," the "way of the gods," *devayāna*—that "It resides in my heart."[7]

---

7. A systematic and documented study of the legend of the Grail following an interpretation of this kind will be found in Julius Evola, *Il Mistero del Graal e la tradizione ghibellina dell'impero* (2nd ed., Milan: Ceschina, 1964). [See *The Mystery of the Grail: Initiation and Magic in the Quest for the Spirit,* trans. Guido Stucco (Rochester, Vt.: Inner Traditions, 1994). —*Trans.*]

III.2

The Instant and Eternity[1]

One may say that the sacred differs from the profane in that it turns essentially toward the past, to fix the stages of a development that necessarily finds its apex in a "present." This present is the metaphysical point to which eternity converges and the worlds dissolve in an amplitude that has no bounds, a duration that has no rhythm, a beatitude that has no end. The present is the eternal: the past is the vestibule that shows the way and admits to eternity. To repeat and retrace the whole cycle that ends at this point means to carry with one all the experience of the ages, all cosmic evolution, to resolve its plot in the eye of God.

Faust could not halt the instant because he could only grasp its transience, the immediate iridescence of illusion, the vertigo that drowns rather than transfigures, the unstable and evanescent phantasm, and not what persists in God as an infinite instantaneity, which is the mystery of the eternal present. These are the two aspects of the "instant," depending on whether one takes the human or the divine standpoint. It is a matter of two apparently opposed and divergent points which denote two worlds, two rhythms, two realities, of which one is absolute and essential, the other fallacious and illusory. Faust's command *verweile doch, du bist so schön* ("stay, you are so beautiful") is a lyrical and not very original substitute for the abyssal fullness of the Ineffable

---

1. [This article, by Guido De Giorgio (1890–1957), was added to the 1955 edition of *Introduzione alla Magia*. —*Trans.*]

96

in which the mystery of divine gestation is accomplished. The myth of purification through aesthetics is the feeblest bridge that modern imbecility has stretched over the instantaneity of the human-cosmic illusion, so as to evade positive certitude of the mystery, of a wall that cannot be crossed except by the vertiginous flight of the wing, which is the Spirit of God.

This is why the modern world oscillates between a dead past and a nebulous future, between what is no more and what will never be except in anticipatory and constructive hope. Traditional wisdom, on the contrary, turns to the past, lives it, fertilizes it, *actualizes* it, and enters into it, carrying its entirety into the present and renovating it in the *ver aeternum* (eternal spring) that the Ancients attributed to the golden age, indicating the perennial germination of the Truth, the teeming of transfiguring states, the assumption into the life that knows neither birth nor death, but is fulfilled in the bliss of the knowledge that is realization. For the moderns, on the other hand, the past is past; it is dead, finished, done with, closed, irremediable—the *déjà vu, le déjà vécu* ("already seen, already lived") to quote Bergson, whose obvious psychological attitude shows all the nostalgic sentimentality of the little man terribly enslaved to the little world. There the twilight present wavers between a dead past and a future not yet born, simultaneously a clouded sunset and a dull dawn: in sum, a veritable pause of agony. From this false vision of things comes the *myth of the future,* the reaching out toward what is not, toward what will never be, because in reality only the present, absorbing the past, is the dynamic point, *the prow of the ship that faces the horizon but never reaches it.*

Modern man is like a pallbearer who sighs for the day that never breaks: the corpse that he carries is the past, the inert and sterile heredity, and the day he awaits is the future, the imaginary offspring, the radiant achievement of an uncompleted, chimerical birth. You will notice that all the moderns, the "great men," are expecting the definitive judgment of their work by the future, perhaps because they feel consciously or unconsciously that nothing they have done is linked traditionally to the regal river of the past; nothing capable of resisting the wavering compass needle of the present, a fleeting instant and an accidental moment, with anything deeper than the marginal friction of the passing cloud. This is why ancient man is a bearer of worlds; he has not left the past behind him, but gathers and brings it along so as to construct in reality a sole incidental point, *only the present, actuality*—whereas modern man, sloughing off a burden too heavy for his feeble shoulders, is light, inconsistent, and, for fear of being overwhelmed by the sidelong gusts of wind, anchors himself to the machine that represents both his cradle and his grave. For the myth of the future is connected to that of speed, which, if one understands its function and internal workings, is the abolition of the past into the already traveled, the imperceptibility of the present, minimized in the *continual expectation of the future.* Readers who want to go more deeply into these matters and to examine them for themselves will find more than one easy path for the comprehension of some greater truth: they need only establish, with a certain insistence, some *critical* heights from which the perspective on events is more clear and secure.

We can see that ancient and modern man are in absolute contrast, like antipodes in the literal sense, tied to the same stem but facing different skies, differently constellated, even though the same impassive sun illuminates them in what for one is day, for the other, night. For the Ancients, indeed, the past is everything; for the moderns, nothing, even when they delude themselves by distractedly seeking solutions to present problems, the so-called warnings, teachings—all sentimental fantasies exploited with cynical opportunism according to circumstance, and offered to the credulity of the simpleminded for even more pitiful deceptions. The rhetoric that has triumphed as never before in today's turbid and filthy Europe resorts to the most bestial sleaziness to capture the assent of the hearkening masses, and uses the past as a remedy for every evil, a universal panacea, a prop for the present, but for momentary use as though to ward off the *vae soli* (woe to him who is alone)!

In reality, modern man has already done with the past, he no longer lives it and finds there nothing but dust and ruin: he studies it, catalogues it, and ignores it. The more minute his investigation, the more it becomes dry bones, then each tries to galvanize in his own fashion these bones set in the sleep of death. In this way the moderns turn to the past when they study it with the same illusion that they obey when they believe, for instance, that photography is closer to reality because it denatures it completely, fixing in its instantaneity what has already happened. But let us see, apart from study, whether the moderns make use of the past for their life. To speak of the past is to speak of tradition, which is intimate and dynamic connection, not external adhesion, not opportunistic support, not simply classification or arrangement. In other words, between past and present there must be *continuity, immutability,* or, better put, a rhythmic development as smooth, continuous, and internal as to be almost undetectable. Antiquity is indeed characterized by this constant tonality that remains virtually unchanged from one epoch to another; the change that happens and must happen takes place in the depths, in the inner strata, almost invisibly, in such a way as not to disturb the regularity of rhythm.

It is often said that ancient civilizations were immobile, or appeared to be; but this is the very thing that shows their greatness, this fundamental stasis that drowns out all conflicts, that brings all the rhythms into the central vein, in the *traditional type,* which only remains in the interest of its determining efficiency. This is why one who wishes to remain in the pure ambience of truth, which is the traditional, always refers to the past to retrace the links of certainty and to integrate them into his experience, which in this regard is recapitulative and conclusive, not repeating externally but integrating its rhythm, which is nothing other than his own vision, formerly unknown but now regained and vivified. It is very difficult to express certain things to those who live in dualistic positions, thinking that there is something other than the Truth, which is God eternally present: Truth, where one only *becomes what one is,* thereby surpassing the sphere of human limitations to live in the very pulsation of the infinite.

When we say "ancient," we mean everthing that is worthy, perennial, traditionally authentic in the past of East and West, no matter whether remote or recent, doctrinal or social, because in its variety of expression it reflects the great light of the Higher World. Beside the Sacred Books there are the symbols, there is sacred art; there is every form of that activity which in the past was always connected to a truth of a superior order, even in humble utensils and in the making and purpose of common objects. The past, as we understand it and as everyone should understand it who seeks only God's truth, is a creative rhythm, an inexhaustible fund of wisdom that is rediscovered every time it is actualized by a new experience. But it is above all the reality of vibrant life, because it is vivified by perennial inspiration from the traditional spring. The moderns, on the contrary, consider the past as a relic, admiring its age and approaching it with the curiosity of a photographer or an archaeologist. Which of them *accepts it integrally,* takes in all its fullness, not to extract fragments for admiration, but to incorporate it in his experience as a creative wholeness?

How many admirers of Dante's work do not stop at praising his poetry or expression—things absolutely exterior and superficial—but absorb its doctrine, the knowledge of every plane of being to which it applies, and the whole of the Celestial Journey?

The past is nothing if not integrated, lived, confirmed by one's own experience, by one's own life, integrated and raised in the great shudder of eternal actuality. The moderns, rather, when they are not fornicating like robbers in a graveyard, turn their backs on it while contemplating the hypothetical "sun of the future" that will never shine because the future does not exist except as the ineffectual terminus of laborious fantasy, a mirage and nothing more, a false projection spasmodically colored by its own insufficiency. The incompleteness in the face of Truth, the incurable sentimentality of him who neither knows nor can bear the weight of taking on the world in the divine instant, have created the myth of the future. With his back obstinately turned to that which is, he curiously awaits that which is not, that which will be, and expects the confirmation of a dream from an illusory reflection of the dream itself in a nocturnal parade of phantasms that the present only generates in the spontaneity of its flow and its mirage. What a strange speculation on the future, that makes one forget the treasures of the past and the tangible immediacy of the present, in which alone one really exists, along with all the worlds, in the essential unity of the point, the jewel of all jewels, the eternal eye of God!

We would like to say more, but prefer to cease with these words of

Zarathustra: *Diesen Menschen von heute will ich nicht Licht sein, nicht Licht heissen. Die—will ich blenden: Blitz meiner Weisheit! stich ihnen die Augen aus!*—"I will not be a light to these men of today, nor be called a light. I will blind them: O lightning of my wisdom, put out their eyes!"[2]

---

2. [Friedrich Nietzsche, *Also sprach Zarathustra,* chap. 85, §7. —*Trans.*]

ABRAXA

Communications

What I have to tell you now is not part of high magic. You know that the true magus will never make mere phenomena the goal of his work. But it may happen that, just as you don't hesitate to use a lever to lift a rock, or a car to get you somewhere, an initiate may develop certain abilities that moderns foolishly call "supernatural," though for him they are as external and insignificant as a lever or a car may be in someone else's practical life. And he uses them with the same indifference and naturalness.

Telepathy: not even today's "critical minds" contest its reality. But they only know of it as an incidental fact: they observe the "phenomenon" when it occurs, or better, when it *wants* to occur here and there. Science for them means to register, not to determine. *Creating* and *directing* the phenomenon does not enter their heads. But that is where our science begins.

You can be sure that if your faculties are sound, your thought can transcend the condition of physical space, and that what telephones, radios, and the like make possible today, you can achieve with a suitable mental technique and an act of the spirit. Yes, it will be an infinitely longer and more difficult business—but you will then have a real *power,* which, unlike that of machines, no circumstance can touch or revoke.

If it is not a matter of higher realizations, every psychic transmission by immaterial means involves two suitably prepared people: and the practice will be much easier if they both form part of a "chain." As for the technique, you will easily be convinced that it is only an adaptation of the same internal instruments as you have needed for the true *opus magicum*.

For now, we must distinguish the one who must prepare for receiving and understanding from the one who must prepare for emitting and sending. The latter needs only one thing: *fixed* and *subtle* thought. "Fixed" means that the mind that formulates the thought, identifies with it, and absorbs it must forget, cancel out, and dissolve any extraneous sensation, staying firm and *constant* toward its object, whether an image or a verbal phrase. If verbal, say it inwardly, distinctly, and perfectly defined. "Subtle" means that "silence" must surround you, and you must not "will," but only "conceive," *think*. And the awareness that "*I* am thinking," "*I* am sending this thought," must be totally absent; instead, your thought or imagination must be like something you remember or recall; it should have the nature of a *breath*, a *wave*, a *whisper*. Deep calm must reign in your soul and body—*and then, like one who luminously releases a seal on the silent thresholds of sleep.*

A special discipline is also needed for the person who is receiving someone else's thought, message, or even influence, when the two of them are more or less at the same point of development. But an Adept is said to be able to transmit his thought to anyone, by direct action, without any prior refinement of the receiver's subtle hearing.

In the other case, the procedure is no different from that of someone who chooses a single awareness from his general awareness, and isolates in his soul-life the Unmoving that stands at the center of the network, receptive to all the vibrations transmitted from its distant margins. Here too not only "silence" is required, but you must make a habit of a minute examination of all your sensations, all your psychic and emotional states, all your mental associations. You must *see* and *separate*. On the one hand, you will find thoughts, states, and associations that you can explain, whose direct or indirect causes you can easily see. But on the other hand, you will discover things that have come to you *from below*, slipping in from behind—or simple "states," sudden memories arising without cause, unrelated images. In this way the frontiers of your awareness and your subtle intellect will expand. Once the first steps are taken, the next will seem easy to you. To notice immediately what belongs to the processes of your individual psyche alone, and what comes in from outside or from below—this is the goal of the discipline. It will probably take months. But you will have to reach that point. It would be wasted labor if your effort were only justified by the phenomena of spaceless thought that you want to produce. But you know that this is also the path you must take for occult defence and inner mastery; you know that it is already a spagyric operation, and not of the small but the Great Art. And the more *light* there will be in your mind, the more effortless you will find its application.

After this, test it. By degrees. Two vases, of course. But both androgynous, only dissimilar in power, as in the sign of our Magic.[1] Test the first contacts on a single train of thought. Both of you should sit in the same space, in half-light, in calm, hieratic, and ritual immobility. You should have decided what to direct: it could be a symbol, or a phrase. The point of departure for both of you is that the mind should meditate, contemplate. Having suspended it there, and each having complete control of his own thoughts, feelings, and imaginations, look at each other. This is called the *preparation through union,* or if you prefer, by syntony. It is the task of the first phase.

In the second phase, one of you should remove the support, make a void, wait attentively. At a given moment, a mental stream will form. Take care not to disturb it. Survey it, register it. And then look: you will see what thoughts, images, sentiments, or perceptions reflect what your companion or your master has thought. By repetition, you refine yourself. With vigor, with fervor. The subtle ear will awaken: it will discern, in the mass of psychic formations, those which are messages and communications. And reaching this point will also represent a conquest on the higher path. For you will detect the same character of extraneous and *suggested* things in many thoughts and states having no relation to

---

1. [The "operation with two vessels" typically involves a man and a woman (see *Introduction to Magic*, vol. I, 218–27). However, in the present case a difference of gender is not assumed (both being "androgynous" for the purpose). To avoid forcing any supposition on the case, I follow the Italian in using the masculine pronoun for both participants, but this should be understood in its traditional, gender-neutral usage. —*Trans.*]

the present practice. "The backstage of consciousness," which you have already been told about.[2] Or you will even isolate, like a precious vein, influences that want to guide or warn you.

Once you have reached this form of receptivity, and more or less completely confirmed real transmissions, you should remove the support represented for you, and also for the other, of proximity in space and physical closeness. You should repeat the first operation with the two of you being not in the same room but separated, for example, by a wall; then at two different places in the same city; and, finally, in different cities. At first, agree on the timing. Then even let that go. Keep in mind that these are not harder tasks, *because hermetic thought knows no space:* it is all the same to it whether two people are one meter or a thousand kilometers apart. Instead, they are phases of the destruction of the *idea* of space in both of you, because that is the limitation, the obstruction: *the phantasm of space that you carry in your mind, unconsciously.* And you can only destroy it by stages, using the suggestion of different distances, of less-distant transmission.

Whoever takes the part of transmitter, when the other is not present, should first imagine the latter's figure, making it appear before him just as it was in the first phases of physical proximity. Then make the image rapidly recede, while keeping it clear and distinct in every detail. You then perform a kind of projection, of a sort that you have already been told about: you imagine a ray that goes out from the middle of your brow and shoots in a timeless instant to reach the same point on the brow of the other person's image. This is one method. But your subtle intellect may suggest others, or you may find them in the treatises on applied magic, Eastern or Western.

By virtue of such practices, two beings who are treading the esoteric path together remain in contact without regard to distance, and can communicate, understand, and agree with one another. And if one of

---

2. See *Introduction to Magic,* vol. II, 53–58. One might refer here to what Islamic esotericism calls the *khawātir*; the term for ideas that come inexplicably to consciousness, originating from an unknown psychic region. There are distinct types of *khawātir,* which may come from the higher world, from the simple individual subconscious, or even from demonic influences. (Note by UR)

them is close to having the status of an Adept, the messages can also send to the other one help, support, warnings, and advice for inner actions and the conduct of life. But little by little you will approach that higher plane on which it is no longer an individual who inspires and guides you, but the force of the Tradition itself.

Just as any inferior practice can always serve as support for a higher realization, this technique of active and controlled "telepathy"—to use the banal modern term—can help you to develop a special awareness: it is that *the mind has no space,* and, in the end, no plurality. It is the awareness that the I can speak through your mouth, just as it can speak through someone else's, because it has nothing to do with the "person." And when you begin to intuit and to *live* this truth, the power of tranmissions will be raised as a consequence. And little by little you will be able to go deeper: the attitude that you have created for receiving messages from other beings, or for sending them to others, will help you to be able to hear or speak a word that no longer belongs to time or man.

III.4

PICO DELLA MIRANDOLA

The Dignity of Man[1]

I have read in the ancient books of the Arabs that Abdala the Saracen, when asked what was the most admirable thing in this world, replied that there was nothing more admirable than man. This agrees with the saying of Hermes: "Man, O Asclepius, is a great miracle!"

Thinking over the reason for these sayings, I was not satisfied by what many assert about the superiority of human nature, such as that man is the medium between creatures, familiar with the higher, king over the lower, of keen senses and enquiring mind, interpreter of nature by the light of intelligence, midway between eternal stability and temporal flux, the bond and even marriage of the world (as the Persians say), and according to David, little lower than the angels.

These are great things indeed, but not so essential as to justify the privilege of supreme admiration. For why should we not admire more the angels themselves and the blessed choirs of heaven?

At last I came to understand why man should be the most fortunate animal, hence worthy of all admiration, and what condition he has been given in the universal order that is enviable not only by the beasts but

---

1. [The Italian text states: "Translated by B. Cicognani from Pico della Mirandola, *Opera* (Basel, 1601), 107ff." I have followed the original Latin text as found in Pico della Mirandola, *Oration on the Dignity of Man,* ed. Francesco Borghesi, Michael Papi, and Massimo Riva (Cambridge: Cambridge University Press, 2012), 108–20, while preserving certain interpretations in the Italian translation that reflect the views of the UR Group. —*Trans.*]

by the stars and even the ultramundane intelligences. It is a thing wondrous beyond belief! . . .

God the supreme Father and architect had fabricated what we see as this mundane dwelling, the most august temple of divinity, with laws of secret wisdom. He had decorated the supercelestial region with intelligences, quickened the ethereal globes with eternal souls, and filled up these excremental and foul lower parts with a host of every sort of animal.

But once he had finished the work, the Artificer wanted someone who could ponder the rationale of it, love its beauty, admire its magnitude. Therefore, when it was all finished (as Moses and Timaeus testify), he finally thought of producing man. But it was not among the archetypes that he fashioned his new progeny, nor in his treasuries that he endowed his new child, nor was there any seat in the whole globe where the contemplator of the universe might sit. Every space had been filled; everything was distributed among the highest, middle, and lowest orders. But it was not in the Father's power to fail his last creation, as though he were exhausted, nor had the supreme Wisdom hesitated for lack of resources in the matter; nor would beneficent Love allow that one who was called to praise divine generosity in all creatures should be forced to condemn himself.

Finally, the Supreme Maker ordained that he to whom nothing of his own could be given should share in everything that had been given separately to the others. Therefore he made man, a work of indefinite type, and put him in the middle of the Universe, saying:

"We have given you, Adam, no assigned seat, no particular feature, no peculiar gift, so that whatever seat, feature, or gift you may consciously [*tute*] wish for, you shall have and possess through your will and your purpose.

"The nature defined for other beings is constrained by the laws we have prescribed. You are not under any close constraint, but you will define it by the free will that we have put into your hands. I have placed you in the center of the world, so that you can more easily look around at whatever is in it. We have made you neither celestial nor terrestrial, neither mortal nor immortal, so that you yourself, as a free and honorary modeler and sculptor, shall make the form that you have consciously chosen. You may degenerate to the lower, brutish regions. You may, by the decision [*sententia*] of your own mind, be reborn into the higher, divine ones."

O supreme generosity of God the Father, supreme and admirable felicity of man, to whom it is given to have whatever he longs for, to be whatever he wishes! The brutes, as soon as they are born, carry from their mother's womb (as Lucilius says) all that they will possess. The highest spirits, right from the beginning or shortly after, were what they will be for all eternity. But to man, the Father has given at birth every type of seed and the germs of every kind of life. As each one has cultivated it, so it grows and bears its fruit in him. If he is vegetal by nature, he will become like a plant; if sensual, he will become brutish; if rational, he will become a celestial soul; if intellectual, he will be an angel and a son of God. And if, unsatisfied with the fate of any creature, he retreats into his own center, a spirit alone with God, he will surpass all things in the solitary darkness of the Father that is above all.

Commentaries

The reader may have noticed a recurrent theme in the first three articles of this part. In relation to Havismat's article, we draw attention to a work that appeared later, containing ample and interesting documentation on the sense of time and the timeless past in the traditional world: Mircea Eliade's *The Myth of the Eternal Return.*[1] This book reveals the inner significance of a vast number of rituals: to make of a present act or event—that is, one caught in the stream of history—the repetition of an original act or fact situated in a mythic past and hence itself timeless. In that way the empirical present, the here and now, was integrated into a present of a different type: a metaphysical present without time or history, which alone made it real in a higher sense and filled it with meaning; thus, becoming was transformed and transfigured into "being." One could even speak of a regeneration and a periodic purification of what happens in time by means of these rites, as a revivifying linkage with the origin, with the beginnings or the eternal present, which is beyond time.

This view is also of practical interest. Eliade rightly points out that all ritual and sacrificial actions are basically performed in states that participate in the "present" of the origins. In the ritual, profane and chronological time is suspended, and there occurs a state of consciousness that is free from it, like a new beginning.

---

1. [Mircea Eliade, *The Myth of the Eternal Return,* trans. Willard R. Trask (New York: Pantheon, 1954). —*Trans.*]

This also points to what Ea and Abraxa have said, because by a natural extension, something analogous applies to space. Magical thought is a spaceless thought, free from space and hence ubiquitous. In magical space, no matter where one is, there manifests the space of the "Center" that is always the same as itself. It is no different for the "Center" in itself, in the sense used by Ea in relation to the Grail saga. The localizations of this Center are essentially symbolic, even in cases where its manifestations also have a real basis: such as when in some specific land, in some Realm, something unique, ubiquitous, and suprahistorical is more or less sensed, such as apparitions of a unique *presence,* or that king who is still alive, though one believed that he had to be resuscitated.

These are meanings that, as a rule, should be brought to life in the practical field, beside their value for understanding traditional reality. In either case, the veil of the spatio-temporal mirage vanishes into the sensation of the *central present,* which is also the mode of the Man who is reintegrated and has become alive.

I should add that the constant references to the past by the esoteric sciences should not be taken as a reversion to a time that, though past, was just like our present time. Closer to the origins, time was qualitatively different from ours and closer to what is supratemporal; the veil was thinner there. It is therefore natural to refer to it when one needs to point a way toward what is actually metaphysical.

Those who are interested can also refer to the ideas already developed by F. W. Schelling (*Einleitung in die Philosophie der Mythologie*),[2] who emphasizes the very fact that the difference between "history" and "prehistory" is not relative, as though it were a matter of two periods of one and the same time, but refers rather to two different species of time (as experienced). The time of prehistory is suffused with a supra-temporal element, so as to make it a sort of intermediary between, on

2. [Friedrich Wilhelm Schelling, *Historical-Critical Introduction to the Philosophy of Mythology,* trans. Mason Richey and Markus Zisselsberger (Albany, N.Y.: SUNY Press, 2007), 127. —*Trans.*]

the one hand, what is history and "becoming," and on the other, what reflects the eternal and the identical. It is in these terms that one should understand what in original civilizations seems, to modern eyes, to have a "static" character—whereas it was more like an imprint on temporality of something superior to it.

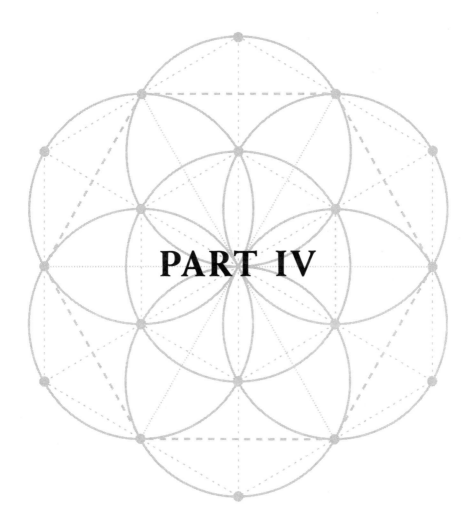

PART IV

IV.1

The Cycles of Consciousness

E_{ditor's note}[1]

The essay published here is recommended to those who would welcome a scheme for translating esoteric phenomenology into the terms of modern psychology. It brings out the natural relationships between our phenomenology and ordinary psychic processes; it shows how the former has nothing "irrational" about it, but is determined by its own rules, linked to special conditions of the human being. In particular, on the basis of what is said in this part about "metaphysical reality," it will be easy to recognize the corresponding organic condition. It will also be instructive to relate Apro's diagram [see figure 1 on page 116] to what Breno has said about the internal conditions of East and West [see chapter I.3 on page 14] and the borderline that separates "mediumism" from "precise clairvoyance." Although Apro has provided some pointers, it remains for the reader to connect our teachings and the various experiences described here with his scheme, for which this diagram will be a very helpful basis.

Regardless of the deep root that justifies both man's own artifacts and man as an artifact or "unconscious prompter of himself"—given that we are concerned here with illustrating the mechanism of conscious-

---

1. [This unsigned note appeared at the end of the current essay. It seems more helpful to place it here. —*Trans.*]

114

ness, and not the deep I that determines it—we will try to assemble the modes of this mechanism into a unitary scheme, so as to understand both its normal forms and the more unusual, extranormal ones.

By *phenomenon of consciousness* we mean any modification of the individual dynamism, whether mental, sensorial, or motoric. The mechanism of the phenomenon of simple consciousness, or the elementary psychic process, can be reduced to the scheme known as the "arc of reflection." This generally means the schematic course within the organism of the vibratory wave produced by an impact or stimulus, propagating as a centripetal current as far as a nervous center, and reflected there in the form of a centrifugal current, until it affects the organ or tissue on which the stimulus acted, and communicates to it the so-called reflex motion.

We interpret the above expression in a more general way, extending it to cyclical systems of actions and reactions that may also be determined on a higher plane, in which case the sensitive and motoric elements are excluded and there may be no accompanying visible, external movement. Such a stimulus is not necessarily mechanical and external: its nature may be organic, psychic, or mental; and the transmission and centrifugal reaction may not occur through the nerve cells, but by means of a more direct relation with ambient or "energetic fields" of a more subtle nature than those corresponding to the physical body, and with whose vibrations man may equally be in touch.

In the processes of ordinary consciousness, the center of the cycle, where the centripetal wave ends and the centrifugal one begins, corresponds to the brain. It can be compared to an extremely intricate *headquarters,* a complex of *teams* that are both registers of facts and assigners of actions. In some cases the cycle may have for its center the sympathetic nervous system.[2] Then the individual is usually incapable of having distinct perceptions. To *recognize* a sensation or a stimulus requires the brain, the true organ on which the function of ordinary self-consciousness is based.

We will call that which manifests specifically through the brain

---

2. [Translating the obsolete term *gran simpatico.* —*Trans.*]

external consciousness, or by the usual term of *waking consciousness.* In contrast, we will use the term *integral consciousness* for immediate consciousness, or the unity of consciousness able to manifest intellectually without the intermediary and the limitation of the brain. The former can be considered as an *external propagation* of the latter, determined by the flow of the volitive current that serves to channel the processes toward the brain.

Beside these two types of consciousness we must consider a third, which occurs whenever the stimuli are not sufficiently intense to cross the threshold of external consciousness, so that the cycle closes beneath them; or obviously when the necessary medium is lacking for the brain to be involved in the process.

These notions suffice for arranging the various processes of consciousness in distinct types. The following diagram may serve as a basis:

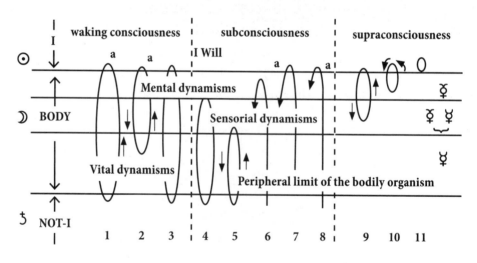

Figure 1

We have divided the intermediate zone between the I and the not-I into three parts, which are three progressive phases of degradation (or reintegration) of spiritual energy, ending with the materialized and motoric form that belongs to the physical structure.

The upper limit could be called *I-will.* Three orders of dynamism follow: *mental, sensorial,* and *vital,* which may be aligned with the three "souls" of Aristotelian doctrine: *intellective, sensitive,* and *vegetative.* Beyond the last of these, one reaches the *peripheral limit of the bodily organism.*[3]

The cyclical processes of the phenomena of consciousness affect in various ways the elements that we have diagrammed. They are represented by curves, some closed and others open. An upward arrow indicates the *centripetal* or *afferent current* (stimulus, reception), and the downward arrow the *centrifugal* or *efferent current,* that is, reaction in general, encompassing all sorts of reactions made by man's being, not necessarily affecting external motion.

WAKING CONSCIOUSNESS

The forms of habitual, external, or waking consciousness can be classified as three principal types of process, corresponding to nos. 1, 2, and 3 on the above diagram.

First, there is the clear perception of an external stimulus, through a current that not only touches the I but causes an active enfolding of the sensation, a distinct *apperception,* which may also be accompanied by a motion (case no. 1). This process takes place every time we form an exact representation of external reality with the mind and senses while awake and in full self-consciousness.

In the diagram, curve *a* of the cycle that goes beyond the plane of mental dynamism is considered as a "variable": it depends on the degree of realization of the I and of the latter's active participation in all the processes and all the reactions.

Case no. 2 shows an analogous process; however, its point of origin is not an external stimulus but a stimulus that comes from the vital functions and is noticed in an equally distinct way. The zone of normal, direct consciousness of the processes usually begins in the field of sensorial

---

3. In the terms of Hermetic esotericism, these elements, *if in the pure state,* correspond as follows: the I-will is *Sulfur* (will ♂) and *Gold* (I ☉); the body, as peripheral limit, is Salt ⊖; the intermediate dynamisms are *Mercury, which acts as mediator,* and inasmuch as it falls under the influence of the Gold principle it is the *active Mercury* ☿ (intellective and, in part, sensitive soul); while inasmuch as it falls under the influence of the Salt principle, it is the *lunar Mercury* ☿ (vegetative and, in part, sensitive soul). (Note by UR)

dynamisms. Only in exceptional cases does it also reach the lower zone of vital dynamisms: then we have the phenomena of *autoscopia,* the direct, supranormal perception of the organs of one's own body.

These two types, 1 and 2, refer to processes that engage and activate the individual's "I-will" center (see the emergence of *a* above the limit of the mental dynamisms).

We now proceed to case no. 3: that of subconscious or instinctive reactions to an external or internal stimulus. This happens when the stimulus is not such as to attract sensible attention, namely in genuine motor reflexes, like starting at an unexpected noise. Perception certainly occurs there, but the circuit closes so fast that the higher dynamisms (somewhat dissociated from the lower ones through distraction) do not have time to inhibit or control the reaction, which is in a way extraneous to the I, and thus confined to a secondary center, temporarily uncontrolled.

SUBCONSCIOUSNESS

Case no. 4 depicts the production of a vague sensation by an external stimulus. There is not enough energy in the centripetal current for the mental dynamisms to intervene decisively and form a distinct perception; or they may lack the capacity to furnish a corresponding image that translates the sensation. The latter is the case with certain indefinable impressions that reach us from the outside (e.g., sensitivity to the weather or to telluric phenomena, the instinctive sense of direction, etc.) without an apperception being able to associate with them. These processes occur through the sympathetic nervous system and form a regressive type of sensitivity. The cerebral center does not take part in them.[4]

Case no. 5 shows an analogous process, but even further down below the threshold of distinct consciousness. The circuit closes, hardly touching the zone of sensorial dynamisms. This chiefly involves the obscure energies of the body's vitality.

---

4. Esoterically, according to the inner aspect, one would say that they occur directly in the "subtle body": in ☿ and partially in ☿. (Note by UR)

Type no. 6 schematizes the process of subconscious reaction to an external stimulus that does not emerge due to a reduction of external consciousness (distraction, drowsiness), resulting in a certain sensitive translation unconnected to a notion of its origin. If, on the other hand, the stimulus comes from an internal source—if it comes from the organic life—then we have case no. 7.

A final and very common type of subconsciousness is the subconscious reaction to an external or internal stimulus that, through an even greater state of reduced consciousness, does not even affect the sensitive soul, and only arouses a certain mental activity that is completely ignorant of its own cause (no. 8). This class includes the processes of mental association, apparently automatic; the spontaneous presentation of images, thoughts, or memories; and also the processes of oneiric cerebration, including the images that form in dream as reactions symbolically translating external or organic stimuli.

We have spoken of a subconsciousness that comes from reduction of the attentive current (will), from insufficient intensity of the afferent currents, or from incapacity of cerebral translation. But we should consider a second type, caused by a disconnection of the higher dynamisms from the lower ones. It may be either spontaneous (as in hysterical analgesia) or provoked (whether indirectly, by use of anesthetics, drugs, etc.; or directly, through special disciplines such as those of the fakirs, or through powerful concentration of attention on a single idea, through hypnotic suggestion, etc.). Here the afferent currents meet a hiatus that they cannot pass, and consequently they turn back and close themselves off below the threshold of consciousness. These forms of detachment are always accompanied by the external context of a more or less deep sleep, or by somnambulism.

Speaking of the subconscious, we must mention *subconscious memory* (cryptamnesia) There is nothing that passes through consciousness (in the broadest sense that we have understood this term) without leaving an indelible trace. Strictly speaking, only the processes of cases 1 and 2 can be called conscious and form part of common memory. But this is a small section of an infinitely larger storehouse, which also preserves the elements obtained through all the other processes that we have described, and which fall below the threshold of external consciousness, or rather through its connections and interruptions. In suitable circumstances, this infraconscious and subconscious material can emerge and manifest either indirectly (through automatic writing, crystal gazing, etc.) or directly. From this there derive phenomena of an apparently inexplicable character, often arbitrarily attributed to transcendent causes, whereas their key is almost always to be found in the subconscious memory, which, thanks to the enormously broad field of subconscious sensitivity, extends much further than normal memory.

One should note, however, that the distinction between conscious and subconscious processes should not be taken in an absolute sense. In fact, the *development* of all the mental processes, including the apparently most aware one of apperception (no. 1), belongs to the subconscious, and completely eludes us. This applies also to the mnemonic processes that are aroused or realized through an effort of attention, which correspond to so-called conscious dynamism, in the sense that one knows where one is starting from and more or less *where* one wants to arrive. But the intermediate phases develop largely in obscurity. As we have said, the energies applied directly to the peripheral limits of the body and even those of vital and partially sensitive dynamisms are like a "means" that is ever more opaque to the light of external consciousness. For in the cycle of the very processes that we call conscious, whether along the centripetal or the centrifugal arc, we must imagine an obscuration of those energies; which is only resolved at the threshold of the peripheral perceptions of waking consciousness (zone of the not-I).

Evidently, from the functional point of view, subconscious facts should not be considered as marginal and parasitic, but as the naturally occulted substratum of the external consciousness. All the modes of consciousness proper to the intermediate phases through which the human being has arrived at his current constitution remain beneath the threshold of external consciousness and are represented by the *inferior functions* (including the various forms of subconscious receptivity). It is precisely these that permit the relationship between the various degrees of the *ladder* of functions immanent in the individual (compare the "little perceptions" of Leibniz's system).

SUPRACONSCIOUSNESS

Case no. 9 represents the supranormal perception of a stimulus of strictly sensorial nature. This is *telesthesia,* or telepathic *sensorial* reception, or psychic perception. As the diagram shows, the cycle closes outside the peripheral limit of the body, and outside the vital dynamisms directly involved in bodily functions. It is an experience that happens in the sensitive soul, under a stimulus that has managed to reach it *directly* without the intermediary of the nerve currents or modifications of the respective centers.

To clarify this, we should imagine that just as man finds himself with the physical body in a "field" of physical dynamisms, so he also takes in other, subtler principles that are also part of his being, thus finding himself *virtually* in contact with other "fields" characterized by less "degraded" forms of energy. But we have to say "virtually" because effective contact only occurs when the higher dynamisms, starting with the sensitive ones, are free with respect to the cellular organism of body and nerves, whose task is to intercept and transform the various types of stimulus.[5] Then they can directly perceive processes and vibrations from those other energetic fields and from the respective "nuclei" to be found there. To the extent that these processes and "nuclei" have no "cyclical" correspondences in the fields of energy degraded to the form of matter and of physically perceptible motion, one may gain telepathic sensorial reception and also experience forces and realities that are purely *psychic,* namely, from a higher plane of existence, set apart from the physical substratum belonging to experience in the world of bodies.[6]

Case no. 10 differs from the last only in that the starting point and lower closure of the cycle occurs at an even higher level. This represents the supranormal perception of a stimulus whose nature is strictly *mental.* It includes the phenomena of intellectual intuition, and also inspiration

---

5. Hermetically speaking, we would say: in the state of separation of the "subtle" from the "gross." (Note by UR)

6. Among other things, we may recall what Henry Cornelius Agrippa says (*De occulta philosophia,* vol. III, chap. 23) about the perception of the "demons," which does not happen thanks to the corporeal sense, but thanks to the sense of the "etheric body" or *eidolon,* enclosed within the human and fleshly vesture. (Note by UR)

and illumination. The cycle, as can be seen in the diagram, does not even touch the sensitive dynamisms: the two ends of action and reaction tend to fuse in a simple act, in a purely intellectual apperception.[7] It is important to repeat here what we have said of the preceding case: that in these forms it is possible to obtain knowledge of beings and forces that have no visible or sensible manifestation in the physical "fields" but that nonetheless must be considered as real. This is why we also mentioned cases of "inspiration." It is a new world of relationships of which the I becomes aware to the extent and on condition (which is rarely satisfied) that its waking consciousness is able to follow the supraconscious.

Cycle no. 11 depicts the limiting case: a circuit that closes inside the zone of the pure I-will, with which the cycle becomes punctual and immediate. It is integral consciousness or self-consciousness in the true and immediate sense of the term: the direct perception of the *one* essence of the I, separated from every modification whether bodily in origin, biophysical, or even intellectual.[8] It is a form that truly has no more physiological correspondences. One cannot speak either of stimulus or of reaction, even in the broadest meaning of those terms. The process of consciousness here is *identification*, direct rapport with the essences; it is *becoming an essence oneself.*

SOME CLARIFICATIONS

In trying to localize in our diagram the field of normal, external consciousness, beyond the lower limit that, as mentioned, falls in the zone

---

7. The expressions of Plotinus, cited in the next part, refer to this condition, relating to the "two that become one" in higher consciousness. (Note by UR)

8. Compare Agrippa, *De occulta philosophia,* vol. III, chap. 55: "Therefore all composition, division, and various discourse being laid aside, let us, ascending to the intellectual life, and simple sight, behold the intelligible essence with individual and simple precepts, that we may attain to the highest being of the soul, by which we are one, and under which our multitude is united. Therefore let us attain to the first unity, from whom there is a union in all things, through that one which is as the flower of our essence; which then at length we attain to, when avoiding all multitude we do arise into our very unity, are made one, and act uniformly." (Note by UR) [Translation by "J. F." from Agrippa, *Three Books of Occult Philosophy* (London, 1651), 525–26. —*Trans.*]

of sensitive dynamisms, we must consider a higher limit that is equally variable, but falls roughly in the upper part of the zone of mental dynamisms. Above and below the area marked by these limits, the light of distinct perception weakens and then fades away. External stimuli rarely succeed in causing a conscious reaction that comes from the pure nucleus of "I-will"; the mental and associative processes themselves rarely close by penetrating the "field" of this *I*, and drawing from it an energetic current by which they could be controlled and directed in every part.

Strictly, one should speak of *two* thresholds of external consciousness, a *lower* and also a *higher* one: they are like two gates—one open and the other closed, respectively—to the physical and the psychic worlds. The former includes processes of the fifth type (case no. 5); under the latter there may develop processes of the second type (case no. 2), to which a consciousness in the true sense usually does not apply, because they happen outside the zone of *mental* dynamisms: the very ones that, through analogous cerebral modifications, determine common self-consciousness, which, as we know, depends on the brain. But then we should speak of two regions of the subconscious: a *lower subconscious* (the zone of automatisms, vital and organic dynamisms, recapitulating the past history of the spirit) and a *higher subconscious* (which is virtually the *supraconscious*), which is the spirit's history to come. Each is a part of the integral being of man, who is both spirit and body, psychic and physical, future and past. We have already mentioned the possibility that through abnormal means and in specific conditions, parts of the subconscious processes of both types may emerge.[9]

---

9. From the esoteric point of view, the lower subconscious and the higher subconscious (supraconscious) can partially be not two different domains, but a single domain realized in two different modes. In the bodily subconscious the "gods" are "asleep," or, if one prefers, the supraconscious of the gods is the subconscious of humans. The supraconscious is the spiritual realization of the invisible forces active in the most obscure bodily processes: forces of a nonhuman character. Thus, in both Hermetism and Eastern esotericism the body is considered as the "material" for the sacred work, and in symbolism "resurrection" is preceded by the "descent into hell" (corporeal subconscious). Hence the relativity of what Apro calls body and spirit, past and future of the spirit: they are two phases of a process that is not linear, but *cyclic*: the "future" of the spirit is a reconvergence in the original stages of "creation," and when the resolution is complete, the circle is transformed into an *act* wherein there is neither a "before" nor an "after." (Note by UR)

Our brain is sensitive to mental energy, but all too often it comes via sensorial energy. It is usually not a matter of a mental dynamism, but of a *mentalized sensorial dynamism.* Thus, our thought has to rely on sensations and images, while *pure thought* (in the *real* sense, not as a philosophical abstraction) is not perceived and falls into the region of the higher subconscious. However, when our brain becomes sensitive to real mental energy, without intermediaries, then our thought will lose its character of an internal phenomenon, unconscious and quasi-abstract, and become a real objective fact. In the current state of consciousness, in regard to its relationships with the not-I, thought is a *sensation of the mental stimulus* rather than a perception of the mental dynamism in itself. Thus, the clear line of separation seen in the diagram between mental and sensorial is more theoretical than otherwise: for ordinary consciousness the two regions have inextricable fringes of interference, and the center of the apparent I, instead of being *in itself,* that is, above in pure intellectuality, finds itself in the middle of this tangle.

We will say something about *integral consciousness.* It should be considered as the true point of departure, the true center that, as its first manifestation and exteriorization, takes on the aspect of individual self-consciousness. When the nucleus of I-will can manifest without limitations or degradations, in its integral dynamic essence, it is a *constructor in action.* The modality of thought can then be called *creative,* rather than *organizing.* Liberating itself from the mental dynamisms connected to the brain, it can project its energy onto physical matter *directly,* or nearly so, such that its creation is emancipated from the normal conditions of time and space and becomes, so to speak, instantaneous.

We see now what are the conditions for the passage from external consciousness to these supranormal forms. As explained, mental energy, sensorial energy, and vital energy should be considered as successively more "degraded" forms of a unique primitive energy, which stems from the integral consciousness and emerges, encountering ever stronger resistances, in the various organs in contact with the external world.

External consciousness corresponds to the state of greatest limitation. To realize the higher forms of consciousness, the I needs to suppress every manifestation in the physiological field, suspending relations with the external physical world, and thus also ordinary waking consciousness. Only by this means will it be able to withdraw into a sensorial field and then into an intellectual field, gradually eliminating all the resistances that obstruct its dynamism or close it within the circuit of the body. The withdrawal of the I from the external environment, with gradual obscuration of waking consciousness, corresponds inversely to the gradual development of consciousness itself, and will cause the emergence of new faculties, more or less subconscious, that gradually reveal themselves. One goes on to cycles of types 9, 10, and 11. As a rule, their nature is to have no phenomenal manifestation. For that to happen would require a current to reactivate the *outer layer* of the integral consciousness, partially "degrading" the latter and reactivating the part of the dynamisms represented by whatever automatism is necessary to translate the modifications of the higher consciousness.

Turning specifically to the *activity* aspect of the I, when it emerges and manifests excluding the more external strata—which are the usual ways of physiological manifestation—there occur the phenomena of *exteriorization* in the strict sense: exteriorization of thought, of sensitivity, of motricity (action at a distance), of visual images (veridical hallucinations), as well as of the vital force itself and even of a part of the organic substance, as happens in the formation of ectoplasm and materializations.[10] Usually, they are all phenomena requiring freedom from the psycho-vital dynamisms with respect to the body, entailing an abnormal dislocation of the individual physico-psychic unity, not always advisable or free from dangers. Moreover, just as ordinary consciousness, which is external, is based on that unity, the phenomenology of exteriorizations develops as a rule in subconscious states (mediumistic trance, magnetic sleep, catalepsy, etc.), whenever it is not guided by a precise method and a sufficient spiritual elevation.

In practice, one can prevent the subconscious from usurping the supraconscious by avoiding actual dissociation and the complete

---

10. To the "dynamic" aspect of "exteriorizations" corresponds the "static" aspect of *rapports*: rapports on the mineral plane (e.g., dowsing), on the vital plane (the therapeutic-diagnostic instinct), on the psychic plane (psychic clairvoyance), and so forth.

suspension of the external activity of consciousness. We will just mention that the principal methods required are of two types. The first consists of attaining an *excess* of internal vital energy, compared to what is needed to sustain normal organic activity. The latter is then not suspended, and consequently one maintains the state of awareness of waking consciousness. Meanwhile the excessive energy remains unused and free to act on other planes. What the mystery literature often mentions as exaltation, sacred intoxication, and the divine "fury" must conceal a method of this kind.

The second type involves making automatic certain dynamisms that usually engage the attention and consciousness, preventing them from turning elsewhere. With certain functions rendered automatic, some higher energies can be detached from the conditions and limitations that those functions impose, and remain free for forms of higher activity. The second method includes the creation of monoideisms,[11] the use of repetitions, and "rhythmicization" in general, which may also be applied to movements and organic functions such as breathing. These are well known and frequent techniques used in all periods by those dedicated to cultivating supranormal powers.

---

11. [Concentration on, or repetition of, a single idea. —*Trans.*]

IV.2

Experiences

I will start by recalling some childhood anticipations of my esoteric experiences. It was in my character, from infancy on, for all my actions to be marked by confidence, together with a singular sensitivity and a drive to mastery. It was a strange thing, given my age, but I remember that the end of each day usually left me with a sense of dissatisfaction and unease, as if there were something I should have grasped and which always eluded me. Yet in the silent night while I was preparing to sleep I was often seized by an extraordinary life force, which bore me, still awake, into a fantastically animated world. I remember witnessing scenes both grandiose and distressing. I felt waves of light passing through me which were fragments of figures coming and going between infinities. I gave a sudden start at hearing someone calling me, whom I could not see. Sometimes I saw my hands radiating a diffused light along my fingers, and my breath itself became a glimmer in the darkness under the covers, where I would often huddle up, quivering.

Gradually, all this disappeared. I kept only the memory of a dream. I was taken up with outward life, student turmoil, nagging intellectual problems. The years passed. My studies gravitated to the natural sciences, which after graduation became the basis of my profession. Little by little and through various circumstances a sort of crisis arose inside me, erupting in the first days of 1928 as a symbolic thought-vision. I don't think it necessary to describe it. I will only say that it gave me the absolute perception of a *task,* united with a clear and natural resolution to act.

The childhood drive to mastery now took on a conscious and higher form. And once again, after many years, it turned toward those invisible worlds that had vanished from my awareness. I felt an inner force that would not relax, trying to escape from human bondage, to become a center, to remain there. I also had forebodings of the dangers strewn along the path, the struggle I would have to bear, the obstacles to be overcome. I also knew what happens to one who fails after his decision, and one who goes astray: he must take up a body again after wanting to kill it, and return with it to where the flame is forever extinguished, in the world of men.

I needed a method. Scientific studies had accustomed my mind to precise ideas, to the system of practical and experimental techniques. This was why the varied and confused material of common mystical and Theosophical literature, which I set out to read, failed to satisfy me. By chance I came across the writings of the UR Group, and was struck by their practical point of view and the unusual clarity of their teachings. I made a general and systematic study of these materials. Resolving to make my own way, I prepared by taking up exercises with the breath force. I had results. A kind of well-being soon awakened in me, encouraging me to persist. I reached the state of lightness and fire that it seemed would fling me into space. The sense of my life began to be quite different.

I was intending to join an active chain, set up according to the instructions in these pages (*Introduction to Magic*, vol. II, 42–52), reckoning that up to a point I was prepared for it, when a rude shock, caused by a serious accident in a chemical laboratory, hit me right in those body parts that I had first "touched." I was forced to leave the city and my work, and go to the mountains for convalescence.

Alone, with long, empty hours ahead of me, I decided to write directly to the leaders of that chain for instructions in more detail, and especially for my condition. They made no difficulty about satisfying me. I recognized the opportunity to abandon the development of consciousness in the middle seat, and to concentrate instead on the other two seats, those of the power of the I and the power of action. To this day my practices follow this direction, so that they are normally not experiences of "vision" but of intensive states that have the function of the force fields of experimental physics. I will describe their main features.

First, I have reached the "silence," which I can realize today to an extent with a simple command.

By maintaining concentration for a long time, the "air" and "fire" states of the spirit are strongly felt.

Having mastered these elementary requirements, I turned to awakening the purified thought in the higher seat.[1] By applying what is said about the attitude needed for esoteric instruction (*Introduction to Magic*, vol. I, 300–303), with conscious thought realized as *power* (vol. I, 262–63), and by meditating on some of the basic texts, I came to see and feel reality in a vast, grandiose, and entirely new way. With a special practice I had been given, I began to modify my sensations, which were many and indistinct, or altered by my abnormal state. With meditation, sometimes continued for hours both by day and night, following the more personal instructions, they penetrated my consciousness deeply, to the point of entering into contact with the forces dormant in the seats of the subtle centers. Then like a memory there arose the comprehension of all the material explained in these volumes, silently summarized and reinforced by the symbolic figure of slaying the Bull. In a state of superior calm, concentration on the seat of the I-will complex has awoken the fluidic force in a remarkable way: thought kindles the fire-force, the creative fire. I "perceive" the world differently. I no longer worry about any realization. The state of power is controlled by the sense of dominating clarity.

I will add some more precise details.

A sense of the sky as *living,* ensouled, moved by visible currents while gradually illuminated by innumerable sparks rushing round, appearing and vanishing at the very moment one sees them.

A sense of nature, which appears as a marvelous creature intent on unveiling itself, so that profound meanings might shine forth in divine

---

1. On the significance of the three seats, see the essay on occult morphology and spiritual corporeity in *Introduction to Magic*, vol. II, 360–66. (Note by UR)

transparency. Sometimes I feel utterly at one with what surrounds me: I grasp other things as though they were parts of myself, springing up from within me. Inside this body, as large as it is real, I feel an energy vibrating that is alive, constant and fervent, calm and intense—like what is reflected in the sky. The blood feels its impact and gives forth a "sound," sometimes of the greatest intensity. In these culminating states, while control seems lost in the face of such an ocean of energy, a danger appears. It would be enough to lose this state for a moment for an "opening" to occur—but it is a state of consciousness that I cannot now describe, however imperfectly: in a flash one *sees*, and finds oneself with deathly cold spread through one's body, rigid as a stone, and stunned. One has to hold steady like the pile of a bridge resisting the fury of the current, feeling its force, impassive and stable before the tumult, the growing violence, and the perils of the whirlpool forming around one.

I also know something of the "dissolution of the mixed" (*Introduction to Magic,* vol. II, 312–20). These uncalled-for dissolutions, once they occurred, left me convinced that they depended solely on the development of the faculties of my being.

Once on New Year's Eve, after partying and drinking a bit, I suddenly felt a blow that snatched away my support and sent me into the void. The impression lasted only an instant, but it was enough for me to understand the meaning and nature of the practices that use violent methods (the "corrosive waters"[2]).

Moments of waking in the night: internal perception of the luminous centers of the body—then the awareness vanishes and I go back to sleep. Sometimes in the morning, apparitions of signs and sigils drawn in lines of fire: a typical one is a zigzag.

Passing from the "volatile" to the "dense": a hard, solid, metallic, heavy sense, mainly located in the zone of the solar plexus; then it spreads to the limbs, which feel super-saturated with power. If I evoke the air, then I feel myself becoming light, airy, but still in an energetic state. A high-frequency vibratory rhythm runs through my members,

---

2. [See *Introduction to Magic,* vol. II, 146–52. —*Trans.*]

and a subtle energy wraps my body like the finest net, sticking close while the body, more extended than the physical one, presses against it in a calm, regular, and continuous way, with a sensation of what I can only call, by analogy, "sonority."

I have practiced the awareness of breathing, following the instructions in *Introduction to Magic,* vol. I, 133–34. I stopped at the second phase, still finding it difficult to understand the meaning of the realization of the "Archangel of the Air." Only one evening I "felt as imminent" the experience, which unexpectedly came and forthwith vanished with a flash of lightning. I was all light-flame: the Infinite. My hair stood on end and a mortal cold rose serpent-like from within, as though it wanted to fling me into the nothingness of a ghastly asylum of death. The next morning—and this too was a momentary sensation—I felt as though the sky was falling on me, as though it were solid, in transparent and luminous fragments.

For the present I persist with the practice of the nocturnal Sun—which so far does not yet illuminate my brief sleep—to which I bring patience and enthusiasm. I experience the knowledge of the "air" with sensations of light-force. The "state of power" kindles ever-deeper forces. One task I now intend is to organize the step-by-step training of the nascent consciousness of the subtle body.

I feel calm, strong, and secure. I am fairly contented with my life here. In fact, thanks to it I have begun to follow the "straight path." I love this place, this solitude among the silent grandeur of the mountains, considering it as necessary and as a period of life that I have willed for myself. I am certain that this is the case.

What Is "Metaphysical Reality"?

Since the expression "metaphysical reality" recurs frequently as a central reference-point for various teachings in this collection, it seems appropriate to define it.

We can begin by taking the literal and etymological meaning. Metaphysics is that which is not physical and is beyond the physical. But one should not identify physical reality with that of "physics," nor metaphysics with what is called that in philosophy. If one sets out by thinking in those terms, one will be very far from the matter in hand, because "physics" as conceived of today is a complex of empirical and inductive knowledge wherein the very significance of immediate and living experience dissolves in mathematical abstractions and general laws, with no value beyond the ability of "prediction." And "metaphysics" today means the philosophical abstraction that escapes even the control of "positive" experimental methods and launches itself into empty speculations and fantasies beyond anything known to the physical sciences.

It will be better to take the term "physical" in the common sense, which blends it with that of "bodily." Then we can define as "physical" that state of being which is subject to spatial and temporal conditions: just as everything that has "body" occupies a certain space and is subject to the changes that happen in time.

If we want to consider things subjectively, it is enough to replace "being" with "consciousness" and thus to define as "physical" everything experienced by a consciousness that has space and time as the conditions of its cognition: that is, the universe made up of bodies and perceived through bodily senses.

Given that, is it obvious what we would call "metaphysical": (1) from the objective point of view, it is any state of being that is not bound to spatial and temporal conditions; (2) from the subjective point of view, it is the experience that a consciousness may have when such conditions cease to be a part of its cognition. *What we understand as a whole by "metaphysical reality" corresponds to an experience of that kind.*

These notions may not be easy for common sense, since generally what man experiences and remembers refers above all to his bodily states. This causes him to instinctively identify "reality" with "corporeity," so that the very expression "metaphysical reality" (with "metaphysical" meaning bodiless) may seem a contradiction in terms. The leap to the "metaphysical" may seem a leap into nothingness, either because he cannot imagine what he could experience once his bodily senses were interrupted; or because consciousness in the metaphysical state would be a consciousness detached from the body: something that in the natural and final course of events would happen with death, or from another point of view would have death as its consequence.

Our readers do not need us to dwell longer on these difficulties. They know that initiation, which leads to realizing metaphysical states, has actually been compared to the very process that occurs in death, but caused voluntarily through an "art" then actively overcome so as to preserve the continuity of consciousness (see *Introduction to Magic,* vol. I, 130–32; vol. II, 182–88[1]). Secondly, what common sense draws from experiences limited to bodily states is contradicted by the results of even an elementary philosophical critique of cognition; this shows that space and time are not constitutive elements of reality, but modalities of human knowledge of reality, which in itself is neither spatial nor temporal, but becomes so because of an inner constitution particular to man, who cannot represent it otherwise. But if that is how things stand, and

---

1. [The author gives references to volume and part (chapter) only. I have specified the articles that seem relevant. —*Trans.*]

space and time are simple laws of the human mind, one can imagine circumstances in which those laws would be suspended and give way to other laws. Then the common experience of reality as bodily would be replaced by another experience, in which "reality" would take on a mode of appearance that is not, and can no longer be, that of bodily things.

Now, with that essential change, and with the transformation of the innermost nature, which at all times and places has been attributed to the power of initiation, it is thinkable that one would experience an abolition of the common mode of cognition, awakening the possibility of perceiving reality from a non-corporeal and "metaphysical" standpoint.

We should note that "non-corporeal" and "metaphysical" are generic terms, referring to a range of states very different from one another, though having in common that they exist outside the physical condition. This is an important caution, given the extremely limited horizons of modern people. Even if they are able to count beyond "one" (or conceive that there could be something other than the physical state), they can rarely go beyond "two," stopping at the duality of bodily/non-bodily, "here" and "there," "this world" and "the other world," and so on, and taking each term as the exact half of the whole. *Such a conception, which is worse than simplistic, needs to be replaced by that of a multiplicity of conditions of existence, among which the bodily and earthly condition is only a particular case, like one section among all the others that can be drawn through the* plenum *of a totality.* Thus, strictly speaking, the generic term "metaphysical reality" will apply to *all* the states of being, once we exclude that of the individual human on earth. For example, when our sciences speak of the Elements, the Seven (planets), the Twelve (zodiac), these are symbolic references to very distinct "metaphysical" states, named by the Ancients as planets and constellations while really they are so many worlds, just like the one that is revealed on the earth through space and time. The term "metaphysical reality" can, however, have a more specific meaning if one takes the term "nature" in the ancient sense of φύσις: as comprehending not only the corporeal world, but basically all that is manifestation, *whereas metaphysical reality is then to be understood as the transcendent, the Unconditioned.*

We will mention in passing that on this basis *the common notion of "death" should be revised and relieved of that character of a supremely important event, unrepeatable, tragic, and final for the being, which it has in the entirely human (and especially Christian) conception of the duality of "here" and "beyond."* Death may indeed have this kind of significance from the point of view of those who have depended entirely on the bodily state, and then find when this has dissolved that they have broken the continuity of consciousness. But in any other case "death" is only a change of state, so that the being may have passed through innumerable "deaths"—and, consequently, innumerable births and lives—beside that of human physical existence. Correspondingly, in the active process of initiation, the neophyte's death and rebirth are only the first element in a series, which may develop in many other changes of state, each of which—for every "planet" or "name" or "deity" or "heaven" or "earth," and so on—equally implies a "death" and a "birth" for him. This gives a glimpse into the true vastness of things, and how today every distance has been shrunk: so rigid has become the gaze, hypnotically focused on this miserable earth, that no sense remains today of the grandeur, spanning worlds and heavens, zones of darkness and zones of light, of the currents of the infinite.

• • •

But "metaphysical reality" may raise a further question of a "philosophical" nature. "Reality," you may say, is not equivalent to "corporeity," but even in this wider sense, what can "real" mean in relation to the I? "Real" seems generally to signify the "being in itself" of things, that is, their being outside the I and independently of the I: hence that which one experiences is not identical to the experience itself (as happens, for instance, in a feeling), but remains something distinct from me, something which exists objectively whether I experience it or not.

This is the view of so-called philosophical "realism," which, however, seems to be just a transposition of what seems obvious when we have to do mainly with corporeal reality: the relationship of the I with regard to things of physical experience has the exact characteristic corresponding to the stance of philosophical realism. But if "metaphysical reality" implies, as we have said, a transformation of the mode of knowing, it obviously cannot be measured by that conception of reality. In fact, as soon as we are not dealing with tangible things existing in space, the seemingly clear distinction between subject and object, between "inside" and "outside," between knower and known—even between knowledge and action—loses much of its clarity and no longer supplies such a firm basis for philosophical realism.

On this subject, there is an author[2] who, in treating the relationships between the modern approach to metapsychology and the initiatic approach, has tried to show how the position of philosophical idealism is preferable, in the following terms.

To admit a metaphysical reality that is knowable only by way of an inner realization—so one is told—would forthwith take on a clearer sense if one granted to knowledge the essential character of an *act* of the I. Now, this is the point of view of so-called modern idealism, which, unlike the philosophies that reduce the knowledge process to a simple reception on the individual's part of vibrations coming from an external reality, has inverted the position. It posits the I as the principle and basis of the cognitive function, which with its act *makes* real, projects the attribute of reality, into what it knows. This idealist concept—the same author continues—may perhaps meet serious problems in the field of common experience. Yet it has the advantage of allowing for a consciousness[3] different from that of a given state of the individual, the necessary and sufficient condition for it being a change of function, that is, of the individual himself: something equivalent to a *transformation of essence,* which is what initiatic sciences always claim. Thus—he

---

2. Emilio Servadio, in *La Fiera Letteraria* (Sept. 30, 1928). Servadio rightly pointed out that the essential opposition is as follows: metapsychology, starting from scientific and positivist premises, tends nowadays to deviate into philosophical hypotheses and spiritualist fantasies; whereas esotericism (Servadio referred above all to the trends of our group) tends to dispense with everything that is "spiritualism" and philosophy, so as to concentrate on reports of *knowledge* and technique.

3. [Following the French translation from the 1929 version: "une *connaissance* différente de celle d'un individu donné dans un état donné" (my italics), rather than the later: "une *condizione* diversa da quella propria ad un determinato stato dell'individuo." —*Trans.*]

concludes—the idealistic concept of reality as a conscious act and reality as a creation of the I could be applied to "metaphysical reality." One could say that "the I itself, ascending, *creates* it at the same time as *it creates itself,* at the limit being the lord of a reality that has no origin but in itself."

Those are Servadio's ideas, with which one may partly agree. With due reservations about the notion of the "I," we can admit that whereas the theory of philosophical realism fits the natural evidence from the experience of the physical senses, that of philosophical idealism is far more flexible, and seems better able to grasp the mode and meaning of "metaphysical" experience. We would also say that the idealistic view, which excludes the notion of an absolutely external reality with respect to the I and to knowledge, is only fully valid with reference to this specific experience, whereas when it claims to apply to the field of common experience, it appears one-sided and only supportable in abstract, "gnoseological" terms.

Moreover, if we consider some cases in which knowledge of a transcendent character has even found expression in a philosophical system—such as Vedanta, Mahayana, and, in the West, Neoplatonism—we find prevalent the same idea of a creative and identifying knowledge of that antirealistic kind. There is a typical passage in the Upanishads, where it says that "the affirmer of the world is the I (*ātmā*)"; by that affirmation it grants an I and a character of reality to the world, which in itself lacks an I. But we can also stay with the West, where we find Plotinus referring precisely to the "incorporeal senses of the heavenly man," that perceive in a different way from the human bodily senses.[4] In his words, "it is true that thought and being are identical, because in the immaterial world the thought is the same as the reality."[5] And again: "We need not look for the intelligibles [the non-corporeal principles of metaphysical reality] outside the intellect. . . . We cannot be truly one with them if

---

4. Plotinus, *Enneads,* VI, vii, 7. [I translate the excerpts from Plotinus with reference to Stephen MacKenna's translation (London: Faber, 1969), but following the syntax and terminology of the Italian. —*Trans.*]
5. Plotinus, *Enneads,* V, ix, 5.

we do not possess them, as is proper to true intellectual knowledge [i.e., metaphysical knowledge]. Only thus will nothing escape it and nothing remain to be sought beyond itself; the truth is there; it becomes the seat of the real beings; it 'lives and comprehends.'"[6] In the νοῦς, in the mind as metaphysical principle of being—says Plotinus[7]—it is evident that for the sage, the two become one: "it must be such that the two make only one, which is a living vision and not merely the act of seeing something that is other." Many other passages of the same kind could be cited against the dualistic-realistic concept of knowing, inspired by the sensible experience of bodies. We will only mention one more,[8] where it is said that the object of the νοῦς is not outside it, but is its very self, such that in the act of knowledge it attains itself, and what it sees is itself.

These expressions assert unequivocally the active and anti-dualistic character of the transcendent cognitive process, but without including the term "create," favored by modern idealists. This requires clarification.

Among the "metaphysical" possibilities there exists a "creative state," and consequently more "creative states" must exist. We will explain this with an analogy. In a certain mode of being, the one in which we are fully present to ourself and internally in command of all the parts of our action, we do something—this state will shape the action itself with whatever form is known, including those corresponding to "things," into objects that seem external, static, and inanimate. This is the *dynamic* plane of nature. Consciousness can make contact with it; on transforming itself, there results an experience in which the significance of its relationship with natural things is precisely that of a "creation."

When we speak of creating something that did not exist before, it is not in the common sense of the term. What did not exist before is the *knowledge* of this relationship. Objectively, no form could exist

---

6. Plotinus, *Enneads,* V, v, 2.

7. Plotinus, *Enneads,* III, viii, 8. [Not III, viii, 7 as stated in the text. —*Trans.*]

8. Plotinus, *Enneads,* II, ix, 1. Compare *Corpus Hermeticum,* II, 12 [not II, 11, as stated in the text. —*Trans.*]. The incorporeal is "intelligence and reason (λόγος) embracing itself, free from all body, unerring, impassive and intangible, . . . containing all, embracing the beings."

that was not supported by a creative process; every form that exists goes back to its creative and dynamic principle, of which it is the expression. With regard to the I, one cannot say that these processes "do not yet exist"; rather, one should say that in bodily existence they pass into a state of silence and subconsciousness, analogous to what happens when an activity becomes automatic. The forces of the dynamic state are part of the I and have never ceased being a part of it. It is a matter of their reentrance into the field of consciousness. Therefore, it is not a question of *becoming* a creator, having not been one before: we are *always* creators, and it is only a matter of becoming aware of it, by transferring consciousness to the corresponding state. For this and similar transformations, the best expression is *reawakening.* Moreover, the notion of "creation" in its modern usage, especially idealist-historicist, carries a disguised "evolutionism": it assumes as the point of departure something that is "less," facing something that could increase it. The initiatic view is the contrary: the "state of justice" of a being, its original state *in signo rationis* (under the sign of reason), does not have a "more" beyond it, but if anything a "less" (hence the Alexandrian doctrine of the *waning* of degrees of light in the πρόοδος, a term that literally translates as "progress"). There is no talk of becoming a god and creator on the part of a non-god and non-creator (the anti-aristocratic position of "rising from below"), but instead of an awakening and a reintegration, or a return to oneself on the part of a "sleeping god" (Clement of Alexandria) or a "swooned angel" (Boehme).[9]

Another clarification is needed when, in the context of "metaphysical reality," one adds to the idea of "creation" that of "domination." The two notions are not, in fact, included in one another: "domination" only applies to the mode of certain specific metaphysical states (personified, for example, in the theology of the divine hierarchies as Thrones and Dominations). The most common traditional expressions—already seen

---

9. We should also mention that the expression "to create a reality that *previously* did not exist," if taken literally and in the ontological sense and not that of inner experience, would raise the problem that with its "before and after" it introduces time into metaphysical reality, whereas time, at least as commonly conceived, is a condition restricted to the corporeal state.

in Plotinus—are "to become the powers," "to be the gods oneself."[10] The apperception of the metaphysical creative functions leaves open the question of how one should relate to them. It is surely possible to seal them with a crown—to use a Kabbalistic expression. But first of all, one would have to decide if this is really what one wants and how qualified one is. The Hermetic advice reported by Zosimus[11] says, for example, that the "spiritual man," "he who knows himself," disdains external magic, lets things proceed according to nature or according to laws, and only seeks the divine gnosis and the domain of the ineffable Triad.

A second question refers to the relationship of the powers. In a certain metaphysical state, the structure and order of the powers of things can be compared to that which, in the microcosm, is given by the nature and constitution of a certain being. One can also change it—but that implies a play of tensions, auto-actions and auto-reactions, which needs to be considered. It implies going much further, to the point of touching and simultaneously "sealing with a crown" the power that in some traditions is called *Chaos,* in others *Death* (the Hindu god Mṛtyu), which is the "materia prima" of transformations. In consequence there follows a transformation (a death and rebirth) and the awakening to another metaphysical hierarchy.

We repeat that this is a possibility and not the only goal, much less the character that every metaphysical experience naturally presents. The way of the dominators is only one of the rays that emerge from the center, and it draws its significance from the existence of many other paths that equally radiate from the origin, where one discovers freedom as the supreme law of the All, as the justification of the double path of light and darkness, uranic and telluric.

---

10. Compare *Corpus Hermeticum,* I, 25–26, 43.
11. Text in Berthelot, *Collection des anciens Alchimistes grecs* (Paris, 1887), vol. II, 230.

IV.4

On the "Law of Beings"

KNOWLEDGE OF EXPIATION—KNOWLEDGE OF REVENGE—KNOWLEDGE OF LOVE

My brief considerations in volume I of *Introduction to Magic* (pp. 167–72), under the title "The Law of Beings," seem to have specially attracted the attention of more than one reader. Certainly, one cannot say that the argument does not deserve it: the existence of a law of the invisible world that seems to have the same importance, the same significance, and the same generality as the physical law of the "conservation of energy" has to interest all those who are about to undertake something *practical* in this field. For that reason, I would like to take up the argument again and complete it with some details that are within my competence.

I wrote (pp. 169–70): *"When resistance is created against the vortex of a being,* [referring to the more specific instruction already given here, one can say that this *must* happen every time that 'solar' initiation is in question] *the cause of an effect is produced; all the more so in the case of a magical operation. The effect is a reaction, namely, a power of the being that turns against whoever acts or offers resistance. If the practitioner knows how to resist, the force is discharged elsewhere. BUT AT ANY EVENT, IT IS DISCHARGED. The 'lines of lesser resistance' then consist of those people who are connected through a bond of sympathy, or even of blood, with him who acts."*

The communication signed "Ermo," which has been passed on to me and which I reproduce, is interesting because it leads to an extension of the problem:

Some writings that appeared in the second volume, particularly those regarding magical chains, the solutions of rhythm and liberation, etc. [*Introduction to Magic*, vol. II, 42–52, 108–14], have made me dwell again, through association of ideas, on certain aspects of occult phenomenology which had already drawn my attention; phenomena that I then had to attribute (albeit without being completely convinced) to common "chance," not having been offered a more logical explanation up to then.

Those pages opened a sudden crack through which some light shone on a dark zone of subconscious personal experiences, which I will summarize in a few words and as clearly as I can.

The data referring to the circle of persons with whom one is linked by relationship, friendship, or familiarity, not just through interests but through shared ideals or sentiments, strong physical or moral sympathy, common tendencies—and in some other cases, ties of invincible aversion, whether justified or not—offer the esoterically minded psychologist the opportunity to make the following curious observation.

Identical or analogous happenings are often found to occur in such a circle: happy or sad circumstances that have almost equal reactions on those concerned.

Sometimes one or more persons belonging to the "circle" are affected by a happy or a sad event; while at other times when one of them is affected by a misfortune, suddenly another—as though on a rebound or through a law of equilibrium—receives some such "gift" at random, as it were. And the stronger the ties of sympathy or aversion that bind the members of the group, the more this obscure law of interdependence manifests.

I could cite particular cases with precise elements and dates, if the interest here were not rather in the general law. Readers with a good memory and a suitable power of observation may arrive at similar conclusions.

These cases have also been noticed by persons who are entirely detached from our studies; persons whose seriousness, balance, and lack of prejudice can give no motive for suspicion.

What causes should one trace for phenomena of this kind? Should one resort to the "law of Beings," to *karma,* to ancestral heredities? Does it allow one to believe in the possibility of *unconscious chains* (magical ones)? Or should one simply attribute it to something like that law of *elective affinities,* displayed in Goethe's famous novel of that name?

Perhaps these problems are unimportant to the study of transcendent esotericism. But one should not deny their importance to those who are trying to understand better the backstage of what is happening around them.

For my part, it is beyond doubt that phenomena of this kind are real, and that they do not obey mere chance.

Ermo himself offers the right key to many cases, in speaking of "unconscious chains."

It is not only through magical operations that two or more persons can reach a state of genuine rapport, so as to form a single body, as it were, in regard to some reactions. Every time that two or more persons establish a sympathetic bond that really goes deep; or every time their lives are oriented to a unique and distinct fundamental tendency, a commonality of vibrations is produced and sets up an occult rapport of "vital forces," automatically and without regard to spatial distance.[1] The individuals then find themselves in the state of "communicating vessels." This is a real fact, which becomes established once the necessary conditions are present.

We must therefore admit that there are natural or elective chains that behave like those created by conscious magical art. This explains the phenomena to which Ermo has drawn attention. It is not rare to

---

1. In the latter case, we recall that the "subtle body" is to an extent unaffected by the spatial condition. On the subtle plane, "distance" is given only by affinity, by syntony of the internal vibrations, or its absence, by their intimate concord or discord. (Note by UR)

have the same thought, or for both to have the same memory, sensation, or association. But when the unity is deep, one may say that one "destiny" merges with the other. Whatever affects one member of the group for good or ill tends automatically to extend to the others who are united *in life,* and to take effect in ways that can be quite different, so that the intimate link is often elusive.

I deliberately said "united in life." The seat of the chain's rapport is precisely that animated *something* between the corporeal and the incorporeal, which esotericists call the "vital body." It is connected with the *blood.* From this one can understand why *consanguinity,* the natural bond established by blood, is in itself a potential link in the chain. A reaction repelled by the individual, if it is very strong, forces its way, arouses the bond, which turns from potential to actual—and therefore passes to the blood relatives: unless the person in question has "electively" established and continued closer relations with others, who then become more exposed to the reaction than his relatives.

In past times the strength of the blood was much more alive than it is today. Nowadays the mixing of races and the individualistic tendency have subverted it, dissolving the state of a natural chain that was formerly provided by the unity of family and group. In ancient traditions we can discern three principles that demonstrate the strength of this conception: the principle of *diffusion,* the principle of *concentration,* and the principal of *substitution.*

By virtue of the first, a "fault" (i.e., the cause of a reaction) committed by one member of the community or the family could cause its "curse" to fall on all the others: they must all expiate it. The same goes for the "offense" suffered by one member. If one can admit that cases of physical and psychic heredity exist, it should not be too difficult to allow cases of the hereditary transmission of vital and subtle elements connected to a special influence, just as in a hereditary ailment a certain predisposition proceeds from the transmitted physical elements. To extend the view further, the principle of diffusion can also work in time: the "curse" of a "fault" may extend over generations of the same blood, until its "expiation" is accomplished—unless the reaction has been exhausted through determined events. If instead of a "fault" it is a matter of an "offense," there remains the legacy of the *vendetta*, of reparation: the "offense" against one has aroused a force in the community that *must* be discharged, or else it will turn into a source of disaster, a distortion of the collective or family entity. The contrary case is the diffusion among the members of a "blessing" or "benefic influence" activated by one of them.

By the principle of *concentration*, on the other hand, the "charge" that falls on a community or chain can be gathered and resolved by a single member, who "redeems" all the others. These are the voluntary or designated "expiators"—or else they are the "avengers." Everyone knows how widespread this tradition was in ancient times, especially with regard to sacrifices. Often the sacrifice was presented as preventing a "diffusion": the "curse" that fell on a community or a family through the fault of one of them was lifted from all by another individual, an expiator or redeemer. In the Judeo-Christian myth, Jesus with his sacrifice ransoms the heredity of Adam that weighed on all the descendants of the "first man."

The principle of *substitution* means that an "offense" committed by or to a single member can be redeemed by another member who substitutes for the first. One can be sacrificed for the other, one answers for the other, or one avenges the other. The effect is the same: the cause that was created is discharged.

I have recalled these ancient traditions, which refer to the state of a chain given naturally in former times by blood, because it extends to various analogous unities that can still be established today, in other ways. *All the terms such as "fault," "offense," "blessing," "curse," "vengeance," "ransom," "redemption," and so forth, in this context should be separated from any moral significance and understood positively as dynamisms of subtle forces, obeying the law of beings and responding to a precise determinism,* which the Ancients showed that they knew and which gives a positive foundation, one might say even a *physical* one, to many usages and traditions that are considered barbaric or superstitious today, or have become so.

For instance, I would like to address the ancient *law of vengeance*. It is sheer ignorance to see in it nothing but the codification of a purely subjective fact based on instinct, passion, and impulse. On the contrary, to any chain-bound group it is a justification based on unadorned reality. The offender's action has created a reaction, because it has broken an equilibrium. Until the reaction is exhausted, the unbalanced factor will remain in the chain, *and will attract to it exactly what the offender should suffer as the effect created by his cause.* Vengeance, on the other hand, defuses the imbalance and restores the state of equilibrium. This knowledge applies not only to chains, but also to relations between individuals, so long as a relationship "in life" has been established: if one person offends another unjustly, then either the latter, reacting, restores the unity of his energy, in which a new cause has arisen; or if he does not do so he *must* suffer the reaction himself, which, as "vengeance," would have struck the former, following an inflexible law. Look deeply at the sense of disturbance and the secret of the *mortal* pallor which appears on his face when he is *mortally* offended, "in his life," and you yourself may find the confirmation of what I have said.

But beside vengeance there is another possibility: *love.* Here the occult dynamic reveals a law that throws a disconcerting light on the meaning and secrecy of certain special teachings. Love, understood as the act of profound sympathy, whereby one is, as it were, identified with another person, creates a *rapport* in the objective sense explained above. *It then creates a path for every energy in action or reaction.* Every unresolved reaction tends to follow that path.

He who knows how to resist, by loving, *can then guide the reactions where he will.* Thus, you understand what is meant by the precept LOVE YOUR ENEMY: it is the way of projecting onto himself the reaction that he has determined.

You also understand why *love is forbidden to the absolute magi*—love in the pure and true sense. *For love's sake, they must not love.* The legend in the East, especially in China, depicts them closed off in a terrible isolation.

I would like to touch on another point, about the "rapports" that are not natural or "elective," but established sacramentally. Today, when the sense of so many things has been lost, one no longer knows the *real, physical* value that consecrations can have, for example, those of baptism or matrimony. These sacraments today are mostly only relics, mere formalities.

In ancient times things were different: a "sacrament" was an act of power that created a "union in life." The act of baptism or equivalent rites in other traditions acted magically on the "vital body" of the person consecrated and attached him "in life" to the trunk of a tradition: his vital force henceforth received the quality of the community and remained occultly bound to it. The act of matrimony sealed "in life" the union of two existences. The operation did not require the subject's participation in order to be effective: his intention could also be absent (as in infant baptism), partial, or even contrary: but just like the physical body, the vital body is susceptible to suffer violence, and all that was required were the *objective* conditions that gave power to the rite. For once the chrismatic seal was placed on him, any infraction constituted a direct action against the collective entity that its power had established—and it imposed itself, for the same reason as explained in the case of "offense," which he who had broken the sacrament would have to *expiate:* it was necessary for the cause, which would have been produced within the chain, to be eliminated. An objective, unsentimental, positive logic now appears in many ancient usages, institutions, and legislations that have been discredited or made the object of open condemnation by the modern mind, which can no longer understand them.

The major obstacle is in the repugnance felt in recognizing that there are laws in life that may to a large extent be set in motion by the inner attitude of the soul, by its decision and its action, but which are in themselves as rigorous and objective as the laws of physics, so that like those they leave no room for the demands of sentiment, morals, or human justice.

One should consider, moreover, that in its earthly existence the soul largely lives on credit, thus it cannot presume to extract itself from what happens to that which does not depend on it, but on which in a certain respect it depends. Man as a pure "I" belongs to himself, and he alone is the cause of his destiny. But already as a mind, then as life, and then as body, man ceases to belong solely to himself, and he shares the destiny of collective entities, beside which his own action and disposition cause new and more special associations that complicate the knot with additional threads. To protest against the fact that one can respond for others, or suffer the action of others (even unknowingly), shows ignorance of these common destinies that belong to everything in man that is not his pure "I." The unjust fact of "contagious" reactions and communal happenings, to whose minor forms Ermo has drawn attention, is found on a grand scale in cataclysms, epidemics, and wars. One does not usually protest, because one does not suspect that these happenings are rebounding discharges from specific causes, obeying the law of beings, that will strike a whole community without discrimination. If a man compromises his own life, he drags into the same fate either the lower or the nobler functions of his organism, which certainly were not to blame except by being parts of his body. One should think the same of the individuals who are more or less deserving, with respect to the collective destinies, once a link in a chain is established.

In physics, the law of action and reaction is based on that of the conservation of energy, which applies to every "closed system." The esoteric extension of these concepts leads to fairly disturbing realizations that are nonetheless real, such as:

> *What one acquires, another is fated to lose.*
> *For one who advances, one or more go back, so that the total is always a fixed quantity.*
> *To every divine ascent there corresponds a demonic fall.*

However, one should not forget that all this concerns rapports that are not linked to intentions. In other words, it is not the case, for example, that he who rises should intend to push others down, or that he who acquires should steal. This happens automatically, in virtue of an impersonal law. And vice versa: those who take the downward path do not know that by so doing they are opening for others the possibility of taking the upward one. Thus there is neither blame for the one, nor any merit for the other: in pure esotericism these human concepts have no more place than what they are allowed by the dynamics of material forces.

The importance is in having a total vision, grasping the *simultaneity,* the collective movement of all the paths, which are each its own, yet interwoven in a solidarity of actions and reactions. I can clarify it with a miniature example: the reaction that I have provoked, if I can resist it, discharges on others, provoking a given event in their life: *now it may be that that event, of which I am the cause, can enter into the other's life just as it was needed to resolve causes latent in him, according to* HIS *free path of ascent or descent:* the two paths are independent, yet one has served the other.

One should perhaps imagine a simultaneity of this sort, the same solid rapport of actions and destinies extended to an unimaginable complexity and a marvelous and *magical* coincidence, applied to everything—to the multitude of creatures, to their lives, their realizations—ever free yet satisfying the rigorous determinism and the nonhuman justice of the "law of beings."

IV.5

Various Commentaries

Many people make facetious remarks about those dedicated to magic, expecting that by waving their magic wand they should prove to the firstcomer, with visible marvels, that magic is not an illusion.

We will set aside the possibility that there may still be someone who can satisfy those frivolous persons in such a way. What is important here is to reflect on how a serious mind might become convinced of it.

As Ea has already noted (*Introduction to Magic,* vol. I, 257–65), the misunderstanding arises largely through thinking of such operations on the model of modern mechanisms and devices: you turn the switch and—click!—the lights go on; you wave the wand and say the mantra and a group of chairs starts dancing the foxtrot, or a "god" jumps out and offers the guests a goblet of genuine ambrosia.

If instead one began to compare magical operations with the most elementary processes of the creative spirit, the idea would seem very different. We do not know, for example, how dashing off a few lines or associating a group of abstract thoughts may sometimes happen by itself, and at other times be impossible, or only possible with great effort. No one asks poets to create on demand—and the theory of "genius," of inspiration, of creative intuition seems to have something to be said for it.

If one does not deny that a certain inner state, not always present and sometimes "capricious," conditions the creative forms that are simply subjective, why should be it so different with the magical act? That is a spiritual creation of a very different quality, requiring a miraculous concomitance not only of the spiritual faculties but also bodily and sub-conscious factors, extra-subjective influences beside the "enthusiasm" or "fire" that unites it all.

There may be some who can dispense with many of those conditions—though it would be quite a rarity if they cared for recognition by the facetious persons mentioned above. But beside the absolute, the relative also has its value and deserves consideration: hence it says nothing against the reality of magic that many degrees require special circumstances, special environments, special inner states—conditions that one cannot always have to hand. It is all the harder if the person who counts for something from the point of view of the invisible lives in the disintegrative atmosphere of the modern city, which imposes a handicap on all his superior faculties.

Another subject for consideration: do those people understand *what is meant by* a "power" of a *magical* character, even an apparently irrelevant one? They may retort: "But we're not asking him to throw a mountain into the sea: just magically levitate this vase a few inches!"

Someone who says this may not have realized that a power of this kind, from the purely physical point of view, is indubitably greater than what it would take to magically cause a little cerebral lesion, by which a person could be incapacitated. And since there is no reason that an objective power should discriminate between one person and another, this could be done, for example, in the brain of a dictator—with all the ensuing consequences that could affect the fate of an entire nation.[1]

Thus it is natural that there should be "conditions" for the power of producing certain extranormal phenomena, when they are not the involuntary, unaware or semi-aware ones of mediumism and even of mysticism, but are really *magical:* decisively intentional, done in clear consciousness and in perfect and *free* will of the I. These conditions are

---

1. As a retrospective historical curiosity, certain of our adversaries, referring to this note, put about the rumor that we were intending to act on Mussolini through magical means, and he almost believed it. We had to expose the origin of this rumor to avoid unpleasant complications.

not "moral" in nature: it is not the moralistic "purity" of the magus who has already become an altruist, a humanitarian, devoted to "evolution," incapable of making any "bad use" of the "powers." The true conditions are instead established by the existence of "entities" that have their own ways and act in given directions that manifest in events of this world. And it is they that one has to deal with. The "power" of man, to be unconditioned, requires him to measure himself with them—since, everything being interconnected, the capacity to produce a seemingly trivial disturbance in the weft of events can give them a very different course and sway the highest causes to different results. This is why orders of "conditions" exist, as many as there are "consecrations," that is, the tests to be passed in the dynamic relations with the "entities."

Thus, the person who could be asked to perform, on demand, the most banal physical phenomenon that revealed a magical character *in the absolute sense,* exempt from any internal or external law and condition, would be one who had already achieved the rank of a "king of kings."

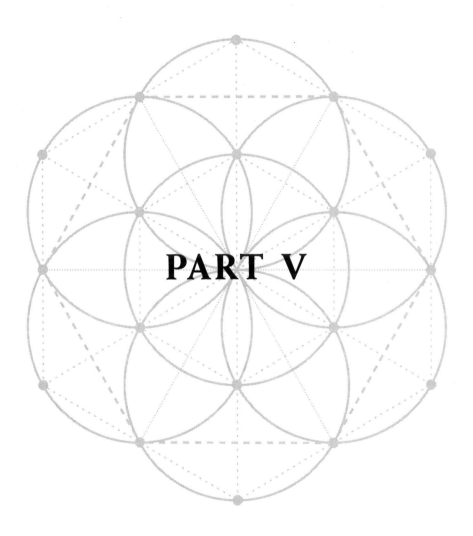

PART V

V.1

Maxims of Pagan Wisdom

It is for the gods to come to me: not for me to go to them.[1]

This reply, given by Plotinus to Amelius, who invited him to approach the gods with the prescribed rituals, reflects the spirit of the "solar" path. The surpassing of the religious attitude; the transcendent dignity of the man in possession of Wisdom, whom Plotinus terms the σπουδαῖος; his superiority not only to the natural world, but also to the divine world: all these are affirmed here.

It is a matter of an inner attitude that is fundamental for practice.

One must create a quality in oneself by which the suprasensible powers (the gods) are *constrained* to come, like females attracted by the male. This quality is summarized in one verb, which means nothing and yet means everything:

TO BE

BE, CONSIST, make yourself a CENTER. Through "ascesis," through "purification," through what Plotinus himself will explain. You have heard tell of the "dry way." This is an aspect of it. Separate yourself from those who are attracted to the invisible worlds through vague neediness, soulful yearning, and confused vision—more "nonbeings" than "beings."

+

---

1. Porphyry, *Life of Plotinus,* §10.

You must make yourselves like the gods; not like good men.
The end is not to be sinless, but to be a god.[2]

These maxims cleanly separate the initiate's path from the path of men. The "virtue" of men, in the final analysis, is a matter of indifference: the image of an image, as Plotinus says. "Morality" has nothing to do with initiation. Initiation is a radical transformation from one state of existence into another state of existence. A "god" is not a "moral example": it is an *other* being. The good man does not cease to be "man" through being "good." In every time and place that understands what "initiation" means, the idea has always been the same. Thus, in Hermetism: "Our work is the conversion and the changing of one being into another being, of one thing into another thing, of weakness into strength . . . of corporeity into spirituality."[3]

+

Sinners can also draw water from the rivers. The giver does not know what he is giving but simply gives.[4]

How does man stand with respect to the all? As a part? No. As a whole that belongs to itself.

Lacking unity, things are deprived of "being." The more unity, the more being they possess.

Every being is itself by belonging to itself; and belonging to itself, it concentrates itself. As Unity, it possesses itself, and has all the grandeur, all the beauty. Therefore do not

---

2. *Enneads,* I, ii, 7; I, ii, 6. [The excerpts from Plotinus's *Enneads,* whose Italian translator is unattributed, are so different from the standard English translations that, with due attention to the latter, I have chosen to reproduce the former, also correcting without notice some errors in the Greek orthography and in the references to the *Enneads. —Trans.*]
3. N. Flamel, *Il Desiderio desiderato,* §6 (ed. Salmon, vol. II, 307). [The quoted passage has been translated from the Italian, as the source is not readily traceable. —*Trans.*]
4. *Enneads,* IV, iv, 42.

*run and flee from yourself indefinitely. Everything within
is now gathered into its unity.*[5]

The essential element for the condition of "being" is *unity*.

UNIFY YOURSELF—BE ONE

This bundle of energes, this horde of beings, sensations, and tendencies
that make up you: bend them beneath a single law, a single will, a single
thought.

ORGANIZE YOURSELF

Bend your "soul," use it in every way, take it to every crossroads until it
is inert, incapable of its own movement, dead to every instinctive irra-
tionality. Just as a perfectly trained horse, when ordered, goes to right or
left, stops, or leaps ahead, so your soul must be to you: a thing that you
hold in your fist. Unchained, you will be ONE: being one, YOU ARE—
and it *belongs to you*. Belonging to you, you will possess grandeur.

Ancient classical wisdom distinguishes two symbolic regions: the
lower, of things that "flee"; the upper, of "things that are." What flow
or "flee" are the things that cannot attain the realization and perfect
possession of their own nature. The other things, *are*: they have tran-
scended this life, which is mixed with death and is a ceaseless running
and aiming. Their "immobility" and even the ancient astronomical designation of their "place" are symbols, denoting a spiritual state. To be
one, no longer dispersed, follows.

+

What is the Good for such a man [for the σπουδαῖος]?
*He is himself his own good. The life that he possesses is
perfect. He possesses the good in that he seeks nothing else.*
*To take away what is other with respect to your own
being is to purify yourself.*
In simple rapport with yourself; without obstacle to your

---

5. *Enneads,* II, ii, 2; VI, ix, 1; VI, vi, 1.

*pure unity; without anything mingled within this purity,
being solely yourself in pure light . . . you have become a
vision.*

   *Though being here, you have ascended.
   You have no more need for a guide.
   Fix your glance. You will see.*[6]

With marvelous conciseness, this expresses what is to be called "good"
in the transcendent sense: the absence of anything that can penetrate
you and draw you out of yourself by a desire or impulse. Plotinus takes
care to define the spiritual significance of such a concept, saying that
the superior man can still "seek other things, inasmuch as they are indispensable not to him, but to his neighbor: to the body that is joined to
him, to the life of the body that is not his life. Knowing what the body
needs, he gives it: but these things in no way intrude upon his life."[7]

   "Evil" is the sense of *need* in the spirit: that of every life incapable
of governing itself, that stumbles around, desiring, striving to complete
itself by obtaining something or other. As long as this "need" exists,
as long as there is this inner and radical insufficiency, the Good is not
there. It is nothing that can be named: it is an experience that only
an act of the spirit on the spirit can determine: separating itself from
the idea of any "other," reuniting with itself alone. Then there arises
a state of certainty and plenitude in which, once given, one asks for
no more, finding all speech, all speculation, all agitation useless, while
one knows of nothing more that could cause a change in one's inmost
soul. Plotinus rightly says that this being which totally possesses its own
life possesses perpetuity: being solely "I," nothing could be added to it
either in the past or the future.

+

   *The state of being is in the present being.
   Every being is in act, and is act.*

---

6. *Enneads,* I, iv, 4; I, ii, 4; I, iv, 9.
7. [*Enneads,* I, iv, 16. —*Trans.*]

Pleasure is the act of life (ἡ ἐνέργεια τῆς ζωῆς).
Souls can be happy even in this universe. If they
are not, then blame them, not the universe. They have
surrendered in this battle, where the reward crowns virtue.[8]

Plotinus again specifies the meaning of "being": it is to be present, to be in action. He speaks of "that sleepless intellectual nature" (ἡ φύσις ἄγρυπνας), a strictly traditional expression. We know of the terms "the Awakened," the "Ever Wakeful," and the symbolism of "sleep," which besides may be more than symbolism, referring to the continuity of a "present being" that undergoes no alteration even in that change of state which habitually corresponds to sleep.

Being, then, is being awake. The experience of the whole being gathered in an intellectual clarity, in the simplicity of an act: that is the experience of "being." To abandon oneself, to fail—that is the secret of nonbeing. Fatigue in the inner unity, which slows and disperses, the inner energy that ceases to dominate every part, so that as it crumbles a mass of tendencies, instincts, and irrational sensations arise: this is the degradation of the spirit manifesting in ever more deviant and senseless natures, to the limiting point of dissolution that is expressed in *matter*. Plotinus asserts that it is incorrect to say that matter "is": the being of matter is a nonbeing. Its indefinite divisibility indicates the "fall" from unity that it represents; its inertia, being heavy, resistant, and blunt, is the same as applies to a person who is fainting, cannot hold himself upright, and collapses. It is of no importance that physical knowledge has its own and different "truth." Corporeal being is the nonbeing of the spiritual.

As the present state of culmination, "being" is identical with "good." Thus "matter" and "evil" are identical in their turn, and there is no other "evil" beside matter. Here we must abandon current opinions. The "evil" of men has no place in reality, hence none in a metaphysical vision, which is always a vision according to reality. Metaphysically, the "good" and "bad" do not exist, but rather that which is real and that

---

8. *Enneads,* I, v, 1; I, v, 4; I, v, 1; III, ii, 5.

which is not—and the degree of "reality" (understood in the spiritual sense already explained as "being") measures the degree of "virtue." In the view of ancient classical man, only the state of "privation of being" was "evil": fatigue, abandonment, the sleep of the inner strength, which at its limit, as we have said, determines "matter." Therefore neither "evil" nor "matter" are principles in themselves: they are derivative states due to "degradation" and "dissolution." Plotinus expresses himself exactly in these terms: "It is by failure of the Good that the darkness is seen and that one lives in darkness. And evil, for the soul, is this failure that generates darkness. Such is the first evil. The darkness is something that proceeds from it. And the principle of evil does not reside in matter, but before matter [in the cessation of action, which gave matter its origin]."[9]

Plotinus adds: pleasure is the act of life. It is the view already affirmed by another great mind of the ancient world—by Aristotle, who had taught that every activity is happy inasmuch as it is perfect. Such are happiness and pleasure in the form of *purity* and liberty: those things that spring from the act that is perfected, and which thereby realizes the one, "being," the Good—not those passive things, seized by means of the turbid satisfaction of desires, needs, instincts. Once again we are led to the nonhuman point of view of "reality." Even in the case of happiness, the degree of "being" is the secret and the measure.

Consequently, Plotinus affirms that souls can be happy even in this universe, thereby bringing to light an important aspect of the pagan concept of existence. If "virtue" as dominating spiritual actuality implies power, one may understand how the "good" is no more to be separated from "happiness" than glory from victory. Whoever is defeated by an external or internal bond is not "good": and it would be unjust for such a being to be happy. But it is only the being that passes judgment on itself, not the world.

Obviously, things are different for those who reduce "virtue" to a simple moral disposition.

It is all very well to say "my kingdom is not of this world" and wait for a god to give happiness in the beyond as a reward to the "just" who,

---

9. *Enneads,* I, viii, 5.

lacking power, have suffered injustice in this life and borne it with humility and resignation. The truth of the warrior and hero of the ancient classical world was otherwise. If "evil" and all its materialization in onslaughts and limitations by lower forces and bodily things has its root in a state of degradation of the good—it is inconceivable, and logically contradictory that it should persist as the principle of unhappiness and bondage in regard to him who has destroyed that root, having become "good." If the "good" exists, then "evil"—suffering, passion, servitude—*cannot exist*. Rather they mean that "virtue" is still imperfect; "being" still incomplete; "purity" and unity still "tainted.'"

+

> *Some lack arms. But he who has arms should fight—no god is going to fight for the unarmed. The law decrees that victory in war goes to the brave, not to those who pray.*
> *That cowards should be ruled by the wicked—that is just.*[10]

Here is a fresh affirmation of the virile spirit of the pagan tradition, a new contrast with the mystico-religious attitude, and a disdain for those who deprecate the "injustice" of earthly things and, instead of blaming their own cowardice or accepting their impotence, blame the All or hope that a "Providence" will take care of them.

"No god is going to fight for the unarmed." This is the anti-Christian cornerstone of every warrior morality;[11] and it relates to the concepts explained above, concerning the identity (from the metaphysical point of view) of "reality," "spirituality," and "virtue." The coward cannot be good: "good" implies a heroic soul. And the perfection of the hero is the triumph. To ask a god for victory would be like asking him for "virtue"; whereas victory is the body in which the very perfection of "virtue" is realized.

---

10. *Enneads*, III, ii, 8.
11. Admittedly, popular Christianity also knows proverbs such as "God helps him who helps himself." (Note by UR)

Fabius's soldiers, when they set out, did not vow to win or die, but vowed to fight and to return as victors. And so they did. The spirit of Rome reflects the same wisdom.

+

> *From fear, totally suppressed, [the soul] has nothing to dread.*
> *He who fears anything has not attained the perfection of virtue. He is a half-thing (ἤμισύς τις ἔσται).*[12]
> *Impressions do not present themselves to the superior man (τῷ σπουδαίος) as they do to others. They do not reach the inner being, whether they are other things, pains and losses, his own or others'. That would be feebleness of the soul.*
> *If [suffering] is too much—so be it. The light in him remains, like the lamp of a lighthouse in the turmoil of wind and tempest.*
> *Master of himself even in this state, he will decide what is to be done.*
> *The σπουδαίος would not be such if a daimon were acting within him. In him it is the sovereign mind (νοῦς) that acts.*[13]

Plotinus admits that the superior man may sometimes have involuntary and unreflective fears, but more as motions that are not part of him, and in which his spirit is not present. "Returning to himself, he will expel them. . . . Like a child who is subdued merely by the power of someone who stares at him."[14]

As for suffering, he can at most cause the separation of a part of himself not yet exempt from passion: the higher principle is never overwhelmed. "He will decide what is to be done." Should the case arise, he can also quit the game. We should not forget that according to Plotinus the σπουδαίος is his own "daimon" and lives somewhat like an actor playing a freely chosen role. Against the Gnostic Christians, Plotinus

---

12. *Enneads,* I, ii, 5; I, iv, 15.
13. *Enneads,* I, iv, 8; III, iv, 6.
14. [*Enneads,* I, iv, 15. —*Trans.*]

retorts drily: "Why find fault with a world you have chosen and can quit if you dislike it?"[15]

Like the νοῦς in man, one can define exactly the principle of "being" made from pure intellectuality: it is the "Olympian mind," with respect to which the "soul" principle (ψυχή) represents something peripheral: mostly it is a depth that remains hidden and latent. But then it is not the "I" but a "daimon" that acts in every deed. Plotinus says precisely that all that happens without deliberation unites a daimon with a god. Now we will see how he describes the opposite condition.

+

There the reason for being . . . does not exist as a reason, but as being. Better said, the two things are one.

Each should be itself.

Our thoughts and actions should be our own. The actions of every being should belong to it, be they good or bad.

When the soul has pure and impassive reason for its guide, in full dominion of itself, wherever it wants to direct its energy: then alone the action can be called ours, not another's: from within the soul as a purity, as a pure dominating and sovereign principle . . . not from an action that is diverted by ignorance and split by desire. . . . Then there would be passion and not action in us.[16]

+

The sensations are the visions of the sleeping soul.

Everything of the soul that is in the body is asleep. The true awakening is to exit from the body. To exchange existence with another body is to pass from one sleep to another, from one bed to another.

Truly awakening is to abandon the world of bodies.[17]

---

15. [*Enneads,* II, ix, 8, trans. MacKenna. —*Trans.*]
16. *Enneads,* VI, vii, 2; III, i, 4; III, i, 9.
17. *Enneads,* III, vi, 6.

Since materiality is the state of unconsciousness for the spirit, any reality that appears through the material senses is a sleeping reality. But we should not interpret the exit from the body and the abandonment of the world of bodies in a crude way: it is essentially a matter of an inward change, integrating oneself with the "sleepless intellectual nature." And this is the true initiatic and metaphysical initiation.

Plotinus aptly compares the change of bodies as passing from one bed to another. Even though it has a consistency, the doctrine of reincarnation could not be better stigmatized as it is by this pagan initiate. On the "wheel of births" one form is equivalent to another with respect to the center, which is equally distant from any point on the circumference. Metaphysical realization is a *fracture* in the series of conditioned states: a bursting open to transcendence. One does not reach it by following the traces of those "fugitive" natures, those who pursue a goal that they have placed outside themselves: in the world of bodies and becoming.

+

> *All that one sees as a spectacle is still external; one must bring the vision within; make yourself one with what you have to contemplate; know that what you have to contemplate is yourself.*
>
> *And it is you. Like someone possessed by the god Apollo or a Muse, he would see the divine light blazing within, if only he had the power to contemplate this divine light in himself.*[18]

---

18. *Enneads,* V, viii, 10.

LEO

Human Rhythms and Cosmic Rhythms

There is a correspondence between the human being and the world of natural phenomena, even though in today's consciousness the sense of it has been lost, or at best felt only in a superficial way. In the waking state, human consciousness lives in a world all of its own, in which the sense-perceptions are ordered by its knowledge, aspirations, and activity. Thus, all the subtler influences that constantly impinge on it are deformed or transformed, because they are automatically referred to the common experiences of daily life.

But when one succeeds in attaining a state of inner silence and, thanks to the methodical practice of concentration, comes to grasp what presents itself to us through the currents of subtler forces that are mostly unknown, beside the ordinary perceptions of the external world—then one becomes aware of a cosmic rhythm manifesting around us in time, to which a human rhythm corresponds in the innermost part of ourselves. One of the stages of human development consists precisely in losing the sense of space while retaining the sense of time; a stage that corresponds to the part of the subtle body that is in direct contact with the physical being of man.

Hence there is a subtle sense of time that corresponds to cosmic events, to the alternation of cosmic phenomena; day and night, the week, the lunar month, the year, and the seasons are then felt and lived inwardly in intimate correspondence. Knowing and feeling them puts one in harmony with the subtle body's activity and prepares us for living consciously in it.

We see, for example, what happens during the twenty-four hours of the day—before and after sunrise and sunset. From sunrise onward, the human complex in all its parts—physical body, subtle form, and ego principle—tends toward an ever tighter union that reaches its maximum at midday. Here too is the zenith of waking or external consciousness, and the subtle elements find themselves completely immersed and fixed in the physical organism. Sensorial observation is more intense, and that which is material is more conformable while kindred to us.

In contrast, at sunset these elements find themselves in a looser union, to which corresponds a greater imaginative and speculative activity, a greater receptivity to the psychic states of other beings; memory may become poorer in facts but richer in delicate associations and intimate tones. All this grows toward evening until the detachment becomes more marked and, at its limit, passes into the state of sleep: the physical forces of the sun cease to act, and the spiritual ones enter, which tend to attract the subtle part of man into their realm.

Detachment becomes complete in sleep, and then man becomes a cosmic being in the integral sense of the word: his physical part lies in bed, but his spiritual essence is free from it, and regains contact with the cosmic spiritual essence. The initiate, the "Awakened one," can carry with him the memory of the waking state; others, if the physical body is in a quiet state, may bring back a vague sense of harmony and restoration. In any case, knowing what happens at night can help the memory of this order of experience and reduce the almost mortal sense of interruption that nocturnal sleep gives us.

Upon waking, the degree of fixity of the elements of the human being is not yet as strong as when the day progresses, and an activity in the spiritual direction may be enriched by a content different from that of ordinary consciousness. Intuitions of a higher degree are more possible in the first hours of the morning than in the rest of the day.

Naturally, man has lost inner sensitivity, and his main activity happens when his being is completely materialized—namely, at midday. A brief characterization of man's conditions of activity would be that in early hours of the morning he is "mystical," "intellectual" in daytime, "fantastic" in the evening, and "cosmic" at night.

Man has lost his sense of the seasons, but he should retrieve it consciously and deliberately. The year, like the day, has its rhythm, and to feel that is to become more complete, richer, and more secure. We will see now how the rhythm of the year unfolds and how man can behave toward it, harmonizing with it.

We must start by saying that the frequent expression in Hermetism and esotericism, "man is a microcosm," is to be taken literally. The human being is a product of the cosmos, and wherever individual consciousness does not reach, there the cosmic forces are always active and dominant. This is not the place to go into details—we will just say that before birth the forces of the planets and stars converge in the formation of the subtle elements that will give rise to the form of the newborn's physical being.

It is these forces that draw the organs out of plasma and coordinate their relationships. Just as the bodily organs constitute an adjustment of forces and entities, a true system, so beyond it there is a planetary system with its cycles and its laws. In man, however, the presence of consciousness produces a perturbation of the laws and correlations, which requires a series of adaptations. When these are not possible, illness arises. Sensible consciousness itself *burns* and consumes the body and leads to death.

It is however possible for man to find inner equilibrium in rapport with the cosmos. Spiritual development can make of him a cosmically conscious being. The very fact of these micro-macrocosmic relations means that when man descends into his own interior, he can rise from his inner sense to the cosmic sense, and thus reestablish contacts and unity. In distant periods, before human materialization had reached the point of completely imprisoning the spirit, it was still possible to have an immediate sense of these relationships. Traces of this period recur in less distant eras, in which one could still live "astronomically," so to speak. It was not, as today, simply a matter of being hot or cold, but people lived differently in the different periods of the year, and celebrated the critical points of change and renovation with magico-religious rites.

If we observe the course of the year, we see first, in springtime, a reawakening of the earth: the elementary forces that were dormant in it are summoned by the solar forces, which irradiate earth not just with light and heat, but also with occult, creative currents: there is a sense of rejoicing that spreads from this encounter—the luxurious sprouting and flowering of plants gives rise to new expansion of other occult forces. The "elementals" of the earth are freed and follow their upward course. Some talk of nature's dissipation and waste in making myriad seeds and germs, more than the earth could ever receive and raise. But humans only see the flower, the fruit, and the seed in view of reproduction of the physical species, whereas in reality this abundance is an external sign, a sort of symbol of the expansion and energetic ascent of the elemental beings from the earthly womb toward the planetary spaces—like a bridge between earth and cosmos through mysterious exchanges of life.

Summer fruiting establishes an active harmony, a cosmic commerce that unfolds in the fullness of peace. Then comes autumn, when the earth begins to recall the elemental beings to its bosom; the external signs are the withering leaves, the wilting stems, the slowing of the sap. Little by little everything dies, and it is winter. The elementals sleep in the bosom of the enclosing earth, subject to it and its laws, until in the spring and summer they live in the streaming toward the planets and the other astral essences.

And what of man? This stellar-planetary being is a guest on earth, where he descends solely to take up the burden of the coarse material body, to isolate himself from the cosmos and to become *himself*. When he remembers his origin, he may be able in spring and summer to become aware of all that lives and moves around him. To know what is happening around him is the first step toward realization. Then he will try to concentrate and to *feel*. Looking at the plant life that buds, flowers, and fruits, he may little by little see in inner images the revelation of the occult forces, the elemental essences freed from the earth, and he himself may expand with them in a profound harmony. This happens especially at certain fixed times, the critical points of the seasons.

Some religious festivals commemorate their beginnings and ritually renew their significance—for example, in the Catholic tradition there are: Easter for spring, Saint John the Baptist for summer, Saint Michael for autumn, and Christmas for winter.

Autumn and winter: when the elemental forces retire and sleep in the earth, what happens in us, without the communication that they set up between us and our stellar origins? The contemplation of nature withering and dying carries us earthward, and we cannot follow it without drying up ourselves. That, then, is the moment to retreat into ourselves: the cosmos that we have lost outside us, we will find within us. It is the opportune period for opening the inner eye and rediscovering the forces of the planets and stars *in us:* our microcosm will be animated and become alive. We will feel in ourselves all the reality that we formerly found outside—and the warmth of the blood, untouched by the external ice, affirms our independence from the earth, our perennial vigil while nature is asleep.

Thus man, by going deeper within himself, can know the world from his inner form. Looking outward with the *awakened* gaze, he recognizes himself. The science that looks at nature from the outside finds only dead things. The path to the true knowledge of nature, through the spiritual knowledge of her, passes through the interior of man.

Experiences of a Chain[1]

(REPORT)

Our group consisted of five persons, always the same ones.

Three of them had never pursued any occult discipline before, but had had spontaneous experiences. The fourth had followed some yoga practices studied in Ramacharaka's popularization. The last, who took on the direction of the group, had in his time been part of the "chain" of Giuliano Kremmerz. All five persons were male.

Our meetings began toward the end of 1927. A strange coincidence: without anyone having thought of or intended it, we noticed that our first meeting was held exactly on the date of the autumn equinox.

The sessions continued every Tuesday and Friday, almost without interruption. None but these five ever took part, except for a visit from the director of a larger chain, who was passing through our city in September 1928.

Our directions were those published in the "Instructions for Magical Chains" in volume II of *Introduction to Magic* (essay II.1, pp. 42–52). The participants followed separately, and as far as possible, the individual discipline and the ritual of the nocturnal Sun.

---

1. [This article was omitted from the 1971 edition of *Introduzione alla Magia,* though it had been included in the 1955 edition. We restore it here both for its intrinsic interest and because a later article, "Metapsychology and Magical Phenomena" (IX.5), specifically relates to it. —*Trans.*]

The sessions always took place in the same room. We have used perfumes of natural myrrh, then incense. In the last sessions, which were attempting a material realization, the environment was lightly saturated with the vapor of rectified ether.

INTERNAL PHENOMENOLOGY

At the beginning of summer 1928, all the members were distinctly noticing the "presence" that had already established itself. Today, the simple fact of finding ourselves together, unintentionally and even in public places, is enough for it to form through us and be perceived. All five do not even have to be there.

When one is in a "circle," the "current" is often felt as a real "impetus" that leads to an internal "frenetic state" with perceptible speeding up of the blood circulation. One of us has found it hard to attain the mental speed needed to accompany and guide the "current" with the imagination that serves to form it. Another has been seized by sudden and strange sensations of panic. A special case happened to the director of the chain while we were evoking the sun rising on the group: he felt the reality of a force of such magnitude as to paralyze his ability to speak the ritual formula of identification: *"His Light is our Light, our Light is His Light, His Force is our Force, our Force is His Force."*

We frequently noticed the spontaneous formation of lines and images, extremely rapid, before the will intervened, and with a vivid luminosity.

There was a noteworthy session almost coincidental with the first anniversary of our group. For a moment, we all *saw* the pentagram forming and closing around us with lightning-swift lines of fire. At the moment of passing from the contemplation of the Sun to the formation of the "current" departing from the upper seat, we all had the sudden perception of a light which, in a strange and impressive way, lit up the whole room, like an instant illumination. The director then no longer saw the surroundings, but only the great pentagram in the "void," with the persons contained in it; that, for just an instant.

The states of "light" during the passing of the "current" to the upper seat, and "heat" at its passing to the lower one, are now noticed very distinctly. They can also happen by themselves. Each of the members has "learned" these states of the spirit, so as to be able to reproduce and use them without much difficulty in his individual practice.

In one session last autumn one of us happened to lose consciousness and fall into a state resembling catalepsy: something that certainly impressed us at the time. At another session (during the formation of the collective current) he only felt himself separated from the body, unable to make the slightest movement, and the phenomenon lasted for a few seconds. Both the director and another of us have often perceived the figures of all the rest as though transfigured by a luminosity, in which the usual physiognomy totally dissolves.

EXTERNAL PHENOMENOLOGY

In one session, during one of those "frenetically lucid states" mentioned above, in the phase of the collective "current," we suddenly noticed a short circuit in the room's electrical system. Especially in the first sessions we habitually heard short, dry sounds in the furniture and on the walls.

We thought of trying to induce the phenomenon of abnormal growth in a plant, placed at the center of our circle. Although we tried it repeatedly, this experiment has not yet succeeded.

The experiment of the real evocation of fire did, however, succeed. It had been tried without success on some easily inflammable substance, but of chemical composition. Following instructions we had been given, we placed in the center of the circle a piece of burnt wood recently extinguished, and it began to burn again visibly and held its heat even after the session was finished. The phenomenon was reproduced a second time. This is how we proceeded: first we contemplated the flame still burning, to immerse ourselves in the process of fire and to *live it*. Then, in the circle, having brought the "current" to saturation point and concentrated it at the level of the "seat of fire" (solar plexus), we vitalized with it the imagination of the fire, which, receded into the invisible state, was now summoned to manifest itself again through the wood.

Another experiment that succeeded is the magico-psychic action on a distant person. She was not forewarned or given a suggestion, though endowed with a more than ordinary sensitivity and linked to one of us in emotional sympathy. We decided to have her found in a specific place. The technique was the same: first, contemplation and *comprehension* of the image, then visualization and *fixation* of the person at the agreed-on place, operating in the state of saturation of the current brought to the height of the "seat of the heart." The person in question reported that at a certain moment she had almost lost consciousness of herself. She had automatically dressed and gone to the place we had decreed; there she regained full consciousness and was very much surprised to find herself there, remembering nothing.[2]

We tried other experiments, though so far without definite results. For example, we have tried to draw the pentagram inside the circle through the exteriorization of mental power. Using iron filings, we have not succeeded. We are about to try again with some other material, following instructions requested and received. However, in answering the request for this report, we all want it to be known that we place little importance on the material and phenomenological side of the chain's experiences. If they interested us, it was only because they proved that the force created by the chain is not illusory, but real and objective; and thus also that the perceptions and spiritual states produced by it are not reducible to cases of suggestion and hallucination. Beyond that, the true center of our work remains spiritual elevation and transformation, with the help that can come to each from the greater power made by uniting our own powers in a single one.

---

2. We can see, therefore, that this phenomenon is entirely different from that of a command based on suggestion. It is a matter of a veritable *action,* executed by a real force; not by "suggestion." (Note by UR)

On the Limits of
Initiatic "Regularity"[1]

René Guénon holds an outstanding position among the few Western writers who have contributed direction and clarity to the field of esoteric sciences and traditional spirituality, not from mere erudition but from genuine knowledge on an initiatic basis. We generally recommend the study of Guénon's works to those readers who do not know them, because they are unique in kind and in value, and can be integrated as complementary to much of what we have been teaching, at least regarding the essentials. However, we must have reservations on some particular points, because Guénon's orientation derives from a line of thought different from that on which our formulations are based, and also because his discourse is essentially theoretical, whereas ours is essentially practical. It will be useful, therefore, to consider briefly how things stand in this regard, so that our readers can decide how they can best make use of what Guénon teaches and integrate it with our own program.

Concerning our differences in doctrinal matters, we will just mention them here without more ado. We disagree with Guénon about the relationship between royal and priestly initiation; about his scheme of the Lesser and Greater Mysteries; and about the restriction of the term

---

1. [Article not present in the original *Krur*, but added to the 1955 edition. —*Trans.*]

"magic" to its lower and pejorative meaning. The three points are partially linked to each other. But what we will address here is the problem of initiation in general.[2]

Guénon's view can be summarized as follows. Initiation consists in surpassing the human condition and realizing higher states of being, which is impossible with the individual's resources alone (12). This may have occurred in primordial times, to a human type very different from the current one, but nowadays it needs an external intervention, namely the transmission of a "spiritual influence" to the aspirant (24, 32). This transmission occurs ritually with membership of a regular initiatic organization. Such is the basic condition, without which, for Guénon, there is no effective initiation but only a vain parody of it ("pseudo-initiation") (21). The "regularity" of an organization consists in being connected in its turn, either directly or via other centers, to a supreme and unique center; furthermore it consists in its linkage with an unbroken chain of transmission that continues in time through real representatives, while going back to the "primordial tradition" (60). For the transmission of spiritual influences influencing initiatic development to be genuine, it is enough that the prescribed rituals are performed exactly by one regularly assigned to this function; yet it makes no difference whether or not he understands the rites and whether or not he believes in their efficacy (105). Even in such cases the chain is uninterrupted, and an initiatic organization does not cease to be "regular" and able to confer initiation, even when it only includes "virtual initiations," because they lack true knowledge (52). It is well known that the Church has similar views about priestly ordination and the efficacy of rituals correctly performed.

As for the neophyte, to obtain the transmission of "spiritual influences" he needs to be *qualified* for it. One of the qualifications applies to the physical plane, requiring the absence of certain bodily defects that are considered as signs of corresponding internal negative disposi-

---

2. We refer principally to Guénon's book *Aperçus sur l'initiation* (Paris, 1945), which for the reader's sake we cite in the Italian translation, *Considerazioni sulla via iniziatica* (Milan: Bocca, 1949). [Page numbers in parentheses are adapted to refer to René Guénon, *Perspectives on Initiation,* trans. Henry D. Fohr, ed. Samuel D. Fohr (Hillsdale, N.Y.: Sophia Perennis, 2001). —*Trans.*]

tions; others are a certain mental (or "speculative") preparation, and the presence of a precise aspiration—or, as we would say, vocation. In general, a state of disharmony and imbalance disqualifies one from receiving initiation (101–2, 297). With the transmission of the "spiritual influences" one becomes a "virtual initiate"; an inner change takes place that—like the membership of the organization to which one belongs—will be indelible and hold good once and for all. All the same, effective initiation needs active, "operative" work to actualize it (190), which one has to do for oneself and which no Master can do in one's place (given that there are various degrees of initiation, this is probably understood for every degree) (25, 206). Only the representatives of an initiatic organization can direct, control, and support this development and prevent possible deviations. The connection with higher states of being, established by the transmission of the spiritual influences, does not always need to be conscious in order to be real (103).

Guénon distinguishes sharply between mysticism and initiation, because the mystic is not "active" during his experiences, and usually lacks even the means to interpret them properly—but above all because he is independent, and that does not satisfy the basic condition for initiation, which is attachment to a "center" and a "chain" (23–24). Secondly, Guénon denies any possibility of what he calls an "ideal" attachment to a tradition, that is, any attachment not made in the ritual manner mentioned above, and through contact with representatives of the tradition who are living, existing, present, and authorized. Lastly, a "spontaneous" initiation is equally excluded, because that would be the equivalent of a birth without parents, or the growth of a plant without a prior seed, which in turn goes back to other plants born from one another (25).

This, in brief, is the Guénonian scheme of "initiatic regularity." Let us see now what we should think about it.

There is not much to object to in the scheme as such; only that it seems to be a purely abstract scheme, in view of the situation that exists for the vast majority of those to whom Guénon's own writings are addressed. We may agree with this scheme; but after that, when we ask how one can actually come to receive initiation, we do not get much light from Guénon, but rather the contrary. He says, in fact, that he only wants to clarify the concept of true initiation. As for bothering with the practical problem, namely to tell one where to turn and, in short, to give solid directions, that is something—as he states (2)—that in no way concerns him and which has absolutely no part in his project.

For the individual, although he hears Guénon speaking all the time about "initiatic organizations" as if they abounded on every street corner, at the point where he wants to get serious and not just have doctrinal explanations, he finds himself facing a dead end, because the scheme of "initiatic regularity" must be really absolute and exclusive.

We are thinking, of course, of the Western man. In the East—from the Islamic lands to Japan—there may still exist centers that preserve enough of the traits indicated by Guénon. But one cannot be too sure of that, even if one is resolved to travel somewhere to receive a regular and authentic initiation. One would have to be lucky enough to make contact with centers of absolutely supratraditional purity, so to speak, because any other case would involve initiations whose jurisdiction (as Guénon himself admits) is within the limits of some actual religion, which is not our own. And there is no question here of "conversion" or otherwise. What is in question here is a complex of physical, subtle, racial, and ancestral factors, of specific forms of worship and divinities, and ultimately of the factor represented by one's mentality and one's own language. It would be a *transplantation* into a different psychic and spiritual soil. This is certainly not something for the majority, nor to be accomplished with a simple trip abroad.

If instead one turns to the tradition that has come to predominate in the West, one will get nowhere, because Christianity is a mutilated tradition that has lost its superior, esoteric, and initiatic part. Inside traditional Christianity—which is as much as to say in Catholicism—there is no initiatic hierarchy; the prospects here are limited to mystical developments through individual initiative, on a charismatic basis. Only occasionally some mystic has gone further and risen to the metaphysical level by an entirely individual path. As for the few scattered mentions in the first centuries of our era, or those believed to be found in Hesychasm (Greek Orthodox Church), for which some Guénonians have gone hunting, one can and should exclude them here.

If after admitting all this one is still searching, what one hears from Guénon is anything but reassuring. He admits, in fact, that all that exists in our time in the Western world are initiatic organizations that have ended up in a degenerate state: "vestiges uncomprehended even by those who have them in their charge" (238–42). Not only that: what he adds in clarification only leaves one more perplexed, and, moreover, it reveals the dangers that stem from unconditionally accepting the abstract scheme of "initiatic regularity."

We cannot refrain from expressing our dissent on two specific points. The first is that even through debased organizations one might be able to obtain something resembling a true initiation. We believe that the continuity of "spiritual influences" is illusory when there are no longer any qualified and conscious representatives in a given chain, and when the transmission has become almost mechanical. In such cases it is possible that the genuinely spiritual influences have "retired," so that what remains and is transmitted is only something degraded, a mere "psychism," open to dark forces. For someone who really aspires higher, membership in such an organization would often become more a danger than a help. Guénon seems not to think so, but believes that if the external, ritual continuity is maintained, one can always obtain what he calls "virtual initiation."

Our disagreement is more serious when Guénon says that the result of investigations which he made long ago is "the formal and indubitable conclusion" that, "aside from the possible survival of certain rare groups of medieval Christian Hermetism, among all the organizations with initiatic claims that exist in the West today there are only two, however degenerate . . . that can claim an authentic traditional origin and a real initiatic transmission: Compagnonnage and Freemasonry. All the rest is only fantasy or charlatanism, when it does not conceal something worse"[3] (34, n. 6; cf. 96). Now, we are not bringing

---

3. [Guénon's text is abbreviated after the ellipse that Evola inserts after "degenerate." I have adapted Fohr's translation accordingly, also with reference to the French original. —*Trans.*]

in irrelevances by saying that there are sufficiently certain signs of persons in the West who possess, or have possessed, effective initiatic knowledge, without having belonged either to Compagnonnage or to Masonry. That aside, we will say that Compagnonnage is a residual initiatic organization with guild origins and a very slight importance, of which not even the name is known outside France. We do not have enough data to pass judgment on it, nor do we believe that it would be worth the trouble. But things are different where Masonry is concerned. Guénon may have had in view some surviving nucleus of ancient "operative" Masonry having no relationship to what modern Masonry really is. As for the latter, at least four-fifths of it has absolutely nothing initiatic about it, but is a fantasy system of degrees built on the basis of an incoherent syncretism, making it a typical case of what Guénon calls "pseudo-initiation." Beyond this artificial edifice, whatever "nonhuman" content is to be found in modern Masonry has, if anything, a worse than suspect character; many things justify the suspicion that in this regard it really is one of the cases of organizations whose genuinely spiritual element has retired and in which the remaining "psychism" has served as a tool for dark forces. Anyone who holds to the rule of judging things by their fruits will recognize the precise "direction of efficacy" of Masonry in the modern world. Its constant revolutionary action, its ideology, its campaign against every positive form of higher authority, and so on, leave one in no doubt of the nature of this occult depth of the organization, except where it is reduced to a pure and simple mimicry of initiation and of the initiatic hierarchy. Guénon does not feel disposed to accept an interpretation of this kind (191). But that does not change things. The responsibility that he takes indirectly with such matters—despite not intending to "maneuver anyone either toward or away from any organization" (2)—is his alone, and we cannot share it in the least degree.[4]

To sum up, the practical problem that pure "initiatic regularity" poses for the Western man is fairly dismal. We need to see what other

---

4. It is also debatable that Masonry is "a purely Western initiatic form" (35, n. 7): one would have to ignore the whole part that the Hebraic element plays in its ritual and "legends."

prospects, legitimate and well founded, can be considered to place it in a better light.

We should acknowledge the merit of Guénon's concept, in highlighting the difficulty of initiatic realization under present conditions, and of setting a limit to exclude certain views on "individual initiation" and "auto-initiation" which some (like Rudolf Steiner) even hold to be the only kind that Western man should pursue. But there is no need to fall from one extreme to another.

It is very true that, thanks to the process of involution that humanity has undergone, certain possibilities of direct realization that were present at its origins, if not altogether lost, have at least become extremely rare. But one should not fall into an equivalent of the Christian concept, according to which man, irremediably stained by original sin, can do nothing for himself in the supranatural field—the equivalent of "grace" and the "sacraments" here being the indispensable intervention of one who can ritually transmit the "spiritual influences" (the basis of everything, for Guénon).

Another important consideration is the following. Guénon himself has stressed that one of the aspects of this involution is a *solidification*, meaning either that reality today presents itself in the rigid forms of soulless materiality, or—we would add—as determined by an internal closure of the human individual. One would think that under these conditions the power and hence the aid of "subtle influences" in the ritual field—not only initiatic but also religious—would be very much reduced and in some cases absolutely nil. In the end we have to ask ourselves what really is the nature of these "spiritual influences," and if the one who possesses them as a "virtual initiate" is thereby protected from every kind of doctrinal and deviant error. To tell the truth, we know all too many cases of persons—and not only Westerners—whose "initiatic regularity" is correct in the Guénonian sense (most of them being Freemasons), but who betray such incomprehension and confusion about everything that is truly esoteric and spiritual that they seem far inferior to persons who have not received this gift, but have a good intuition and a sufficiently open mind. Here too one cannot avoid applying the maxim: "I shall judge them by their fruits." Then we should be under no illusions about what, in the present state of things, the "influences" in question can give on their own.

That said, one should keep the following in mind as a general principle and crucial requirement: the man who has come to be born in the present epoch has accepted what the Theosophists call a collective *karma*: he has associated himself with a "race" that "wanted to do it on its own," throwing off even the constraints that served only to support and guide it. The extent to which this man who "wanted to do it on his own" and has been left to do so has only headed for his own ruin, is obvious to anyone who knows how to read the face of modern civilization. But the fact remains: today in the West he finds himself in an environment from which the spiritual forces have withdrawn, and the individual cannot put much reliance on them unless by a happy combination of circumstances he is able to open the way to a certain extent by himself. There is nothing to be changed there.

Since we find ourselves in a situation that is already an anomaly, for all practical purposes in the initiatic field we also need to consider paths that are themselves exceptions, rather than the regular ones.

Guénon himself admits up to a point that such exist. He says that the spiritual centers can intervene outside the forms of regular transmission, admittedly in ways extremely difficult to define, "whether in favor of individuals particularly qualified but isolated in a milieu where the darkness has reached such a point that almost nothing traditional remains and initiation is precluded, or in view of a more general but more exceptional goal, such as reforging an initiatic chain that has been accidentally broken" (64). But Guénon adds: "it is essential to remember that even if an apparently isolated individual succeeds in gaining a real initiation, this initiation is spontaneous in appearance only and will, in fact, always involve some kind of attachment to an effective chain"[5] (64–65). Now this is precisely where we must agree, and see *where the initiative comes from* that determines the contact. We call it contact because the essential thing is not a "horizontal" attachment to

---

5. [Or "an effective center." Evola translates Guénon's "*un centre existant effectivement*" by "*una catena effettivamente esistente*." —*Trans.*]

some organization with historical continuity, but a "vertical" attachment, as the inner participation in supraindividual principles and states. Any particular organization of men is only a sensible manifestation of these, or even, in a way, merely an incidental exteriorization.[6] Thus, in the present case, one can always ask: Is it really the intervention of a center that has determined the initiation—or, on the contrary, is it the active initiative of the individual advancing himself to a certain point that has brought about that intervention?

In this context we can mention a qualification that does not enter at all into Guénon's scheme, an active qualification created by a special discipline, a special individual preparation, that does not only render one "elect" but, in certain cases, actually *imposes* election or initiation. Many examples illustrate this possibility, from the symbol of Jacob wrestling with the angel until he compels his blessing, up to Parsifal (in Wolfram von Eschenbach) who opens the way to the Grail "with arms in hand," something "never heard of before." Unfortunately, one finds nothing in Guénon's books that might be an active preparatory discipline, which in some instances could lead without any interruption of continuity to actual illumination.[7] Nor does Guénon indicate any practical discipline for the work of actualization that makes a "virtual initiate" into a true initiate, and finally an adept. As we have said, Guénon's domain is that of simple doctrine, whereas it is essentially the practical domain that interests us.

But even within the doctrinal domain, on another occasion Guénon has written something that could cause disorientation. He refers to an Islamic teaching, according to which: "one who presents himself at a certain 'gate,' without having reached it by a normal and legitimate way,

---

6. Besides, concerning the Rosicrucians, Guénon speaks of the collectivity of those who have reached a specific stage superior to that of common humanity and attained the same initiatic degree (238). Consequently, it would be inaccurate to speak of "societies" and even of "organizations." Elsewhere Guénon has stated that the initiatic hierarchies are nothing other than the degrees of being. All this can therefore be understood in the spiritual and metaphysical sense, and not the personalized and organizational sense.

7. This is typically the case in the asceticism of original Buddhism, which even has a technical term to define "those who have woken themselves by themselves."

sees it shut in his face and is obliged to turn back, but not as a mere profane person, for he can never be such again, but as a *sâher* (a sorcerer or magician working in the domain of subtle possibilities of an inferior order)."[8] We must express definite reservations against this. First of all, if someone who has reached that "gate" by an other than normal way has a pure and upright intention, that intention will certainly be recognized by the person in charge and the door will be opened, following the principle "Knock, and it will be opened to you."[9] And should the door not open in such a case, that will only mean that the aspirant is faced with the test of opening it *himself* using violence, following the principle that the threshold of Heaven suffers violence.[10] For, as a general rule, as Éliphas Lévi very rightly says, initiatic knowledge is not given, but one *takes* it: that being moreover the essence of the active quality that Guénon himself admits, within certain limits.[11] Whether one likes it or not, the highest type of initiate will of course always have a certain "Promethean" trait.

Guénon is right in not taking seriously "initiation in the astral" (21, n. 8; 34, n. 6), if he has in mind what some "occultist" circles mistakenly think about it. But here too these ideas may simply be a distortion of others, which should not be lumped together with them.[12] Apart from the fact that *in every case* true initiation occurs in a condition that is not ordinary waking consciousness, it is possible to raise oneself actively to states in which the essential contacts for supraindividual development are favored. Islamic esotericism mentions the possibility of

---

8. [René Guénon, *The Reign of Quantity and the Signs of the Times,* trans. Lord Northbourne (London: Luzac, 1953), 317. —*Trans.*]

9. [Matthew 7:7. —*Trans.*]

10. [Alluding to Matthew 11:12. —*Trans.*]

11. It is on this basis that the principle of "incommunicability" should be understood, in one of its aspects. True metaphysical knowledge is always an "act" and whatever has the quality of an "act" cannot come from elsewhere; according to the Greek expression, one can only obtain it καθ᾽ αὐτὰ (by oneself).

12. One may also recall the very important part that initiation received in dreams plays among primitive peoples; on this, see, e.g., Mircea Eliade, *Shamanism: Archaic Techniques of Ecstasy,* trans. Willard R. Trask (Princeton: Princeton University Press, 1964). [Note adapted to cite English edition. —*Trans.*]

attaining *shath,* a special inner state that among other things eventually makes one able to get in touch with Khidr, an enigmatic being in whom resides the principle of a direct initiation, without the intermediary of a *tariqa* (organization) nor a *silsila* (chain).[13] Although considered as exceptional, this possibility is admitted. The essential thing here is the *nyyah,* the upright intention, not to be understood in the abstract and subjective sense, but instead as a *magical direction of efficacy.*

We now come to a further point. As we have seen, Guénon excludes "ideal" attachment to a tradition, because "one can only attach oneself to something that currently exists"[14] (33), meaning a chain of which living representatives still exist in a regular filiation. Lacking that, initiation would be impossible and nonexistent. Here too there is an odd confusion between the essential element and what is incidental and organizational. What is really meant by "currently exists"? Every esotericist is well aware that when a metaphysical principle ceases to manifest perceptibly in some environment or period, it is not because it is any less "current" and existent on another plane (which, after all, Guénon more or less accepts—compare 239–40, n. 6). Now, if "ideal attachment" means a simple mental aspiration, we can agree with Guénon; but things are otherwise regarding the possibilities of an effective and direct *evocation* on the basis of the magical principle of analogous and syntonic correspondences. In short, Guénon himself admits—and perhaps even more than he ought—that "spiritual influences" also have their own laws (162). Is that not basically equivalent to admitting, in principle, the possibility of a decisive action on them? One could even

---

13. On this, see, for example, an article by Abdul Hadi (*Études traditionnelles,* August 1946, p. 318). He speaks of two chains, of which only one is historic and its initiation imparted by a living master (*sheikh*), authorized and possessing the key of the mystery: it is the *et-talīmurrijāl,* dependent on men, distinct from the *et-talīmur-rabbāni,* which does not involve a living man as master, but an "absent" master who is unknown or even "dead" for many centuries. This second path is connected to the notion of the *Khidr* (*Seyidna El-Khidr*), through whom one can receive initiation in a direct way. Such a view is especially important in Ismailism. Among the Rosicrucians, the mysterious figure of "Elias Artista" was in a certain way equivalent to Khidr.

14. [Preferring "currently" or "presently" to Fohr's translation as "actually" (original: *esistenza attuale*). —*Trans.*]

imagine it being done collectively, by creating a psychic chain to serve as a body that, based on "syntony" and, precisely, on "sympathetic" correspondence, would attract a spiritual influence in terms of a "descent" from a plane where the conditions of time and space have no absolute value. The attempt could succeed or fail. But it is not to be excluded, nor confused with simple, inconsistent "ideal attachment."

Finally, Guénon denies that an initiation can be realized on the basis of what has already happened in previous existences (146, n. 3). We agree if he is referring to the reincarnationist theory, which we accept as little as Guénon does. But we do not agree if he also excludes what one might call a special *transcendent heredity* in some individuals that confers a particular "dignity" as to the possibility of achieving initiatic awakening by a direct route. This is explicitly recognized in Buddhism. Guénon's image of a plant or a living being that is not born without there being a seed (which would be the "beginning" [*inizio*] defined by the ritual initiation from the outside) is only valid within certain limits. If it is made absolute, it contradicts the fundamental metaphysical view of non-duality and, in short, reduces all beings uniformly to a lowest common denominator. There are some who may already carry within themselves the "seed" of awakening.

With that we have shown the essential elements to be considered vis-à-vis the unilateral scheme of "initiatic regularity." In a way, we would be disqualified if we did not allow this scheme its due value. But there is no need to exaggerate and lose sight of the special conditions, indeed anomalous ones, in which even the best-intentioned and qualified find themselves in the West. Who would not be delighted to discover initiatic organizations such as Guénon conceives of them, even if not in the aspects that make one think of a bureaucratic system of formal "legality"? Who would not seek them, simply asking to be judged and "tested"? But that is not the case, and on reading Guénon one finds oneself rather like someone hearing how nice it would be to meet[15] a certain fascinating girl, but on asking where she is, getting all excited, is answered by silence or "It's not our concern." And as for Guénon's

---

15. [Originally *possedere*, "possess." —*Trans.*]

indirect hints about what may survive in the West of regular initiatic organizations, we have already stated our reservations about them.

There is one further question that we should really have put at the beginning by saying that the very idea of ritual initiation as Guénon expounds it seems very weak to us. There is too little in the transmission of vaguely defined "spiritual influences," which one may not even be aware of, making one into a "virtual initiate" while being exposed to every error and deviation just like the most "profane" person. As far as we know, and from what one can assume from specific traditions, including those of the ancient Mysteries, real initiation is more like a sort of surgical operation, resulting in a lived and extremely intense experience, and leaving (as one text puts it) "an eternal trace of fracture."

Meeting someone capable of giving an initiation in these terms is not an easy matter, nor dependent on one's qualification alone. (For reasons already given, in the modern West the principle that "when the disciple is ready, the Master is ready too" is under various restrictions.) In this case it is essentially a matter of elements that are, so speak, "detached" (in the military sense), which one may or may not encounter in one's lifetime. One should have no illusions about finding a true and proper "school" with everything needed for regular development, with an adequate system of "security" and controls. The "schools" in the West claiming to be such, with "initiates" who almost list their qualifications on their visiting cards or in the telephone directory, are vulgar mystifications, and the more so, the more they claim. One of Guénon's merits is having treated many of them with the scathing criticism they deserve.

What then of those who have taken on the karma of the civilization into which they wished to be born, being very sure of their vocation, wanting to go ahead on their own, trying to make direct "vertical" or metaphysical contacts rather than the "horizontal" membership of organizations that have appeared historically and might have supported them? They naturally embark on a perilous path, which is something we must explicitly emphasize: it is like venturing into a savage land, without any "credentials" or a reliable map. But in the end, if in the profane world it is considered natural for a well-born person to risk his own life when the goal is worthwhile; there is no reason to think differently about those who, in the circumstances, have no other choice when it comes to the conquest of initiation and shaking off their human bondage. *Allah akbar!* one might say with the Arabs: "God is great"—while Plato had already said: "Every great thing is perilous."

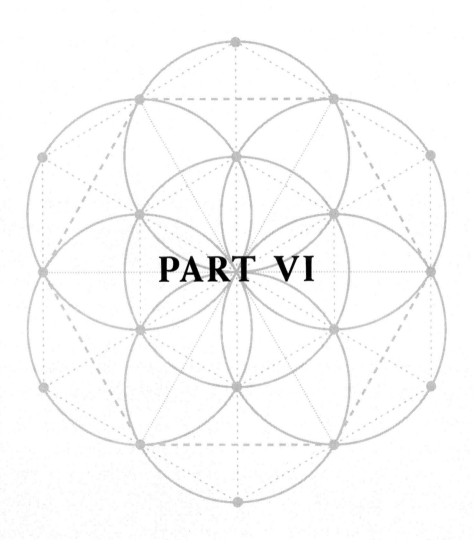

PART VI

C. S. NARAYANA SWAMI AIYAR[1]

Transmutation of Man and Metals

Alchemy today is no longer understood, as it was in ancient times, as the Science and Art of transmuting man and metals by means of *yoga* and as the *rasavatha* ("killing" or fixation) of mercury, but merely as a method for obtaining gold and silver from base metals.

Ancient Hindu Alchemy is a Science of the spirit and of man's spiritual form, of matter and of every sensible manifestation. It treats the astral and elementary aspect of the principles and the influences that they exercise on each other, especially with regard to man. It is the science of the soul of all things, which teaches us how every manifested creation can be transformed and brought ever higher in strength and potency, by means of dissolution, adaptation, transposition, and readaptation, and thence regeneration, determined by the change of polarity, in a transcendental mode. It teaches the secret physics and chemistry of the universe and of the soul, and treats the process of *projection* of life and the rebirth of man in the divine spirit, beyond the material ele-

---

1. [One of Evola's commentaries in the second volume, "Anticipations of Physical Alchemy" (*Introduction to Magic,* vol. II, 176–78), presented extracts from a paper by this author: "Ancient Indian Chemistry and Alchemy of the Chemico-Philosophical Siddhāntā System of the Indian Mystics," in *Proceedings and Transactions of the Third Oriental Conference, Madras, December 22nd to 24th, 1924* (Madras: Law Printing House, 1925): 597–614. Evidently, Evola contacted the Indian alchemist and received the present contribution from him, which is not the same as that paper. Since the English original is not available, this is necessarily a retranslation. —*Trans.*]

ments of his physical body, by means of internal transformations. Thus, it treats the essence of things in the light of nature and applies the powers of the spirit to produce material changes and material results, arising from the invisible ether (*ākāsha*).[2] Human greed has made of this magnificent science something that merely aims at making gold and silver.

In order to understand ancient Hindu Alchemy, one needs to know the relationships between man and the physical matter of the universe, between man and the planetary world both from the material and the spiritual point of view. When a man's material part is ennobled by his spirit, and vice versa, when the spirit is dignified through the material nobility of man (and both paths are valid), that man becomes a divine being (*deva*), a participant in both the masculine and the feminine principle of divinity. Without this spiritual training and this self-education, Alchemy is a simple pastime of a materialistic sort invented by the modern West. Nor can one become a "Philosopher" of the science of Nature through the curriculum of today's Western university culture.

As the basis of our studies, the disciple is taught about the arising of the living universe from primordial chaos, where the spirit is in the dual mode of self-containment and infinite spiritual space (*akhanda-ākāsha*). First of all, this space, which is the substance of life, manifests the *Shiva* form and the *Shakti* form,[3] and from this differentiation there originate forces of attraction, adaptation, separation, readaptation, and therefore of integration and disintegration, which produce the forms of energy and power in motion in space and time through the nonmaterial "great atoms" (*paramanu*) and the "great elements." The latter proceed from one another by densification: from Ether comes Air; from Air, Fire; from Fire, Water; from Water, Earth.

Beginning from these principles the ancient Hindu wisdom has developed a system of natural and spiritual sciences that need to be studied before one can comprehend the alchemical treatises, to which

---

2. Which is the same thing as the Western alchemists' *Quintessence* and Paracelsus's *Astral Light*. (Note by UR)

3. That is, the masculine and the feminine principle, which are, respectively, at the basis of every "being" and every "becoming."

the masses rush in the hope of making gold. Since heavy and dense gold is one of the solid bodies produced by the process we have mentioned that begins from *ākāsha,* whoever hopes to attain gold must know this process. He therefore needs the science of the cosmic spirit, of psychic matter and of matter as such; of the forces whose action works in the bowels of the Earth and which produce the natural kingdoms, until they culminate in man and in divinized man. Nature is the great Alchemist, and man can reproduce her work by practicing developments, adaptations, orderings, dissolutions, readjustments and regenerations, resurrections, transpositions and transmutations of one thing into another, step by step, from the lowest to the highest, always bearing in mind the forces and states of formation.

Granted that, we proceed to the practical side.

• • •

There are two paths: *devayāna-mārga* and *vajrayāna-mārga. Devayāna-mārga* is the path taken by the *rishi* (the Awakened One) and the *mūni* of the ancient temples; and even today it is attempted by many. As regards our subject, it uses practices with the breath (*prānāyāma*) described in the treatises (*shāstra*). The vital force (*prāna*) that is manifested in man in the form of breath is controlled and furnishes the method for experiencing the inner light that exists in every human being.

In principle, breath control is practiced three times a day: morning, noon, and evening. Its phases are called *recaka, puraka,* and *kumbhaka.* In *recaka* the lungs are purified from every residue of air by forcibly expelling the breath. In *puraka* new, pure air is inhaled. In *kumbhaka* the breath is held as long as possible without strain, then slowly exhaled.

In the yoga schools *prānāyāma* is begun at the age of seven and continued three times a day, from this young age. The method is called *Upanayāna* and is connected to a ritual; the word also has the sense of "being led"—to the *extra eye.* That is, the Master (*guru*), as an experienced person, leads the disciple to realize the "third eye," the internal eye of mental vision. Then one has liberation (*mukti*) and the perception of the light of nature.

We come now to the application and to physical regeneration. Ancient Hindu science teaches that the father's seed deposits the principle of life in the nucleus of the mother's ovum in the form of a *power* wrapped in *prāna;* a power that immediately goes into action by qualifying the vital ether in the principles and the elements, so that the organization and form of a new being is produced in the maternal substance, phase by phase, through the proper combination, dissolution, and recombination. The action of this power ceases when the baby comes into the light: it then becomes a dormant force that resides in the *mūlādhāra* (a point at the base of the spine) and which no longer acts in the vital centers already formed in the body.

The yogi awakens this power by using the fire ignited from *prāna* by means of breath control (*prānāyāma*). Our treatises teach that the breath takes two directions alternately, these being two currents (*nādī*). One starts from the left nostril and is the *idā-nādī*, also called *chandra* (Moon); the other starts from the right nostril and is the *pingalā-nādī*, also called *sūrya* (Sun). The purifying action of *recaka* is done with the right nostril; the *puraka* with the left, and the *kumbhaka* stops both directions, while the mind concentrates on a point between the eyebrows.

Once that practice is mastered, concentration is transferred from this point to the *mūlādhāra* and always kept there while the breath is held.[4] Ritual positions of the body (*āsana*) integrate the psychophysical action and lead to the awakening of the inert and dormant basal power; this occurs as though by a chemical action of oxidization and superoxidization produced by the solar current on the *mūlādhāra,* which instead is dormant when the lunar current predominates.

Thus the active mind and the active will make contact with the power that has produced the organization of the body, and together

---

4. The preliminary concentration between the eyebrows, as indicated by the name of the subtle center that refers to it (*ājñā-cakra*), leads to the realization of the mental power of command and "projection," which stabilizes the masculine and positive pole in relation to the feminine power that is to be awakened at the base. On all this yoga, see J. Evola, *The Yoga of Power: Tantra, Shakti, and the Secret Way,* trans. Guido Stucco (Rochester, Vt.: Inner Traditions, 1992). (Note by UR) [Adapted to cite the English edition. —*Trans.*]

with it they recapitulate all the phases of that organization.[5] It is achieved in the body, rising from the the base along *nāladhanda,* which is the direction of the spinal column, from the base to the top of the head, traversing the seats of the elements, reaching the cerebral mattter that is the ultimate transformation of the vital ether and of the imponderable substance, or *liquor vitae* (liquor of life).

Mastery of the practice is usually reached after three years. By continuing it for two more cycles of six years each and following all the prescribed rules, the *bramachāri* becomes a real yogi. When the exercises are begun at the age of seven, the action proceeds alongside the natural organic processes and forces that manifest in childhood (from 7 to 14) and adolescence (from 14 to 21). They produce physiological transformations; there develops from the vital fluids, from chyle and chyme, and from the mesenteric glands of the lower intestine, a very special animal fluid called the *seme,* which flows along the direction of the spinal column like the mercury in a barometer tube, forming the current *sushumna.* It reaches the centers of the cerebral region at the age of 20 or earlier, depending on the nature of the vital elements inherited from the parents.

The first symptom of awakening the basal power is heavy perspiration. By persisting in the practice and concentrating the mind on the *prāna,* physical and even psychic disturbances may be experienced, such as a shaking and trembling in the whole body. Persisting further, one hears in the brain a tremendous burst of tone: and if the yogi is frightened by this internal manifestation of "sound" (*nada*), his fear may lead to epilepsy, asthenia, even insanity—to which there are living testimonies. But it can also happen that due to the sudden fear one falls into a state of apparent death, and then there is another danger: that of being taken for dead and being cremated or buried. This is why it is unwise to embark on these practices without the help of an experienced master. Even practicing breathing in unusual rhythms can cause pulmonary disturbances of various degrees.

---

5. Thus, a regeneration takes place, accompanied and supported by the active mind and the will: one could call it a "rebirth in the mind and in power." (Note by UR)

This is the *devayāna-mārga*. We will now speak of the other path, which is the *vajrayāna* known to the school of the Siddhas. The Siddhas maintain that on the first path it is very difficult to be sure of the result, and also to maintain perfect awareness in the state of dissolution (*laya*). Furthermore, they note that the human body is subject to every kind of disease and disturbance, so that it is possible that death will supervene before one has reached liberation; nor do they set their sights on liberation after death (*videha-mukti*) or in another birth, being uncertain, among other things, that someone who has once died as a human will return to a human form of birth.

The Siddhas thus aim first at fortifying the body and *conjoining body and soul* in a mode of existence related to the primitive ethereal state of the *ākāsha*. This process has been called *kāya-siddhi*, or "completion (or perfection: *siddhi*) of the body." The body—*kāya*—becomes a *vajra-kāya*, that is, a body endowed with high resistance (literally "adamantine"—*vajra* = diamond) and inexhaustible vitality. Life is prolonged, and in this way the Siddha follows simultaneously *bhukti* and *mukti*.[6]

The principles of the royal Science and this Art are explained in the Siddhānta tradition under the names of *rāsavāda* and *cāmikara-vidyā*, in a language that is plain and transparent only to the initiates.

It is a matter of transforming one's own *rasa* (mercury, *liquor vitae*) into a higher, ethereal form—fluid gold and Sun—and then turning it into dense matter; an operation that in Tamil is called "killing mercury."

The course consists of two cycles of six years each, during which *prānāyāma* is practiced uninterruptedly. During this time the material part of man is fortified by chemico-metallic substances prepared in such a way that they can be absorbed and assimilated by the cells and tissues, which "fossilize" the physical and transmute it into a mercurial body that resists the attacks of age and time. The blood acquires a chemically

---

6. *Bhukti* is said to be the opposite of *mukti*, or that which must be renounced by those on the path of the ascetic yoga of knowledge who aim at the Great Liberation: all that the body and the world have to offer. On the path of Siddha and Tantra, however, one thing does not exclude the other. (Note by UR)

higher density and viscosity; there is a mineralization and a densification, and at the same time the body is reduced to the natural elements in the ethereal state, through accommodation, dissolution, reaccommodation, polarization, combination, and recombination. The combined action of the psychic transformations and the chemico-physiological transformations brings about the amalgamation of the soul and body, to the point of producing an inner vision, concentric, resplendent, and refulgent,[7] and to liberation in life (*jīvan-mukti*).

At this stage the matter is soul and the soul is matter, being interwoven almost to the point of identity. The body, composed of the five elements of the *siddha,* is transmuted into an immortal ethereal (*ākāsha-hamsa*) body, which can pass together with the soul into the ethereal (subtle) state and become the body of an intrastellar being.

In practical physical alchemy one begins by following a suitable diet and by freeing the body, within and without, from any bad secretion and concretion, through medical means. Then one introduces doses of myrobalan plum and pepper, burnt salt and alkaline salt.

After the third year the body should have become able to retain this salt completely, so that no trace remains in the sweat or urine. The salt is combined in turn with borax, potassium chloride, ammonium sulfate, mercury chloride, mercury sulfate, yellow arsenic, sulfur, fool's gold (pyrite), and gold. The combinations are ten in number, and there are ten assimilations that follow the steps of initiation (*dasha-diksha*).

One can see that it is impossible to follow this path on one's own, because one may know how to obtain these compounds, but not when the moment comes to use them so that they cause no harm. Bear in mind that these are substances that can be tolerated and assimilated by the *siddha's* body only after reaching a certain stage of development, and not by the body of an ordinary man.

It would take a large volume to tell you everything about chemistry

---

7. We have already had occasion to mention that the term *vajra,* which defines this type of life and is also an attribute of the "perfect body," contains beside the idea of "diamond" (hardness, incorruptibility) that of "lightning." This relates to traditions concerning the body that is radiant or wrapped in an aura of fire, etc., common both to the East and to the ancient West. (Note by UR)

as a synthetic science directed toward action on the metals. I have written a book on the subject, but so far have not been able to publish it. Here I have kept to the aspect that concerns man and the human body, to demonstrate that Hindu alchemy works through the powers of the spirit and the powers of matter, and that it aims to join the one with the other, bringing the body to the primordial state, ethereal or mercurial.

And even though Sir John Woodroffe, for all his application to the study of Hindu tantric literature, and although he has made the texts better known than any Indian has yet done, speaks about the effects of the practices in question with discreet mistrust, I submit this essay through you as a contribution.

TIRUVELLORE (CHINGLEPUT),
SEPTEMBER 1928

EA

On the Symbolism of the Year

In speaking of the Hyperborean tradition (*Introduction to Magic,* vol. II, 370–78), we mentioned the part played in it by solar symbolism. We would like to take up this special aspect of the subject with reference to the material collected by Herman Wirth in a work that was also mentioned there.[1] This may also serve as a sort of counterpart to what Leo has said from the standpoint of inner experience, in his essay on "cosmic rhythms" in the previous part (V.2, pp. 164).

Among those rhythms, one of the most important corresponds to the annual cycle of the Sun. For example, many dates consecrated by operations of ceremonial magic and various traditional rites are based on it; dates that are not arbitrary or conventional, but have been fixed with a view to the power belonging to the symbol and to "sympathy."

Herman Wirth defines the symbolism in question as specifically Nordic-Atlantic, for the following reason. Once the orignal Hyperborean homeland had become frozen, given the extremely bitter winter lasting for months, the experience of the sun's light and its annual alternations must have been experienced in a much more lively and dramatic way than ever before, or anywhere else. It is thus under-

---

1. H. Wirth, *Der Aufgang der Menschheit* (Jena, 1928). We must advise the reader that we are referring here to that which is traditionally viable in that work, with the strongest reservations toward the many chaotic and disputable things in it, which from the scholarly point of view have undermined the value of its fundamental ideas.

standable that the symbolism in question would have arisen only in Nordic-Atlantic centers, namely in the lands where the various branches of the Boreal stock came to settle. In the Southern regions, on the other hand, lacking a contrast of this kind, it was not so much the *principle* of light but its effects that would have been felt, in terms of exuberant fertility connected with the earth, and such effects must have presented themselves as more immediate material for symbolism. Not only that: in the warmer climes and especially in the tropics, sun and heat often take on the character of demonic forces, in contrast to the purely spiritual character of solar and light symbolism that prevails among the races of Boreal origin.

However, in both cases we must take issue with the "naturalistic" interpretation. In primordial times, natural phenomena were never treated religiously in themselves, but rather for their value as revelations of the supranatural. The essence of the original religions was not a superstitious divinization of natural phenomena, as modern interpretation maintains, but the reverse: the natural phenomena were valued, in antiquity, as perceptible manifestations and symbols of divine essences; only thus did they appear real, whereby the sensible, naturalistic element was not primary but secondary, and it only took precedence in cases of cultic degeneration.

This also applied to the Sun and to the "year," with all the elements connected to them in the Nordic-Atlantic cycle. Here gods and sacred structures did not express allegorically or "poetically" aspects of the annual course of the Sun, but vice versa: the whole year presented to the senses an eternal and incorporeal "story" in terms of cosmic symbols. While in the Kabbalah the year was considered as "faithful testimony" of the "living Lord, king of eternity,"[2] and in ancient India as equivalent to the body of the "sacrificial horse,"[3] in the Nordic-Atlantic cycle the Sun's annual course was related mainly to the fundamental idea of a death and a resurrection.

The sign of the Sun as "life," "light of the world," in various forms

---

2. *Sefer Yetzirah*, IV.
3. Cf. *Bṛhadāranyaka Upanishad*, I, i, 1, 8.

of primordial symbolism is also that of Man. And just as in its annual course the Sun falls and rises, thus Man too has his "year," he dies and rises again. While it is true that this meaning also appears in the daily course of the Sun, with sunset and the return at dawn, one should keep in mind that in the Arctic regions the whole year takes on the characteristics of a single day and a single night. The symbolism that follows the Sun's annual course, while it makes various aspects or "moments" of the divinity correspond to the various phases of the Light, conjoins the latter to astral signs and series, of which the most familiar and recent is the zodiac. On that point Wirth states that signs of this kind, while in the first place they had a sacred significance, served at the same time as the basis for the notation of time; not only that, but they were also the signs of a unique alphabet, each of them corresponding to a linguistic sound and root. According to Wirth, fragments of similar "sacred series" are to be found in inscriptions of what are considered the earliest writings—predynastic Egyptian, archaic Chinese, South Arabic, runic, and so forth—and can be successfully integrated with them. The significances of divine beings, constellations, suprasensible forces, and parts of cyclically conceived time thus come together in signs, which he takes to be those of an original sacred tongue.

In the northern homelands one of the events of the "year god" had a special importance: the one where the Sun reaches the lowest point of the ecliptic and the light seems to fall into the abyss, yet it rises again, resplendent. This is the *winter solstice*. At this point the system becomes complicated by a new element, expressing that in which the Sun, "Man," or the "Light of the Earth" seems for a moment to submerge itself. "Water," "mother," "cave," "abyss," "tomb," "serpent," "mountain," "house," "house of strength," "house of the deep," "house of the mother" or "of night," and so forth: these are all aspects of the archaic hieroglyphs referring to it, and they constitute equivalents from which one can understand various others present or latent in symbols, rituals, myths, and cosmogonies of more recent civilizations.

The "year god" descends to the "waters," the "mother," or the "cave" to find new strength. On his return, his sign is merged with that of the "tree"—the "tree of life," the tree whose roots are in the abyss, and which is associated with the "serpent" or "dragon," and so on; while the same significance attaches to a whole group of divine figures in the act of rising from waters, rocks, caverns, and the like. It is interesting that in Paleo-Egyptian and Sumerian his hieroglyph of the rising sun also has the meaning of "opening the mouth" and "word." This could be related to Wirth's idea that it opened a "sacred series," following the principle that it also had an alphabetical value and, by extension, a linguistic one. The ancient Egyptian statue that became *sonorous* as soon as it was touched by the light of the rising sun might incorporate in stone this side of the solar mystery.

On the other hand, in ancient Rome the day of the winter solstice, the 25th of December, counted as a "solar birthday" of the "invincible god"—*natalis solis invicti*—and we know that this festival, with the same date, finally passed into Christianity. There, moreover, the birth also appears as that of the *Word* (the Logos) made flesh, "light of men." An analogous, hidden survival is the Christmas tree and the custom of lighting candles on it at the exact solstitial date.[4]

One of the Hyperborean symbols associated with the symbolism of the year is that of the *ax* ("ax-god," "man with the ax," also "spine god," etc.). The ax here alludes to the power that splits or divides, and which refers precisely to the winter solstice, in that it cuts the course of the sun and of the year into descending and ascending arcs. Once the division arrives, the "son" is born, the sign of the "new year" appears, and also the "new light" and the "new sun"; the mouth is opened and "the word is born" (the Logos). We would also mention the equivalence of the striking and shattering power of the "ax" (likewise of the "hammer"—another Nordic symbol, e.g., that of Donar-Thor) with that

---

4. [At this point of the original article (1929), Evola inserts an explanation of why the title *Krur* was chosen for the third year of the monthly journal. Whereas the first two volumes had as logo the image of Mithras killing the bull, this one has a stick figure with uplifted arms rising above two wavy lines. To "satisfy the legitimate curiosity of our friends," Evola explains that in ancient Sumerian, the root *k-r* stands for the "place where the celestial light is reborn"—hence the symbol of waters—while "man," the "tree of life," and "resurrection" are shown by the ideogram resembling a capital Y (the cosmic man with raised arms) and expressed in Chaldaean and Runic with the phoneme *u-r*. Hence "KRUR." —*Trans.*]

of lightning, and the fact that it establishes a relation (esoterically, of course) between such a power, separation (as in the Hermetic "separation"), and the solar *initium* as a "new life."[5]

In hieroglyphic terms, since one of the commonest signs for the sun is the circle, either plain or with a central point ⊙, its division gives ⊕, a sign that includes the "double arc" (also related to the "double ax" or two-bladed ax) and similar dualities. If the two phases, ascending and descending, of ⊕ are considered according to their generic aspect of higher and lower arc, the symbol may change to ✕ and also to ⊖, the two halves then representing "heaven" and "earth." Morever, their synthesis in the sign ⊕ ("circle with cross") seems to be one of the most ancient and revered symbols in the Nordic-Atlantic order, and is also found in megalithic structures. The duality mentioned forms the basis for various concordant developments of signs, which Wirth has sought to trace in alphabetical-linear glyphs from distant prehistory, following the paths from North to South and from West to East traversed by the Boreal race and by those who split off or derived from it. We reproduce some of these typical series as Wirth has reconstucted them.

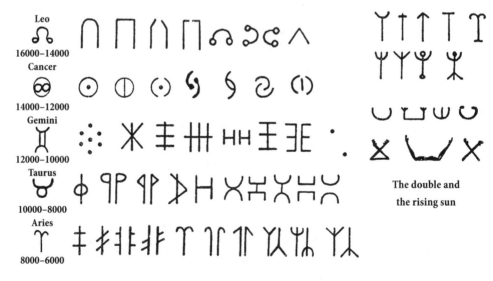

Figure 2

---

5. One may note the survival in the fact that the "hammer" is found in the Masonic gavel, the Master's attribute in lodge rituals.

The year, and the sequence of the "sacred series" of symbolic alphabet and calendar, are said to begin from the point of the "god in the waters" or "in the cave"—that is, the winter solstice (the "solar birthday" thus being identical to "New Year's Day" in modern terms). However, due to the precession of the equinoxes, this point of the solar orbit falls from age to age (at intervals of about 2,000 years) under a different zodiacal constellation, whose sign may provide the key to various versions of the "sacred series," which may thus be situated historically with some approximation.

The most ancient of these versions has as its key the eminently solar sign of Leo ♌: the corresponding age, also called the age of the "Wolf" or the "Bear," falls between 16,000 and 14,000 BC. The development of the fundamental sign with its gemination is shown in the first line of the diagram. There follows the age of the "Two Serpents" under the constellation of Cancer ♋, between 14,000 and 12,000 BC; then that of the "Reindeer" or "Elk" (Gemini ♊, 12,000–10,000 BC); the age of the "Bull" ♉ or "Buffalo" (10,000–8000 BC); the age of the "Ram" ♈ (8000–6000 BC). The shapes of the designs illustrate the development of the basic signs corrresponding to each one. We have reproduced these signs from Wirth.

This presumes that the catastrophe of Atlantis occurred in a period contained between "Taurus" and "Aries." After the Hyperborean cycle, a center was founded in that land that ensured a certain connection between the various forms derived from the primordial tradition, at least as regards the West Atlantic area. In fact, we seem to be missing developments of the "sacred series" based on the next signs corresponding to the winter solstice: from 6000 to 4000 BC there should have been the sign of Pisces, and from 4000 to 2000 that of Aquarius. Instead, we find a regrouping on a different basis: the key point of the series is no longer the sign of the winter solstice, but that of the spring equinox. At least that is what Wirth believed he could reconstruct; thus, for the age from 4000 to 2000 BC, Taurus returns; between 2000 BC and the Christian era, the sign of Aries; and, finally, from AD 1 to 2000 that of Pisces. As we know, these last signs correspond to symbols and symbolic animals of the more recent cults: the Ram (Lamb) and the Fish in

Christianity; the Bull in Egypt, Greece, Persia, and so on. But this does not exclude revivals or survivals of more remote solstitial cultures, for which the material that would have to be treated is extremely complex. Theories such as Wirth's present an excessive schematization and need to be integrated with a broader and stricter type of research.

Because of its special interest from the initiatic point of view, we have reproduced some ideographic developments of the single "ascending arc," which, as we have said, have the convergent values of "heaven," "resurrection," "awakening," "Man-with-raised-arms," "Tree," "rising Light," and so forth. Such developments seem to derive from the last Nordic-Atlantic versions of the "sacred series." They are found in the prehistoric signs of Central America, in the Pyrenees, in northern Europe, and in northwest Africa; also in the predynastic Egyptian, Creto-Minoan, archaic Chinese, and other linear scripts. They hark back to the dynastic Egyptian hieroglyph of two raised arms, *which is that of the* "ka," *the* "double." This sign is thus a kind of synthesis of the initiatic mystery, precisely through the convergent meanings of "heaven," "birth of light," "rebirth," "rising sun," and "double."

Considering the sun as a celestial symbol, in order to frame what has been said about the "year god" within a universal symbolism that is properly differentiated, we will do well to examine briefly various forms of the appearance of the principle of light.

The highest and most primordial of them all is the purely *uranic.* The sky in its character of luminous, sovereign, distant, and immutable reality stands here at the center and provides the basis for a cycle of corresponding divine figures. Historically, that corresponds to the Boreal cycle and is found where traces of that cycle are preserved.

Right after comes the *solar* phase, in the Nordic-Atlantic form of the symbolism already described. The Sun takes the place of the sky and assumes prime importance. But the values of the preceding phase often persist here, in that the solar god is considered essentially in his aspect of pure light, as for example in Apollo's symbolism—itself of Hyperborean origin: he personifies precisely the principle of immutable light, in contrast to Helios, who is the sun in its aspect of a being and a light that rises and sets.

When this principle of death and rebirth predominates, we find ourselves in a third phase, which is a real decline in spiritual level. Here the solar principle ends by losing its autonomy: it becomes the cosmic "masculine" that has as its counterpart the feminine, namely, the earthly principle, the Goddess of the Earth and of Life. Here we have the cycle of divine couples and a "lunarization," because the Sun comes to be affected by that law of transformation, of mutability and non-polarity, for which in other phases the moon had served as the fitting symbol.

In the last phase, to be considered as complete degeneracy, there is not only the couple, not only the principle of the pure celestial light that has taken form in the Sun associated with the Earth, the Waters, the Mother or divine Woman, but it enters a relationship of subordination to this second principle. It is the Mother of Life who now comes to the fore; it is the Isiac principle that incorporates the idea of immutablity, primordiality, and sovereignty. In astral symbols, as in ancient Babylon, the lunar rather than the solar divinity is preeminent, and the dyadic relationship already appearing in the Nordic-Atlantic phase turns into that of the masculine as the son and lover, who only shares in immortality and has his fleeting life renewed through his relationship with the divine Woman or the earth Mother.

The symbolism of the year as explained here with reference to Wirth's researches has an intermediate place among these phases. It no longer belongs to the purely "polar" stage, the uranic and Olympian one, but precedes the forms of lunar and telluric involution. In its highest aspect it has a visible reference to the authentically initiatic mystery, as a mystery of transformation.

VI.3

The Magic of Victory

You have heard tell that there exists a *way of action*. It has become very remote from the man of today: because although it concerns experiences of realization that were not exclusive to the domain of the Mystery, its presupposition was still a *sacral* orientation, and a ritual adherence of the "within" to the "without," which have long been lost to common consciousness.

I will nevertheless try to capture here, in their spiritual significance, some ideas that may make a certain misunderstood aspect of ancient civilizations transparent for you, so that you can assimilate something of their light, should your life encounter the situations I will now describe, or if your special vocation should create them.

And as starting point I will take what a historian of religions has said:[1] *"Primitive religious thought confuses in a single notion the idea of the double soul, that of the Fury and the Erinyes, that of the Goddess of Victory and the Goddess of Death. . . . A curious conception of a divinity that at the same time is a goddess of battles and the double of man."*[2]

Do not smile at expressions like "religious thought" and "primitive"—

---

1. The order of ideas expounded here by Abraxa has since been taken up and developed with additional reference to the spirit of the ancient games in Julius Evola, *Revolt against the Modern World*, trans. Guido Stucco (Rochester, Vt.: Inner Traditions, 1995), 129–42. We reprint Abraxa's essay because of various details of a more technical kind that it contains. (Note by UR) [Adapted to cite the English edition. —*Trans.*]

2. A. Piganiol, *Recherches sur les jeux romains* (Strasbourg, 1923), 117–18.

or at "confusing" notions, or the "curious" ideas of the Ancients, who surely couldn't yet see as clearly and disctinctly as we do today! You know that those are just a historian's *fixations*.

But you, instead—*understand*.

For you, these associations hide the secret of the *heroic initiation*.

That which in the lucid classical and Roman world took as its vehicle exploits and contests in which the pallid "spiritualists" can see nothing but "brutality."

But now, penetrate the *meaning* of those divinities and notions, as follows:

The vital power that is not you, that holds you together with your body, animating, moving, and controlling it where your consciousness cannot reach, or when it is absent; the power that is your true, deep soul, and which—not you—has willed how you should be, has formed you thus, before you acted, on its own model, then joined you to the modes of external consciousness and inner sensation that correspond to *this* organism of yours—understand that this power is the *double*. You do not know him: he stands *behind* you—so that you cannot *turn around*. He is the daimon, your *numen*.

You lead your transient life until you are detached from your numen—until you and he are two. He is bound to your life like the flame to the burning wood. He is inside the substance of your being like a fire lighting it up (and for such a light, you exist), but which yet devours and consumes it. In the end, when the coarse compound can no longer support it, the flame breaks away and the body collapses. The flame will attach itself to a new wood. Somewhere else a new light will begin to shine.[3]

---

3. To this idea, often repeated by Abraxa, there is a Taoist correspondence. A text of Chuang-Tzu reads: "A bundle of wood exists as a bundle so long as it is tied together; when it is untied, it is no longer a bundle. Man is like that: he is a man so long as all his parts, all his organs are connected and coordinated: when that union ceases, the human individuality ceases." Moreover, he compares the latter's life to the fire of a bundle which is being burned, and which can be transferred to another bundle once the first is exhausted: "The bundles are tied up and untied in turn, as people live and die, appear and disappear." (See C. Puini, *Taoism* [Lanciano, 1922], 70). (Note by UR) [For various interpretations, see the note in *The Complete Works of Chuang Tzu,* trans. Burton Watson (New York: Columbia University Press, 1968), 53. —*Trans.*]

But meanwhile you understand the first association: *of the daimon, the double—with the goddess of death.* Hold once again in your mind the sense of this transcendent power of life, the root of life, and how corrosive and mortal it is in its total operation. Return to the teaching that I have repeatedly given; that which is at the center of our Art.

In symbolic terms it is said that Water is interpolated between Earth and Fire, and that on contact with the second, the first is not destroyed. Thus, either in subtle and everyday modifications that dull bodily consciousness fails to grasp, or sometimes in more abrupt forms to which I have already drawn your attention, fleeting apparitions of the numen, daimon, or double are produced within the soul's energies, which then enter an unusual state. But this is something you know already, concerning operations aimed at a not so different goal.[4]

You also know about the propitiations and attitudes. You know that the magus grabs these contacts, slips inside, *fixes.* He sets up a relation of masculine to feminine. From a proclaimed life, he passes to a life that proclaims itself. He emerges in another condition of existence, and in that *there is no longer anyone behind him.*

Remembering all this, apply it. The contact is not established (or, if it is, you cannot perceive and use it) until by means of an abnormal state of external consciousness you have arrived through "exaltation" at approximating the level and the "frequency rate" corresponding to the double. The means are many. But now you are approaching knowledge of the second assimilation: *the double, the transcendent part of the human being, goddess of Death, is related to the Furies, the Erinyes, the goddesses of Battles.*

On the path of *action,* it was *dance* that was anciently used as a frenetic method of attracting and manifesting divinities and invisible forces in the human soul: it is the bacchic and maenadic theme—the

---

4. Compare especially what has been said (*Introduction to Magic,* vol. II, 335–47) on the *sexual* aspect of this power. The double is what the Romans called the *genius,* which is akin to the *genus* (cf. the expression *lectus genialis* in the sense of a marriage bed).

transport to contacts through vertigo. Into the life liberated through rhythm there enters another life, as the emergence of the abyssal root of the former; and they were dramatized as Furies and Erinyes, savage natures with attributes like Zagreus's "Great-hunter-who-overwhelms-everything": forms, therefore, in which your daimon appears, taking on the quality of the state that has "extracted" him.

The *agonal game* is a higher degree.

Even beyond that, the heroic intoxication of battle.

Either one, where there was light, would have contained the possibility of a special intitation. And as the frenetic approach obtained through the maenadic state—in making the two one and flashing from the contact—the knowledge of the double is phenomenalized as a sensation, or even an image, of Furies and Erinyes. At the level of the exaltation of battle and of the heroic impetus this same experience takes the form of goddesses of war, Valkyries, the stormy Virgins of battle. And what finally corresponds to the magical accomplishment of the experience, to the domination of the Masculine over the Feminine—is the apparition of *Nike,* the *goddess of Victory.*

Now you have grasped every part of the identification. The "curious" concept of a divinity who is simultaneously a goddess of battle and the daimon of man, who is the power of death, who is an unchained "subterranean" force—now speaks to you.[5]

As phases of the same experience developed from action, the Fury—the goddess of Death—Nike or Victory objectify, respectively, the release, the sensation of the critical passage to the transcendent power, and finally the triumph over it.

While the frenetic life of the Bacchantes and Corybantes vacillates between the insidious vertigos of formless dissolution and ecstatic escapism, at the center of the warrior's rite stands the virile hardness of *Iron,* assuming the function of the "Gold" principle used in the pure

---

5. The same author cited by Abraxa states (p. 118) that it was from the Fury that Victory inherited the attribute of a book in which the double (called by the Etruscans *lasa*) recorded the actions of the person behind whom he stood. It was a matter of a "body of memory" actually enclosed in human form and susceptible, as we know, to manifest through a timeless vision in moments of deadly peril. (Note by UR)

Hermetic Art.[6] And you know of the pressure of the rhythms; of balancing on the crest of the wave; standing up to the wave. These acts of the spirit, on the plane I have been speaking of (which is not that of contemplative experiences), awaken in you like souls of wars and contests, to be consecrated and crowned by total victory. It will not seem strange to you, then, that in ancient times a Victory would often acquire a sacred character: that in the *Imperator,* the hero, the general acclaimed on the battlefield, there was the sense of the sudden manifestation of a force of a higher order that glorified him.[7] *When, due to a consciousness difficult to recover today, the visible and the invisible, that which is physical and that which is metaphysical, are preserved in mutual parallelism, a victory could be the body of a corresponding mystical and magical fact, which determined it along the paths already opened by the energies that come from the internal to the external: the victory could be the visibility of an initiation and an epiphanic mystery that were being accomplished at the same time.*

While the warrior challenged the Fury and Death externally and materially, at the same time he was meeting them internally, in his spirit, as powerful dangers of the deepest nature emerging from where man's consciousness cannot reach. Understand victory in its possible meaning of immortalization, which is equivalent to that of the "initiatic death."

You can then read beyond the symbols of "triumphal death" and of Victories or kindred divinities who *lead* the warriors' souls to the "heavens": they are symbols of that heroic initiation that is mediated by Victory,

---

6. In pure Hermetism, the appreciation of Iron is not wanting. For example, Braccesco (*Espositione* [Venice, 1551], 58*a–b,* 59*a*) understands by *Mars* the "fixed sulfur"; he says that "on Mars depends the perfection of the elixir," and that its property is not found in any other substance, "but that it treads the fire under foot, and is not conquered by it but admirably reposes in it, rejoicing in it." "The body of iron is the strongest of bodies, and the stone therefrom, and the *will* of these is more in it than in any other body, hence the wise have chosen it."

7. One of the Roman military rites that, like so many others, had a symbolic content, was to raise the victor upon shields. Ennius assimilates the shield to the celestial vault— *altisonum coeli cupleum,* and it was sacred in the temple of Olympian Jupiter and of the Sabine Semo Sanctus. The ritual thus expressed the raising of the Chief through Victory above the celestial world. (Note by UR)

the *Janua coeli* (door of heaven) through which one passes to an *other* life. It takes the place of Hermes Psychopompos, of Miryam, of Sophia, at the same time expressing to you the special quality that has the raw, virile, and inflexible temper of Iron, infused by the warrior's spirit in its realization.

I will speak briefly of another detail. Often the victory of a general was considered, in the ancient Roman tradition, as an independent divinity, whose mysterious life became the center of a special cult. And festivals, sacred games, rites and sacrifices were intended to perpetuate its presence.[8] The *Victoria Cesaris* (Caesar's Victory) is one example.

If you have understood, this should not seem absurd or superstitious. By becoming the power of active (solar) initiation, *every victory creates an entity* that is henceforth disjunct from the destiny and individuality of the mortal man concerned. It is a force that rules by itself without needing material; it is virtually the principle of an effective influence and of a "tradition"—in the magical and technical sense that you should already have grasped.

Such an "influence" is not "sanctifying"—but indeed *triumphal.* Rituals that work through the traditional laws of sympathy can attract it. The sacrificial act may give it a temporary body in which to manifest and multiply. The institutional cult makes of it a latent and occult "presence" behind a race: something that like "fortune," energy, or inspiration can supplement the human forces of the relevant stock every time a state is produced that can create a contact. Thus, the commemoration of Caesar's death in Rome was fused with that of his victory, and he was celebrated as a "perpetual victor." They are aspects of the "warrior tradition" that is effective and has an occult soul of its own. Know that, infuse the ritual with it, all the more invisible as it is more manifest. That will also give you the way to understand Rome.

Rome did not know the spirit in the mystical or philosophical forms, to which it always felt a barely concealed indifference: it knew it above all through *action,* and bore witness in institutions and traditions where action—even in the *certamina* (contests) of the circuses—became a symbolic rite and a sacrifice; and in the glory of the Empire.

---

8. Op. cit., 124, 147, and 118. [Presumably referring to Piganiol; see note 2. —*Trans.*]

VI.4

ARVO

The "Origin of Species," According to Esotericism

Readers will not have failed to notice that one of the points at which esoteric teachings go straight against the current concerns "evolution."

"Evolution" is a kind of fixation of the modern mind. It is a veritable "complex," which thanks to that "subterranean logic" of which Iagla has spoken (*Introduction to Magic*, vol. II, 53–58), controls the minds of many who think themselves devoted to the "scientific" method and objective research. They need to realize something that applies to many other things: that certain possibilities of understanding, seeing, and verifying are the effect of a certain change of attitude, rather than the reverse, as rationalism believes.

With regard to "evolution," one might be surprised, for example, by what has been said about the Hyperborean tradition. The idea that a great unitary civilization may have already existed in the interglacial and Paleolithic period, from which derive the fundamental symbols, the roots of language, and the writing of the oldest cultures—such an idea must seem revolutionary to modern opinions, which believe that they are settled once and for all on a positive basis. And it is not just a question of simple evolutionism in the history of civilization: it begins to affect other areas of science, which, in one form or another, hold to the Darwinian hypothesis on the origin of species and the animal descent of man.

Thus, the problem has to be faced fairly and squarely. I will therefore summarize what esoteric teachings have to say on the subject, without going into details that would take me too far afield, beyond what can usefully be discussed in the present context.

First, I must state, without dwelling on it, that even in the field of profane science evolution is not treated today in the way that Darwin expounded it in his own time. The Darwinian hypothesis has undergone many criticisms since then, and real difficulties that were not seen at first have forced it to be modified.

Where it has proved weakest is in its attempt to deduce the variety of species from a kind of automatic play of conditions in the material environment, from natural selection, and from the hereditary transmission of acquired qualities. As against this, the "vitalistic" point of view, which continues to gain in prominence, gives vital energy precedence and preeminence over all other conditions. Henri Bergson is among those who have ventured into the strictly scientific field to oppose Darwinian evolutionism, showing how its shortcomings open the field to the hypothesis of an evolutionism no longer bio-materialistic in character, but "creativistic."

Even the biologists have recognized how the variety of species resists the attempt to deduce one from another in a simple and linear way, as Darwin had supposed; they have come to admit that there are "leaps" from some species to others. The hypothesis most in vogue today is that of Hugo De Vries, who calls on internal "mutations" that are unpredictable and essential in order to explain such leaps within the evolutionary scheme.

All the same, this is just one hypothesis among others, and only interesting for pointing out a difficulty that largely persists even after introducing the enigmatic concept of mutation. I note in passing that this difficulty exactly parallels the one that physics has been wrestling with of late, when with Planck's "quantum" theory and Heisenberg's principle of indeterminacy it has been forced to stop and face *finite* quanta of "action," without being able to explain them further or to identify a continuous process that leads from one to another.

Nonetheless, since the evolutionary hypothesis, however modified and revised, continues to be current in biology, we must examine its general foundation. We know what an impressive wealth of facts Darwin and his school have gathered in the fields of morphology, embryology, paleontology, and even geology. No one is thinking of denying these facts. What is debatable, and should be shown up as arbitrary or at least one-sided, is their interpretation, whereby these facts are used in Darwinism as proofs and support for the materialist concept of evolution. That said, I will proceed directly to the fundamental argument.

Although one may have succeeded in identifying a continuity of forms and links, allowing for passage from one species to another right up to man, all that has done is to establish a line, while no one can say what direction it has taken. Thus, every fact adduced in support of evolutionism could be simultaneously adduced in support of the opposite thesis: an *involutionist* thesis, no more, no less. That the lower species should be the preceding degrees of the higher ones is no more true than that they are *degenerative involutions* of the latter. *The presence of intermediate stages* (even if they are stages of *transition,* and not *crossbreedings* or even *sortings*: another possibility that the evolutionists do not think of) *you cannot tell from that alone what direction the process has taken.*

That is the fundamental point. We will now see what can be added to it.

Let us begin with the so-called primitive peoples, from the point of view of their mentality and their civilization. Who is to tell whether they represent the earlier states of present humanity, and not the involutive and residual forms of an even more ancient humanity? The fact that primitives tend more to disappear than to "evolve" gives one pause. Furthermore, one should consider that an "even more ancient" humanity may have been *different,* such as to leave no traces where forms of civilizations closer to us have established and superimposed themselves; thus, all that is left of them is their descendants, degenerate but nevertheless from the same stem. Modern ethnological studies of the presumed "primitives" have in fact found in them not an inferior degree of the same mentality, but an *other* mentality, an *other* civilization. From that, by "integration," one can go back to that "even more ancient humanity." Modern explorers of prehistory, such as Leo Frobenius and Herman Wirth, have followed this very method.

Going from primitive man back to the anthropoid and ape (assuming that one make the necessary leaps in order to reach the other animal forms over the transformists' barriers), one can say the same; to the point that many animal species could be considered as degenerations or degradations of even more ancient nonanimal forms. Our point of view, to be precise, is that *man does not derive from the animals, but if anything, there are various animal species that derive from man, in a way that I will now try to explain.*

The main obstacle to this point of view is the fact that man's traces stop at a certain geological period, whereas those of prehistoric animals continue back to much earlier periods. But this very fact can be interpreted in different ways, by those able to bring a certain broadmindedness to the idea of transformations: *the fact that the mineral traces of man are more recent may simply mean that man was the last to enter the process, under a certain involutionary aspect, by which such traces could persist as fossils, hence be discoverable.*

The misunderstanding about "cavemen" comes from not reflecting that it is natural for some of the earliest traces to be found in caves, which for many causes could not be preserved elsewhere. The idea of man's recent appearance on earth is based on the same kind of oversight. I am not asking for a simple admission that man descended from heaven: it is enough to get over the concept of corporeality that I would not call "material" so much as *mineral*; enough to think of the possibility of a body whose most physical element (which today is the bony system) was composed of a substance insusceptible to preservation through the process of fossilization. Then the fact that no traces exist in the most remote geological periods leaves one indifferent and able to entertain the existence of primordial human lineages (of which the anthropoid apes would be the first, degenerate materializations) coexisting with even more advanced forms of the involutive process, which would be represented by the earliest animals of prehistory. This concept has nothing intrinsically absurd about it. By analogy, every manifestation necessarily has an inverse character: that which is most primordial, most internal, most central, can only be the last to appear in the movement toward the external.[1] And at the center and origin, according to esoteric teaching, stands Man himself.

Of course this Man is not the same as the man of today, but corresponds to him in the sense that today's human may be considered as the closest manifestation and most direct descendant of the primordial Man. As such he represents the origin, the axis, whereas other species represent lateral or divergent directions, not to say by-products.

With an image already used by Ea, I can perhaps indicate better what would otherwise take a long conceptual detour to be understood.

Imagine something like an attack, an attempt at conquest. A group of tightly unified forces faces the danger, turning toward their object. The struggle begins. In the exposed front line some are beginning to fall, others advance. They meet resistance and the mêlée begins. The onslaught weakens. Few manage to keep up the original direction; they leave behind a trail of those scattered, captured, sacrificed, or struck down, being most of those with whom they set out on the enterprise. The squad of survivors holds firm and advances: still fighting, they manage to force a path and finally reach the goal of the campaign, seizing and holding it and planting their own flag there. Behind them in every direction lie the attempts by the same will that were aborted, frustrated, or caught in dead ends.

Let us now take "conquest" to mean attaining the physical state of existence in the conditions we know today. Humans are the ones who have reached it, and the others who have swerved or deviated are various animal species. Man in his current state expresses the form that can preserve and support in the material condition the lineage of a primordial humanity. Originally, many animal species were included in it, certainly not in the forms in which they appear today, but in their principial forms. Their biological origin was in a degenerative specialization, a branching out from the original into divergent directions, each expressing the exhaustion of an attempt, the halting of a wave of assault,

---

1. The same occurs in every *finalistic* process: the *goal* or end precedes as an *idea* all those conditions that are necessary to actuate it, and as a *reality* it appears last, after them.

from which those who have "broken through" have separated and left them behind.

It is interesting that ideas of this kind have even appeared on the margins of modern culture, without any connection with traditional teaching. In the works of Edgar Dacqué, for example, we find a very similar concept and a diagram that makes it much clearer.[2]

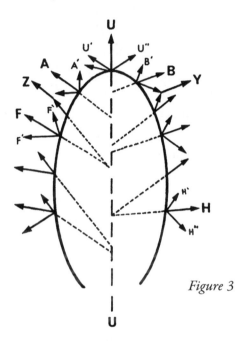

Figure 3

At the letter U,[3] where the central direction emerges, is man as we know him. A, B, etc., can be considered the closest approximations, for example, diluvial man, the anthropoid, the apeman. Lower down and further back in time there are other attempts, more elementary and divergent, the first to appear in the completely "densified" form of existence as we know it, and accessible to paleontology; their zone extends outside the curved line of the figure. The various points of exit on this curve, from each of which a group of secondary directions and

2. E. Dacqué, *Leben als Symbol* (Munich and Berlin, 1928), 171; cf. Dacqué, *Urwelt, Sage und Menschheit* (Munich and Berlin, 1927).

3. [The first letter of *uomo,* Italian for "man." Not all the letters cited in the text appear on the diagram, but this does not affect the sense. —*Trans.*]

deviations proceeds, represent the "types" of each species. These second-ary deviations (directions U' U", A' A", B' B", F' F", etc., with respect to the directions U, A, B, and F, which also continue on the exterior the direction coming from the axis) are the transformations that each spe-cies has undergone in an incomplete struggle, though adaptation, selec-tion, and so on—in other words, through the factors to which Darwin tried to reduce everything. On the contrary, the passage from one spe-cies to another does not happen on the periphery: there one can only find *crossings* (as in Z and Y) misinterpreted by evolutionists as "transi-tional forms." Instead, what determines the "passage" is the separation and emergence of a new branch that starts from the central direction (the one leading to man) as a new effort after the failure of the preced-ing ones.

Here we can also restore the true significance to another fact that seemingly confirms evolutionism, namely the theme of ontogenesis repeating phylogenesis. That the development of the human embryo passes through a series of phases with some resemblance to the forms of animal life simply means this, from our point of view: that every human realization contains in abbreviated form and recapitulates all the attempts whose possibility was included in the original stock. *But it repeats them exactly on the basis of the original impulse, which goes beyond them all;* a thing self-evident in that an embryo aborted at any phase always remains a human embryo, not that of a fish or another animal species.

It is in a very special sense, and not the material one or valid for biological considerations, that one can say that since the central line UU passes through the origin of various types of animality, man, before appearing as he is here, lived in the hierarchy of animal forms. This does not mean any of the animal forms that appeared on earth histori-cally prior to man: it means rather what corresponds in the ancient mys-tery traditions to the "sacred animals." In the cult of those "animals," often found in devolved and limited form among certain primitive peoples, is concealed the memory of that knowledge, that coessentiality, referring to other planes or stages of existence. The "sacred animals" are powers of life that formed part of primordial man, and from which he separated himself in order to go further; they are not single animals, but "group souls," the daimons, whose body is the comprehensive life of a given animal species—and each of them is a transcendent experience, exhausted and abandoned on the trail of the past through a sort of catharsis or purification. But as I have said, having originally been part of the universal man, and since earthly man is the most direct expression of the origin, there remain rapports and occult correspondences: those which esotericism considers by naming the members, the functions, and the energies of the human body after the zodiacal symbols or other equivalents.

Our diagram is shaped more or less like a branching tree, which should be imagined in its outer part as in a continuous movement of expansion and return, like that produced by a heart. That represents the appearance of the individuals of each species, and their dissolution into the original stems to which they belong, and in which is preserved the obscure will that continues to blindly assert itself in the fruitless effort that constitutes it.

It is as though each of these efforts, aside from any factor of fall or deviance, is an approximation of the central will that only succeeds in its realization through man. Likewise humanity itself is a vast reiteration of attempts and approximations, which only in the rarest of men attains a perfect realization of the type. In a way, the struggle depicted in our earlier image is still undecided: if man represents, at least on earth, the last position conquered, that position, being the most advanced, is the hardest to hold. The scattered, the fallen, the deserters, and those swept away by animal passions who are reabsorbed and dissolved in forces that take them back, through contacts with the occult forces of animality—they are without number.

The doctrine of metempsychosis now appears in its correct light. It is true, in the sense that there is a real possibility of an involutive process. But a human soul does not, as crudely imagined, pass into the body of an *individual* animal: instead, it is reabsorbed into the entity or archetype which is the matrix of animal births of a given species, whose occult direction resembles that which informed the whole life of such a man.

Recalling what has been said many times in these pages, one may moreover state that, apart from such "sacrifices" of humans to the "sacred animals," there exist other possibilities and centers of reabsorption. In general, the degree to which human life accepts collective influences also marks that of reabsorption and remolding in the matrix of humanity, with the individual serving as material for other attempts, other shots, which may more or less approach the center of the target.

Much could be said about this, explaining the esoteric view of conditioned immortality and of reincarnation; for example, for the correct interpretation of phenomena like those of a certain "heredity" which—we mention in passing—are not based on transmission from one individual to another, but rather on a kind of "habit" contracted by the *"genius"* or *"manes"* of a given lineage. This is why each individual nucleated on it usually carries a determined and characteristic attribute, going back to a collective influence.

Perhaps I will have the chance to add something about that. Here I will end by saying that our ideas are best reflected in the Aristotelian and scholastic terms, where the "type" is the *materia* and the individual the *forma,* so that the more there is of individuation, the more there is of form and perfection.

All that which is still collective in life is what is still incomplete in man. By separating from all that is not himself, by absolutely individualizing himself so as to be nothing else and only that, man goes beyond the fate of rebirth because he has accomplished its very purpose. Without further oscillations or deviations, he then incarnates the pure, central direction, so as to "have no more daimons" and to make a single thing on earth with his "idea" and his "Name."

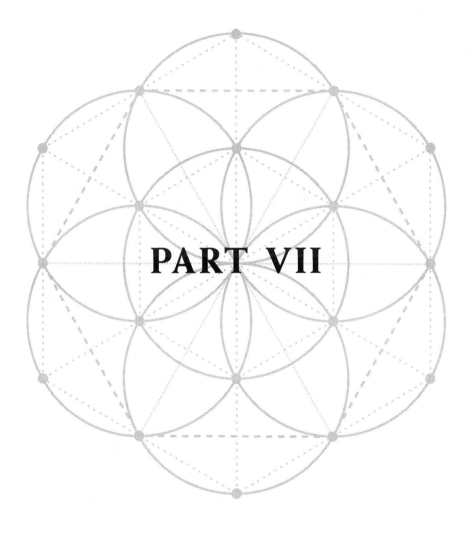

PART VII

Various Commentaries

MORE ON SURVIVAL

On Pacts, Fear, and More

Some readers have been left rather disconcerted by the initiatic doctrines of the afterlife given in these pages. The concept of the "dissolution of the mixed," the exhumation of something like the ancient concept of Hades, from which only a privileged few can escape to become truly immortal, the consequent denial of the current Christian view of the soul as being automatically immortal in every human being, the expectations for its afterlife being only the consequences of its conduct on earth (measured by the standards of morality and divine commandments): all these themes seem uncomfortable.

That does not prevent them from conforming to the point of view of *reality*, whereas those reactions only obey sentiments or intellectual confusions, chief of which is to confuse immortality in the true and absolute sense with an approximate survival.

If we were in an ironic mood, we might ask whether, after due consideration, the idea is really attractive that every person survives *for all eternity*, with all that he is, corresponding to his I, to his individual personality, hopefully with those relationships between "spirits" in the hereafter that resume the social routines of earth, of which Swedenborg has spoken in such grotesque visions as to make one skeptical of the other aspects of that personality, still so esteemed in spiritualist circles.

But even following the esoteric ideas about the decomposition of the personal unity (a unity that is anyway quite relative in most cases), there might be *fiches de consolation* (compensation payments) and the case might not be hopeless. We might maliciously suggest that some "bit" of the I could survive as a psychic, dynamic, and mnemonic complex for a while—not too long, but enough to have the satisfaction of influencing some circle of worthy spiritualists; to creep into the "spirit" (*sit venia verbo* [excuse the word!]) of some Anglo-Saxon spinster and inspire her with more than enough "revelations" to found a new "spiritualist" group; to amaze the professional psychologists by giving rise, through psychic influence, to infant prodigies, miraculous calculators, talking horses, automatic writers, and those who "recall" past incarnations; finally, to disturb those who have gone to live in the place linked to some strong passion of theirs (haunted houses), though usually without this "bit" of the I being able to perpetrate mischiefs such as the first fallen angel was guilty of in Anatole France's *Revolt of the Angels*.[1]

Irony apart, there are doctrinally viable possibilities between the two extremes: that of the absolute immortality of the adept who achieves the Great Liberation, and who in Hellenic tradition is the "Hero" who takes up residence in the Elysian Fields, and the fate to be expected after death by one who has led an earthly life totally given over to materiality, passions, and instincts. If intermediate degrees are allowable, and if one prefers to think objectively instead of on the basis of simplistic sentiments and empty hopes, it should be obvious that the condition for these intermediate possibilities depends on how much one has already realized in one's own thought and will, by living, *objectively* (this "objectively" to be underlined), in a certain detachment from the naturalistic individual complex founded on the body and the experience of the physical world.

Let us take some of these intermediate cases. Men whose whole life and conduct have been rigidly dominated by a single ideal, which they elevate above their own person and to which everything—instincts, feelings, happiness—has been subordinated, have unknowingly created

---

1. [The angel came to earth, studied in a library where he discovered the true nature of the universe, then returned to heaven to lead a revolt. —*Trans.*]

a certain objective basis for survival. The nature and value of this ideal, as one can see, is of little importance: it is only that it has had the power to cause a certain "self-transcendence." This was already mentioned in vol. I of *Introduction to Magic* (pp. 144–50).

Another case is dedication. Typically, a woman who has given herself totally to another, in a relationship of love and sacrifice, in "living for him" or "*burning up* for him," has already nourished a "transcendence" that may help her to preserve a continuity in that "alteration" that is death—even to ensure a degree of effective survival. The same can be said for a similar relationship, but one referring to God—not with words, prayers, and devotions, but with enthusiasm and a constant referral that puts him above all else. Here too we must maintain the objective point of view: it does not matter if "God" exists as a theistic theology conceives of him. The important thing is not the object of devotion or the rational basis of a faith: it is rather, and only, in the *fact* of an orientation that causes a certain structural change in the occult makeup of the human being that is efficacious in the face of death.

Another case is the deathbed conversion. In the state of extreme psychic instability due to the feelings that erupt at the approach of death, the act of absolute concentration or desperate belief in a point of light, which as "God" is the very image of the transcendent state,[2] may have the effect of an initiation, and *rip* the consciousness from that support whose destiny, with the body's dissolution, it would otherwise share.

This glance at a few prospects may suffice to overcome a too rigid and schematic set of alternatives. Survival, therefore, while wholly ensured by initiation (so long as the initiation succeeds, of course) may also be obtained in part, even involuntarily, through ways of life and attitudes that indirectly determine certain subtle processes—even ways of life and attitudes colored by idealism. Utter dedication to an ideal, to another person, to "God" whether in life or at the last moment—are like mountain passes leading to intermediate forms situated between the "realm of the dead" and the "isle of Heroes."

---

2. On this, see the remarks on the *Tibetan Book of the Dead* in *Introduction to Magic*, vol. II, 132–37 ("Initiatic Consciousness beyond the Grave").

• • •

Continuing the theme of the after-death doctrine, we draw attention to a little-known classical text that is among the most explicit on the problem we have already treated (*Introduction to Magic,* vol. I, 144–50). It is a minor treatise of Plutarch called *On the Face that Appears in the Orb of the Moon.*

The basis here is the threefold division of the human being into body, soul, and mind. Soul is understood as all the emotional and intellective faculties of the ordinary man, while mind (νοῦς) should properly be considered as the supranaturalistic principle of the personality, which so rarely appears in common life that one can say that if man knows something of a soul, he has no idea of what the νοῦς is, the spirit in him. While the nature of the soul is *lunar,* that of the νοῦς is *solar* and uranic.

With these assumptions, Plutarch relates the doctrine that man undergoes *two deaths.* The first happens on earth and in Demeter's realm: it occurs when the body separates from the other two principles and returns as a corpse to Mother Earth, of which, according to this interpretation, Demeter is the goddess. But in a following phase there occurs the dissociation of the soul-complex; this is the *second death,* which takes place not on earth but symbolically in the moon and under the sign of Persephone: the soul itself then separates from the properly spiritual and suprapersonal principle, from the νοῦς, and is reabsorbed into the vital substance of the cosmos, to be understood as the root of mortal existence subject to the destiny of birth and rebirth in the "cycle of generation." The teaching related by Plutarch agrees exactly with the Hindu, which describes it as the opposition between the destiny of those who go beyond, and the destiny of those for whom the second death represents in a certain way the end—the end of individual existence. This second possibility is linked to the so-called *pitri-yāna,* which Hindu teaching also connects with the lunar symbol and the location of the moon; those who follow this path reach the "seat of the moon" in which they are reabsorbed, as though into the stock of new mortal births.

The reabsorption of the "soul" and the consequent end of the conscious individuated principle of a simply human nature may take a long time. Plutarch says that in the "moon"—that is, in this phase of intermediate existence preceding the second death—the soul may retain as memories and dreams what made up its earthly existence. Not only that, but tendencies, passions, and impulses may still be active in it, when these had a special intensity in beings much attached to earth and to life. In that case the reabsorption of the soul under the sign of Persephone is delayed. That is a favorable circumstance for those for whom the second death is the terminus of their posthumous journey, because it still ensures a certain individual survival. But for those in whom the condition for moving on is the detachment of the νοῦς from the soul and its purification from the latter, it would be a stoppage, a restraint, since the second death signals the achievement of liberation, of "rebirth above." Once it is detached, the purely intellectual principle passes beyond the lunar sphere, which is to say the sphere of mutability, of disorder, of becoming, and is integrated into the principle that is coessential with its nature, symbolized by the sun. For the nature of the νοῦς is said to be solar, while that of the soul is lunar. Plutarch calls those who reach such a realization the "victors," to whom is due "the crown of the initiates and of those granted a triumph."

Here we must point out that the ontological distinction between soul and spirit (νοῦς), which as we have seen is of capital importance in exoteric doctrine, was already rejected in one of the first church councils and condemned by Catholicism, which stops at the body-soul duality. This is despite the distinction having been admitted by the early Fathers and found even in Saint Paul (e.g., Hebrews 4:12). Moreover, without reference to it there is no possibility of understanding whatever truth may lie in the Catholic myth of "purgatory," the place more or less corresponding to the intermediate existence that, for those who are going beyond the second death, represents a phase of catharsis, consuming the residues of "soul" that entangle and hold back the νοῦς, the solar spiritual principle.

We do not need to emphasize the danger of not distinguishing the soul from the spirit: it opens the way to every humanizing contamination and every prevarication of sentiment, to the point of losing any sense of what transcends the sphere that the ancients connected to the lunar symbol. Among other things, it has given birth to the error of the soul's immortality—we call it an error, because the soul as such is not immortal, but mortal. Thence arises that confusion, overwhelmingly typical of Christian mysticism, of the emotional, psychic, and sentimental domain with the genuinely spiritual and supranatural order.

• • •

There is a certain relation to the "Law of Beings," on which Iagla wrote in a part IV chapter, in surviving popular beliefs about the "pacts" by which one becomes bound to invisible powers through one's dealings with them.

Whatever positive value can there be in things of this sort? In principle, they concern a low magic that relates to the world of passions. The premise is the idea, familiar to our readers, that every human passion has its "demon";[3] in other words, that which manifests in man as passion also exists objectively as a suprapersonal force. Such a force is everywhere and unambiguously defined: the demon of a passion does not *have* that passion (as a man can have it, or not have it, or have different ones): the demon *is* that passion, and its whole being is made from it.

When a man feeds a passion, the corresponding demon arises in him and tries to mingle with his soul as wine with water. The passions of man constitute the life of the demons, who feed on them in a literal sense; and in this way they are able to take on bodies according to their particular thirst. Hence common expressions such as "he's the very *incarnation* of hatred," or of love, avarice, and so on, are often literally exact. To kindle a passion in oneself and cultivate it is in the occult sense to *evoke:* one's own "vital body" enters into sympathetic rapport

---

3. [I have translated the Italian word *demone* as "daimon" when the context suggests the Greek δαίμων, a generally positive concept exemplified by the familiar spirit of Socrates. Here the same word is rendered as "demon," to suit the more negative connotations. —*Trans.*]

with a given order of vibrations, and spontaneously offers itself as the instrument for the demon to manifest and act there.

Such ideas may seem crazy to most people, who know nothing of the secret dynamics at work in the "affective" states of the human being. But those who have eyes to see will understand on this basis certain possibilities that sometimes occur even today in folk magic. Someone yearning for the satisfaction of some passion, and who looks for extra-normal means for it, if he lacks the "dignity" required to operate with his own energy, resorts to something that, by the law of its own being, has every interest in the satisfaction of that passion: namely the relevant demon. It is a matter of finding some method for completely *opening* the "vital body" to it: then a rapport is established in that body with a force that, being free from the conditions of the physical body, may enable various extranormal possibilities.

The methods for this contact may vary widely, perhaps dramatized by apparitions, ceremonial apparatus, commands, blood pacts, and so forth—but the general idea is always as indicated.

Thus, the very fact of such a conjunction in the vital body creates a *pact* and gives a certain significance to the popular expression: that the price of the pact is to "sell one's soul." Without excluding the possibil-ity of dramatizations, which remain purely symbolic, the significance is as follows: that the rapport established in the vital body, especially if "sealed" with a formula of power, constitutes an occult *intoxication* in the truest sense, which tends to expand. The extranormal satisfaction of a passion multiplies it fatally, for the very reason that the "opening" that it has requested has brought the demon inside the person's "life" to a degree not otherwise possible. In extreme cases, one can say that such a person no longer lives for himself, but for the one whom he has invoked. He either submits, terrorized, to the "invasion" of the passion, which flames up and against which he can do little, since it has become a quality penetrating his very life; or he makes himself its instrument, so as to truly become the "incarnation" of a demon.

"Taking a soul," therefore, should be seen as no more than the natu-ral impulse of a force that has no body, and longs to have one; which has no consciousness, and longs to assume one, in order to manifest on a plane and in a condition of existence that to a certain degree is barred to it. Thus, to be accurate one should not speak of an intentionality and of "wickedness": the action follows from their "own nature" of a certain category of incorporeal beings.

Nevertheless, all this borders on "black magic."

• • •

Every idea when joined to an emotional state modifies the rhythm of the "vital body" and synchronizes it, according to its own nature, with some field of occult influence. Whoever devotes himself to esoteric practice should be aware of this fact.

Thus, *fear* "opens" it, in the same way as *desire*. For example, someone knows of a magical action against him: a curse, hatred, or incantation. If he "believes" in it and begins to be afraid, it greatly facilitates this action. A positivist mind, seeing real results, would naturally say that they are created by "auto-suggestion." In the cases under consideration, that is a very superficial view. Something else is happening: the thought of the possibility of the threatened effect has opened, by means of the state of fear, the doorway to the *objective* action of the enemy: it has infused the subtle body with a vibration in sympathy with that of the action itself. It has not *determined* the result (which is all that the thesis of autosuggestion can offer, and besides fails when the effects come to impact the external world), but has *conducted* the force that produces it, and which otherwise might not have found the way to get so far.

On the "Sacred" in the Roman Tradition

In 1929 there appeared a book by Vittorio Macchioro entitled *Roma capta: Saggio intorno alla religione dei Romani* (Rome Captured: An Essay on the Religion of the Romans), published by Principato. It was noteworthy for the seriousness of its documentation, its clarity of exposition, and the lively sense of the tragedy in which the ancient sacred tradition of Rome found itself involved. We certainly differ in more than one point from Macchioro's interpretation. Along with almost all contemporary historians of religion, he lacks those doctrinal and traditional reference points that alone allow one to grasp the positive essence of anything referring to premodern forms of spirituality. All the same, his book offers us much material that is already partly organized, and usable for whoever wants to explore in depth the world of Roman spirituality, before the period in which extraneous influences altered it. We have made use of it in this essay, intending to shed light on other aspects of the Roman tradition, beyond those already treated in previous essays.

Sallust called the early Romans *"religiosissimi mortales"* (very religious mortals; *Cat.* 13), and it was Cicero who declared that in its sense of the sacred, ancient Roman civilization outdid every other people or nation (*omnes gentes nationesque superavimus; Har. resp.,* IX, 19). This and many other testimonies found in a whole series of ancient writers make nonsense of the views of those who see and value in Roman civilization only the profane aspects, civil, political, and juridical. However, this should not cause misunderstandings regarding the use of the word "religion." The primordial "religion" of the Romans, which was traditional and rooted in the mysterious origins of the "sacred city," has very little to do with what is usually understood by the word today.

First point. Early Roman "religion" almost totally lacked the *personification of the divine,* to the extent of an absence of images. The ancient Roman generally felt a deep-seated aversion to image-based thinking. In the secular field, this was one of the reasons for the contempt in which the artist was held by the early Romans, and their original pride in having very different ideals than those of creating pictures or carving marble. Hence in the sacred domain of the early Romans there was nothing of the sort of mythology they were wont to ascribe to Greek *decadence.* Still less did the Romans conceive of the gods as philosophical abstractions, theological concepts, or speculative theories. Thinking along those lines had no more place in Roman realism than the exteriorization of the figurative arts.

The Roman, then, knew the divine neither as "thought," nor as a mythological world, nor even as hypostases supporting a simple faith. The Roman knew the divine as *action.* Before any concept of *deus* (god), the Roman had a living sense of the *numen*: and the *numen* is the divinity understood less as "person" than as power, as a principle of action; it is not the depiction of the entity that interests one (at most, the original Romans represented the *numina* by symbolic objects such as the lance, fire, shield, etc.), but its positive action. On this basis one may well say that ancient Roman "religion" was "experimental" in character. Servius, in his commentary on the *Aeneid* (III, 456), highlights this point by saying that the ancient Romans, *maiores nostri* (our elders), rested their entire religion not on faith, but on *experience: maiores enim expugnando religionem totum in experientia collocabunt* (the elders by subduing religion assigned everything to experience). We can add to that the testimony of Lactantius (*Inst. div.,* IV. 3), who tells us that Roman "religion" did not have the purpose of seeking the "truth," but only of knowing the ritual: *nec habet inquisitionem aliquam veritas sed tantummodo ritum colendi.*

One is therefore justified in speaking of an *active-intensive conception of the sacred* that is specifically Roman. The ancient Roman seems to have preserved such an adherence to the sphere of essentiality as to exclude from his original traditions any fantastic or mythological form of suprasensible perception. We are well aware that the traditional mythologies, with their various figures, are not creations of human fantasy, but systems of forms in which fantasy, with its images, transmits, embodies, and dramatizes suprasensible experiences. But we also know that these modes of experience, mediated and mythologized, are inferior to a direct and absolute experience, formless and imageless, mute and essential. The Roman conception of the sacred seems to have been at this very level. One can see in it the coherent, sacred counterpart of that realism, that intolerance of the inessential, the superfluous, the sentimental and the subjective, that in the first ages were always the watchword for the Romans on the ethical, political, and social planes. And just as the Roman disdain for aesthetes and "philosophers" concealed the awareness of a higher *ethos*—that inner lifestyle of self-possession which caused the first ambassador from an already declining Greece to declare that he found himelf in the Roman Senate not among a horde of barbarians, as he had feared, but as though in a "council of kings"—likewise in the apparent poverty of the original Roman cult, in its dry and naked forms, alien to any mysticism or pathos, any fantastic or aesthetic frills, we have something superior to the exuberant mythological and theological creations of other civilizations, something mysterious and potent, scarcely conceivable in its grandeur: a breath of the *primordial*.

In ancient Rome, the counterpart to the conception of the god as *numen* was that of the cult as *pure ritual*. Ritual accompanied every aspect of Roman life, both individual and collective, both private and public, both in peace and in war. The most ancient Roman religion was bound up with the so-called *Indigitamenta*. *Indigitare* more or less means "to invoke." The *Indigitamenta* were books recording the names of the various gods and the occasions on which each of them could be effectively evoked, according to its own nature and, as it were, its own jurisdiction. These names were therefore *nomina agentis* (proper nouns of agency), having a practical, not a mythological origin. They also contained mysterious connections following the ancient idea that a name contains something of the power or soul of the thing named and evoked. The Roman formula that always accompanied the ritual is characteristic: *"I know that I am naming."* It expresses the deep awareness of the act, its responsibility, the participation in its "fatal" aspect, which can transform it into a command of the invisible.

Not prayers or dogmas, therefore, but rituals. The relations of the Romans with the sacred began and ended with the ritual. Macchioro writes:

> Roman religion never had a theoretical, ethical, or metaphysical content; it never possessed or wanted to possess a complex of doctrines about God, the world, or man: it was fulfilled by ritual alone. Outside the ritual there was no religion, either good or bad, true or false. To accomplish the ritual exactly meant to be religious. One who altered the ritual left the confines of religion, however pure and sincere his intention, and fell into superstition.[1]

The core of Roman "religion" was thus the determination of the *true ritual* that was efficacious, fitting, and decisive. This gave rise to a *ius sacrum* (sacred law), or

> a fixed, traditional ritual, which coincided with religion and as such could not be changed in any detail without destroying the rapport with the god inherent in its very performance. The smallest infraction of the *ius sacrum,* even through inattention, created a *piaculum* (infraction), and in consequence the whole ceremony had to be repeated. If the one guilty of the *piaculum* had committed the error deliberately, the rapport between him and the divinity was broken forever and he was outside the *ius sacrum, impius* (impious) and subject to divine punishment. If the *piaculum* was involuntary, the rapport could be reestablished through an expiatory sacrifice.[2]

---

1. [Vittorio Macchioro, *Roma capta: Saggio intorno alla religione romana* (Rome: Principato, 1928), 36. —*Trans.*]

2. [Macchioro, *Roma capta,* 38. —*Trans.*]

We must be clear about this "divine punishment" and "expiation." They had nothing to do with "sin" or "repentance." In a laboratory, one may have spoiled an experiment through carelessness or imprudence. Then it has to be repeated, even if one has not suffered the consequences of the mistake, which may have been caused by some tiny detail. One should think of the ritual in the same manner. When ancient Roman tradition speaks of someone "struck by lightning" for having altered a sacrificial ritual, this "divine punishment" should only be seen as the impersonal effect of forces evoked and mismanaged. As for the expiation or the expiatory sacrifice, there was no sense there of a moral act of contrition, but of a sort of objective operation of disintoxication and reintegration on the part of whoever had rashly opened the door to forces polarized in a negative sense, and hence impaired the objective ability to "evoke" and *indigitare* in the person responsible.

Not only Roman life but also Roman greatness was centered on the ritual and its well-defined tradition as something of transcendent action. Valerius Maximus (I, 1, 3) states that the Romans attributed their good fortune to their scrupulousness in ritual. According to Livy (XVII, 9), after the terrible Battle of Lake Trasimene it was not a priest but a general, Fabius, who said to the soldiers: "Your fault is more from neglecting the sacrifices than from any lack of courage or ability." Plutarch (*Marc.*, 4) records that in the most tragic moment of the Gallic War the Romans "reckoned it more important for the salvation of the city that the consuls should practice the divine things (the rituals) than that they should defeat the enemy." The mystery of the origins was supreme: "Rome could not have acquired such power by itself if it had not somehow had a divine origin, such as to offer to the eyes of men something grand and inexplicable" (Plutarch, *Rom.,* I, 8). As the last echo, the emperor Julian (*Contra Eracl.,* 222c) did not hesitate to say that he could not compare to the ritual knowledge of the gods "even the domination of all the barbarian lands together with the Roman ones."

Someone who cannot appreciate the virile, austere splendor of this spirituality, whose world of *numina* and *rites* harbors no "religious intimacy," no sentimentality or theological speculation, may be led to define the Roman vision of the world as a "magical primitivism" like that of uncivilized peoples. Macchioro himself seems to have been of this opinion. But our readers already know enough to avoid such incomprehension. They know that although "magic" may also have been an ancient traditional science of a fairly low order, which the Romans themselves banned more than once, it can also denote a spiritual orientation that relates to the "religious" (in the common, devotional sense) as the masculine to the feminine, as the "solar" to the "lunar." As for primitive peoples, readers also know that they represent for us the twilight fragments of very ancient races and civilizations, of which even the names are lost to us today. And because what is at the origins is not inferior but superior and closest to spirituality; the fact that certain traditions among primitives only survive in materialistic, bestial, degenerate, and superstitious forms should not prevent us from recognizing the meaning and dignity that are due to them once they are restored to their origins. That is largely valid for what is "magic" among primitives and not sorcery. Not in degenerate forms, as in those pitiful residues, but in forms still luminous and self-aware, early Rome incarnated that original spirituality, impregnating its whole life with it and secretly sustaining its greatness through none other than ritual and the tradition of ritual.

We pass on now to another feature of the Roman concept of the sacred: *immanence*. But one should not think here of the speculations of modern "idealist" philosophy. To explain it, we will compare the style of Roman spirituality with that of the Greeks. While the latter was, as we might say, under the sign of *space,* the former was under that of *time*. For the Greek, the gods, as objects of pure contemplation, live as eternal essences in the absolute space of the supernal world; for the Roman, the gods, while losing nothing of their metaphysical dignity, manifest essentially—as *numina*—in time, in history, in human events; and the Romans' chief preoccupation was to reach an equilibrium, to propitiate an encounter between divine and human forces, or rather to ensure that the former should augment or direct the latter. The whole Roman art of augury reflects a similar idea: and since, in turn, the weave of augural and oracular answers was inseparable from the totality of Roman achievements, one could say that for our ancestors all Roman history had the character of a veritable sacred history, a history continually overshadowed by divine significances, revelations, and symbols. Only all this had as its counterpart not an ecstatic and passive attitude, but an active and warlike one. It is well said that the Roman *made* his history sacred, actively involving invisible forces in it and working in union with them.

A special aspect of "immanence" concerns the *human symbol.* We know that at the Roman origins the pontifical and kingly dignities were united in a single person; also later, and before Augustus's restoration, some sacred functions were the prerogative of political leaders such as the consuls and many other typical Roman figures. Even more characteristic examples could be found in the specifically sacred domain. Here is one cited by Karl Kerényi. In Greece, the statue, in its perfection and completeness, symbolized the Olympian god. In Rome, the same god had instead a living symbol consecrated to him: the *Flamen Dialis.* This pure and majestic figure, closely linked to the idea of the State, appeared in his whole life as a living symbol of the divinity—so that he could actually be called "a living statue of Jupiter." And the significances preserved in the imperial era were no different, albeit in already fading reflections. The imperial cult itself is one witness to it. The human figure of a ruler incarnated a divine symbol.

Another aspect of Roman "religion" concerns the afterlife. At the origins, the afterlife as a "religious" problem was of no concern to the average Roman. Being a virile realist, alien to any vain speculation, shut off from the agitations of hope, fear, and belief, the Roman was uninterested in it. He could stare into the void itself with a clear and calm eye. He had no need for afterlife prospects in order to give his life a meaning and an inner law. Thus, the original conception of the afterlife in Rome was chiefly that of a night, a state devoid alike of joy and pain: *perpetua nox dormienda* (endless sleeping night), says Cato; *ultra neque curae neque gaudi locum esse* (the place of neither sorrows nor joys) are the words attributed to Caesar himself. The success in Rome of Lucretius's revived Epicurean philosophy is significant here. It does not denote a materialism, but again a realism. The ancient Roman soul reacted against the mysticism and mythologizing imported from Asia and decadent Greece; to a great extent it was at ease with a conception like

Epicurus's and Lucretius's, in which the explanation through natural causes served as a weapon to destroy the terror of death and the fear of the gods, thus liberating life and making it calm and secure. Meanwhile for the better sort there remained uncontaminated the Olympian ideal of the gods as impassive and far-off entities, from which there is nothing either to hope or to fear, and who are of value to the Wise solely as the model and limit of perfection.

Nonetheless, the afterlife problem was not totally solved within the religious problem of the individual soul's fate. The ancient world always recognized man as a much more complex entity than the simplistic pair of soul and body: as an entity comprising various forces, and in first place those of his stock and race, which had their laws and special relationships with the living and the dead. *The part of the dead that stands in essential rapport with such forces is that which above all concerned the Roman:* not the dead person in himself, but conceived of as a force that subsists and lives on in the deep stem and destiny of a family, a clan, or a race, and which is capable of action. And here again we find the marks of the general Roman concept of the sacred: in place of the soul, a *power;* in place of sentimental intimacy, the objectivity of the *ritual.* Originally, the Roman considered the deceased not as a personal being but as an impersonal energy, to be treated like all the other presentiments as invisible counterparts of the visible. As Fustel de Coulanges says, the dead did not love men, nor did men love the dead. There was no relationship of regret, sorrow, or piety, or at least this was something subordinate and "private" compared to the essential purpose, which was to *direct* the energies freed by death so that they could be made to act in a "fortunate" rather than unfortunate direction.

We must now consider briefly the development that the Roman concept of the afterlife underwent. Originally, it rose from the substratum of the spirituality of less civilized Italic peoples, whose horizon stopped short at the *"way of the underworld":* meaning that the dead generally blended back into the impersonal energies of the bloodline, and that their union with the living only continued as such, not as transfigured and transfiguring natures. That is the meaning of the ancienc concept of the *lares,* which is actually more Etruscan than Roman. The *lar* is the *genius generis* (family genius), the vital force that generates, pre-serves, and develops a given stock and which simultaneously serves to receive the energies of the dead: a substance in which the dead continue to live and to be obscurely present in a family. The cult of the *lares,* in its original form, was, as we have said, neither Roman nor even patrician in character. Its origin was Etruscan and Sabine. Servius Tullius, a king of plebeian extraction, is said to have introduced it into Rome. The mythologem that makes the *lares* the sons of "Mania the dumb" or of Acca Larentia, identical to the goddess Dia, and which sees their region not in the high heavens or in a symbolic place on earth, but in the underworld or subterranean zone (Festus: *deorum inferorum, quos vocant lares* [of the gods of the underworld, whom they call the *lares*]), derives from the southern and Asiatic civilizations of a chthonic and matriarchal type. One feature of the cult of the *lares* was that slaves had a prominent part in it, and indeed it was the only cult in Rome that had slaves among its ministers.

Nonetheless, the true Roman spirit appeared through a later purification of this cult. From the concept of the dead dissolving in the obscure and naturalistic energy of the ancestors, it moved to that of the dead as a "hero," a divine ancestor, principle of a supranatural heredity that the family or clan ritual served to perpetuate and confirm in his descendants. Varro already assimilates the *lares* to the *manes,* calling them "divine spirits" and "heroes." Thenceforth, their assimilation to the heroes of the patrician Hellenic cult became ever more frequent, thus reaffirming in Rome the fundamental beliefs belonging to all the great Indo-European civilizations of the Hyperborean stock. Writers such as Censorinus and Plutarch tell us of a duality, a double "genius," one light and the other dark, until in traditions taken up by Plotinus the *lar* is conceived as the soul of those who in death have been liberated and become eternal spirits. Whereas the *lar* was originally depicted as a snake, the ambiguous creature of the humid earth, it later assumed the virile figure of the *pater familias* (family father), in the act of sacrificing. Thus, the *lar* regained the "regal" significance contained in the original word, for *lar* is equivalent to the Greek *anax,* meaning "leader," "chief," or "prince."

It is an aristocratic vision that corresponds to the highest and purest consciousness of Romanity. The destiny of those who will be only shades in Hades now becomes secondary. The dead one who remains united to the living is not the simple vital energy of a stock, but something transfigured, a luminous principle that has as its body the perennial flame ritually burning at the center of the ancestral home; not an abstraction or a pious memory, but a *force,* active for the protection, "fortune," and grandeur of its descendants, while these, faithful to their tradition, keep the contacts intact by means of the ritual.

A final aspect of Roman "immanence" is revealed here. The Roman union of the dead with the living is only one form of the unity of divine and human forces, unfolding on the plane of action and history. Once again, the imperial theology will represent a limit to this process with its symbolic divine genealogies. The "genius" of the rulers is already a genuine force from the "upper world," connected through mysterious channels to the invisible influences of a certain bloodline and to the supraindividual element that, despite everything, was present in the imperial function.

VII.3

Liberation of the Faculties[1]

The forces that can lead to initiatic realization cannot become active until they are freed from impediments, both inner and outer.

In this article we consider only the external impediments and offer some rules for life by which one can proceed to their removal.

I.

The first condition is the mastery of absolutely clear thinking. To this end one has to get free from the *wandering of thoughts* even for a very short time: a few minutes will serve, though more would be better.

One needs to become master of one's own thought world. We are not masters of it if outer circumstances such as our job, habits, social pressures, time of day, obligations, and so forth, impose a certain thought and manner on its development. In the relevant span of time one must, of one's own free will, unburden the mind from the usual everyday train of thoughts, take a specific thought and place it through one's own intitative in the center of one's mind. It does not have to be a lofty or interesting thought. In fact, it will help for present purposes to start by choosing a thought that is neither interesting nor important. This will better stimulate the autonomous activity of thinking, which

---

1. [Added to the 1955 edition. —*Trans.*]

is the main thing: whereas if one chooses an interesting thought it will pull the mind along with it. This discipline is better served by thinking of a pin than of (a) Napoleon.[2] You must tell yourself: "Now I will start with this thought, and through my own intitiative connect everything that can be objectively relevant to it." The chosen thought should end by standing in the forefront of the mind with as much presence and liveliness as at the start. This exercise should be done daily for at least a month. You can take a different thought each day, or keep the same one for several days. After doing this, in a second phase one tries to bring to full awareness that inner sensation of firmness and security that will soon appear when one observes one's own mind. In the third phase, one concludes the exercise by concentrating one's own consciousness in a place a little above the root of the nose, between the eyes, and with active visualization causing a feeling of a flow that goes horizontally from the brow round both sides to the back of the head, then going down the middle of the back along the spinal column, pouring the accumulated feeling into those parts of the body, together with the words: FIRMNESS AND SECURITY.

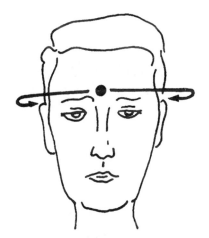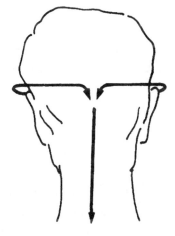

Figure 4

2. [The phrase *"pensando ad uno spillo, che non ad un Napoleone"* could mean either Bonaparte himself or the standard gold coin named after him. —*Trans.*]

II.

After practicing these exercises for about month, a second discipline is added.

Pick some action that you would certainly not do in the normal course of daily activity, and every day impose that action on yourself, spontaneously, as though it were an obligation. It will help to choose an action that can be repeated every day for quite a long period. Here too it is better to begin with an insignificant action, which otherwise would not be done and which you need to make yourself do. For example, you might decide to water a plant in a pot at the same time every day.

After a while, add a second action of the same kind, then a third, and so on, up to as many as you can do without affecting your usual occupations.

This discipline may also last about a month. As far as possible, continue the first exercise during the second month, without making it an absolute duty as in the first period, but also without neglecting it, otherwise you will soon find that you are losing the fruits of the first month and regressing to the lazy neglect of uncontrolled thoughts. You must absolutely ensure that the results, once achieved, are not lost.

With this second discipline, by performing a self-directed action, one becomes aware, through subtle observation of one's own soul (second phase), of the acquired feeling of the inner impulse to the activity, and then diffuses this feeling into one's body, making it flow from the head down to above the heart.

III.

In the third month a new discipline must take the central place in one's life, aiming to establish a certain equilibrium of soul in the face of the alternations of pleasure and displeasure, joy and pain. One must consciously substitute a state of mind impassive toward any alternations of exaltation or depression. It is a matter of watching yourself so that no joy transports you to excess, no sorrow drags you down, no experience makes you inordinately attached, no prospect fills you with hope or fear, no situation upsets you or makes you lose your presence of mind, and so forth. Do not worry that this exercise will make you indifferent: you will soon see how in place of what is lost through this discipline, purified faculties arise in the soul. Some day, observing with subtle attention, you may feel an interior calm within the body (second phase). Direct this feeling of calm in a similar way to the two cases described above, making it radiate from the heart to the hands, along the legs, and finally toward the head (third phase). The feeling should always be brought back to the heart and freshly radiated out from that center. Naturally, that cannot be done after every single exercise, because this is not really a case of a single exercise but of an attention continually directed to your own inner life. But at least once a day you should put yourself in mind of this inner calm, and then do the exercise of radiating it from the heart. As the illustration shows, the radiation traces the outlines of a pentagram:

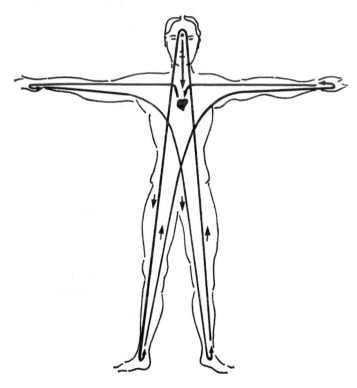

Figure 5

IV.

In the fourth month, as a new discipline, one should cultivate so-called *positivity*. It consists of considering, when facing every experience, every being and thing, what is *positive* in them. This faculty of soul can best be conveyed by a Persian legend about Christ. One day, while he was walking with his disciples, he saw the rotting corpse of dog by the roadside. All the disciples turned their heads away to avoid the disgusting sight. Only Christ stopped and, thoughtfully contemplating the creature, said "What magnificent teeth this dog had!" Where the others had only seen the ugly and repulsive side, Christ was able to see that, despite everything, there was beauty there. In such a way one should try to discern a positive side in every manifestation and every being.

This discipline is related to what may be called the suspension of criticism. There is no need to believe that you will end up calling black white. All the same, there is a big difference beween the judgment that stems only from one's particular individuality and defines the positive and negative, the fair and the foul, in function of that individuality, and the attitude of one who is able to participate impersonally and with open mind in any external phenomenon or being, asking himself in every case: "How does this thing or being come to be this way or that?"

Someone who spends some time—say about a month—in this discipline of trying to consciously see the positive side in all his experiences will gradually observe a dawning sense as though his whole skin were becoming permeable, and his soul opening to secrets of every kind and to subtle processes in the environment that completely escaped his attention up to then. The actual purpose of this is to combat the negligence and lack of attention to these subtle things that is innate in every man. When you notice that the feeling described above manifests in the soul as a kind of blissfulness, try to direct this feeling, by means of thought, toward the heart, making it flow from there toward the eyes and thence into the spaces before and around you. You will soon observe that it sets up an intimate rapport with this space, as though you are expanding beyond yourself: you come to consider the part of the world surrounding you as still belonging to yourself. This discipline takes much concentration:

above all, you must be able to notice that every passion, every sudden and violent movement, has a damaging effect on this attitude. As for repeating the exercises of the first months, the rules apply as given above.

V.

In the fifth month one tries to cultivate the attitude that meets every new experience with a completely free and open mind. One has to completely avoid the mentality that says when confronted with something new: "I've never seen or heard anything like it, so I won't believe it—it's an illusion!" As a discipline, you must be ready to expect something new at each moment. Everything hitherto regarded as normal, everything that has seemed possible, must not be a drag that prevents you from accepting a new truth. If someone says: "Look, the church tower is leaning over tonight," you must be able to think that, in principle, the current knowledge of natural laws can be modified or improved in consequence of such a seemingly inconceivable fact. Someone who in the fifth month devotes himself to this kind of discipline will notice a feeling arising in his soul, as though there is something moving in the space that was mentioned in the fourth discipline—as if something was coming to life there. This feeling is extremely fine and subtle. You need to pay close attention to these subtle vibrations of the environment (second phase) and to make them flow, in a way, into all five senses; notably the eye, the ear, and the skin, in that the latter contains the sense of heat (third phase of the discipline).

At this stage of esoteric development one pays less attention to the impressions from reactions of the inferior senses, those of taste, smell, and touch. It is not yet possible to distinguish the many negative influences that mingle with the positive ones acting in this field. Therefore, the practioner leaves any extension of the discipline to the lower senses until a higher stage is reached.

VI.

In the sixth month you test yourself by repeating all five exercises sytematically and in order. The effect will be a particular mental equilibrium. You will observe the total disappearance of any vexation or disappointment when faced with the world's phenomena or beings. The calm comprehension of things that hitherto remained completely hidden from the soul will become possible. Even the gait and gestures are transformed under the influence of these disciplines, and if you notice, some day, that even your handwriting has taken on a different character, you can say that you are on the point of entering a higher stage of development.

A complete initiatic discipline comprises three parts. The first is the contemplative realization. The second is the continuous attention to everything occurring in us, and everything that we experience. The third is to pervade the subtle, occult part of the body with specific states; and it is to that section that these disciplines apply. They touch on various zones:

    I. head and dorsal spine
    II. from the head, through the heart, to the body
    III. from the heart to the whole person
    IV. from the heart, via the eyes, to the environment.

As for the fifth discipline, it favors a returning motion: from the ensouled environment back to us.

Two last points: *First:* the six exercises paralyze the harmful influence that can come from other esoteric disciplines, enabling only their beneficial side to remain. *Second:* they ensure a sound basis for the work of concentration, meditation, and contemplation.

COMMENTARY[3]

In order to grasp the importance and true significance of the disciplines described here, one must take into consideration what even modern psychology has suspected: that in the human being there exist so-called "complexes," nodes of psychic energies having their own life, to the

---

3. [In the Italian editions this commentary is printed entirely in italics. Given that neither the essay nor the commentary is attributed, this emphasizes the (internally obvious) fact that they are by different authors. —*Trans.*]

point of being largely independent of the waking I. Up to now, attention has mostly been concentrated on those "complexes" that have a pathological nature. But formations of this kind, deep and tenacious, also exist in the more normal person. Their effect is that no impression or experience goes straight to the I, but undergoes alteration due to prior impressions and experiences, so that we react in an instinctive and automatic way along lines already defined in the past, even when we have largely managed to master those reactions in the conscious zone. There is therefore something in the human soul that tends to cancel out any new development; and it is through this that there acts the paralyzing and perverting influence of obscure forces—forces that may be called those of the *counter-initiation*.

This can be verified in various psychic domains, namely in the field of *thought* and in those of *will, feeling/emotion, judgment,* and *memory*. The four disciplines described here aim to plant a principle of active autonomy in each of these domains. This is obvious in the first two exercises: rigorously developing a train of thought on a theme that does not specially interest us, concentrating in a mode of active consciousness, and, likewise, regularly performing a certain act that also has no special interest or importance, thereby reinforcing a positive attitude of the thinking and emotional faculties, limiting the force of automatism and of disorderly and fleeting impulses. Some may recall that in Ignatius of Loyola's *Spiritual Exercises* one of the main preliminary tasks of active asceticism is to master what he calls the *inordinatae affectiones* (disordered affections).

The third exercise aims at developing equanimity, namely attaining balance vis-à-vis pleasure, pain, and emotional reactions in general, so that these reactions do not manifest automatically in us. One must actually become able to stop the immediate reactions that such experiences or sensations tend to cause; later, in full mental equilibrium, one can freshly consider each impulse for acceptance or rejection. When we have a perception or an experience, if something similar has been associated in the past with pleasure or displeasure, our memory not only recalls it but automatically refers to the emotional complex that stores it in us, and our reaction to the outside world is immediately influenced by it. Through the third discipline, on the contrary, we develop the ability to stop an automatic reaction in the emotional field, so that we maintain an attitude of freedom whenever a given experience occurs, and evaluate it in the light of our current, perfectly conscious state. This grants the third liberation, the *liberation of emotion.*

As for the fourth discipline, that of making oneself consider only the good and positive aspect of things and beings and refusing to see the other aspect, it should not cause misunderstandings. This is not a matter of strolling through the world like a naïve idealist, seeing everything as rosy, falling into every enticement of life, and forming a false vision of reality. Its purpose is to acquire, during a certain period of time, the faculty of seeing things positively, because the positive and creative aspect of things is the one that relates to the real, supraindividual I, while the negative aspect refers to the contingent and limited individual. This is the path that must be taken to reach the fourth liberation, the *liberation of judgment:* it enables one to sharpen a flair for judgment, whereby one goes straight to whatever in beings is supraindividual in character, whatever is linked to a higher order, to what alone is effectively real. In such a way one can even have a presentiment of whatever in a particular life transcends that life and preexists its mundane and human birth (cf. *Introduction to Magic,* vol. I, 138–40).

The last discipline has points of contact with the previous one, but is different: it consists in accepting nothing as definitely prejudged, and bringing everything into the full light of our consciousness, as if the facts and impressions were being presented to it for the first time. This leads to a *liberation of memory.* If when faced with any fact I immediately start judging it, I automatically set in motion a certain content of my memory, rather than actually encountering it. But if instead I say: "I want to examine the matter afresh," I face the perception with my present judgment in an objective way and can also see, bit by bit, what the content of memory stems from. I can follow the path of recall up to a point that is not a void, but an objective field that I can freely explore and which is spread out clearly before me.

It is in this sense that the disciplines described here may well be considered as preliminary instruments for the initiatic work of the *liberation of the faculties.*

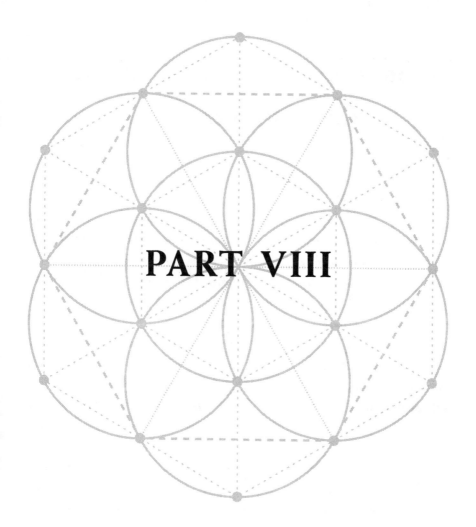

PART VIII

Starting Magic, According to Giuliano Kremmerz

It will be helpful for our readers to revisit some of the matters already treated, by way of the form they take in the Kremmerzian teaching. This is, moreover, the same system as has figured in some writings by our collaborators, notably Abraxa. The object is to indicate the convergences, and also to shed light on some particular aspects.

What follows is compiled from passages taken from Kremmerzian works that are not easily found (Commmentarium, La Porta Ermetica, Avviamento alla Scienza dei Magi, *the four Fascicoli,* I dialoghi sull'Ermetismo),[1] *and then reassembled, with some modifications of form necessitated by this compilation.*

Our *purity,* understood integrally, is the conscious and unalterable *neutrality* of consciousness. Any hatred and any love, indeed any self-interest of the Hermetic operator, renders success in vain, canceling and destroying the hoped-for result.

The development of the Hermetic intelligence is facilitated through

---

1. Since then, Kremmerz's works have been reprinted by the publisher Universale di Roma. [For his *Opera Omnia* in Italian, see the material archived at www.giulianokremmerz.it. For a selection in English, see Giuliano Kremmerz, *The Hermetic Science of Transformation: The Initiatic Path of Natural and Divine Magic,* trans. Fernando Picchi (Rochester, Vt.: Inner Traditions, 2019). —*Trans.*]

complete equilibrium, both physical and mental, in a regime of life that is sober, unforced, and observed in silence, realizing the vanity of words.

Detach yourself mentally from the environment, as from something that must not and cannot offend you. Say: the unjust cannot succeed in upsetting my equilibrium. The image of the completely integrated man gives the impression of the most perfect neutrality; like a just Lord; the specter of God as imagined by believers: a judge, generous and magnificent bestower of gifts, with the lofty sense of the giant who would not smite a feeble man.

The perfect man is not altogether body nor altogether spirit, but the integration of the powers of the spirit in the body that feeds it and serves for its manifestations, in a constant equilibrium that prevents the excess of either factor.

In physical life, use everything and abstain from everything at will. With a sober way of life, the body is strengthened. If you are sick, then fast. Apply this regime to passions and desires. The passions are sufferings for desires unobtained or insufficiently satisfied. Desire soberly, and when desire becomes excessive, abstain from it. What most distances you from power is the desire for pleasure.

A Master must be superior to good and to evil, because his state of continuous equlibrium depends on his neutrality to both, so as to develop the inner powers and make use of them in all ways. Every operation carries the impress of the operator's state of balance or imbalance.

You yourself are the laboratory, and you must see it as clearly as in the light of day. Reflect on your actions and meditate on them. The characteristics, the impulses, and the constant style that they maintain reveal to you your ancient being, your forgotten history and what you have been. Form the habit of frequently examining your conscience.[2]

• • •

One's own body, like one's soul, can be accustomed to cold and to heat. Thus, you should dominate it: prohibit and command it; give and take away from it. Your physical body and soul should obey and be constantly

---

2. [*Coscienza* serves in Italian for both "conscience" and "consciousness." —*Trans.*]

under the orders of your intelligence, which has the right to blow hot or cold on them. Thus, eat and fast; wake and sleep.

Your thought acts with such certainty on the body that with sufficient training you have the latter entirely under your command. Have no fear of contagions, infirmities, disturbances of any kind. It is enough to *think* that such things will not happen in your organism.

Educate yourself step by step. With the sensations of heat and cold: on a cold day, for example, think that you can do without an overcoat, because the cold does not hurt you, but energizes you. In the heat, start willing your skin not to perspire; then the external heat will not bother you. Attend to the various needs. To habitual ones: do not abstain from alcohol, if that is your habit, but *will* that the need for it shall cease. To physiological ones: *will* that sleep should come at a certain hour of the evening, or on the contrary, *will* that it should not come until a certain hour. Fast, not for penitence, but to inhibit the stimulus of hunger from arising before a certain moment.

In this way you can work directly on the organism, through little disturbances that can affect it. In weaker persons the will is *imaginative;* in stronger ones it is simply *enunciative.* Then you will have no need for "suggestion": it will suffice to will with conviction, as the musician uses his instrument.

Hermetic education thus tends to render the integrating faculty of the human intellect the absolute master of its animal vesture, so as to make the latter an obedient and ready servant of the psychodynamic authority that is in us. Purify yourself of every obstacle to the free exercise of the intelligent will: *free yourself from every necessity.*

• • •

Since man is conceived of as analogous to the cosmos, magic has as the basis of its precepts the analogous laws of the things and acts that compose him. For example, washing oneself is the analogical symbol of the evident virtue of water that cleans the stones that it washes over; fasting is analogous to the liberation from obstructions; chastity, to the state of freedom, rather than that of sexual passion, which is suffering. Wash yourself so that the acts of your hands do not only clean your body and outer senses, but above all the hidden being that has received dirty impressions in the course of the day. Be temperate by habit and fast at the new moon[3] by eating only once—because you know that at the first day of appearance the moon is virginal, innocent, and pure, analogous to the lunar or astral body of man, which at birth lacks the stigmata of the new human life. Be chaste, by not entertaining the state of passionate disturbance—neither obey, nor provoke, nor satiate yourself with it.

To accomplish a ritual needs no "faith." All that is needed is that it be performed without any alteration of the form. With all due precision, like the countryman who goes to his garden, hides the seed in the earth, and waits till it becomes a sprout, then a tree.

• • •

Realization, both high and low, is an act of *love*; whether for good or ill; for that which brings help and that which causes harm.

Any idea of personal advantage muddies and halts it—whether the reward is moral or material, it is the same. If a lover "prays" for his lady, he obtains nothing unless he converts his love of her to the love of a mother who sacrifices herself for her child. Ask yourself, if someone else's infirmity were to pass into your body, whether you have the strength to suffer in their place without complaint or regret. If you can say yes to that, you are ready to obtain the thaumaturgic virtue.

State of love: subtly, kindly, you must feel all the expanse of a state of tender responsibility, as you would feel spontaneously for a child who was speechlessly begging for help. Like the host who opens his door to a friend and envelops him with his hospitality. A sentiment that is kindness, compassion, charity, being like the protector who lets the other rest in him and will see to everything. He wraps the other in a wave of goodness, thinks of him and *gives him* (there is no other word) calm, insensitivity to pain, life.[4]

---

3. [The text has *plenilunio* (full moon), but the rest of the sentence implies the new moon. —*Trans.*]

4. All things being equal, it is only necessary to change the quality of that which is given, and which as a *state* or fluidified image is first aroused in you, when one wishes to direct the operation to a contrary or simply a different result. See "The Magic of Effigies,"

Know only the love that unites two souls without desires, without exceptions, without partialities, without advantage, and who at the same time live by the same desire, the same partiality, the same advantage, in a communion of profound goodness where no shadow is possible. This love is called Beatrice, because it is Light, Purification, Beatitude. It is neither an art nor a science. It is a spirit that the Hermes[5] heralds, *as the dawn the Sun.* It must be invoked. If if arrives, do not reject it, for it will not return. If it arrives, receive it. That which you love will be taken by the same love, and if it is more perfect it will give you all you ask of its spirit.[6]

This is the first little key.

• • •

Hermetically speaking, prayer is an act of the concrete fluidification of the will. To formulate the idea, and desire[7] its realization, is *prayer.*

The imagination of things that is well defined, pictorial, minute, chiseled in its finest and clearest details, is will in action, is creation. To conceive, imagine, depict the idea, then to feel oneself in the state of *truth,* accord, and consciousness with the thing thought of, is an act of will, whether or not the word expresses the volitive thought. The will is perfect when the idea formed in consciousness is the idea as seen. Peace between the imagined idea and consciousness, will in action, love that intervenes and makes it fruitful.

In the consciousness thus integrated, with the profound will, beyond any environmental influence, belief, or passion, the Hermetic

---

(*cont. from p. 251*) *Introduction to Magic,* vol. II, 229–36. For good as for ill, Kremmerz has said, the condition is *love,* understood in the Hermetic sense as the simple force of *enveloping* and *penetrating rapport.* (Note by UR)

5. [See below for a definition of what is meant by *l'Ermete,* "the Hermes." —*Trans.*]

6. Such a love ceases to be necessarily linked to a specific being. We note too that the abovementioned allusion to love between two persons is mainly intended to explain, by analogy, what kind of state is in question: a state that one must reach in magic in order to evoke *in oneself* without reliance on, or bondage to anything else. (Note by UR)

7. Evidently, this is a different species of "desire" from that of which Kremmerz himself says, in conformity with what has always been the magical teaching, that it paralyzes realization (cf. *Introduction to Magic,* vol. I, 261–62; vol. II, 173). (Note by UR)

power manifests spontaneously, without effort, through the imaginative act alone. *The imagination is the instrument of creation of the integrated consciousness.* It is enough to create a thought-form in such an inner condition for the form to be realized, not as the result of an effort, but as that of a state of being that is independent and intimate, knowing no obstacles. The conception, in magic, is a flash, a lightning operation that implies the most perfect education both of the physical and the mental body.

Thus: close your eyes; create an image and look at it. In the dark, you will see with a sight that is not of the senses. If several persons close their eyes in the same way and open the intellectual sight—then communion with the light is established through rapport. The rapport between the astral vibrations perceived by the individuals forms the *astral current,* which in turn you need to learn to control.

Hermes should make you understand the mental motion outside any body, surface, or space: a free motion in a nondimensional intellectual environment, or one that contains all dimensions. The human mind, hermetically penetrated in this function, gains from it a divine virtue that changes into miraculous powers.

• • •

Magic is the state of *mag,* which is an intensive state of trance that puts our fluidic body in direct communication with the cosmic astral current; projecting it out of the physical body *like a shadow without light,* since the astral light is *black* light.[8]

When the intellectual center predominates over the peripheral extremes in contact with the external world, it is possible to detach and isolate the fluidic body from the outside, liberating the mental power,

---

8. In the *Dialogues,* Kremmerz further explains the doctrine that the spirit is breath, and as breath it goes, after death, to be blended and dissolved in the mass of cosmic ether. Only the magus, when performing the projection, does not emit his spirit (air, wind, breath), *but a second self* that contains the spirit and supplies it with a humanlike body, invisible to the physical eye, indestructible, capable of doing with mental power what ordinary man does with his limbs, and no longer needing a physical body to transport itself. (Note by UR)

which then *sees*. It renders the animal senses inert, to give complete freedom to the *other,* to the Hermes, which is the communicating sense between the ultrahuman and the human. It is not passive ecstasy that views the manifestations, but power to *direct* them, giving them energy.

All that is thought of in the astral is realized in action: things hermetically thought are true facts, because they become real. To enter in every mode into contact with the world beyond, and to work actively in it, in order to have the reactions or effects in real, common life.

. . .

The spirits of the elements, or elementals, are condensations of etheric matter,[9] with their lives and finality determined. According the element that predominates in its specific function over the others that are still present, they belong to one of the four classes of elementals: those of Fire, Air, Water, and Earth. All these families are innumerable, constantly being reproduced, reconstituted, enlivened, and renewed. Every spirit, of limited life. Every life, of intelligence relative to its function. Every elemental, inexorably striving for its end.

Immobilized by that end, they can become immortal when through human agency they acquire the hermetic property of the human mind: with the volitive and negative liberty that becomes more precise and free in them than in incarnation. These entities therefore preserve the inexorability of their original character when they are attracted into the orbit of ends that sympathize with their temperament.

The mental hermetic force, when at its most active, has powers that dominate the elemental spirits, to the point of being able to dissolve them and, in the ultimate degrees of magic, to make them immortal.

There is a vast legion of elemental spirits desiring immortality—so say the sacred books; and as a fatal condition of the path, you are for the most part in contact with them, *because they are all elementals of Fire, they thirst, and you have the water to quench their thirst.*

The ether is made from Fire, of fire that is inconceivable until your

---

9. Our readers, given what has been said several times, surely have the means to give expressions of this kind their proper sense. (Note by UR)

spirit has attained a special state. The object, to be precise, is: (1) Reduce man to the etheric state;[10] (2) reduce the etheric to the state of Fire;[11] and (3) reduce the evil that comes into contact with us by means of the integrated purifying movement.

The Symbol: Hermes who loves Venus.

The Name: Pyromagia, or eonic Magic.

The Form: The red robe with a triple knot on the silken cord.

The Mystery: The initiate closed in the deep darkness of his cowl.

The End: The Hermaphrodite, indissoluble unity of complementaries.

The Sign: The raised palm—the Flame.

The Means: Silence.

---

10. We meet again the connection that formed part of the earlier chapter (VI.1, 188) on Hindu alchemy. The formulation in Taoist alchemy is also identical to it. (Note of UR)

11. This is what has also been called *ignification of the astral light.* (Note of UR)

VIII.2

First Ascent

Life is a journey during the nighttime hours.

PANCATANTRA

The following description of the first ascent of one of the most arduous peaks of the Dolomites (see also Rivista del CAI, May–June 1929)[1] *may be of interest to our own readers, regarding the possibility that even today, in special circumstances, one can have experiences whose significance is not unrelated to the so-called "path of action."*

In the heart of the mountain, one of the grandest of the Alpine range, between precipitous buttresses and towering walls there hides a peculiar hollow of snow.

It is like the atrium of an immense rock-temple, wrecked in the forgotten past and worn down through the millennia, among whose colossal ruins there rises, still intact, a single strange idol, like the changeless symbol of an archaic faith lost in the flux of time and buried in the inmost instinctual urges: the faith in Mother Earth and in the Sun God.

The rock-idol—which now has a name,[2] petty and vain like all human things in the face of primordial nature—suddenly breaks out at

---

1. [Domenico Rudatis, "Il Pan di Zucchero della Civetta," *Rivista mensile del C(lub) A(lpino) I(taliano)* XLVIII/3 (1929): 153–91. —*Trans.*]
2. ["Pan di zucchero" = Sugarloaf. —*Trans.*]

the topmost level of the snowy hollow, with its sheer eastern wall made whiter and smoother at the base by the subsidence of the snowfield; and it thrusts into space, stubbornly keeping vertical and smooth—and smoother still in the upper part, toward the summit. Framed by the mountain's central node and a marvelous north-facing row of peaks and pinnacles which it arrogantly dominates, it appears from the west slope, opposite that of the hollow, as a colossal pilaster jutting not far from the wall but with its smooth face soaring and severely sheer.

Man, when admiring his own constructions, delights in his work, and when he sees something similar in nature he cherishes the illusion that nature is reflecting human creation and acting as humans do. Thus fooled, he exalts his own efforts and himself, enjoying and finding beauty in natural things. This is the beauty most easily and commonly felt. But there is another beauty that is not bound to individual tastes, not the "prettiness" of the empty modern mentality, nor the philosophers' vague idea of "the Beautiful": a higher beauty that fascinates us even though inexplicable and disdainful of pleasure: the expression of power.

The inviolate idol of the snowy hollow possesses such beauty. With its austere grandeur and its unadorned nakedness, utterly devoid of any ornament, it reveals an immutable nature, an infinite self-assurance, a measureless might. It resembles no human construction, but in its extreme simplicity and severity of line it displays an individuality, emanating a mysterious suggestion of shattering hostility and a strange fascination.

Other peaks possess the beauty of power in an extraordinary way, through a combination of size, shape, and surroundings, and the different architecture of each expresses it in its own style. For as Nietzsche says, "architecture is a sort of eloquence of power expressed through forms." Both high and low, among the formidable crags and in the lofty spaces around them, the power is in the contrast, the give and take of forms and elements, which the eurythmy of the rock-faces translates in primordial symbols.

Climbers from various countries had attempted the conquest of this peak many times, in vain.

An alpinist challenge may reflect an individual's character: here, as in few other human activities, his feeling and will are truly his own.

In the most difficult climbs, the will to power is affirmed and realized in the purest way. But this affirmation has always to be set and kept at the center as the absolute signifier of values, because outside the naked will to power every will disperses in the agitated passivity of desires and impulses, in which the relative incapacity of the I to realize its own autarchy becomes objectified. With this absolute centrality I felt the problem and the search for its solution. It was a search lived as the prelude and root of the action, an intimate measuring of oneself with the difficulty, a first effort and inner development to prepare oneself for the difficulty itself, an exaltation and liberation of the immanent power. To search for oneself and to find oneself in the solution of the problem, as though on the threshold of a new existence, free and heroic: that was really what my search was. Action—in alpinism, as elsewhere—is a blind and extroverted chasing after desires, a merely external impulse, when one relies on vanity, when it serves more or less directly the incentive and opinion of others.

I roamed alone and half naked in the ecstasies of freedom, and alone I interrogated the haughty sphinx in whose face the impassibility of eternal things seemed to smile at the inanity of every effort.

Until, having found an ideal companion, in perfect harmony of will and action, the peak was attacked. But the day, clear and promising as we left, soon became overcast and ominous, and very soon the storm broke. The rain suddenly started battering violently all around on the parched rocks. We holed up wretchedly in a small alcove a little below the crest. The air was filled with electricity, and at every moment we expected some discharge to burst with thunder on its jagged outline. The rain fell thick and furiously, the wind kept driving the thick, dark fog. Our "idol" was perhaps the god of hurricanes: we could not even see it.

When we left the alcove, we were numb with cold and immobility. The freezing rain did not let up. Our soaked boots, the crumbly rock, our frozen hands and the water made the descent quite dangerous.

Slowly the weather calmed down and we returned to the refuge.

Toward eleven, the sky had rapidly and definitely cleared, so that we felt sorry not to have persisted.

Since our ideal was a route of ascent directly from the base, we decided for that day to try reaching the first projection that offered itself on the lower part, and thus see whether next time we could try a direct climb, instead of via the crest.

Intending to make this a preliminary and partial attempt, we took only a 42-meter rope, a few spare meters to make rings, some snap rings, five spikes between us, and each his ice axe; all the rest was left on the edge of the moraine. And up we went through the ice field and the adjacent scree.

The first contact with the rock found me respectful, as though timid and honored at the same time, but suddenly the difficulty stared me in the eye with a sense of mystery and secret delight. The horizon and the mountain vanished without my noticing, feelings and emotions melted away as a torrent loses itself in the alpine lake, into whose limpid mirror my consciousness seemed to have been transformed, allowing me to look into the depths, into the I, with an unknown transparency, reflecting the will to a naked action, an end in itself.

The divine game had begun, and its intoxication possessed me.

The real opponent in the climber's game is not the mountain in its stolid materiality, nor any abstract spiritual idealism, but the difficulty: that is what arouses power. It is the insatiable and tireless lover that multiplies its own offerings the more it is loved, that is no sooner possessed than it transforms and seduces one anew with other bewitching aspects until you possess it again, in an incessant combat of love and conquest.

The first gully, formed by an angle and perpendicular, ended in a hollow beneath a ledge, in which, already wakened from the first feelings of difficulty, I joined my companion. Above us the wall leaned outward, at first overhanging then gradually showing an open and superficial gully leading up to two small black hollows, round and regular, side by side and quite odd, like an owl's eyes with a fixed stare of defiance and ill-omened, which we had noticed from the snowfield that morning. From a foothold protruding to the left of the ledge, my friend carefully surveyed the overhang and attacked it.

I could see nothing as I carefully watched the slow motion of the rope, while time passed in serious and silent expectation. But in the unknown silence there was the invisible rhythm of action, till at last a shout told me to advance.

I hung on with three fingers of each hand to a single hold, brought both my feet level with my hands, simply propped up with my whole body behind; grasping with just three fingers, I withdrew one hand, and with great effort managed to grab a higher hold, then adjusted the position of my feet. Thus, I entered fully into the difficulty that followed intensely for a considerable stretch.

Every slightest protrusion or prominence that the fingers could grab, every roughness on the rock on which the soft boots could rest or prop themselves, was a subtle trick in the contest, a turn of skill, a thrill of the tense nerves, a joyous rhythm, a surge of power that had a relevance and a value more essential than fame, wealth, honors, and all the shams of so-called civilized life.

When I reached my companion, he pointed up with a grin: "Look, we're already at the 'eyes'!" And indeed those two empty sockets were there, as though astonished at our victory.

We went on without a break, straight up with a fine climb through an odd series of superimposed niches. Having crossed the frightful threshold of the overhang, we felt that we had completely penetrated our sphinx's realm, and the rocks, the patches of overhanging wall, the very air, and the silence—it all had the enchantment of the unknown, as of fabulous regions.

It became less difficult, and we now found ourselves at the opening of a first large cavern, black and dripping. A little slope of damp ground rose toward the back. To keep my boots dry, on the ascent I had tried to take advantage of a projecting rock, but at the first touch it split and collapsed. I dodged quickly to one side to avoid being hit by it, but it was not enough: one foot remained under it. I feared a fracture. When I freed my foot, the boot had a wide split on top and venous blood was clotting around a wound that was painful, but not serious.

My will had become colder and sharper, as though tempered by suffering this injury, and the ascent continued through extreme difficulties. Once we had passed the cavern, our project of making a preliminary attempt could now be counted a success. But who remembers even vaguely the plans they have made? The real climb overrides projects, intentions, and goals! Precisely because it is ascent and conquest.

The intensity of action had done away with our concepts, sensations, and memories, like useless coverings wrapped around a sick body when it really needs the sun. Nothing more intervened in the contact between us and the mountain. Distant alike from fears and hopes, there was that lucid exaltation in us, dry, interiorized, that the feeling of strength and accumulated willpower drew from the difficulties joyously overcome.

We decided to press on.

My friend went up in a straight line on the clear and smooth face, whose steepness and difficulty gradually increased.

He mastered it with the calmness of conscious strength.

It was a splendid battle! In the immense and silent abyss, the blows of his axe as he planted some safety spikes accompanied our song of life with the threat of the unpredictable.

As the ascent progressed, the face gradually lengthened, widened, and steepened. The view ran uninterruptedly over the smooth and vertiginous uniformity of the growing overhang. Above us our savage idol now showed her higher and more terribly polished part.

We began creeping up through a passage closed in like a chimney, then my companion directly engaged the face above it.

My mind, concentrated on the action, could not be distracted by thinking; the power of the impulse after the difficulties we had left behind gave it no respite. The difficulty on this stretch continued at the highest level.

It was a little before six in the evening when we reached the top.

At that instant the pincers of the difficulties opened up, silently releasing the soul and the senses in the superhuman freedom of the boundless horizons that were suddenly revealed.

The sky was opalescent; a pearly sunset illuminated the horizon, all embroidered with distant profiles. The day died slowly in the exalted quietude and the uncontaminated solitude of the peak. The mysterious breathing of the beauty ensouled us with its more intimate and profound rhythm. And only then did we truly know the sense of the virginity of the summit, consisting not in novelty, but in a purity, a pri-mordiality, and an absolute simplicity of rapport with the forces of the earth and with ourselves.

We had nothing to drink or eat, but we did not even know the exis-tence of hunger and thirst, though we had drunk nothing since morn-ing and not eaten since the previous evening.

Perhaps we too, and I too, could almost say: "The airy spirits of the heights brought me food," as the Tibetan yogi Milarepa sings in his magnificent *Song of Joy,* on returning from long isolation on the snowy peaks of the Himalayas.[3]

We only just woke to awareness of the time—and down we went, pursued by the ending of the day. Some twenty minutes had flown by on the summit.

This descent was wondrous and reckless, packed with sensations that reached unknown inner depths.

Haste and difficulty quickly compelled us to let ourselves down with the rope. I skimmed down it, grazing the smooth, sheer faces, con-stantly amazed at having ascended them.

We became more and more worried at using up our scanty equip-ment. The difficulty was not in sliding down the rope, but fixing it first and releasing it afterwards. To find a crack for the spike or a projection for the loop of rope was a problem, a pain, on this smooth and compact rock. Meanwhile the evening was starting to submerge the mountain, first darkening in the rifts and chimneys, and little by little all the lights turned gray, leaden, indistinct, as though stupefied by the twilight.

And we had no candle or torch, nothing beyond the minimal climb-ing equipment that we had taken with us at the start.

The shadows turned blue, then ever darker on the gigantic rock idol, making it grim and horrifying like the image of a savage and incomprehensible deity.

We continued to descend, our energy and will stretched to break-ing point in a desperate chase after the fading visibility. My companion hammered with epic fury.

---

3. [See Milarepa's song in *Introduction to Magic,* vol. II, 220–26. —*Trans.*]

He retied the knots on the rope loops by pulling the ends with his teeth, wrenching savagely like one possessed. And down we went on our rope, as fast as a spider seeing its web ruined.

Retrieving the rope became a worry that only ceased when the freed cord whizzed through the air to fall beneath us. Every delay in slippage, every tangle that needed undoing, was a loss of precious time.

The darkness weighed down around us and seemed to slowly penetrate the rock face. Little by little the horizon, the sky, the mountain all disappeared in the darkness of night: a night with no moon and few stars, so dark that it seemed one would never see day again.

I kept glancing down at the abyss, at whose base one could still see vaguely, like a glimmer, the white expanse of the snow, now the only and increasingly blurred sensation of the end, where the invisible walls were lost in the depths.

It was no longer possible to tell exactly where we were going. We knew that to stay on the right track we had to continue along the perpendicular, and no more. While I was thinking that we must make a bivouac, but that there was no space in which we could huddle, my friend said, without any conviction, that a few more descents would bring us to the snow.

The value, the complexity, and the significance of all the impressions of these nocturnal hours surpassed any ability to depict them.

Sometimes an acute shudder of supernatural isolation invaded me for a few instants.

Then the will suddenly reasserted itself as soon as a cry, rising from the abyss of silence, darkness, and the unknown told me that my friend had managed to find a stopping point.

Sensations alternated in my mind of an eternal night, and of an endless descent inflicted by destiny. I seemed to be realizing materially the esoteric truth that "life is a voyage through the night hours," as one of the strangest Hindu texts says.

I remember the final spike, kept as a last resort, which my companion placed in a crack found by touch, and hammered in frantically in the darkness without missing a blow; and a later descent using a minimal projection that would not be seen by day, but to the hands searching for it in the darkness seemed monumental. While I held my feet on it to tie the rope, my friend's voice suddenly gave a cry from below. He had reached the snow!

It was the end of the battle, the conclusion, the salvation after the interminable assault!

The very nearness of safety made me feel all the more the risk of the final descent. I caressed the projection as though trusting myself to the benevolence of its friction holding the rope, and went down taking meticulous care to keep it well stretched against the rock face. Once more the thought that the rope would slip from its hold obsessed my imagination with the expectation of a fatal fall: it vanished as I felt myself regularly sliding, then surged up and disappeared again as I was heading straight down into the crevice between the snow and the rock. Knowing that on one side the crevice formed a deep wedge, I aimed for the opposite side, where my companion was already awaiting me. We slithered chaotically down the snowbank and were back beside our rucksacks on the moraine.

When the lantern was lit after all that darkness, it was as splendid to us as a miniature sun! To look around us, to be sitting together, rope and axes put casually aside, stretching our legs and simply resting, with enough space to do it—to have any space at all—seemed unheard-of, prodigious! It was a respite enjoyed by every fiber of our being, the release of all tension in an echo of joy.

It was about an hour before midnight.

The air brought us no sound from the scattered villages sleeping in the low and far-off valleys.

We spoke by fits and starts, laughing and enjoying the little food we had, our muscles and nerves completely relaxed in a serenity of life, pure and joyous as infancy, stretched out in our little circle of light broken by the rocks, at the feet of the giant vanquished by day and again by night, which we felt invisibly and solemnly looming over us.

What joy of memories and power of sensations our souls had gathered in that brief time of our lives!

Certainly, the conquest of our peak was within the reach of very few, because its formidable smoothness daunted and dampened the impulse of any vainglorious desire and any foolish enthusiasm, without which man can seldom stir himself. Yet it was not the success but the resonance of the act in itself that seemed to have given the whole of nature as a gift to the soul, as though reborn.

No "sports record" as such can give this gift. One must be able to get it from an infinitely higher ascent: aiming to perform it only as the inner violation of one's own limits, as the mediation of a pure act of power, to transcend it, to purge the action from impulse and emotion and resuscitate it as freedom.

Any motive, noble or ignoble, is still always dependence; causality is a chain. But on the mountain you learn to shake it off and break it.

The world of rocks awakens nostalgic echoes of absolute freedom. "How beautiful they are, how pure, these free forces not yet stained by spirit!" wrote Nietzsche in his youth after returning from a mountain storm—but meaning by "spirit" human feelings and passions.

How important is a climb in itself? Perhaps little. What is important is the power that we can awaken in ourselves by sporting with danger, then the will entirely wills itself.

It is an immense joy to ascend and cosmically rejoice in the rocks, the sun, the elements, because only in this immediacy of rapport can one breathe the heights, the extension of the senses, the liberty.

If the *Pancatantra* says in its enigmatic way that "life is a journey during the nighttime hours," all existence is sleep and mortal torpor unless it has a sense of the end of the journey and the reawakening to day.

In the mountains we can feel the shudders of this great reawakening.

In the moutains we can find the unconquered and primordial essence of nature and of life, the light of the inner day.

In the mountains, when the abyssal voices of nature, the spare and dispassionate action, and the intense sporting with danger converge, breaking through the limited sense of life, across the threshold of the soul come subtle sensations vibrating in impossible rhythms of nonhuman music; and consciousness, as though emerging from the Nietzschian *eternal return,* as though sighting the center of the infinite circle of becoming, as though unwinding the first turns of the veil of Maya, perceives the illusion and the vanity of things; it recognizes the absolute unreality of goals, reasonings, hopes, and norms, and foreshadows its essential and positive solitude; and a sense of acting, existing, and consisting in naked power first lurks, then appears on its horizon like the imminent hurricane in the black and impenetrable night: it is the I, the All, which flashes before the image of its mask!

This is the life to be sought in the mountains, and it is the most vertiginous.

This is the reality that we have approached.

This has been our ascent.

ABRAXA

Knowledge of the Sacrificial Act

In order to introduce you to another formation, adaptation, and resolution of our fundamental ritual—a more severe and trenchant one—I would like to speak briefly about the mystery of the *sacrifices* used in Magic.

To sacrifice is to invoke, strip, dominate, transmute, in order to project—or to absorb. The operation takes as its center the body and the *blood* of a victim, because the forces you are dealing with are of such a nature that you should not offer yourself *directly* as a "magnet" and a body for their manifestation and incarnation. The ritual rhythmicizes and measures the identification: certainly you must feel in your spirit and control the forces that descend on the victim, but the integral reception should be only in the flash of the climactic moment of the kill, when the power is liberated and dominated—or projected—in a single action.

In sacrifice as in any ceremonial ritual, the key and the pivot are the purification and magical dignity of the operator. These are two conditions under which the power of consecration, imposition, and invocation is developed, or integrated, within you, which is to animate, magnetize, and enliven the ritual.

With strict abstinence, chastity, fasting, silence, isolation, and observation of all the rules that are known to you relating to spiritual and ritual purity, you must first loosen the bodily and material bonds, so that you are gradually unburdened of the dark cloud of desires, imaginations, and affections, and the solar I begins to shine in you.

Calm, free from all fear and doubt, in control of heart and mind, stopping all motions of the unstable soul and wandering thoughts, establish yourself by degrees in that I, and raise yourself to the inner light and to contemplation.

Depending on your ability, the period required will be shorter or longer: days, weeks, months. Only when you feel yourself *saturated,* in complete certitude and in equilibrium of the inner force with the magnetized and exalted sensibility, can you embark on the sacrificial action.

Before all else, formulate and fix firmly in your mind the goal and meaning of the action. Consider its parts.

First of all, the *consecration* of the victim. It is the operation through which you *open* it, specifying it as the receptacle and entry point of an entity or a force.

An animal, lacking the degree of closure that individuation brings to human consciousness, is by nature more prone to "intercourse." Only a veil separates it from the primordial powers and from the demons, or gods, of life. And the custom in certain traditions of *inebriating* the victim is intended to give an extra push to the sacralizing work that summons these powers into it, destroying its predispositions and "impurities" and making it *divine.*

I know how much more you would like me to tell you. Nonetheless, what can help you here is not what is susceptible to being *told.* It is by *seeing* that you will know. You may be sure that effective knowledge is not learned for one occasion and for one particular goal: it is what is already understood in the transformed inner vision of things, without which Magic is inert and vain. When everything speaks to you *in the language of a symbol,* that is when you have the beginnings of *expertise.*

When you no longer see the earthly animal solely as an earthly animal, you will also know the direction of sympathy and efficacy for the action of the spirit (whether or not linked to a formula or a ritual) with which the complete actuality of a power is attracted and fixed in the victim's body, which already contained it in dormant form.

Even if your consecrating virtue is complete, you do well to conform to the correspondences taught by Tradition, where every animal species is already "sacred" to a particular divinity. And when you impose a concrete goal on the sacrifice, choose for the victim that animal whose god represents the direction concordant with the nature of that goal.

However, you know that in high Magic, it is a degradation for the immediate motive to be any personal intention. The higher significance in the sacrifice is liberation, renewal of liberation, immortalization, creation. And as for the mystery, you may know it from the myths of the ancient Wisdom.

Therein you will find the doctrine about gods *created* by sacrifice, who derive their origin and essence from sacrifice, who exist through sacrifice or are confirmed and renovated in their mode of life. You will recognize this in many primordial myths: that the heroes or gods who fight against monsters, dragons, serpents, bulls, and other wild forces, and those forces themselves, *are one and the same thing.* For a force to fight against itself or even kill itself—this is the very act that makes a god. The "god" emerges from the power of chaos that reacts against itself, that shatters itself, thus freed to rise to a higher plane, making itself the principle of a law, of a power of order: thus Marduk, conqueror of Tiamat the dragon of chaos, is the cosmic regulator.[1]

This is the meaning of the sacrifice in its universal sense and on the transcendent plane. Once you comprehend that, you can come down to the sacrificial actions of men and establish the twofold direction in which they can be efficacious: through the sacrifice one can kindle and renew the very act that originally constituted the essence of a god, and which, through the violence done to chaos, was transformed into the "spirit" of a law of life or of nature; or else you can attract and confront forces still in the free and wild state, then by means of the sacrifice exert the dominating and transfiguring action on them.

Without falling into a lower magic, you can see for yourself that an immediate and specific realization can also result from adapting one or another of the sacrificial meanings just mentioned. For in the first case, by reproducing the *spirit* that constitutes a law you have the

---

1. More generally, consider the whole cycle of myths in which the generation or creation of men and of things proceeds from a sacrifice. (Note by UR)

means, through placing a command in it, of dominating that law; and in the other case, when the act is the creation of a new entity, you only have to give it as its "soul" the idea of your goal. You can do all this in the instant of the kill that frees the energy from the body, strips it bare and fixes it.

In ancient times, the temples and other places consecrated to sacrifices that were regularly performed were already saturated with occult influences and virtual presences. Today, only the subtle intellect can lead you to discover the place best suited to you. If you do not have your own operating chamber, shut off from outside influences and magnetized through rituals, you had better choose open spaces among the great natural forces, on mountains or by the sea: today, when every building is infected by the fumes and rotting ferments of the human mass.

Once you know and have firmly fixed the meaning and the goal, then act. With your mind in the Sun, and with the sign that follows and confirms the mental action, enclose yourself and the victim in a pentagram, drawn from right to left. If you have companions in the chain (and they too must first have gone through the spiritual and ritual purification), they should be arranged in an inner circle, forming a current, everything being enclosed by the interwoven rays of the pentagram.

The better you know these invocations, the greater will be their virtue of magically exalting you. Use them, placing the "direction of efficacy" in the god summoned by the ritual.

All the rest falls beyond the capacity of words: how at a given instant you *feel;* how after contact is established you should increase by degrees and uninterruptedly the intensity and saturation of the presence, magnetically concentrated on the victim; when the limit is reached at which the act of killing must strip and fully release the force; what are the skill, boldness, and rapidity of spirit by which you seize that force in the pure state, confronting and coercing its ambiguous and frightening nature, in the state in which the power, able to manifest destructively toward any closed circuit of the body and of matter, is absolute; how you can control, channel, and direct the efficacy of the energy transmuted and now passed into you—or the revelation of the god who works this—especially when you must make it the body of power of the imagination-command of a magical projection; by what ways you fix or guide it into your own body, into the chain, into other beings, animals, or things—the "digestion" of this efficacious energy—all that can only be told by your spirit, to your spirit. You have been told repeatedly about the internal structures of the actions and states in the instructions for Hermetic practice (*Introduction to Magic,* vols. I and II, passim).

Keep foremost in mind that the action only works when the saturation and the sense of certainty are absolute, when the rhythms coincide of themselves to produce the spark that makes a single thing of you, the victim, and the summoned demon.

I will give you some ritual details, adapted from formulae of the most ancient traditions. But avoid formalizing yourself. If you do not *feel* these formulae, leave them alone. They are only an outline for you. Perhaps you yourself will find and animate others of the same type.

Once the pentagram is drawn, do not move. If you have a chain inside it this will steadily accelerate the current, from left to right, raising the Sun, following our ritual. As soon as the presence or the magnetic saturation is detectable, spread your arms and *declaim:*

> By the virtue of the sacred word that turns Earth to Fire and Water to Air—and Fire to Earth, Air to Water.
> By the virtue of the power in action that unveils and strips bare.
> By the force of this living current of well-being.
> I (Name)
> Evoke from the invisible and living world of Light,
> X (Name of the God)
> On the Earth, in the Earth I evoke you.
> Burn this shadow, rend this shadow, conquer this shadow.
> Come, come, come!
> May the marvel be great,
> May the force be complete,
> Rapid as a thousand lightnings,
> As a thousand thousand Lights!

After speaking the formula, raise the right palm, then sign the victim's head with the right thumb.

Here is one formula to follow:

> *As this animal is in my power, and depends on me to kill or to spare it,*
> *Thus you depend on my power.*
> *Your life is my life and my life is your life.*
> *I dominate your life.*
> *I liberate your life.*

At the moment of killing, one part of the power rises, another incarnates, and the body of its momentary incarnation is the *blood* spilled from the victim, which is magnetized and saturated with a supranatural magical virtue. Certain ceremonial forms, not wholly distinct from lower magic, make particular use of this *blood* for communion, operation, consecration.

But you had better follow the part of the force that rises to the world of the gods, which is their "food" and ambrosia, the draught of deathlessness[2]—not that which is attracted to the world of men, and which is by nature obscure, dreadful, and difficult to control.

If you always act from the Light, fear will never get a hold over you. The moment of sacrifice was often considered as a solemn and fearful moment, and those forces that, liberated and uncontrolled, break into the world of men through the opening given to them are demonic powers of deception and malice.[3] In the Athenian Buphonia sacrifice, the sacrificer fled, throwing aside the ax, as though in a catastrophe— and similar things can be found in other traditions, together with rites

---

2. In this context, recall the Eastern doctrines about the draught of immortality (*amṛta*) created by the sacrifice, which is enjoyed at the same time by the god and the sacrificer. Cf. *Bhavagad Gita*, IV, 31: "Those who feed on the remains of the sacrificial ambrosia go to the eternal Brahman." (Note by UR)

3. This is so even when a god presides over the sacrifice, because in the sacrifice the chaos that had been dominated in him is reawakened and unfettered. Thus, one can say that the sacrificial action that fails wounds and harms a god. (Note by UR)

of purification and expiation performed by those who had taken part in the sacrifice, participating in the astral vortex of which it was the center. But all this happens only when the mind is unsound, the force unready, and the spirit impure.

Among our ancient traditions I would remind you of the sacrificial actions of the builders, destined to *create* an entity that would remain bound to a house, a temple, or a city that was to be built, as though it were its "soul." You see there clearly expressed the idea of the efficacy of the sacrificial operation for aeonic creation.

You can also revisit what I told you about the divinities who are personifications of "Victories" (see chapter VI.3, pages 204–9). You can recognize in the rhythm and progression that are developed in the heroic experience the exact phases of a sacrificial action: the emergence of the "daimon" or double, then the manifestation of Nemesis and the Furies as "goddesses of battles," then fighting and subjugation of the forces unleashed, culminating in Victory. Just as sacrificer and victim coincide here in a single being, there, as in the sacrifice, the victory can *create* a god, or bring one back to life. And as periodic sacrifices reproduce by analogy those which originally made up the substance of a god, they feed this same substance actuated and dominated within human consciousness. Thus, in Rome the bloody games and contests evoked divinities, but also, through an equivalent state identical in magical efficacy to the sacrifices, evoked the Victories, conceived of as *entities,* mystical epiphanies of which the real victories recorded in history had been only traces, signs, and symbols.

Various Commentaries

ON SACRIFICE

In the preceding article by Abraxa, sacrifice has been considered in its initiatic, magical, and operative aspect. In order to give it a more general context, it may be useful to mention other sides of the sacrificial rite, well known to tradition and belonging to a more limited domain.

The first case concerns what was alluded to when speaking of the "law of beings," about the possibility of deflecting the effects of certain created causes (see *Introduction to Magic,* vol. I, 167–72). Here it is a question of *expiatory* or *vicarious victims,* upon which a force that would normally strike another object, another being, or even a community is made to discharge itself. This situation is obviously different from what Abraxa was considering.

We meet another aspect of the sacrifice specifically in the Hebraic and Judeo-Christian tradition. It is the sacrifice as *ransom,* differing from the previous one by its moral aspect and by its particular assumption. Namely, it presupposes a nature that was originally evil, or a fault committed that the sacrifice expiates through bloodshed. In the latter case the sacrificial theory tends to be "de-realized" in that it no longer concerns relations between forces, but justifies itself in legalistic terms. Thus, in the crudest interpretation of the myth of "original sin," the fault is understood as an offense and transgression toward the Creator, who has to be placated by offering him a sacrifice. Naturally, this all belongs in the field of pure exotericism.

There is more foundation to the concept of a fault in objective and amoral terms, like a poison that has to be eliminated if there is fear of its associated effects. There is also the idea that specific attitudes and specific actions confer on certain forces or entities a power over man and, as it were, infect his blood with them. Hence another aspect of sacrifice: as purification, a recurrent aspect in ancient Greek ritual. Related to that, the sacrifice can also take on the sense of an offering that transfigures, elevates, reintegrates.

The ritual *killing,* when connected to a meaning of this kind, may undergo an interiorization. Thus, Hindu tradition recognizes the equivalence between the literal sacrificial action and ascesis, or yoga. The view here, in comparison to the Judeo-Christian view just mentioned, is broadened and purged because it does not involve the concept of guilt or "original sin." It simply derives from what is called the *samsaric* state of existence. Sacrifice or ascesis are both effective for "killing" a current of samsaric force, to obtain from its death a higher life.

In some developments of Christian mysticism one comes close to meanings of this kind, when Christ's sacrifice was not conceived of as a vicarious expiation to placate the divinity, but as the indication of a sort of action through which one "dies" to be able to rise again and attain "salvation." But we will address this in one of the next articles. As confirmation of the exoteric nature of Catholicism, it is interesting that such an interpretation has been condemned in a conciliar decision.

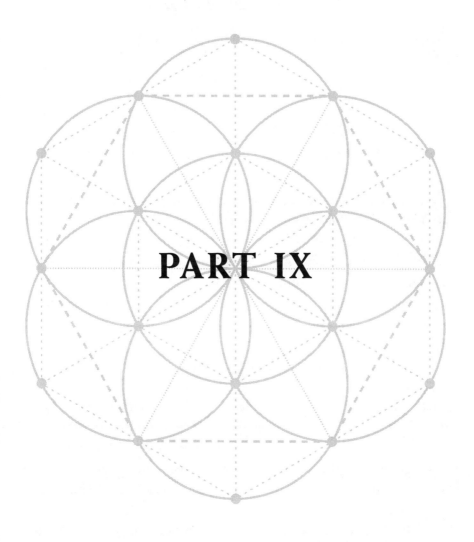

PART IX

Noise

Silence, silence: its voice has such power that nothing can suffocate it. The synonym of eternity, it is hidden behind every appearance of our life: it is the history behind our news, the abyss of our heights. While we wander among thousands of beings who brush past us and are similar to us, while we all have identical goals, though some of us are going north and others south, suddenly a voice resounds that cuts through the street clamor: "What will become of them in fifty years?"

When this question flashes into our mind, our companions dissolve as though under X-rays and show the skeleton beneath their phantom appearances. They are phantoms clothed in black, and nothing more. The one at the head of them all who seems to have defied the common law is the first to vanish. We are walking through the paths of a cemetery; the houses and grand shops lining it are so many tombs, like the ancient mausoleums flanking the Appian Way.

Still the line goes on: and the phantom beside us seems to be different from us, seems to have avoided the flash of revelation. But it is pallid like us: it is our living mirror.

Everyone has armored his own skeleton with a different armor, confident in having found what none will attack: but it is enough to look into his eyes to see in their depths the same fear as in a thousand other eyes. So as not to teeter, he hangs on to something outside himself, created by him and needed by him. He needs it because it *makes a noise,* because with its din it covers up the silence.

What would machines be good for, if they weren't noisy? The first requirement of the machine is to make noise. First it must make noise, then something else, anything else! Admittedly, everyone who invents a machine is thinking only of what it will produce: but go down there into his mind, where even he dare not tread, and you will see that at the root of his need for work is the need for noise, always noise to suffocate that silence that never sleeps. Let the drive belt stop for just a minute, and the motor stop, and you will see him who was drunk on it sober up and stagger, as if one of those soldiers of the great army of life had been caught in the gearwheels of death and was scarcely left with one sleeve of his garment.

To be among many, so as not to be alone—so that when one is silent, the other speaks—that is the battle tactic. The Napoleon who gave this rule did not have an armed enemy before him, but he had other beings similar to him, slaves like him and, like him, fighting a battle in which they would have been defeated. What does it matter? Their sons are there to win the battle that the fathers lose. Not a moment of truce— that is the important thing: and the steering wheel left by the fallen is taken in the hands of the survivor, so that he will drive the machine further on, where the other could not go.

A strange enemy, an extraordinary purpose! The more one wins, the more one has to win; the further one goes, the further off one is. The more the motors of life rumble, the more one hears that silence which will not vanish, as the drop of oil will not blend with water. The faster the machine goes, the more it seems to be standing still.

Listen while they speak in dreams, these great captains out of uniform: look at their hearts through the slackened armor. They dream of being alone, and in the horror of their solitude they turn to ice. Because they sleep so little, they are such early risers. They are wearier in the morning than in the evening. Look at them: unarmed all night, they have fought with the enemy whom they fled from in the day under the pretext of heading toward him: and now they run, run, run for fear that he will reattack, seize them by the throat, and stare into their eyes. They run like someone fleeing from a burning house, they run like someone still spattered by the blood of the murder victim.

They have burned up their life, they have killed themselves. How can one not pity them?

IX.2

PAUL MASSON-OURSEL[1]

On the Role of Magic in Hindu Speculation

The most ancient of Indian texts, the *Atharvaveda,* consists of a collection of magical formulae. The Tantras, in which the latest Hindu syncretism comes to expression, provides magic with various practical or speculative methods acquired through an experience of almost three millennia. Thus, magic in India is found both at the beginning and end of an immense and complex evolution.

In the process an extreme variety of cults and philosophical reflections often managed to derive both religion and metaphysics from magic. But even then, the magical views and methods remained unaltered.

What we call magic is the human presumption of acting on nature in an immediate way, by means of states of consciousness or psychic operations. To cure a fever with quinine assumes that one believes in the intrinsic value of a material substance. To cure the same fever with verbal recipes implies faith in the efficacy of a word that is psychic, both on the level of its pronunciation and its comprehension. Magic should be defined through the mental character of its means. In particular, we

---

1. [A prefatory note reads: *"Report written for the 'Group of Ur' by Professor Paul Masson-Oursel of the École des Hautes-Études of Paris."* This translation takes account of the presumed French original, in Julius Evola, *Tous les écrits de Ur & Krur . . . signés Arvo-Agarda-Iagla* (Milan: Archè, 1986), 297–305. *—Trans.*]

should avoid calling its methods arbitrary: the rules of magical causation show no less rigor than what we moderns call natural laws.

The necessary and sufficient condition for magical efficacy is the exact knowledge of the appropriate recipe, and of the occasion on which it is to be used. The magical spirit is not suited to approximations, any more than the positivist spirit is. For India, in every circumstance, in every respect, there is no truth but the exact, *satyam;* nothing correct but the timely: the action performed at the right moment, *kalpa;* nothing regular but the canonic, *pramānam.*

Now, the distinction between the psychic and the non-psychic does not enter into Eastern thinking in the same way as in European philosopy. Often these two forms of existence are not at all opposed to one another, but continuously connected by means of certain mixed or intermediary functions. When they are opposed, as for the Jains, the Vaisheshika, and other schools, it is in this sense: that the spirit is life, *jīva,* whereas materiality is reduced to particles capable of only motion or repose. Or for the Samkhya or yoga, it is in the sense that the spirit sees and enjoys, while nature "evolves," acting and transforming itself.

Moreover, "seeing" according to the Hindu view has nothing of the passive θεωρία of the Greeks, the reflection of an image in a mirror. To see is to shine, as much as to be illumined; it is to comprehend clear ideas, rather than to possess them innately; to assimilate through analysis and synthesis. The fusion of psychological terms with prefixes of *vi* or *sam* is the indisputable sign of this.

To enjoy is not limited to feeling an external influence: it is more a case of penetrating, elaborating, creating forms as much immaterial as material.

To live is not to contemplate but to exploit a fund of mnemonic or operative resources, inherited from the past; to create without limits new resources for the future.

If spiritual existence is equivalent to action, why should the spirit not be able to act beyond itself? It may be impeded by the fact of finding itself wholly or partially enclosed in our body, like balls in a sack. Yet India has never conceived of the "interiority" of consciousness like that. The spirit escapes from the body not only in death and in its image—sleep—but also in most of its perceptions. It perceives in the measure that it illuminates or forms its objects. Given such a theory of knowledge, magic is in no way paradoxical or transgressive, as our modern Western prejudices would have it.

• • •

According to Eastern scholasticism, as in our own, human activity admits of three modalities: words, thoughts, and actions.

Words are the essential part of primitive magic. The Vedas control nature through them, not only as *mantras*,[2] but also as hymns praising a divinity. Inasmuch as words are audible and articulated, they exist absolutely, and this is why they can command events. It is said that they were "seen" by the *rishis* of deepest antiquity, or else received as sonorous revelation, which means that these sounds exist in and of themselves, like the Ideas of Plato. The sacrifice sets these operative formulae to work and only has recourse to the gods—personified cosmic or ritual forces—insofar as they obey the verbal injunctions. When the formulae are pronounced in full observance of the science of the word, they are in reality more sovereign than the gods themselves. The *Pūrvā Mīmāṃsā,* an exegesis of the Vedas, is equivalent to a grammar of Vedic sounds. Later, Tantrism established a similar grammar for sounds in general, compared to other modes of expression. In fact, colors, contacts, odors, and tastes also offer languages that can correspond to that of articulate sounds, following precise rules. Hinduism inherited the dictionary of these parallelisms and equivalents from Brahmanism, and conceived of them both as an integral science and as a universal technology.

The supreme status of Vāc, the word, and above all that of Brahman, the ritual formula, testifies to the prestige that India attributed to the word as key to knowledge and power. The groups immune to this prestige are few and mostly isolated: the deniers of the Vedas (*Vedanindaka*), freethinkers or sophists; materialists, Buddhists, and Jains, indifferent to the Vedic tradition and much more concerned with thoughts and

---

2. On the *mantra,* see the special study devoted to it in *Introduction to Magic,* vol. I, 338–45.

acts than with words. Yet one cannot ignore the late formation of a Hindu-influenced Buddhism, which teems with *mantras*.

• • •

To admit the autonomy of thought to the point of universal jurisdiction is not a magician's attitude, as we see it. By labeling this attitude as rationalism, we even claim the contrary. It is not so in India, since the civilization of that country has never believed that man lacks that regulating function that, following certain Greek schools and certain Cartesians, we call *logos* or reason. Ancient Buddhism, without postulating an absolute Spirit, expects the salvation given by enlightenment from thought alone, that is, from an exhaustive discernment that frees one from transmigration inasmuch as it suppresses "ignorance" and "attachment." This integral intellect is not magic at all: but that does not prevent that when preaching to the ignorant, to make himself accessible to inferior minds, a Buddha proceeds with a spell (*nirmāṇa*), just like the Asuras of the Vedic pantheon. Mitra and Varuna possessed their phantasmagoria (*māyā*) as an instrument of action to maintain the law (*ṛta*). Magic puts itself at the service of the *dharma,* even when a purely intelligible law is recognized under that name.

Intellectualist on principle, Buddhist philosophy has investigated the contents of those forms of existence that it calls the *dharmas*. The school of the "Lesser Vehicle" (Hinayana) has classified them; the school of the "Greater Vehicle" (Mahayana) has criticized and often dismissed them, declaring their vacuity. It goes so far as to posit this paradoxical equation: *saṃsāra = nirvāṇa,* in other words, that relative and painful existence does not differ, at base, from absolute liberation, nor being from nonbeing, nor happiness from misery. This shows at least that India may mistrust the magic of ideas, while only in exceptional cases does it doubt the magic of words.

Nevertheless, it believes in a certain magic of thought. A disposition of the spirit or an intention are not reduced to subjective epiphenomena: they act on reality both near and far because they are part of that reality. In Buddhism the thought of the *bodhi,* the wish to promote the well-being of all creatures, contains an efficacy of the utmost impor-

tance. For every Hindu the last thought at the moment of death partly
decides the destiny of the soul. Subtle techniques, cultivated assiduously
and traditionally, train the individual to immerse himself with sufficient mastery in the anonymous and universal spirituality, to find there
a long-forgotten past and to influence other minds at a distance. To our
eyes these efforts seem like "occultism," but to the eyes of the East they
appear as positive duties.

• • •

The magic of action, in short, is not conceived of except through a
purely spiritual activity. To give form by means of material operations is
no longer magic—no more in Asia than in Europe.

India very soon became convinced of the fact that action enslaves.
Whether good or ill, it demands retribution, and consequently after
death sows new births ad infinitum. Thus, *karman* brings about
saṃsāra, and reciprocally liberation requires the extinction of *karman.*
However, one still entertains the possibility of a certain salvific action:
the sacrificial act; and one continues to admit that beyond the intellect the operation in which an *ātman* or a *purusha* depends on itself
alone, without contamination on the part of cosmic relativity, shines in
absolute freedom. A Jain, a Brahman, and a Buddhist usually agree in
giving to this nonaction, which is the only true action because it is perfect autonomy, the name of *vīrya*; and when the theorists fail to discuss
it, it is because such an affirmation goes without saying. It is only the
Europeans who deceive themselves about it.

This pure act, to which certain Greeks have attributed a "geome-
trizing" quality, was readily admitted by the Hindus to work extraordinary marvels. Yet its spontaneity had nothing accidental or capricious
about it. Although activated by it, the worlds that it creates are not contingent, since Shiva or Vishnu institutes them by means of a regular
necessity, in the same way that the Buddhas, in the unlimited realizations determined by the *sādhana,* all follow the same career at more or
less length: their works of perfect beings, even if they differ from one
another, only do so in their more or less perfect and profound assimilation to total spirituality. And since here Buddhism and Brahmanism

meet, we have certainly arrived at one of the fundamental convictions of that whole civilization.

Hindu realism is not a realism of sensualists nor of arithmeticians, but of magicians—Hindu idealism is not an idealism of aesthetes or geometers, but again a magical idealism. Why should one be surprised, if over there the real is measured by *doing,* more than by *being?*

Esotericism and Christian Mysticism

More than once it has been said in these pages that Christianity represents a religious system that contains various traditional elements but lacks an esoteric and initiatic counterpart. Compared to what was normal in the principal ancient or non-European traditions, this is quite an anomaly, and it certainly does not support the claims to superiority asserted by the religion that has come to predominate in the West.

As for those traditional elements, they do not apply to Christianity as such, namely as a pure evangelical doctrine, but to the *corpus* (body) of Catholicism, in relation to the symbols, myths, rituals, and dogmas by which it defines its orthodoxy. Here a number of elements take a simple religious form and value, while also being valid on a higher plane and thus *catholic* in the etymological sense of "universal."

Catholicism lacks an esotericism because in its hierarchy there is no regular élite with adequate authority that, through possessing the requisite knowledge, would be conscious of the deeper dimension of those elements: the metaphysical and meta-religious dimension.[1]

---

1. Referring to one of the "intellectual gifts of the Holy Spirit," Thomas Aquinas mentions the comprehension of the profound meaning of the symbols and Holy Scriptures. But this remains no more than a statement, because neither in Aquinas nor in the other Church authors is there any concrete example of this kind of interpretation. In the

As regards the experiential side, one would have to tackle the very complex problem of the significance of everything ritual and sacramental in Catholicism, deciding on the analogy or the difference between the religious and the initiatic levels. At the basis even of a religious tradition, as Catholicism is, there is a spiritual influence and its transmission in an uninterrupted chain through regular and well-defined rituals. In Catholicism this continuity centers on the so-called "apostolic succession." The main aspect of the transmission is bound up with the ordination of priests and bishops. The other sacraments, beginning with baptism, are intended to admit, integrate, and confirm the individual within the traditional current, by means of the transformation in his nature supposedly produced by the virtue of the principal rituals.

Naturally, this structure does not belong to Catholicism alone, but is found in every traditional form, even if not specifically initiatic. But in Catholicism the claim is more explicit that the ritual has the effect of a supranaturalization and a divinification of human nature,[2] which original sin would otherwise have rendered corrupt and helpless: hence the idea that the Christian represents the spiritual man par excellence

---

(*cont. from p. 287*) Church Fathers, for example in Origen, one finds the distinction between three meanings of the scriptures: corporeal (historic), psychic (moral), and pneumatic (spiritual), the last of which is to be discovered "anagogically" by using a "spiritual intelligence." This proposes to "transform the sensible Gospel into the spiritual Gospel," on the principle that "the Savior has chosen to make symbols of his own spiritual actions." But in practice it is reduced to an allegorical interpretation of the Old Testament that aims to make it a prefiguration of the New Testament; and its final conclusion is always the Christian mystery, whereas the esoteric interpretation would relate this mystery—as a particular expression—to a metaphysical, universal, and supra-Christian plane. The fact that these authors touch on so many points of Judeo-Christian scripture that do contain initiatic elements, without even mentioning them, shows the difficulty of crediting them with the gift of "gnosis."

2. In this respect, the words of the liturgy for Holy Saturday concerning baptismal water are typical: "Who [i.e., the Holy Spirit] by a secret mixture of his divine virtue may render this water fruitful for the regeneration of men, to the end that those who have been sanctified in the immaculate womb of this divine font, being born again a new creature, may come forth *an entirely celestial offspring*." [English translation of the Tridentine text from William Whitmee, compiler, *Lent and Holy Week in Rome* (Rome: Valentini, 1896), 386, adapted to reflect Evola's wording. —*Trans.*]

compared to the non-Christian, and that salvation is only in the mystical Body of Christ, which is to say in the Church as a community and chain formed by ritual and endowed with the corresponding spiritual influence. Objectively speaking, this claim can only serve for Catholic "internal use" and has no justification, because any regular tradition can make the claim with as much right as Catholicism. Every regular tradition is likewise based on an influence from above, which transforms the individual's naturalistic element and gives rise to a new current among the forces of the world. In point of fact, one cannot see where the Christian has shown himself superior to members of other traditions, or that he possesses a spiritual dimension absent elsewhere.

It is more important to point out the seldom-mentioned fact that in Catholic orthodoxy the ritual is thought to possess the same characteristics of objectivity and independence from sentiment, from "psychology," and even from morality, as belong to the magical and initiatic order. This is visible in the baptismal ritual, given that its effect is supposedly independent of any intention or merit of the person baptized (as is obvious when applied to newborn infants); likewise, in the fact that the sacred quality induced in a regularly ordained priest is acquired once and for all, and cannot be lost through moral turpitude or even lack of faith. The same applies in principle to other rites and sacraments of Catholicism.[3]

When the conditions are present for the real efficacy of the ritual, and when its survival is not merely on the level of devout fervor and mysticism, one may admit that there is a certain nonhuman and sacralizing power in Catholic ritual and sacrament. But even then, one cannot confuse the order to which it belongs with the initiatic order, much less think that the former could take the place of the latter. René Guénon has defined the difference as follows: religious ritual enables a participation in the suprasensible order, but keeps within individual limits, whereas initiatic ritual realizes participation of a supraindividual

---

3. Strictly speaking, Catholic theory exceeds all bounds in its belief in the magical power of the ritual. An example of this is the power to "absolve" through the ritual of penance, which would certainly suspend the karmic law of cause and effect.

character; the former aims at "salvation" of the individual's soul, in terms of prolonging its individual existence after death; the latter aims, instead, at true immortality. But the most essential difference is in the presence or absence of the theistic premise in the concept of the sacred. Everything religious, and especially Christianity, has as its limit the idea of a personal God, distinct from the creature. The idea is foreign to it of a plane on which this distance is abolished by the supreme metaphysical identity, which is what is meant by initiatic "liberation" and "awakening."

In a complete tradition, religion and initiation are two domains that do not exclude one another, but while keeping their distinction allow for a passage, whereby that which has a religious value can at a higher level take on an initiatic one. However, when this is not the case, as in Catholicism, the religious rituals seem somewhat like a meaningless and deceptive parody of initiatic rites: a parody sometimes verging on profanization when on the experiential side the highest peak is represented by *mysticism* alone.

It is an absolutely essential point, though generally unknown, that mysticism and initiation are two different things. There is a common tendency to reduce very different states to mysticism. There are certainly cases in which the mystic passes beyond the sphere defined by his path and arrives at transcendent realizations; but that implies a veritable *metanoia* (see *Introduction to Magic*, vol. I, 49, 58) and is always an exception—to say nothing of the fact that such realizations, under those conditions, almost always seem fragmentary and confused. Furthermore, mysticism in Christianity takes a typical form, set up as though in a closed system, where those exceptions are extremely rare.[4] In Catholicism especially, mysticism is presented as the simple continuation of the religious and sacramental experience, and the *cognitio Dei experimentalis* (experiential knowledge of God), which is its essence, despite the doubt that certain expressions may arouse, remains in the field of subjectivity and emotionality, and has little to do with pure

---

4. After the period of the Greek Fathers, it was almost exclusively limited to German mystics, most notably Meister Eckhart.

intellectuality, with the effective destruction of the human nature, and with real deification.

• • •

At any rate, it may be useful to our readers to go deeper into the matter, considering in various instances the meaning of Christian ascesis and mysticism and evaluating them from the esoteric standpoint.

The first thing to mention, in the history of Christian mysticism itself, is a process more or less of degradation. If we go back to the first centuries of the Church, we find in the Fathers a number of elements still connected to initiatic teachings, for the simple reason that they developed in a milieu where currents of past and present mystery wisdom and Neoplatonism were still alive and influential. But from Augustine onward, and especially later with the Spanish mystics, we find a growing humanization and psychologization of Christian mysticism, which even the Thomist current could not avoid. The subject of mystical experience is increasingly the soul, not the spirit: the emotional aspect prevails, and moralizing views take precedence over ontological and existential ones.

The basic characteristic of Christian mysticism is passivity. According to Aquinas's own conception, "The fundamental element of mystical contemplation consists of a passive movement of love for God, which usually leads to a certain feeling of his presence."[5] This "is not the product of our activity, although usually preceded by ascesis and meditation and normally accepted as the reward of one's own efforts. But it depends on God's initiative; and our spirit finds itself passive there, although it reacts vitally under the divine impulse."[6] This idea of passivity is underlined by the theory of a double grace, one called "sufficient" and connected to the normal Christian life, and the other extraordinary, due to the mystical gifts of the Holy Spirit, which alone would permit a properly supranatural development. The

---

5. Fr. F. D. Joret, *La contemplation mystique selon S. Tomas d'Aquin,* Italian translation (Turin, 1942), 11, and chap. 5.
6. Joret, *La contemplation mystique,* 9.

very arising in the soul of love for God—which takes the place here of the fire of the initiatic intellectual ascesis—is taken as an effect of divine grace.

Christian ascesis, especially at its origins, has shown some positive aspects as preparation for contemplation. We will mention them.[7]

A first directive of ascesis is isolation and simplification. It is justified in terms of an analogy that refers less to Christ than to the Father, and reflects the earlier pre-Christian ideal of "deification." "The man who through the gift of grace and his untiring ascetic efforts may come to resemble God must need also be an image of the simplicity and unity of God. . . . As his deification increases, the man approaches ever nearer to the perfect divine simplicity that asks nothing outside itself and is sufficient unto itself. It is evident that a theology that [like the Greek] assigns such an important part to the concept of deification and conceives of God primarily under the aspect of a unique, simple, and self-sufficient being should see the ideal of Christian perfection in the man who is completely free from all passions and who aspires toward God by reproducing, as far as he can, his unity and simplicity" (*AC,* 34). The anchoritic ideal was originally no different, except that the external, material isolation in that case must have had only a symbolic and ritual value, hence that of a discipline limited to the starting period. At a higher degree, the *extra mundum fieri,* isolating oneself from the world, had no need to happen materially, but only in the spirit. In that respect Christian and initiatic ascesis can agree.[8]

Ascetic detachment can also take the form of *instabilitas loci* (shifting of place) and *xeniteia* (living abroad). The detachment from one's own land and family or tribe, the refusal of a fixed abode, wandering, going to foreign and distant lands—all that can also have a symbolic and ritual value, to impress the idea that one is not in this world as in a permanent seat and as though in one's native land, but

---

7. We refer here to two works by Fr. A. Stolz, *L'ascesi cristiana* (Brescia, 1944) and *Le Teologia della mistica,* 2nd ed. (Brescia, 1947), belonging to the movement that is trying today to revalue Greek Patristics. We refer to them, respectively, as *AC* and *TM.*
8. Compare in Islam, which has no monastic asceticism, the concept of *zuhd,* which is not a renunciation made materially but an inner detachment.

as travelers and exiles, not forgetting one's celestial end and origin.[9] As we know, this meaning was very much alive in original Buddhism, and we might add, with special reference to the active way, that it was not foreign to the chivalric ideal, in the form of the "knight-errant." But it should be borne in mind that Christianity lacks premise for the coherent realization of this kind of meaning, because it rejects the initiatic theory of the preexistence of the soul before this earthly life. Only with reference to such a theory can earthly existence signify a transit, for one who has come from afar and who is turning again toward other states of being.

Christian ascesis also knows the use of *silence*. "It is not just a renunciation of communication with other men, but also a positive factor of inner life" (*AC,* 62). We know of the part that the discipline of silence played among the Pythagoreans, and also of the meaning of yogic and initiatic silence. However, Christian ascesis almost wholly lacks the practice of the most interiorized degree of this discipline, which is silence not only of spoken words but also of thoughts (Ibn-Arabi's "not talking to oneself"). True, it knows the so-called prayer of quietude; we find the expression *quies contemplationis* (the quiet of contemplation); and Saint Gregory, among the conditions for mystical contemplation, mentions freedom from the *noise* of thoughts (*TM,* 112). But Christian ascesis has no precise and active method for it, such as is known in the East. And in monasticism, which replaces the hermit by the conventual ideal, more consonant with the collectivizing trend of Christianity, there is also a hypertrophy of the liturgical element, which predominates over the individual discipline of silence even in contemplative orders like the Carthusians, Carmelites, or Camaldolites.

In Christianity the state that we call "silence" tends less to follow techniques than to cultivate certain inner conditions. This includes the so-called cognition of external things. It is "strictly knowledge of Satan's dominion, by seeing the power that he wields over the world of the senses and in recognizing the true place that material things

---

9. *AC,* 53–60. From this viewpoint, persecutions, expulsions, and the like may serve as extraordinary means used by God to remind us what our true homeland is.

ought to have within the divine plan. This is knowledge that should not remain purely speculative: the soul must at the same time put it into practice, freeing itself from the intemperate affection for creatures, incompatible with the life of union with God." Some maintain that such "knowledge" has to be received from angels, because no natural and human science can give it to the soul (*AC,* 130–33). Initiatically, this corresponds to the "separation of the real from the unreal," which is achieved essentially by way of pure intellect, disconnected from the emotional entity; the neutralization of the "demonic" forces is a natural consequence of it. Secondly, and with the same intention, it is said that the Christian's soul must know what it is before God, which is equivalent to "being convinced of one's own nothingness, being freed from egotism and released from one's own will." Such a discipline, however, suffers the distortion of the Christian way of understanding "mortification" and the passive "creaturely" attitude. Initiatically, it is a matter of "disidentification" and surpassing oneself as a simple individual being: a process that does not happen through abasement and humility, nor with reference to the image of God as a distinct being, but in conceiving of one's own person as an incidental mask, irrelevant to the true I, like the consciousness of an actor who does not confuse himself with the part he is playing. In any case, these are the two chief ways, following the knowledge of external things and of oneself as an individual, in which the Christian ascetic tries to favor the *quies contemplationis* (silence of contemplation) and to be no longer subject to the things around him, nor to passions and vain desires.

If we now go beyond the preparatory degrees of Christian ascesis to consider those which lead to realization and to mysticism proper, the fundamental and almost exclusive reference point is the imitation of Christ on a sacramental basis. Here we leave behind the purely devotional and emotional forms that are of no value to us; how they could have taken root in generally active and willful races, like the Western ones, remains an enigma. The mystical outlook as found on a slightly higher plane is as follows: Christ has transfigured human nature, which he assumed by incarnating, in the body of the Resurrection and Ascension. And the glorification of the body of Christ must be understood in the deepest sense, wherein the Redemption is the restoration and perfection of our bodily life in Paradise. Christian ascesis therefore regards the Christ event as the path to glorification, referring to the restoration of the Adamic state in which the body was completely subject to the soul, and the sensorial part to the spirit. And since in Christ's redemptive work the path to a renewed harmony between soul and body passed through his death, and because we too must follow this path so as to ensure our body's victory over the effects of original sin, so Christian ascesis has as its pivot the concept of mortification, of dying and rebirth in Christ (*TM,* 182–83).

This is supposed to have already been activated in the sacramental domain, starting with baptism. It is believed that the redemptive and sanctifying grace in which man participates through baptism already contains the seed of the mystical, supranatural life, because one is baptized in the sign of Jesus's death and the crucifixion of the former man. While in baptism the faithful imitates and follows Christ in death, in the Eucharist, which is the food and nourishment of new life, he participates mystically in the sacrifice, in the resurrection and the ascension: a participation that is real in the sacramental mystery, even though accomplished in a veiled and invisible way, inaccessible to our experience (*AC,* 71–79). This is why the idea prevails in Catholic orthodoxy that there is no real discontinuity between the sacramental life of the common believer and the mystical life: the latter is not exceptional, but already contained as a seed in the former. The mystic, instead of leaving the seed of union with God dormant, activates the energy for realizing this union as an *experience* (*TM,* 44–50). A more concrete interpretation is as follows: the ritual (sacramental) participation in the death and resurrection of Christ does not transform the whole man at a stroke. Instead it is the inward man (ἔσω ἄνθρωπος, Romans 7:22) that is to be transformed. Thereupon the ascetic, helped by a special grace, must little by little kill off the "laws of sin" in his limbs and thus, following the new supranatural principle of life that he has received, prepare a new body for the resurrection of the flesh, after physical death has finally divested him of the "body of sin" (*TM,* 39–42). However, in dogmatic terms this realization is postponed until the time of the Last Judgment. It is not admitted that it could be achieved while alive.

We will now see how to evaluate this whole doctrine from our point of view. We hardly need point out here that the scheme of a death which opens the way to the supranatural order is not specifically Christian; even if it is not indispensable for every path of spiritual realization (because the latter does not necessarily always involve a crisis), it can have initiatic value. What is specific to Catholicism is the idea that it is not an exceptional and perilous initiatic operation, but the religious rite open to all that has the power to induce a supranatural quality in man, even if only in germ and potential, and to bring it about from the outside, without the subject participating or even being conscious of it, as is obviously the case with infant baptism. Moreover, if, as mentioned, there is talk about ulterior actions of grace and the Holy Spirit to favor mystical development, this view potentially involves a dangerous confusion of levels. If sacramental death, resurrection, and glorification are conceived of in terms of *reality,* they cannot be anything but symbols and prefigurations, allusions to an order that transcends the generic sacralization associated with the religious life. It is quite wrong to suppose that the Christian who has been baptized and has participated in the other sacraments of his tradition finds himself at any advantage for the future realizations of an effective initiation. The Alexandrian distinction between the *pistikos* and the *pneumatikos,* that is, between the simple believer and the gnostic or initiate, holds good. Mystical experience may implant the idea that it does not necessarily imply a break, but can be quite a natural development of the life that the Christian already believes to be supranaturalized through the sacraments. But neither the sacramental nor the mystical life goes beyond the subjective, psychological, and moral plane, whereas initiation has an ontological and supra-individual character. In regard to the former one can at best speak of *sanctity,* not of *deification.*

As for formal correspondences, we can mention one detail: baptism is a simple ritual imitation of contact with the "Waters," of the "dissolution" in the life principle that is prior to and above any individuation or form: an experience that in its radical, exceptional, and even dangerous character can obviously have nothing to do—unless, if you insist, invisibly—with Christian baptism.[10] The notion of the "glorified body," in which the law of death is vanquished, entered Christianity directly from the earlier mystery traditions, but in becoming the dogma of the resurrection of the flesh or of purely eschatological prospects in the afterlife, it lost its concrete and initiatic significance. Much the same scheme is found in the Eucharistic rite of *transmutatio:* the bread counts as body, the wine as blood and soul. Both elements are *transformed* and when, after that, a piece of the host is placed in the wine, it signifies the joining of the transfigured soul with the body in the manner of the resurrection body or the immortal body of Christ. Nowadays it seems very superstitious to suppose that there is anything more than a simple allegory in the eucharistic participation, with the effects of moral elevation and, if you like, mystical transport: certainly not what always counts as the extreme limit of realization possible for an adept in this world. In regard to all this, anyone who has a notion of what is really involved would more likely think of a profanation.[11]

Apart from the hoped-for intervention of grace, no precise path is indicated for the Christian mystic in the domain of realization, namely of the development and actualization of the influences induced in the sacraments. There are only the simple, subjective attitudes corresponding to the so-called theological virtues of faith, hope, and love. "Mortification" is imagined in essentially moral terms, with due emphasis on everything that is suffering and "penitence." This is utterly incompatible with what suits a sane and normal Western human. Due to the sense of "guilt" and congenital sinfulness of which everyone is supposed to be conscious, we know what a pathological course Christian mysticism has often taken. Besides, prayer and oration, itself understood as a gift of the Holy Spirit, is thought of as the fundamental mechanism of

---

10. The Gospel mentions a baptism of fire, beyond of that of water. This double baptism and double regeneration correspond with two phases of the initiatic work, called in Hermetism *albedo* and *rubedo.*

11. See the essay on the "immortal body" in *Introduction to Magic,* vol. I, 196–202.

the mystic way, so that some consider ecstasy itself to be a degree of it, indeed the highest.[12]

Already for Pseudo-Dionysus the Areopagite, the basic phases of Christian mysticism were the purgative life, the illuminative life, and the unitive life: a formal scheme that can also be valid in the context of the initiatic path. However, things are very different in reality. Thus, concerning the last phase, Guénon is absolutely right when he points out the confusion in the mystics' use of the terms "union" and "unitive life." "This union does not, in fact, have the same significance as in yoga and its equivalents, to which the similarity is altogether superficial. It is not that it is illegitimate to use the same word, because even in current language one speaks of union between beings in many cases in which there is evidently no identification between them, to any degree; but one must be careful not to confuse different things under the pretext that a certain term designates them both."[13] However, it is significant how often the symbolism of marriage is used for the mystical union. Does that not indicate a unity that maintains the distinction, as happens in the uniting of a man with a woman, in the same way that in prayer, even at its highest degrees, there remains the relationship between a "I" and a "thou"? In Christian mysticism one can only speak by analogy of a *cognitio Dei experimentalis*—experiential knowledge of God. A state of "eccentricity" (in the sense of non-centrality) is essential

---

12. *AC*, 121. A contemporary writer, Frithjof Schuon, who has tried to find initiatic perspectives in Christianity, believes that the active counterpart of the passive participation mediated by the sacraments is the practice of invoking the salvific name of Christ (with special reference to the Eastern Church). This is one of the most primitive techniques for "killing the *manas*," that is, neutralizing the mental I, analogous to the ceaseless repetition of a "divine Name" in Islam. The abuse of the liturgy in the Catholic contemplative orders, objectively speaking, has no other result. Beside the negative aspect, it is problematic that the "virtue of the name" should also facilitate certain states of illumination. It is surely a chancy thing to do, and one needs to have confidence in the protective action of the sacraments in order to exclude the possibility of action by very different extrasensible influences, once the *manas* is "killed." In any case, the mystic has little chance of correctly interpreting the phenomena that occur, because he stays on an emotional rather than an intellectual plane, and the Christian devotional setting with its various images may serve to mislead rather than help him.

13. "Contemplation directe et contemplation par réflet," *Études traditionnelles* VI (1947), 140.

to it, almost without exception. For that matter, the very word "ecstasy" indicates the same thing, for it means "going out of oneself." Initiatically, it is more a case of the opposite, namely going into oneself and making oneself "central." Thus, someone has rightly spoken of yogic states not as "ecstasies" but as "instasies" (*enstasi*).

One might be tempted to relate the phase of illuminative life to the effects of the intellectual gifts of the Holy Spirit mentioned above, which according to the Thomist scheme are six in number: (1) the ability to discover the substance beneath the accidents; (2) the internal sense beneath the words of the sacred texts; (3) the truth beneath the symbol; (4) the spiritual reality beneath the sensible species, that is, beneath phenomena as they appear to common experience; and consequently also (5) the hidden effects of a cause and (6) the hidden cause of certain effects.[14] Formally, these might be powers of an initiatic character, more or less connected with "intellectual intuition." But it is enough to read Saint Thomas's own examples to see that there is nothing of the kind there; in fact, it does not go beyond a theoretical scheme.

Concerning the purgative life, still for the sake of indicating reflections of initiatic views, we quote as follows: "Many writers of Christian antiquity assert that the soul, on exiting this world, must pass through various abodes of demons in the airy regions. The demons examine the soul to see if they can find something of their own there. . . . The soul is unable to continue its journey until it is purged of all these stains. At the same time, besides being purified, the soul is instructed by good angels in every divine science, so that it will be able to understand the Mysteries of God. This entire process of purification and instruction is repeated until the soul has reached perfect purity and the fullness of knowledge." This gradual purification after death "is generally not mentioned [by Catholic theologians] in all its particulars. It has, however, been applied to the anticipation of our ascent that is experienced in the life of prayer, and in that application the aforementioned doctrine expresses absolutely unarguable truths" (*AC,* 128–29). Now, in all this it is easy to see a reflection of the mystery doctrine, especially

---

14. Cf. Joret, *La contemplation mystique,* 274.

the Mithraic account of the passage through the septenary or planetary hierarchy (see *Introduction to Magic,* vol. I, 98–128, and vol. II, 246), which has nothing to do with the world of prayer but with that of initiation, in which exactly seven degrees appear as so many "purifications."

Other "residues" of interest are the views found in the early Christian writers about the restoration of the Adamic state, understood as the first goal of Christian regeneration. The Church Fathers continually insist that one must achieve the perfection belonging to the primordial state by going in search of the lost earthly paradise. It was an old Christian idea, maintained up to the sixteenth century, that this place, from which our first parents were expelled, still exists in a high region inaccessible to men, unless they have been helped by exceptional divine grace, as was the case for Elijah, Enoch, and Saint Paul himself (2 Corinthians, 12:1–5). Its inaccessibility was expressed through the symbolism of deserted and unattainable places, and also by that of the angelic guard with a fiery sword or a zone of fire encircling the paradise. This reproduces the initiatic doctrine of the "center" in its relation to the primordial state: always present from the metaphysical point of view. And the symbolism of the belt of fire to be passed through is no different from that of the baptism of fire, also going back to the motif of Hercules who won immortality (ascending to Olympus to marry Hebe, eternal youth) only after the fire on Mount Oeta had consumed his human nature. This motif ties in with many others of initiatic origin, for example, a virgin enclosed by a circle of fire, who will belong to him who can cross it without perishing. Obviously, the Catholic concept of purgatory, in its projection to the hereafter, reflects the more general motif of purification.[15] Moreover, we see there a hint of the initiatic idea that Paradise and the Kingdom of Heaven represent two distinct "places."[16]

---

15. It is said that only those purified through fire can enter into Paradise. Saint Ambrose (In Ps. 118, serm. XX, 12): *Omnes oportet per ignem probari, quicumque ad paradisum redire desiderant.*

16. *TM,* 25–26, where this passage from Saint Ambrose is cited: "Paradise is a permanent region of heaven, but it is, so to speak, the ground floor of the kingdom, the foundation on which is built on high the kingdom of heaven properly so-called. It is the lower region of the invisible heaven, from which the elect, each according to his

Still keeping to early Christian thought, once it is admitted that the Adamic state can be regained through the high degrees of mystical contemplation, even magic intervenes when the privileges of this state are listed. The first is the gift of knowledge, or gnosis—by which it is recorded that Adam gave the animals "each its name"—the name, in the ancient conception, expressing the very essence of a thing or a being. Saint Thomas also writes about this: "This upright stance (*rectitudo*) of man as originally and divinely instituted consisted in the fact that the lower part of his being was subjugated to the higher part, and the latter was unobstructed by it. Thus, the first man did not find in external things an obstacle to the pure and stable contemplation of the intelligible effects, perceived by means of an irradiation of the primal truth" (*TM,* 89). This already relates to the second gift, which is *apatheia* in the more general sense of immunity to passions, of not being led by impulses, of a natural sovereignty over the instincts.[17] According to the Fathers, man as microcosm comprises the whole creation, hence the power that man possesses of self-domination manifests likewise in the macrocosm: the dominion of man over nature is the reward for the complete victory that man wins over himself. The hierarchical relationship between the powers within man translates into that between man and the world (*TM,* 84). In this way the saints were already promised an unlimited power over creation, as in Mark's Gospel (16:17–18): "in my name they will cast out demons; they will speak in new tongues; they will pick up serpents, and if they drink any deadly thing, it will not hurt them; they will lay their hands on the sick, and they will recover." That these powers are the very same as in high magic or theurgy needs no emphasis: Agrippa or Paracelsus would not have put it differently.

(*cont.*) own merits, will sooner or later ascend toward the various higher regions of heaven." In Christian terms, this distinction is also expressed by saying that Christ's grace is superior to Adam's grace and leads to a perfection that is beyond that of the ordinary paradisal state.

17. There is an interesting view expressed by Saint Augustine (*De civ. Dei,* XIV, 15), according to which at the same point at which the soul was separated from the divine world, the body in turn ceased to be subject and obedient to the soul, and entered the state of passivity defined by concupiscence.

Lastly, as the third prerogative of the Adamic state there is the gift of immortality, *athanasia,* "bodily immortality being the sign and proof of the internal presence of God." Hence "a restoration of the primordial state would also include the reacquisition of immortality" (*TM,* 82–84).

In the origins of Christianity, when like an echo the ontological idea of *deificatio*—assimilation to God and participation in his nature—still predominated, thanks to the preceding mystery tradition, over the moral ideas of faith, charity, and merits to be rewarded in the afterlife, some prospects of the kind were still half-open that, once the accretions were removed, look onto a higher world than that of mysticism, of which the latter is only a feeble and largely humanized echo.

A last point. We know what an important part Mariolatry, the cult of the Virgin as "Mother of God," plays in Christianity. In its outward aspects and from the historical point of view, this cult testifies to the influence on Christianity of gynocratic views, namely those of the preeminence of the divinized feminine principle (Magna Mater, the Gaia of Hesiod, etc.) as in the archaic, pre-Indo-European period of the Mediterranean region. Nevertheless, an esoteric interpretation of it is possible, and surprisingly enough is hinted at by the same Catholic author whom we have been repeatedly citing, when he says that Mary "is the highest ideal of the ascetic," because "the ascetic tries to form Christ in his soul, to make it the 'bearer of Christ' and the Mother of Christ" (*AC,* 192). Yet this symbolism, traceable to the initiatic sphere, basically contradicts the principle of passivity belonging to the mystical path of Christianity and so much emphasized by insistence on the indispensability of grace (i.e., of action by a force that is psychologically experienced in terms of grace) for any supranaturally efficacious initiative. But if in Christian symbolism the Virgin is impregnated by the Holy Spirit, following initiatic symbolism the "virgin birth" is strictly speaking the birth that has no need for external aid, the endogenesis due to a pure and intact force. As an Indian text says, Kumarī, the Virgin, "is the power of the will."[18]

---

18. Note the correspondence with the expression that Dante uses of the Virgin (*Paradiso,* XXXIII, 34): "Queen, who can do what you will."

Another mystical interpretation of the "Mother of Christ" makes her the representation of the Church, the mother of the supranatural life (*AC*, 193). This is in relation to the supranaturalizing influence that is supposedly linked to its tradition, its organization, and its rites.[19] Usually this point is related to the exclusivist doctrine typical of Catholicism. Since mysticism is considered as a development of the individual's experience of immersion in the current of divine life, brought about by the sacraments and especially the Eucharist, and since it is the Church, understood as the mystical body of Christ, that carries this current, the obvious conclusion is that there can be no true mystical life except within it (*TM*, 77). Moreover, non-Christian mysticism, lacking union with Christ, can only be naturalistic, if not actually due to demonic influences. (This view obviously considers Christ solely as a historical personality believed to be the Redeemer, not as a suprahistorical and universal model for imitation.) This would lead one to presume that in the non-Christian mysteries there can be no question of true deification, but only of more or less contingent psychic states (*TM*, 61–71). The famous principle *Extra ecclesiam nulla salus* (no salvation outside the Church) generally sanctions the idea that only redemption of the Christian type can bring about a liberation from the diabolic power, expressed as breaking the circle of the demonic forces that surrounds us; whereas to succeed in making one question its power and think that redemption under the sign of Christ and the Church is superfluous would be the most dangerous victory that Satan can credit to his activity (*TM*, 66).

We have already said that all this can only be valid for the "internal use" of the Catholic Church. Likewise we have mentioned that these opinions have an exclusively practical justification, no different from that of similar exclusivist views found in the external and exoteric

---

19. In the initiatic sphere the symbolism of the Lady has in many cases been applied to the force, the doctrine, or the organization that is its depository. Thus, in the case of the medieval chivalric initiation of the "Fedeli d'Amore" [see *Introduction to Magic*, vol. II, 99–107. —*Trans.*], the Lady represents either "Holy Wisdom" or some organization belonging to this current. The moment of transition to the active state is often symbolized by marriage or even incest (where the Lady or the Mother becomes the initiate's bride).

forms of many other traditions. They have no basis whatever outside the sphere of jurisdiction of each tradition.

In this context one can finally ask the question of how useful it may be, for those with an initiatic vocation, to join and participate in a religious tradition—which in the special case of a Westerner is Catholicism.

As a conclusion from the preceding investigation, it seems clear that Christianity has a unique character compared to other traditions. On the one hand it is not a pure religion of the "Law," like ancient Judaism or orthodox Islam, but emphasizes inner experience. On the other hand, it ignores the experiential plane of esotericism and initiation, which puts it on a lower level than the traditions where that plane is adequately considered. This intermediate nature of Christianity allows one to characterize it precisely as an essentially *mystical* religion, which has absorbed and adapted a number of esoteric elements in its mystico-sacramental form.

Now, a current defined in these terms has a chiefly psychic and collective character, rather than a spiritual and metaphysical one. At any rate, that appears obvious enough in what the Catholic tradition has become in our time, bringing to mind those cases of institutions from which the authentically higher influences have largely withdrawn. But because psychic institutions of that sort keep some of their vitality and their force of inertia, to join it may serve more as a fetter for someone with an initiatic vocation than as the basis for higher development. One joins a "chain" from which it is difficult to disengage and whose subtle influences are difficult to control. Thus, already on the doctrinal side it is typical that those who most sincerely live the Christian faith sacramentally and mystically are the most "caught up," the most fanatical, the most unable to recognize and respect what is prior and superior to their tradition, and what has manifested in the world and in history in other equally legitimate forms.

In every respect, and especially in the case of Christianity, one must judge that the relations between the external, religious path and the metaphysical are minimal, and that one can be immersed in the mystical-devotional current to the point of attaining relatively high degrees without perceiving anything of the initiatic and metaphysical order. With its systematic and closed character, its elements that are only a reflected image of the mystery of transformation and deification—merely formal and as we might say "lunar"—Christianity is perhaps the least of the traditional forms to be recommended to one who wishes to enter the "direct path."

GIC

From "The Song of Time and the Seed"

I

Time does not pass: — it transpires
in hymns of eternal seeding
in the bodies and teeming rainbow
of every solar season;

Make your limbs radiant
with a sense of incisive light
that sculpts and repeats its songs
in the dawns of the native word.

At the borders of every land
its torrential motion frees
the space of the soil, the turfs
in sonorous turquoise horizons.

And it breaks in violent splendors
into the element's darkness
to fringe the silver secret
in corollas of days and nights.

II

Splendors enclosed in you, never unveiled
unless as glimmers and appearances
of weightless breaths of essence, envious
of the mystery in which they were born.

They sing in the swarm of the silences
the event of the spirit, dispersed
in the universe's vegetal ardors
and the native groan of the senses.

But an indestructible aura of health
in the persistence of breathing scans
the celestial intervals and the volutes
of the mystery fed by your own blood.

III

The live event of being woven
by impalpable pulsations of time
or unloosened — flesh and bone — inside
the mines of accomplished songs,

Consumes and revises in us the weight
of a spirit ardently extended
in the unconfined harmony
of generations of mornings . . .

Time — nourished in all the pores
by interior morning moods
of spaces woven from slow promises
of yearning of blood and promises of flowers —

Joins us inexhaustibly
to the voluptuous organicity
of every breath that thinks or rests
in the word and inside the seedling.

IV

The fatal consumption of myself
is a sacred complex of figures
of night and dawn incised in the reflection
of my indestructible natures.

This being, bound — by fits and starts —
to the buds and shoots of a whole
immemorial trunk — but intact —
inside which the fruit becomes seed again.

If it is crushed into arid salts of bone,
it rises in hidden saps of heaven
in the earthly magic of the stem
which testifies the native force
of sex projected into thought.

V

The light dilated in calm vehemences
of porous tides of elements and of flesh,
crystallizes in heaps of fruits
and in ecstatic reposes of juices.

Your memory which breathes its calyxes
and the shining aromatic throbbings,

Rises toward the furrows and the fractures
of the sleepless stars and of the eternal dawns
where it ferments and reechoes the germs
of your awakenings and of your natures.

IX.5

Metapsychology and Magical Phenomena

A specialized journal of metapsychology has published some critical views aimed at negating "magical" phenomena, as being indistinguishable from what modern metapsychology studies and calls by the general term of "psychic (or parapsychological) phenomena."[1]

Metapsychology has arrogated to itself the status of a "science," and whatever it happens to observe, it tends to set up as the common denominator for facts ranging over a far wider field. The effect of this can only be a lamentable confusion, and often in practice a way of dragging the higher down to the lower. In fact, the material that falls under the observation of modern metapsychology belongs only to the lowest grades of the extranormal sphere, and it could not be otherwise. It is quite possible that mediums, sensitives, somnambulists, and at best some savage witch doctor or a person with natural gifts of healing or clairvoyance would consent to serve as "subjects" to the metapsychologists. But no adept, or even a "saint," would lend himself to this. And if the *experimental* attitude is reduced to a plain, external observation of the "facts,"

---

1. [The 1929 text begins thus: "In no. 7 of the journal *Luce ed Ombra* (1928), under the title "Commentary on certain magical experiences," there is reference to the phenomena obtained by the group of Genoa, a member of our chain, and whose report figured in issue 5 of *Krur.*" See V.3 of the present volume for the report in question. —*Trans.*]

it is obvious that no real discrimination or comprehension is possible. The same extranormal phenomenon—say, an apport—can be produced by a "medicine man,"[2] a saint, a medium, and by an intitiate. For the metapsychologist the same thing is happening in all these cases, namely an "observed psychic phenomenon," whereas if one does not stop at the crudest exterior level, very different things are going on. The so-called "positive" approach is thus condemned in advance, because it misses any qualitative difference between extranormal phenomena; and for the very reason that it does not understand that any phenomenon of this kind is part of a whole, of which the "factual" aspect is only a portion, owing its significance to the whole, case by case. Strictly speaking, everything in metapsychology should be reduced to the collection of *traces*. But it does not limit itself to that. As we have said, due to the drive to reduce the inaccessible to the accessible, and by the nature of what without exception falls into the metapsychologists' hands, this branch of research only serves to muddy the waters, to elevate to first position an order of phenomena that, however sensational they may sometimes be, are still of a lower and insignificant nature, and it ends up by obstructing the understanding of what relates to the truly suprasensible.[3]

But let us turn to the first question, concerning the relationship between magical phenomena and psychic phenomena in general. The magical character of a phenomenon is given first and foremost by its *intentionality* (being preceded by the mental representation of the goal); then by the *continuity of the effect with respect to the necessary cause* (even if sometimes insufficient), the latter being the power of the one who

---

2. [In English in the text. Also *medium* is always italicized, as being a foreign word —*Trans.*]

3. The claim put forward by the metapsychologists cannot be better characterized than by the introduction to a collection of works on the subject, published by "Astrolabio": "Using an obvious parallel, we might say that metapsychology differs as much from that baggage of generic ideas with which the ignorant identify it, as someone who knows the nature of electricity and the cause of lightning differs from those who believe that it is hurled by Jupiter's hand." Setting Jupiter aside, one may ask what scientism really *knows* about the *nature* of electricity. It remains in the field of what someone has justly defined as "learned ignorance." And any esotericist should draw his own conclusions from that.

acts, once certain conditions are satisfied; and finally, *the active presence to oneself*, in terms not only of lucid consciousness, but especially of exalted consciousness or supraconscious, at the crucial moment for producing the phenomenon. All this is clear enough, and it would be a contradiction in terms to say that extranormal facts can be also produced in this way by a medium. To the degree that a medium would be capable of it, he would evidently cease to be a medium, and to use the same term for such different situations is absurd and wrong.

The field of initiation and high magic involves disciplines of individuals or of working groups[4] that have nothing to do with mediumism and the field of spontaneous psychic phenomena. Besides, if there is anything that paralyzes what is enabled through mediumistic and suchlike states, it is a preparation of that kind. It is enough to try it, to be convinced. Disciplines of an initiatic or magical type are the best cure for a medium, in other words, for stopping him from being one and, if it is still possible, making him a normal being, which is the starting point for any development in a genuinely upward direction.

Moreover, magic uses specific signs and symbols, follows certain arrangements, chooses its days and hours, and so on. There is nothing arbitrary in all this: every detail has its rationale according to a specific goal, and follows a *method*. In magic it is the precision of this method, united with the discipline of certain internal forces, that leads to the result, whereas there is nothing of the sort in the more or less sporadic and spontaneous "psychic phenomena" that are the objects of metapsychological observation.

With regard to this method and these disciplines, there is a *tradition* in magic. It is a knowledge that comes from afar and has been validated by a long series of experiences. The direct or indirect allegiance to such a tradition is generally another condition for everything of a magical character (even holding good, to an extent, for witchcraft), whereas nothing of the sort is to be found in the persons used as "subjects" and in the isolated cases with which, almost without exception, the metapsychologists busy themselves.

---

4. See, for example, the instructions given in *Introduction to Magic*, vol. II, 42–52.

Let us add that as a rule, magical operations cannot satisfy the conditions that the metapsychologists demand for their investigations, because the presence of profane people who are simply there to watch is an obstructive factor. An operative magical chain is totally active, and such intruders would produce the effect of a faulty conductor introduced into an electric circuit: they would somewhat paralyze and depotentize the whole thing.

On another front, the same thing happens in mediumistic sittings, at their particular level of influences (very different from those of high magic and theurgy) and in their own psychic climate: they are known to succeed all the better when the participants are neither suspicious nor observant, but credulous and even superstitious.

In magic, as well as phenomena that are observed and not intended there can be others that are intended and not observed. That is nothing special when one is in the area of efforts for which today's conditions, both internal and external, are extremely unfavorable. Usually someone with real competence in magic will be able to discern the reason for these negative aspects and to trace them to precise and intelligible causes.

In particular, we must admit that at the moment a door is opened, forces may rush in through the gap thus offered to them and produce unwanted and unexpected phenomena. In *practice* there is again a large difference between magic and metapsychology. In magic, one tries to eliminate phenomena of this kind, though they will happen spontaneously as the operative group gradually consolidates. As a rule, the phenomena are not allowed to capture attention or arouse interest. In contrast, in "psychic" and mediumistic sittings the great object is to obtain any phenomena, so long as they are concrete and visible: not the wish for a specific one and avoidance of any other.

There are phenomena such as a command issued in an extranormal way to a distant person, in which it makes no sense to speak of suggestion, as the metapsychologists do. In this and other phenomena the structure of a procedure of the magical type is clear to see: an image at the center; then a force that galvanizes and saturates it in a continuous process, to the point of crossing the borderline between the I and the not-I, between psychic and physical (or between one person and another) and translating it into a corresponding real event, in which the operators' active force, aware, perfectly rhythmical and harmonized, reaches its conclusion. There is a clear difference here from certain "psychic" phenomena of the spontaneous sort. We recall that the medium Eusapia Palladino, when she was young, even without entering a state of trance would form a certain desire or image in her mind, and sometimes the matching phenomenon would inexplicably follow. What is missing here is the character of *causality* developing in a continuous mode. One readily admits that it is also absent from any form of magic resembling witchcraft, where the so-called helping spirits intervene. But this is certainly not magic of the most advanced order, that of high magic.

In the criticism that has given rise to these explanations, the positivist prejudice (which is equivalent to materialist) inherent in the metapsychological method is reaffirmed when it blames the importance that we give to the "internal experience," which, being unverifiable and inexpressible, is supposed to serve us as a convenient and inaccessible resort. Evidently, what the metapsychologists appreciate, because they can grasp it in their hands, is the mere *caput mortuum* (dead head): that which corresponds in an experiment to the crudest and dead "precipitate." For us, of course, things are the opposite. We have already justified a magical practice not by its results, but precisely and solely by the internal states beyond ordinary consciousness that one must rise to and actively possess (see *Introduction to Magic,* vol. I, 263–64). Initiatically speaking, it is by this criterion alone that operative magic is of any interest. This higher and decisive zone, consisting of pure internal experience, is naturally ineffable and "experimentally" unverifiable by others. To want it to be otherwise is not to know what one is asking. As for the rest—paths, disciplines, techniques, and determinisms of the magical field—they can be expressed in language that is not "mystical" but intelligible and sufficiently exact. It seems to us that the present collection of essays, most of which treat of nothing else, is sufficient proof of that.

IX.6

LEO

The "Plumed Serpent"

D. H. Lawrence was a liberated man. Anyone who has followed his work has the clear sensation of a man who rises up and stands on his own. He was liberated above all with regard to his readers: he had no concerns about pleasing many, nor of pleasing few, and not even of being understood. He did not explain—he went his own way, alone with his vision—without distraction. He is alone with his vision, and to those able to take it in, it appears alive and whole. And his creations have a magical fullness.

The Plumed Serpent may be the most weighty and complete of Lawrence's works. There are no dissertations or arguments there, but instead a psychic atmosphere that makes us live in the soul of a land, where forces still seem to exist that have already vanished elsewhere and passed into other modes of being.

The land is modern Mexico—so little known to most people. Mexico is a country where the aboriginal occult forces have resisted the invasion of the ruling race, and have remained beside it without being extinguished. The events that happened in the years after the book was completed give it a kind of prophetic value. The anti-Christian struggle of recent times—despite its Masonic-anticlerical and pseudo-Jacobin gloss—had in reality a very different significance from what one might at first believe. It is the old pagan soul rising up against the Christian religion; the ancient gods of Mexico have awakened from their age-long sleep, to reclaim their people; one might say that ancient Quetzalcoatl, the "plumed serpent," was returning to manifestation.

We recommend the book to those who may be interested in these happenings, as Lawrence's art has dramatized them, but here we will only describe a climactic episode, not lacking in elements of authentically esoteric value.

The ancient Indian blood that pervades the Mexican race first reawakens and becomes conscious in a group that, having received a European education, experiences the contrast all the more strongly. Others follow it. We find ourselves in a process of veritable evocation. First of all, unseen in the night, the drum sounds to summon the faithful. The rhythm of the drum has a magical character relating to the awakening of psychism; in certain forms it is a way to attain ecstasy and thus contact with suprasensible forces.

The crowd gathers silently around the leaders, and the "saturation" increases with the hammering rhythm until it breaks into a hymn, which really works as a magical formula or mantra. It is then that the ancient god Quetzalcoatl comes to manifestation, to enter once more into contact with the blood of his people. In the book, he declares his own nature in these words:

I am the Living Quetzalcoatl.
Naked I come from out of the deep
From the place which I call my Father,
Naked have I travelled the long way round
From heaven, past the sleeping sons of God.

Out of the depths of the sky, I came like an eagle.
Out of the bowels of the earth like a snake.

All things that lift in the lift of living between earth
*   and sky, know me.*

But I am the inward star invisible.
And the star is the lamp in the hand of the Unknown Mover.

Beyond me is a Lord who is terrible, and wonderful, and dark
    to me forever.
Yet I have lain in his loins, ere he begot me in Mother space.

Now I am alone on earth, and this is mine.
The roots are mine, down the dark, moist path of the snake.
And the branches are mine, in the paths of the sky and the bird,
But the spark of me that is me is more than mine own.

And the feet of men, and the hands of the women know me.
And knees and thighs and loins, and the bowels of strength
    and seed are lit with me.
The snake of my left-hand out of the darkness is kissing your
    feet with his mouth of caressive fire,
And putting his strength in your heels and ankles, his flame in
    your knees and your legs and your loins, his circle of rest in
    your belly.
For I am Quetzalcoatl, the feathered snake,
And I am not with you till my serpent has coiled his circle of
    rest in your belly.

And I, Quetzalcoatl, the eagle of the air, am brushing your
    faces with vision.
I am fanning your breasts with my breath.
And building my nest of peace in your bones.
I am Quetzalcoatl, of the Two Ways.[1]

Little by little a sense of relief spreads through the people: "Quetzalcoatl has come." The original divinity returns to live in them, expelling the alien cult that had subdued the Mexican soul from the outside.

But there is also, on a higher plane, the mysterious stimulus that incites men: "*Go, and once you have gone, you will never be able to turn*

---

1. [D. H. Lawrence, *The Plumed Serpent* (New York: Knopf, 1933), 342–43. Written in 1923, first published 1926. —*Trans.*]

back." Quetzalcoatl's message speaks to them of transcendent self-consciousness. From the esoteric point of view the following message surely has expressions of remarkable inspiration. Here it is, in its sibilant intonation:

> The great Snake coils and uncoils the plasm of his folds, and
> stars appear, and worlds fade out. It is no more than the
> changing and easing of the plasm.
> I always am, says his sleep.
> As a man in a deep sleep knows not, but is, so is the Snake of
> the coiled cosmos, wearing its plasm.
> As a man in a deep sleep has no to-morrow, no yesterday, nor
> to-day, but only is, so is the limpid, far-reaching Snake of
> the eternal Cosmos, Now, and forever Now.
> Now, and only Now, and forever Now.
> But dreams arise and fade in the sleep of the Snake.
> And worlds arise as dreams, and are gone as dreams.
> And man is a dream in the sleep of the Snake.
> And only the sleep that is dreamless breathes I Am!
> In the dreamless Now, I Am.
> Dreams arise as they must arise, and man is a dream arisen.
> But the dreamless plasm of the Snake is the plasm of a man, of
> his body, his soul, and his spirit at one.
> And the perfect sleep of the Snake I Am is the plasm of a man,
> who is whole.
> When the plasm of the body, and the plasm of the soul, and
> the plasm of the spirit are at one, in the Snake I Am.
> I am Now.
> Was-not is a dream, and shall-be is a dream, like two separate,
> heavy feet.
> But Now, I Am.
> The Trees put forth their leaves in their sleep, and flowering
> emerge out of dreams, into pure I Am.
> The birds forget the stress of their dreams, and sing aloud in
> the Now, I Am! I Am!

For dreams have wings and feet, and journeys to take, and
  efforts to make.
But the glimmering Snake of the Now is wingless and footless,
  and undivided, and perfectly coiled.[2]

Could the men of the Serpent accept the message? The book does not answer that; with a profound artistic sense the author has given us a vision that can live in us, transcending the book itself. The events of the novel provide enough for us to feel the soul of a people in its inmost part. There are states not yet entirely forgotten in our own souls, and, in a conscious return, we feel that we are penetrating our own interiority. It is a past that justifies and explains our present.

---

2. [Lawrence, *The Plumed Serpent*, 175. —*Trans.*]

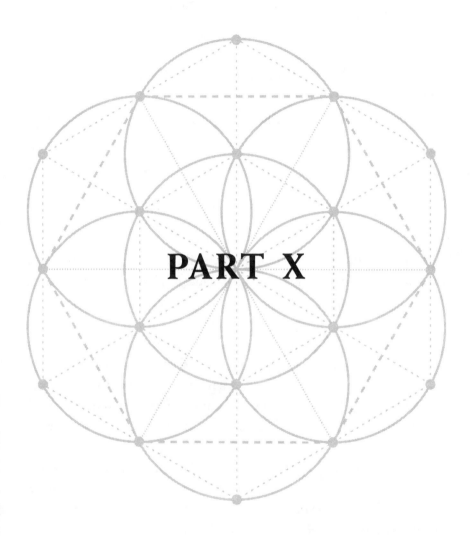

PART X

Remarks on Action
in the Passions

The human psyche can be compared to a body of which only some parts are capable of active motion, flexibility, or agility. In all other parts it behaves like a *rigid* body, incapable of elastic reaction, so that any impact warps, bruises, or fractures it. Typically, everything in the human soul that is sentiment, emotion, and passion is just like the deformation and fracture that rigid substances suffer when they are hit, because they lack the elasticity that restores them to their original form.

Much could be said about this; many exercises could be suggested for those aiming for the initiatic integration of their own being; much food for thought could be offered to the many who think they are active toward things and people, while inside they are passive.

One has to gain the ability to make a real *act* correspond to every passion or emotion: an act that invades the psychic state and, so to speak, works on it *before* the jolt or disturbance of pain or pleasure, instinctive attraction or repulsion, occupies and prevails on us.

In a word, one must learn the secret of *willing* one's passions and emotions—which is obviously the opposite of putting one's will at their service. Instead of *allowing* a passion to take hold, one *grabs* it, asserts oneself, and does so before it has time to pervade us. It is like someone who can catch a missile in midair, and is consequently unhurt by it.

If there is any way to make a passion lose its power, this is it. But it takes skill, because the game is a subtle one. A *willed* passion is no longer passionate: that much is obvious. To the extent that I can say "I *will* this," I can also say "I do *not* will this." But what can I say of the *boldness* required for there to be no residues; of the quick eye and ready hand needed to catch what is out to cheat us?

Let us move to our own field. Following this course may well bring about an occult experience that is anything but negligable, and like any respectable occult experience, not free from danger. When you *will* a passion, you are obviously setting up a *relationship,* because if the thing is real you are reproducing internally the action enclosed in the passion, and *not your own,* and transforming yourself. In this way you can also release it into *someone,* and you know that in some situations "neutrality" is impossible. If it is not you who *enters* and establishes "ascendency," it is the *other* who enters into you: in which case you may consult what has already been written on the subject of "pacts" (see chapter VII.1, page 220).

· · ·

One says "*mine*" in the same way whether of a thought, an image, or an emotion. But it is not difficult to see what a difference there is when referring to activity.

A notion, once it has occurred; an image, once defined in the mind: these become a virtual possession. I can *recall* them. Through recall I can reproduce them, reactivate them, and represent them to my mind whenever I please. But with a feeling or an emotion this is not possible, or only so to a lesser degree. I cannot make a past feeling or an emotion real whenever I like.

Thus, we are back to the case of a rigid and inelastic substance capable only of the possibility of *impressions* (in the literal sense). There is no *agility* here: the active components of the I do not exist. And so they have to be created: to extend the free power of representation that I have for ideas and images to the field of pure emotional states.

To get coldly excited? Exactly. *Hatred, love, fear, desire, anxiety—I must become able to arouse them all in myself with a mental action, at will.* No more or less than that: and to the same degree as when they are aroused by objects, persons, or specific conditions.

This is another of those things without which one will not go far in magic. Ascetic purification is impassivity: the substance that formerly, like lead, could be warped by any impact, is now like a diamond, which nothing can scratch—or like water, which you cannot catch in any way. Magical purification, on the contrary, is an activity sure of itself on every front and on every plane: softening everything and filling it all with actions, without exclusions, doubts or limitations. One confronts the passions and sensations, rips away their strength, invades them where they were about to invade us, transforming their action into our action, and thus making them, as it were, acts of our inner being, which you can move freely from virtuality to actuality and vice versa, as you please.

On deeper examination, every passion, even when tied to a pleasure, always contains in the normal state an element of *suffering*. One should connect these remarks with what has been written about the metaphysics of pain (*Introduction to Magic,* vol. II, 189–92), and also about the relations between feeling and realization (vol. II, 175–76). Anyone may find interesting points for consideration in these connections.

Take, for example, the *sunset.* Who does not know the sickly and conventional references to the effect of sunset on the soul? But those apart, there always remains a consuming and tormenting state of nostalgia, heartache, and grandeur—and you may want to dissolve yourself, attaining something that you neither know nor can express. Unless poetic imaginations and elaborations intervene, it ends there. Yet it is a state of passion. The soul is subjected by it; the pathos holds it and makes it impossible to approach the mystery hidden behind it.

The sadness of this state really expresses the manifestation of a transcendent sensation, to which consciousness cannot open itself; hence it is transmuted into a blockage, an excessive discharge, which gives rise to the emotional state. *The specific passion of the sunset is no less than the cessation of the impulse to open oneself to that light which flowers when the external light fades and dies, so that for the bodily eyes, darkness begins to fall.* The limited being that holds on tenaciously and fearfully to its ego instinctively reacts against such an impulse and invitation that the evening brings, when it happens to abandon itself to the spectacle of things. By its reaction it shuts itself off, and the subtle impulse winds up in the "sublimity" of common sensibility, which is exactly what gives rise to that constellation of vague emotions, and even deep ones, that make up the *pathos* of the sunset.

Needless to say, modern man, obtuse and deaf, does not "have time" to pay attention even to this pathos. With the points of transition abolished, the power of "separation" will surprise him at night like an assassin, felling him with sleep among the specters of artificial lights. To him the "midnight sun" will correspond to unconsciousness.

For the others, this may be a hint—and a task for *activity in passion*. *Knowing* is already a preparation for comprehension; and comprehension, in turn, hermetically prefigures realization: for what we have been speaking of, as for the rest.

• • •

Concerning what Abraxa has written about the possibility of war for arousing states of soul that, taken actively, have the value of *paths,* I would like to quote some observations on war made by Arturo Marpicati that are very characteristic in this regard.

"If the *individual* faculties are dimmed in the monotony of trench warfare, and the field of consciousness is reduced to a minimal circle, during a bombardment the commonest phenomenon for most is the *cessation of mental activity.* We stay put, following with all our being the whine and explosion of shells, but thinking of nothing; the brain clock has stopped. I even happened to surprise myself as 'doubled': *I was no longer consciously present to myself; there was another one of me*; I seemed not to exist and to see myself not existing—*I had the strange sensation of the 'I-spirit' being detached from the 'I-body'* and of being indifferent to it. When the fury climaxed in the paroxysm of pounding artillery fire, *there was no more interest in it:* neither in far-off affections nor in friends close by, neither in life nor in death. One felt already dead . . . the desert was all around. The sense of fatality had flowed in and reigned over all the organs. It took some time after the bombardment was over for the faculties to regain their *normal functions*: something that to many organisms would unfortunately never happen."[1]

Every student of our science will recognize the states in question: mortification, suspension, separation. But here, simply *undergone* and incipient. Gleams of transcendent realizations would disclose themselves if in those moments the action came from within.

In comparison, we recall what Iagla has written, also referring to a wartime experience (*Introduction to Magic*, vol. II, 152). It seems that even in modern warfare certain possibilities, which once served as basis for the "ritual" of the heroic traditions, have not altogether vanished.

---

1. Arturo Marpicati, *La Proletaria, Saggi sulla psicologia delle masse combattenti* (Bemporad, n.d., 22–23). Italics mine.

X.2

Awakening

This is how it began. One day, after long hours sitting on a lakeshore watching the animals, the reflections, the flowers, the colors, and enjoying the peace, something that I have never rightly understood began to flutter in my heart; I say "flutter" now, but no word could ever express the strangeness and the feeling of this movement, if indeed it was a movement. The sensation was quasi-physical, but I did not notice it right away: it was so delicate and light, a fresh, calm, and pure air. I was both surprised and unsurprised to have an absolutely different and novel sense of myself and of things. For the first time I felt my "I-ness," unique, whole, sufficient unto myself, independent of any person or circumstance, eternal, alone, inhabitant of my own universe, suspended in an immense peace, connected to all things by a contact like a "diffusion of myself," agile, rhythmical, simple, pure, and alive, awake in that immense peace in which all beings were dreaming and all things were sleeping. The extraordinary thing is that all this was in no way extraordinary, but profoundly and absolutely natural. I felt exactly as though I had nothing to do with my own thoughts, or with those circumstances that, if they were my limit, were also my liberty; the reality was beneath those things, and in that reality was liberation, and in that liberation was life, the life burgeoning within me.

This blooming of something unknown and yet not new, this diffusion in the tranquil weft of the thing as it bloomed, had, as it were, "unblocked" my heart, had undone the bonds: things did not appear drowsy, muddled, and confused in the disquiet of desires, but free, new, released and shining in the calm and pure light of nature. All the ancient being—the being that called itself by my name—was estranged and distant; yet the elements of that being must have been synthesized and purified and, from that synthesis, the essence had become "I," pure intelligence, released to behold in a timeless world the infinite marvel of all things.

It was the sun in the sky and luminous clouds, birds in the trees and on the lake, far-off voices: immense peace. A sacred and profound peace, in whose substance beings, sounds and colors were woven; a peace that was reality and life, a peace that was made from the inexpressible joy of being itself; all that I had sought was before me; in that vibrant peace life was dancing, and I perceived the dance, the music, and the rhythm; things had all their resplendent original purity, and in the heart there continued to pulsate, not the blood, but that which was the flower of eternity, boundless, luminous, perfect, exquisite, and pure, revealed like a glance between a baby's eyelids. All the truth beyond which there is nothing to be sought, all the peace that is the substance of life, all the grand silence that is the origin and the music of sounds, all the irrepressible joy, all of being become life, it was all there, on that lake, all was finally true, all was suspended, immense, serene—all was in me.

That "I" that appeared to be looking was not myself at all, but something absolutely impersonal living in me. Yet its power was as great as though it had emptied the universe, and in one point, which was "I," all of life was contained, all reality concentrated; outside there were nothing but phantasms, phantasms with which my mind populated eternity. That "I" alone was the absolute inhabitant of its divine world; alone, yet filling by itself its great solitude; alone, yet united to all things; time did not hold it prisoner because it created no time; thus it did not populate with beings and things the frightened realms of unreality, and, being only "I," no place existed for it; thus any sense of going, seeking, expectation had vanished; it was simply life conscious of itself, a dimensionless point; but around life there was singing and dancing, and with its baby eyes it assisted in the grand creation.

• • •

The thing lasted for about an hour; then it was lost, sought, found, and lost again; finally, one of its many flashes remained and illuminated this being which carries my name. This experience has definitively wiped out anything vague, indefinite, or hidden that remained in me; masters, religions, aspirations, occultisms, rituals, neighborly love, and all the rest have vanished from my world. What surprised me for a while is that the thing did not last unless I made it last; and thus I can recreate it when it is lost, because I keep its root in me. However, it is indifferent to everything that interests me, and unreachable through desire; this supreme beauty appears when nothing disturbs the mind, as the sky bends to mirror itself even in a roadside puddle; it gives the sense that all that was done and is to be done has nothing to do with what is; that the path has none of the significances and goals that are attributed to it; that it has absolutely no significance and no goal, because it "is," and by being, all is perfect; it gives the sense of an immense liberty and an unending peace; it is neither love nor hatred, but its nature is harmony, and a certain number, or rhythm, or measure that needs discovering is the key to this harmony. It exists in everything, and yet everything is suspended in it; compared to it, the worlds are playthings, but its grace finds no opposition. It is the dream of a god and I am the dream and the dreamer; it is timeless, or time is that of nature, and all nature is the body of this newborn being. It is very difficult to describe this thing as seen by one deprived of himself, because none of those modes, tendencies, thoughts, or systems that make up the human being, absolutely nothing of that which can be expressed, subsist there. Instead, these things appear like unrealities, artificial products that float on the sea of being until the phantasmagoric force that has created them is exhausted. Yet there is a relation between that reality and this unreality, and the two forces could be elements of an even more hidden profundity.

The "Primitives" and Magical Science

Our readers already know what to think, from the esoteric point of view, about the so-called *primitives* or *savages,* concerning their beliefs, traditions, and destiny.

We repeat: savages are not the remnants of original humankind; they do not represent what we all once were: the pre-civilized condition of the same humanity as has "evolved" to its present state. Between the psyche and the civilization of a man of today and that of savages there is a hiatus, a leap, indeed an essential qualitative difference. The savages are *not* part of the modern Western cycle: *they are part of another humanity, an archaic humanity of which they represent the twilight, degenerate, and involutionary forms.* Thus, rather than a point of departure, they represent a point of closure, the point at which a descending process was exhausted and ceased. They express a sunset, not a dawn, and they carry residues and the last echoes of even more ancient realities, having no counterpart in the cognitions, mentality, and sensibility of modern humanity.

Now, anyone who considers the magical sciences, and esoteric sciences in general, finds himself faced with a system that likewise does not belong to "modern civilization." *Between such a system and what survives in the traditions of primitives, there exist points of contact.* But I hasten to add that this in no way authorizes the conclusion that many

328

draw from the legitimacy and reality of this kinship: the relegation of magic to the "superstitions" of savages.

The situation is exactly the opposite. Magic constitutes a wholeness, a worldview complete in its own way, with its own logic and coherence. That is the positive point of reference which explains it, not that which needs explaining. It is not the "superstitions" of savages that can account for magic, but vice versa: the principles of magic, in their intrinsic validity, may account for what is superstition among the "primitives," but at the same time they can bring to light things that are true and real, fragments of metaphysical teachings and transcendent experiences.

Much has been written in modern times about the mentality and traditions of primitives: heading the list are the names of Frazer, Lang, Moore, Hubert and Mauss, Durkheim, and Lévy-Bruhl. Nonetheless, they have generally not gone much further than collecting materials; nor should one hope for further steps, so long as they remain on the so-called "ethnological" level. Unless the whole thing is to remain a mere object of curiosity, one needs to *know* something; to have had certain experiences; to have been inducted into certain teachings, whose truth is not verified through the methods of modern science, nor framed within the familiar notions of the latter. Only then can one *see* into many things, and know the level on which they may not be mere fantasies and superstitions.

It may interest our readers to highlight some of the principal points, in which one can see the correspondence with the states and the teachings that have often been mentioned here.[1]

I. THE "MANA"

The fundamental experience of the primitive is identical to what stands at the foundation of any magical conception. "To the mind of

---

1. I limit the citations to two fundamental works by L. Lévy-Bruhl, *La mentalité primitive* (4th ed., Paris, 1926) and *L'âme primitive* (2nd ed., Paris, 1927). [In the present version the citations are taken from Lucien Lévy-Bruhl, *Primitive Mentality,* trans. Lilian A. Clare (New York: Macmillan, 1923) and *The "Soul" of the Primitive,* trans. Lilian A. Clare (New York: Macmillan, 1928), abbreviated as *PM* and *SP. —Trans.*]

the primitive there is existent and permeating, on earth, in the air and in the water, in all the divers forms assumed by persons and objects, one and the same essential reality, both one and multiple, both material and spiritual" (*SP*, 16). It is *mana* or *imanu*—what Éliphas Lévi and Paracelsus call *astral Light*, the Brahman and the *prana* of Hinduism, the Hermetists' *Acqua divina* or *Mercury*, the Taoists' *chi*, and so forth.

For the primitive, this reality is neither an imagination nor a concept: it is an immediate datum of experience, a *perception* that precedes all others. Reality, before being nature or world, is *mana*. "[T]his principle is present everywhere at once like an impersonal force, and yet it is individual in certain persons. . . . It was the soul of things . . . intangible, but like air, wind, it could manifest its presence" (*SP*, 17).

In that they are made of *mana*, "primitive mentality considers and at the same time feels all beings and objects to be homogeneous" (*SP*, 19). "He has no idea of 'the natural kingdoms,' or of the essential properties of the forms of being included in them. To him all being is defined (as far as he thinks of defining it) by what it possesses of mystic force, either as a constant factor, or at a given moment" (*SP*, 26).

The relation is obvious between this and the magical vision of the world as power. For primitive and magus alike, all things are realized as power: the mode and intensity of the power, or *mana*, of which it is the manifestation, constitute its real being. The higher the quantity of *mana*, the more a being really *is*. Therefore "primitives live, think, feel, move and act in a world which, in a great many ways, does not coincide with ours" (*PM*, 59). Made of *mana*, the "powers" for him are not ideas produced by reasoning joined to experience: they are "more like direct apprehension or intuition. At the very moment when he perceives what is presented to his senses, the primitive represents to himself the mystic force which is manifesting itself thus." (*PM*, 60). "[I]n their representations the world of sense and the other make but one. To them the things which are unseen cannot be distinguished from the things which are seen. The beings of the unseen world are no less directly present than those of the other" (*PM*, 61).

Hence the error into which moderns fall whenever they ignore the fact that the terms used by primitives designate both material representations of immaterial qualities and immaterial representations of material objects (*SP*, 114). Frequently, the terms only designate the "doubles"—what we would call the subtle forms—of the things named.

Such is the case, for example, in the mention of a "kidney fat" that is extracted by a magical operation, resulting in death (*PM*, 64), or of bodily organs that are removed during regeneration and replaced by other organs, or by crystals or special stones (*SP*, 272). It would be naïve to take all this literally. But that does not prevent it from sometimes being exactly the case among primitives: and then, but only then, having lost the original significance, is it a matter of superstition—or witchcraft.

2. SPACE AND TIME

One evident consequence is that the experience of space and time is not the same for the primitive as it is for the "civilized." For the latter, space is "like a background of canvas, unconcerned with the objects which are traced upon it" (*PM*, 95). For the primitive, on the contrary, it is alive: "to them it will appear burdened with qualities; its regions will have virtues peculiar to themselves; they will share in the mystic powers which are revealed therein" (*PM*, 95). Every place has a kind of fatidic quality: it has its mysterious individuality and its "intensity." But the premise of "sacred geography" is no different, and that has always been a part of the traditional sciences.

Likewise time cannot be felt as composed of homogenous units simply ordered in succession. Instead, it is perceived as *rhythm*, with periods characterized by the typical manifestations of good and evil powers, differentiated by quality (*PM*, 94–95).

Now, practical magic refers exactly to this sense of space and time. Only that presupposition makes sense of the theory of "holy" lands or cities, the traditional centers of spiritual influences on earth, the environments to be "vitalized" through rituals, and everything involved with astrology that relates to specific moments in which the ritual may be integrated with the great forces of things.

In the cycles of festivals on which our own calendrical notation is based there survives the trace of the ancient qualitative and symbolic experience of time. The state of consciousness in which the magical methods are efficacious is that in which the world becomes alive again, and once again everything is the mask or symbol of a "power," more or less directly intuited.

3. IRRELEVANCE OF NATURAL CAUSES

The primitive mentality knows nothing of "chance" and pays hardly any attention to the "natural" explanation of phenomena. It has no interest in *how* things happen, but looks for *why* they do. For any event, and especially for those commonly thought of as fortuitous, it asks the question "Why thus and not otherwise? Why, for example, when crossing a ford, was this man swept away by the current and not another?" For the primitive mentality there is no true solution to this problem unless it goes back to the action of a "power." The primitive ignores all the "two-dimensional" laws and determinisms that the typical modern explanation of phenomena resorts to. If a snake, a lightning strike, another man, or the like has killed someone—for him, all that is just a deceptive appearance: *natural causes never produce anything by themselves;* it is the invisible causes that furnish a satisfying explanation (*PM,* 35–58). Nothing happens down here that has not already happened, as it were, on another plane. What happens visibly is only a conclusion, an epilogue.

It follows from this mental attitude that every thinking process is reduced to a minimum. In the primitive, mental effort is chiefly applied in the third dimension: he does not try to connect one phenomenon with another, but to spy out the occult force—due to an entity, a dead person, or even a magician—without which that "chance" collusion of natural forces would not have happened; or else a natural cause might not have had that effect, for example, the snakebite might not have been fatal (*PM,* 60–61, 91–92).

Boehme wrote: "Believe me, you are not here to fight with inanimate beings, but to fight with gods!"[2] When the primitive comes to feel the strongest action of a power, he lets go: the conclusion, the epilogue,

---

2. Jacob Boehme, *Aurora,* XXI, 121.

does not interest him. He would think it puerile to fend off some natural cause like sickness or danger: the action would still get at him by other means—it is already a *fait accompli*. The only efficacious thing would be to eliminate the supranatural cause, such as killing the person who cast the spell. And vice versa: the primitive exposes himself nonchalantly to natural causes of danger, disease, and so on, because in his mind they cannot do any harm unless a certain *intention* behind the scenes is directing them against him. "People do not die of a cold wind; people only get ill and die by means of witchcraft" (*PM*, 37).

What has to be kept firmly in mind here is that the primitive does not have recourse to "powers" because he is ignorant of natural causes, but vice versa: because he knows the "powers," and the experience of them is the immediate and primary datum for him, he ignores the search for natural causes, and even when a "civilized" man faces him with them, he refuses to acknowledge anything there of interest or adequacy to explain the effect (*PM*, 36–37). Though all this can end up in superstition—which is naturally often the case when dealing with savages—it does not devalue the principal consideration, which is the need to explore the meaning of the event, both in us and outside us, along the dimension of depth.

4. DEATH

A particular idea among the primitives is that *death is never natural*. Death has the character of an accident, a violent and anti-natural fact. Each time it requires a transcendental explanation. "If, therefore, at a given moment death supervenes, it must be because a mystic force has come into play. Moreover, senile weakness itself, like any other malady, is not due to what we call natural causes; it, too, must be explained by the agency of a mystic force" (*PM*, 38).

This belief, strange as it may seem today, echoes an archaic metaphysical tradition—the very one revealed in some "titanic myths": that mortals are beings who have been thunderstruck and felled by a stronger race. Mortal life is a struggle: only the initiate is victorious, and in his conquest of immortality he is simply reintegrating himself in his original state, in conformity with nature. The dim memory of that stage, combined with the general sense of invisible actions affecting man, is what explains these ideas of the primitives about death.

5. "PARTICIPATIONS"

Esotericism teaches, and demonstrates practically, that what lies behind physical, spatial reality is perceived when the incorporeal principles of the human being acquire a certain freedom from the corporeal ones in which they are habitually immersed. One must recognize that where the primitive is concerned, there is nothing extraordinary about this condition. *If his world is not ours, it is because the relationship of the I to its own body is not the same in the "civilized" as in the primitive man.* If we rightly allow that the connection between psychic and physical is unstable in the latter, we can then understand a complex group of phenomena and concepts that would otherwise have seemed fantastic— because what has been verified today in mediumistic and hypnotic states compels one to admit such things, formerly branded as fable and superstition.

The first consequence of this lesser solidity of the bond between "soul" and "body" is that in the primitive, psychic faculties and processes are not so limited by space. The primitive soul lives simultaneously in a psychic environment, in which his elements and energies can meet and combine with those of other beings, and also with "inanimate" things and objects that we consider "external."

"[I]n the representations of the primitives, each man's individuality does not stop short at his personal exterior. The limits which surround it are indecisive, ill-defined, and even variable acccording to the amount of mystic force or *mana* which an individual may possess" (*SP,* 115). One can say that the primitive soul, beside the part attached to the body, has an extra and free part that can "attach itself" to this or that. To his mind the clothing, the remains of food, the weapons, the excrements or fluids, and the objects that a person has made and worked on, or even just touched, may carry something of his "soul," so as to offer a way of occult access to it irrespective of distance.

When studying all of this, two aspects must be distinguished. The first would refer to a degenerative condition, thinking of "communications" made possible through a certain lack of form or weakness in the savage's soul. On this, I refer to what I have already written (*Introduction to Magic,* vol. II, 153–61) in evaluating the views of De Martino, an ethnologist. From that instability there come the "perils of the soul," which I will address below. However, there is a second aspect, namely the fact that "participations" do objectively exist: it is true, for example, that certain objects retain a relationship with their owners, as does everything that was part of their body, and so forth. All this is real *on its own level,* and not limited to the psychisms of savages. Nevertheless, it requires a special internal condition that can be attained either regressively (through dissociation) or integratively (as in the case of high magic), for these relationships to be perceived and turned to one's advantage.

6. THE LEOPARD-MAN

In exceptional cases, where the psychic and subtle principles are especially unstable (whether due to emotion, excitement, intoxication through various drugs, etc.) or when an object or being is supersaturated with *mana,* there may occur genuine irruptions of "power" in the individual who enters into a relationship with that object or being.

The extreme case of such obsessive irruptions is to be found in a persistent belief of the primitives in many different regions: putting on the skin of an animal is reputed to produce a genuine transformation in one's nature (*SP,* 167). There is a typical case of four natives who "confessed that at night they assumed a panther skin which gave them superhuman force. Thus disguised, they entered the huts, and devoured their owners. They did not lose their strength unless someone succeeded in wresting from them the skins they had fastened to their bodies" (*SP,* 165). "There is a general belief in men-leopards. With the aid *of certain drugs and fetishes,* men seem to have the power to transform themselves into men-leopards. In other districts there are said to be men-crocodiles, ape-men, but we never hear of snake-men" (*SP,* 165; italics by Ur).

Possession can happen while the soul remains inside its body, which naturally keeps its usual form;[3] but it can also happen during sleep, when the subtle part of the being is even freer from the visible body. Then there may occur a veritable transference of the "soul" into the body of a given animal, and consequently a literal bilocation or dual presence. There are precise accounts, recorded by explorers, of animals being hit, and of persons who were sleeping far away found wounded and even killed while in their beds. Thus in some circumstances it is not a case of "superstition" or "suggestion."[4]

In short, it is always the instability of the bond between soul and body that can account for the primitives' singular belief: that it is possible for a man's soul to join more intimately with another body, and even with a thing, than with his own body, so that he is more at the mercy of what happens to the former than what happens to the latter.

This can also happen through the violence of a magical operation that extracts a man's "soul" from himself and puts it at the mercy of the magician, with or without the intermediary of objects.[5] "The Baluba sorcerers assert that they can steal away a man's personality, and leave his body a mere mindless automaton, 'an empty ear of corn'" (*SP*, 274). The man may stay alive, but he is like an empty shell, a phantasm whose life gradually ebbs away until, at his death, the magician is the complete master of the vital force and can use it for his own ends (*SP*, 273).[6] In other cases he can substitute himself for the soul expelled from another's body.

---

3. If one thinks that along with a certain power there may be instilled the image of the relevant "type" (leopard, jackal, etc.), one may also conceive of the state of possession sometimes being accompanied by a spontaneous projection of the relevant image, which others may perceive in a sort of hallucination, replacing the human form of the one possessed. (Note by UR)

4. See the instruction about doubling given in *Introduction to Magic,* vol. I, 196–202. (Note by UR)

5. Compare *Introduction to Magic,* vol. II, 229–36, which explains an operation of this kind. (Note by UR)

6. Among primitive beliefs there is also the possibility of extracting the vital elements from certain substances, which remain the same physically but are deprived, for example, of their nutritional powers (*SP*, 278). This may be related to the *vampiric feeding* that others have mentioned in these pages.

7. THE "TOTEM" AND THE "DOUBLE"

Moreover, if the body is the *principium individuationis* (principle of individuation) of consciousness, the lack of a firm and stable bond with a body will also cause the sense of individuality to remain vague, diffused, and connected with the sense of other forces and other beings. Our readers know that this is precisely the danger run by those nowadays who, to achieve the possibilities of magic, try to recapture ancient states of consciousness: it is the danger of losing the sense of personality, of reentering the domain of influences from which one had otherwise succeeded in isolating oneself.

The primitive does not have a true consciousness of his own. Before feeling himself, he feels forces that go beyond him, and of which he is an incarnation. It is chiefly a matter of the *totem*. This is the mythic ancestor whose life continues in that of his descendants in the form of the collective soul of a race, clan, or tribe. The individuals of the clan are its transformations, its temporary incarnations, while it is also considered as the entity, the "spirit" of a given species of animal. But this is not a concept: it is an experience. The primitive feels himself as a species before he feels himself as an individual.

He speaks of the *double:* the *tjurunga* of the Australians, the *kra* of the Ewe, the *ntoro* of the Ashanti, the "onomino" of the Ba-ila. The double is himself, and at the same time it is something other and something more than him: it is the deep root of his being—and while the man dies, leaving only a shade which in turn suffers the fate of dissolution (the *srahman*), the double survives: it has lived in many men, and will live in many more. And in the great majority of primitive beliefs, totem and double are one and the same thing. If one turns back to what has been said about the origin of species according to esotericism, one will easily see the relation of these ideas with initiatic teaching (see VI.4, pp. 210–18).

In the same way, the particular constitution of the primitives causes them to find themselves spontaneously in a relationship somewhat like a magical chain. Then we see all those laws of action and reaction that Iagla has explained (IV.4, pp. 141–49) informing a complex of ideas and norms that are found almost identically in every form of the primitive mentality, and which thus have a real foundation, an objective justification, whenever this state of rapport with the collective consciousness remains effectively alive.

Here I will end these brief notes, in which I have only chosen a few of the many points that might interest us. In conclusion I would recommend reading works on the "primitive" mentality and soul to students of esotericism. The latter, having correct principles at their disposal, may be able to proceed from the degraded residues and even "superstitions" to some things that are only hinted at in certain occultist treatises.

X.4

Two Hyperborean Symbols

Among the Celts, the boar and the she-bear symbolized, respectively, the representatives of spiritual and temporal authority. These were the two castes of Druids and Knights, equivalent to the castes of Brahmans and Kshatriyas in India, at least originally and in their essential attributes. This symbolism is purely Hyperborean in origin, and is one of the marks of the direct attachment of the Celtic tradition to the primordial tradition of the present cycle, whatever elements may have been added to this principal current from other traditions, earlier but already secondary and derivative. The Celtic tradition can be seen as one of those junction points of the Atlantean tradition with the Hyperborean tradition, coming after the end of the secondary period in which this Atlantean tradition represented the predominant form, and, as it were, the "substitute" for the original center, by then inaccessible to ordinary humanity. The symbolism in question may also offer some interesting indications on that point.

---

1. [This essay was one of many additions made by Evola to his 1955 edition of the *Ur* and *Krur* papers. It is a translation of René Guénon's article "Le Sanglier et l'Ourse" (The Boar and the She-Bear), first published in *Études traditionnelles*, Aug.–Sept. 1936. In translating it from French to Italian, Evola made some minor adaptations and abbreviations for a readership unfamiliar with Guénon's style, vocabulary, and references; changing the title is one example. These have been incorporated in the present translation, which otherwise follows Guénon's text as found in *Symboles fondamentales de la Science sacrée* (Paris: Gallimard, 1962), 177–83. The notes are also Guénon's, unless otherwise indicated. —*Trans.*]

First of all, we notice the importance given to the symbol of the boar by the Hindu tradition, which itself issues directly from the primordial tradition and affirms its own Hyperborean origin explicitly in the Vedas. The boar (*varāha*) not only figures as the third of the ten manifestations (*avatāra*) of the god Vishnu in the current cycle (*manvantara*), but the entire cycle of manifestation of our world (*kalpa*) is designated as *śveta-vārāha-kalpa,* the "cycle of the white boar." Given that, and considering the necessary analogy between the great cycle and the subordinate cycles, it is natural that the mark of the former should recur at the beginning of the latter. This is why the polar "sacred land," the seat of the primordial spiritual center of the present cycle or *manvantara,* was also called Vārāhī, the "land of the boar."[2] Besides, since it was there that resided the first spiritual authority, of which every other legitimate authority of the same order is only an emanation, the representatives of such an authority naturally also received the symbol of the boar as their distinctive sign and kept it through later times. Hence the Druids called themselves "boars," although since symbolism always has multiple aspects, one can also see this as alluding to their isolation from the outside world, the boar always having been considered as "solitary." Besides, we must add that this very isolation, which the Celts, like the Hindus, maintained in the material form of retirement to the forest, relates to the characteristics of "primordiality," a reflection of which is always preserved in any spiritual authority worthy of its function.

But returning to the word Vārāhī, which may give rise to some very important observations: it also serves to designate an aspect of the *shakti* of Vishnu (and more specifically relating to his third avatar),[3] which, given his solar character, immediately shows its identity with the "solar land" or primitive "Syria,"[4] which is another of the names for the

---

2. Note that contrarily to what Saint-Yves d'Alveydre seems to have thought, the name of Vārāhī does not refer to Europe at all: that was always the "land of the bull," which refers to a period already quite distant from the origins.

3. The Sanskrit term *shakti* means the "wife," or the "power," or the immanent aspect of a divinity. (Note by UR)

4. The original meaning of the word *Syria,* which does not only correspond to the

Hyperborean Thule, hence for the primordial spiritual center. Besides, the root *var* of the Sanskrit word for boar is also found in Nordic languages in the form *bor;*[5] the exact equivalent of Vārāhī is therefore "Borea," and in fact the common name of "Hyperborea" was only used by the Greeks at an epoch when they had already lost the meaning of this ancient designation. It would be better, despite the usage that has prevailed since then, to call the primordial tradition simply "boreal" rather than "hyperborean," thus clearly asserting its connection with "Borea" or the "Land of the Boar."

There is more: the Sanskrit root *var* or *vri* has the sense of "cover," "protect," and "hide." As the word *Varūna* and its Greek equivalent *Ouranos* show, it designates the sky, both as covering the earth and as representing the higher worlds hidden from the senses. (The Latin word *coelum*, from *celare* [conceal], originally had the same meaning.) Now, all this applies to the spiritual centers, either because they are hidden from profane view or because they protect the world with their invisible influence, or again because they are like images on earth of the celestial world itself. We will add that the same root has yet another meaning, that of "choice" or "election" (*vara*), which evidently applies as well to the region universally known by names such as "land of the elect," "land of the saints," or "land of the blessed."

The reader may have noticed in the above the union of two symbolisms, "polar" and "solar," but in what especially concerns the boar it is mainly the "polar" aspect that counts. One reason is that in ancient times the boar represented the constellation later known as the Great Bear.[6] This substitution of names is one of the signs of what the Celts symbolized by the battle of the boar and the bear, meaning the revolt of the representatives of the temporal power against the supremacy of the spiritual authority, with the various troubles that followed in later

---

(*cont.*) region known as such today (to which it has only been transferred) is "land of the sun." See the essay by René Guénon, "La Terre du Soleil," in *Études traditionnelles*, Jan. 1936. [Note by UR—though not designated as such. —*Trans.*]

5. Hence the English word "boar" and also the German *Eber*.

6. We recall that this constellation has had many other names, including the "Scales," but the Sanskrit word for scales, *tulā*, brings us back to Thule, the Hyperborean center.

historical epochs. The first instance of this revolt was actually far earlier than history as commonly known, earlier even than the beginning of the "dark age" or *kali-yuga,* when it would reach its greatest extent. That is why the name of *bor* could be transferred from the boar to the bear, and "Borea" itself, the "land of the boar," could have become at a certain moment the "land of the bear," during a period of Kshatriya hegemony which, according to Hindu tradition, Parashu-Rama brought to an end.

In this same tradition the most usual name of the Great Bear is *sapta-riksha;* and the Sanskrit word *riksha* is the name of the bear, linguistically identical to what it is called in other languages: the Celtic *arth,* Greek *arktos,* and even Latin *ursus.* But one may ask if this was really the original meaning of the expression *sapta-riksha,* or whether, following the substitution mentioned, there was a sort of superposition of words that were etymologically distinct, but associated and even identified by a certain phonetic symbolism. In fact, the general meaning of *riksha* is a star, or basically a light (*archis,* from the root *arch* or *ruch,* to shine or illuminate); and on the other hand the *sapta-riksha* is the symbolic dwelling of the seven Rishis. Beside the fact that their name refers to vision, hence to light, they are also the seven "Lights" who transmitted the wisdom of earlier cycles to our present cycle.[7] The resulting association between the bear and light is not an isolated case, because we see the same thing regarding the wolf, both with the Celts and the Greeks,[8] where that animal is related to the solar god, Belen or Apollo.

During a certain period the term *sapta-riksha* was no longer applied to the Great Bear but to the Pleiades, which also comprise seven stars. This transference of the name of a polar constellation to a zodiacal constellation corresponds to a change from solstitial symbolism to

---

7. Note the symbolism of the "seven lights" persisting in various initiatic or formerly initiatic traditions. [Guénon's original reads simply: "persisting in masonic symbolism." —*Trans.*] We also note that the seven stars mentioned at the beginning of the Apocalypse (Revelation 1:16, 20) are sometimes interpreted as those of the Great Bear.

8. In Greek, wolf is called *lykos* and light *lyke;* hence the double meaning of the epithet of Apollo, Lycaeon.

equinoctial symbolism, implying a change in the point of departure of the [annual cycle, hence also of the order of predominance of the][9] cardinal points that relate to the different phases of this cycle.[10] The change here is from the north to the west, which refers to the Atlantean period; and this is precisely confirmed by the fact that for the Greeks, the Pleiades were daughters of Atlas, and as such were also called the Atlantides. Transferences of this kind have often caused multiple confusions, when the same names received different applications from one period to another, so that for earthly regions as well as heavenly constellations it is not easy to determine which they refer to in a given case. It is even impossible unless one connects their different "localizations" to the proper characters of the corresponding traditional forms, as we have done in the case of the *sapta-riksha*.

Among the Greeks, the revolt of the Kshatriyas was depicted in the Calydonian boar hunt, which clearly shows a version in which the Kshatriyas expressed their claim to a definitive victory, because they killed the boar. Athenaeus reports that according to the earliest authors this Calydonian boar was white,[11] which identifies it precisely with the *śveta-vārāha* of Hindu tradition. No less significant from our point of view is that the first blow was given by Atalanta, who is said to have been nursed by a bear; and the name Atlalanta could indicate that the revolt began either in Atlantis itself, or at least among the heirs of the Atlantean tradition.[12] Moreover, the name Calydon recurs precisely in Caledonia, the ancient name of Scotland, which apart from any question of particular "localization" is the very land of the "Kaldes" or Celts; and the forest of Calydon is really no different from that of Broceliande, whose name is the same, albeit in a slightly

---

9. [The words in brackets, present in Guénon's text, are perhaps inadvertently absent in the Italian translation. —*Trans.*]

10. The transference of the Scales (Libra) into the zodiac naturally has a similar significance.

11. *Deipnosophistarum*, IX, 13.

12. There are some other curious correspondences in this regard, especially concerning the golden apples that figure in the legend of Atalanta as well as in the garden of the Hesperides or "Daughters of the West," who, like the Pleiades, were daughters of Atlas.

modified form, and preceded by the word *bro* or *bor,* the very name
of the boar.[13]

We should add that the two symbols of the boar and the bear
do not necessarily appear in opposition or conflict, but in some cases
can represent spiritual authority and temporal power in their normal and harmonious relationship, as seen in the legend of Merlin
and Arthur. Merlin, the Druid, is in effect the boar of the forest of
Broceliande (where he is finally not killed, like the Calydonian boar,
but put to sleep by a feminine power); and King Arthur has a name
derived from that of the bear, *arth.*[14] More precisely, this name is
identical with that of the star Arcturus, allowing for the slight difference due to their respective Celtic and Greek derivations. This star is
found in the southern constellation of Boötes, the herdsman—names
in which the marks of two different periods are again united: the
"Bear keeper"[15] has become the Herdsman, while the Bear itself, or
sapta-riksha, has become the *septem triones,* that is, the "seven oxen"
(hence the word "septentrion" to designate the north). But we do not
need to study these transformations, which are quite recent compared
to our theme.

From these considerations a conclusion seems to emerge concerning
the respective contributions of the two currents in forming the Celtic
tradition. Originally, the spiritual authority and the temporal power
were not separated as two different functions, but united in their common principle, and a trace of this union is still to be found in the very
name of the Druids (*dru-vid,* "strength-wisdom," the two terms being
symbolized by the oak and the mistletoe). In this capacity, and also
as representing more particularly the spiritual authority, to which the
higher part of the doctrine was reserved, they were the true heirs of the
primordial tradition, and the essentially "boreal" symbol of the boar was

---

13. [The Italian version here omits Guénon's paragraph concerning the sex of the Great
Bear. —*Trans.*]

14. In Scotland one also finds the surname McArthur, or "son of the Bear," as a visible
sign of belonging to a warrior clan.

15. [Following the French *le gardien de l'Ourse,* not the Italian *il giardino dell'Orsa*
(bear garden!). —*Trans.*]

rightfully theirs. As for the Knights, having the bear (or Atalanta's she-bear) as their symbol, we may assume that the part of the tradition specially destined for them contained chiefly elements from the Atlantean tradition; and this distinction may perhaps explain certain more or less enigmatic points of the later history of the Western traditions.

X.5

Experiences among the Arabs

What I have to relate dates from the period when Libya and Tripolitania were Italian. As a background: already in boyhood I had felt a lively and spontaneous interest in everything to do with the supra-natural and spiritual, reinforced by various readings, even if not very discriminating at the time. My family did not lack ancestors who had shown the same interest, including a practitioner of alchemy who lived in Urbino in the sixteenth century. For my part, I found myself study-ing Arabic, with the idea that the Arab world might hold interesting experiences for me, and accepted that I was destined for a government post in our colonies there.

Naturally, there was no lack of Italians who were curious about the phenomena of which some Muslim circles were said to be capable. And that is just how things began: some Italian officials in contact with Arab notables—mainly through the initiative of Carlo Conti Rossini, secretary general for Tripolitania, who arranged the matter with Hassuna bey Gurgi, the property administrator for the Arab reli-gious communities—got permission to attend some fakir sessions in the *zawiya* (religious school) es-Sagira of Tripoli.

To tell the truth, we were only permitted to attend incognito, in an adjoining room, through a wooden grate that, however, allowed perfect visibility. Arabs were sitting on the ground in concentric circles, and started practicing a well-known primitive technique of ecstasy, con-sisting of repeating formulae and at the same time making rhythmi-

346

cal movements of the body, especially the head, from right to left and from front to back, to the point of resembling the disarticulated head of a puppet—all accompanied by the soft sound of a drum. At a certain point there was a pause and the participants were served the meat of a *urel* (a sort of large desert lizard). After they had eaten it, the session continued up to a certain point of saturation, at which many of the participants started to perform the famous fakiric feats on themselves, sticking large pins, skewers, and daggers into various parts of their bodies. Our guide caused one of them to leave the circle and come to where we were: we could ascertain that the skewers were fixed not only in the muscular and mebranous parts of his body, but also in the flesh and the abdominal cavity. But no blood flowed.

This was not the only session of the kind that I attended. In another zawiya, in Bengazi, I was able to witness other well-known phenomena of fakirism: the swallowing of broken glass, long nails, and burning wicks. I managed to interview one of those who were performing such feats—a fisherman. I asked him what became of the materials he swallowed: nails, glass, stones. He replied that after the session, the Chief of the zawiya placed his hands on his body, whereupon all the things "dissolved" into water which he spat out of his mouth, and nothing remained.

This was the only detail that aroused a certain interest in me, because the rest was more or less known through readings and reports of trustworthy travelers: I had merely been able to confirm it personally and directly. One might say that someone sensed my deep disappointment. As I left one of these sessions, I was approached by an Arab who said: "Leave all these things, they're not for you, they're too low for you, look for something else."

My job required quite a bit of travel all around the colony, including the interior. Wherever possible I did not miss contacting circles that cultivated what we might call the "psychic" side of Islam. I admit that I sometimes used a rather incorrect expedient: I amazed several Arab groups with my knowledge of *dhikr,* secret formulae, and signs. They assumed that it had all been transmitted to me by some master or other, for my qualification and initiation. They did not know that these were things that anyone in Europe could know, thanks to works such as that of Depont and Coppolani on Muslim fraternities, published in Algiers.[1]

The decisive event happened some time afterward at Tert, a place near to Derna. I knew that a mysterious old man lived there, devoted to the ascetic life and enjoying special prestige, despite his miserable economic conditions. I invited him to come to me, which at first he declined, saying that he did not feel worthy to approach a great Italian chief. At last he consented. Then something unusual occurred: an immediate understanding between us. He told me that he *recognized me*, and knew already that we would have to meet. When we parted, he wanted me to accept a ring from him, which I was never to part with: it was of gold, with two sphinxes grasping a sapphire.

On returning to my Arab friends of the coastal zawiya, I mentioned the encounter and showed them the ring. They gave every sign of amazed and awed recognition. They told me that the person I had met was a *Sheikh ál Tariq* ("Lord of the Path"), the name of a particular initiatic rank, and that his ring would have opened any path to me.

Thus, little by little, a change of heart took place in me, whose first result was my "adhesion" to Islam. This could only surprise those who have no exact idea of what Islam itself is. The "adhesion" is merely pronouncing the "testimony" (*shahādah*), having taken a ritual position that must have a certain value of *mudrā* (of "gesture-seal"): the upper right arm beside the torso; the forearm raised with the fingers closed, except the index finger, which points up; the left arm bent so as to hold the right elbow in its hand. The "testimony" is the well-known formula "*lā ilāha ill-Allāh wa Muhammad rasul Allāh*," which affirms the absolute unity and uniqueness of God, adding that Muhammad is his prophet. But Islam is known to accept other prophets, including Jesus himself, for whom it has a particular veneration. Moreover, Islam, because it is only a religion, has neither a clergy nor sacraments; it is reduced to the observance of the Koranic law, as the sacred rule for ordinary life. It thus leaves ample spiritual freedom, requiring only a direct personal rec-

---

1. [The study alluded to here is Octave Depont and Xavier Coppolani, *Les confréries religieuses Musulmanes* (Algiers: Jourdan, 1897). — *Trans.*]

ognition of the sovereignty of the one God and the absolute submission to his will (this being the meaning of the word *islam*).

The principal difference between Islam and Chistianity is worth explaining. Christianity is a sort of blend of common, popular religion (exoteric) with mysticism (esoteric). The rituals, symbols, formulae, and sacraments of Catholicism, for someone who considers them in the abstract—let us suppose someone who knows of them in the distant future, when they alone survive as fragments of the whole religion, in fragmentary state—might present a character that is not only esoteric, but even initiatic. But in current practice that is all adapted to the level of the simple devotional life accessible to everyone, and leads at most to some individual mystical experience. In Islam the two things are quite separate: there is the external religious law (*zāhir*) which concerns the organization of secular life, and there are quite distinct currents that are straightforwardly esoteric, chief of which is the *tasawwuf* (which is more or less so-called Sufism), structured in chains (*silsilah*) and with a secret teaching.

Returning to my own experiences, my insertion into Islam, while in no way prejudicing my previous spiritual orientation, was the premise for any possible contact of a more essential kind. And thanks to the precedents I have mentioned, it was not difficult for me to be initiated into an esoteric confraternity, the *Rifa'ia* of Benghazi. The initiation (*nird*) consisted of certain rituals intended to transmit a specific spiritual energy (*baraka*), rituals that concluded by sipping the same special beverage from the same vessel as the group's *noukaddem* and *khūan*. Certain teachings and special formulae were then communicated to me; some of them had the power to evoke and activate the collective energy of the chain or organization in case of need. Others were able to propitiate—in certain circumstances, not normal ones—the apparition of one of the "Chiefs of the Path." It was in fact stated that one of the supranormal powers of those Chiefs was that of bilocation: they could double themselves or impart particular teachings to the disciple.

It is as well to emphasize that the transmitted influence, the *baraka* received in initiation, was conceived of as something that needed to be actualized if one wanted the initiation to be effective. And this is an individual operation, left largely to one's own capacities, being able only to offer opportunities, putting one to the test of activating and mastering this force and inserting one's own in it. One can be helped and protected, but basically one has to proceed on one's own. The idea of initiation as a spectacular operation from the outside that suddenly changes a being once and for all, without his doing anything, is a mistaken, superficial idea, due to incomprehension.

It was therefore a case of nurturing the seed planted in me; and here I began a period of various events and experiences that are not easy to relate. I passed from one environment to another, in distant places, and I had the sense that through certain secret signs one person was signaling me to another, to test me in various ways, to interest me in things that had no apparent relation to each other, but which I think must have been integrated by someone with the ability to take them in at a single glance.

I will mention experiments attempted in three different directions. The first was that of ceremonial magic (evocative). My guide in this type of experience was my master in Arabic and the Koran, called Ibrahim, whom I had known for some time but whose modest appearance would never have made one suspect faculties of this kind. The phenomena obtained were frequent manifestations of flames, apparitions of immense and strange eyes, and so on. But I was warned not to pay too much attention to the phenomena in themselves; I have the impression that the aim was rather to develop a force for commanding the invisible and control over any emotion. Madness, Ibrahim told me, was the danger that one ran at every step, if one lacked the right orientation (*nyyah*).

Second, there were experiments in sexual magic, with a technique that essentially agreed with what has been explained in these papers (*Introduction to Magic,* vol. II, 335–47). Usually it is persons temperamentally much given to sex who are admitted to these practices, using their inclination as "materia prima." The rule is to manage intercourse with a woman such that it never comes to the normal and animal termination, that of seminal ejaculation. The organizations I entered into contact with used Berber girls specializing in such practices. I believe that each time they received an occult preparation. There were also formulae—*dhikr*—and no girl consented to such practices unless they were used. During the whole night when the experiment was prolonged, use was made of a tea in Arab style, like a strong decoction, with successive infusions of various herbs that must have been related to the degrees and course of the enterprise.

The practice seems to have had two purposes. First, it was self-control, different from the simple resistance of temptation because it accepted all the normal conditions, both physical and psychic, of intercourse with a woman; nor was one required to suppress the sensations that usually accompany it, the only exception being to master and inhibit ejaculation. But the girls involved had precise instructions for using every means to make this happen. One bizarre detail: I happened to see these girls crying when they succeeded in this effort of "diversion," and excusing themselves, saying that they had had to obey their orders.

But the goal to be realized through resistance and self-control was also a means, because the energies aroused and intensified in sexual union of this kind should lead to what some call a "breakthrough," with corresponding forms of illumination and penetration into other planes of being.

Last, I will mention an experiment with the magic mirror. The requirement for this, as for every other experiment in the organizations I frequented, is that the candidate must possess an indispensable gift: the incapacity to be hypnotized. And they used every means to see whether I possessed this gift. A similar detail is interesting, especially in relation to experiments such as those with the mirror. We are told that the premise is a temperament diametrically opposed to that of a medium, or one who easily slips into a state of reduced consciousness and daydreaming. As for the details of practice with the mirror, they are more or less the same as indicated in these pages (*Introduction to Magic*, vol. I, 72–78). For me, a consecrated mirror of black crystal was used. During the experiment, preceded by the recitation of various *dhikr,* an elder of the zawiya stood by me. I was taught a formula to use in case of danger. The experiment went thus: normal perception of the external world was suspended, and I felt myself in a surrounding of diffuse, opaline light, which then became clear azure, a light followed by a sensation of utter darkness (the Hermetic "nigredo"?). After a time that I cannot estimate because the sense of time was completely suspended, there suddenly appeared a vision like an enormous cataract of flames that assailed me like a whirlwind. I admit that I could not hold out. In terror, I spoke the formula that I had been given and immediately returned to the state of ordinary consciousness. The Arab who was assisting me said with a smile: "What a shame, a little more and you'd have succeeded. But you have gone pretty far. Don't be discouraged, and perhaps you will attain the goal in this life."

Not long after this I was recalled to Italy, thus closing the chapter of my experiences among the Arabs. I keep the gold ring given me by the "Lord of the Path," and also an Arabic manuscript of magic entrusted to me by Ibrahim, my master in magical evocation. While drafting these short notes I revisited it, to see if any part was suitable for transcription in an appendix. I have to admit that this was not the case: it was a matter of rituals and formulae for a magical procedure of commonplace character that I would call empirical, with no initiatic or theurgical importance. For the readers of these pages it could be nothing but the object of simple curiosity. Perhaps they would be interested by the following verses that I have translated, and which derive from those Arab circles.

> *Nothing in the world ever had a beginning, nor did the world.*
> *Nothing can ever end.*
> *Do not let eternity weigh on you, seek to fill it with yourself, forever.*

> *No instant of eternal time can say:*
> *I was the first.*
> *No one and nothing can say:*
> *I will be the last.*

> *The word that you speak, even to your dog,*
> *is heard in all the planets*

and in the space between them, full of lives.
Not a word is lost.

When you form a thought in your mind,
which is such a miserable thing
that you despair because it is so small,
it tumbles down like a raging torrent,
and fills another world
which is set in motion.

Neither to east, nor west, nor north, nor south
are there any confines.
The infinite is infinite: space and time.
But an act of pure goodness
conquers myriad centuries.

Do not have vain thoughts, nor say vain words,
the Hero is the one who knows to keep silent.
Be good, but before being good
BE YOURSELF.

X.6

Various Commentaries

In the previous part, at the end of the considerations about Christian mysticism and esotericism, a question was raised that merits some further attention. It concerned the advantage that someone with an initiatic vocation might draw from associating himself with a religious tradition and following its rituals.

The problem only interests us if posed from the practical point of view, and not in general, but with regard to the present epoch and the civilization in which we live.

From the doctrinal point of view, a religious tradition, including Catholicism, may well contain elements, symbols, and rituals that allow for a higher and esoteric meaning. But this does not prevent the fact that a religious tradition may have been imprinted by influences different from those at work in the initiatic chains; and it may well be that such influences, in cases of degeneration (and it is anything but improbable that modern Catholicism is one of these), are reduced to a mere psychism.

With this in view, it is necessary to take up a position contrary to the thesis defended by one author, otherwise deserving of every respect, about the necessity for "traditional exotericism." In his terminology this is more or less equivalent to the religious tradition. Such theses are the consequence of a formalism already highlighted in these pages while indicating the limits of initiatic "regularity" (see V.4, pp. 173–86).

The author in question asks of the person who refuses the authority and significance of a religious tradition "whether he, whatever his potential, is really capable of approaching the initiatic and esoteric domain, or whether it would not be better for him to appreciate the value and range of exotericism [i.e., its religious tradition] before searching further." This is a fair question, if it applies to a sincere examination of one's own vocation; there are, in fact, many cases of people who, even without being aware of it, are seeking in esotericism what is more or less a substitute for religion, whereas they could have found satisfaction in a suitable deepening of the religion itself, if they could have overcome preconceived ideas and a certain intellectual presumption.

However, it is a different matter for one who is certain of a sincerely initiatic vocation. Is there any sense or advantage for him to join even the religion of his own civilization and the land in which he happens to live, and to follow its forms? We believe not, and especially (for the reasons that Ea has laid out) if it concerns Christianity. The author we have referred to poses the problem as though it were the alternative of either giving one's general existence a non-profane orientation, or not doing so, aside from the aspects of it to which initiatic disciplines can specifically apply. We think this orientation wholly desirable, but the author's error is in virtually believing that no other paths exist but that of observing and following the morality, rituals, and rules of one's own religion. We are on his side when he attacks the thesis of those for whom a "profane domain" exists as an autonomous sphere from which one can abstract oneself. As he rightly says, there is no profane domain: only a profane point of view, which is a product of degeneration and devoid of any legitimacy. He adds: "In principle one should not make any concession to such a point of view; but in fact it is very difficult in the current Western environment, and in certain cases and up to a certain point it is even impossible."

That is all very well: it is necesssary that whenever possible one's own knowledge and action should have a non-profane reference point. But this is essentially equivalent to infusing a deindividualized significance into every form of existence that is at all susceptible to it; it is equivalent to making the impulse to transcendence the principal motive force in every experience.

Is all that possible just through observing traditionally religious precepts? One cannot answer that with a simple yes, and especially not in view of current conditions. In general, one cannot simply say yes because esotericism considers two paths as equally legitimate and practicable, called in Hinduism the "Right-Hand Path" and the "Left-Hand Path." As has already been said concerning the relationship between esotericism and morality (*Introduction to Magic,* vol. II, 238–49), precepts, laws, and ritualistic conformity belong essentially to the former path. In the latter all that is deliberately set aside: one frees oneself from it, and the impulse to transcendence is fueled in direct ways that may even involve transgression. Many aspects of the current epoch—which according to Hindu teaching is proceeding under the sign of Kali, who is precisely a divinity of the "Left-Hand Path"—tell us that at such a time the latter is a more suitable path, given the general climate of dissolution and of unconstrained forces.

These are timely considerations, because we know of circles that, on the basis of theses like those of the author in question, try to make tradition in an esoteric sense serve as the sanction for a traditionalist conformism of an infantile sort, ready to find everything right and legitimate. Some have even put on laughably intimidating airs, threatening those who, without having the possibility of joining a "regular" initiatic center (as if they were found today on every street corner), disdain the norms of "traditional exotericism," that is, religious rules, with the danger of rebirth in states corresponding not to the central, human condition, but to the peripheral condition of an animal or even worse.

Practically speaking, since here and now the chief "traditional exotericism" to be considered would be Catholicism, with its devotionalism, its bourgeois moralism, and all its modernizing degradations, we do not think that anyone is running such a risk, nor is less qualified for an eventual initiation, if for example he does not go to Mass or confession, and uses sex otherwise than in regular marriage and for the sole purpose of animal procreation, and so forth.

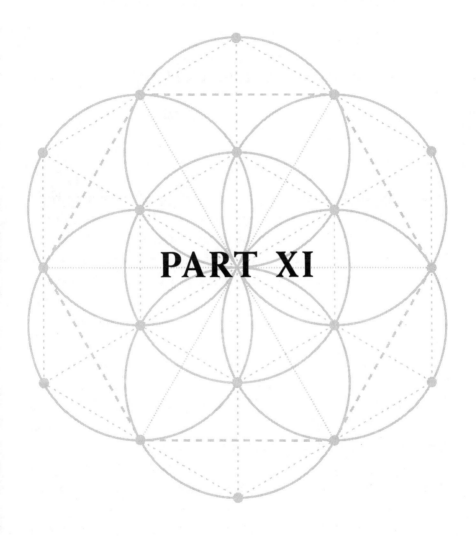

PART XI

XI.1

Notes on "Detachment"

That which the Hermetic tradition calls the "separation of the mixed," the Hindu tradition of Samkhya designates as the detachment of *purusha* from *prakṛti,* meaning the detachment from whatever in the personality is nature, necesssity, or becoming, in order to identify with or liberate the virile principle made from pure consciousness which, immobile yet active in its immobility, is the center of every movement. The separation of the purushic principle is an extraction of the true principle of self-consciousness from the swoon of semi-consciousness—corresponding to man's so-called normal waking state. There is a traditional technique for it, found in the samkhya-influenced yoga of Patañjali, as also in the *Bhagavad Gita.*

This method may be applied in a truly creative form if one can grasp the depth of its authentic occult meaning. Detachment apparently seems a simple operation: man, in fact, has the illusion of experiencing himself as consciousness of being, in that he feels himself living immersed in his thoughts, his feelings and sensations. But in reality his consciousness has sunk into them; one could even say, is woven from them. *Thus, it is not he, but someone "outside" or "above" him that has true consciousness of what is happening in him:* this someone appears as his own I, while it knows itself to be above identification.

Once that is understood, one is on the way to distinguishing the possibility of a real and positive detachment from a detachment that is purely intellectual. True, this detachment is first realized only on the

358

mental plane—and the sensation of being separated from the world of emotions and impulsive willing is equally mental, because whereas we can say that we are clearly experiencing our thoughts in the waking state, we cannot say the same about the world of our feelings, will, and instinct: all we know of those is the reflections in the most external and indeed cognitive consciousness. Thus, those few who begin such an experiment may well mistake for authentic detachment the kind that is quite easily attained, namely the separation of the purushic principle from what one may call the mental *prakṛti*, that is, from the entirety of modifications, motions, and flows that make up the common psychic life of the individual. The technique of "silence" and the reconnection with the originating force acting behind thought can already achieve that. At this point one attains a freedom that has an effective value, but which can give the as yet unintegrated consciousness the illusion of also being detached from the planes that descend to the deepest and organic nature, and of possessing dominion over them. Yet in reality one has only reached a faculty of control over them through the central nervous system, or through that nervous center more particularly linked to the mental life. It is therefore a matter of an indirect control, reflected and peripheral, which has only a preliminary value.

In this regard, we can describe something we ourself have experienced, and which from the methodical point of view seems to us of fundamental importance. There is a point that can be reached in which one is free from the dominion of *prakṛti*, but without the I being yet realized in the true, absolute purushic nature. This is a point that we can call "neutral," because one is "liberated" in a certain way, but not yet capable of "liberating." It is a truly dangerous point, not only because the disciple can fall into complacency and misuse of a certain liberty that he has gained, but above all because in that state there occurs in his physio-psychic life an interruption in the natural direction of all his vital processes, or else an interruption in the rhythm of that physical life understood in the normal sense, which, if it is not disturbed by a transcendent experience, generally passes from the prime of life to the vigor of maturity, and thereafter to a slow decline.

If this interruption occurs, the individual has the sensation of a frightening vacillation of his own physical forces and feels the compelling need to gain vital energies to support and animate his own bodily existence. From that moment on he sees himself as a "fighter against death." And here lies the danger of insufficient knowledge, because two ways are offered to feed the roots of his physical life with another vital energy: a lower and a higher way. The lower way is the easier, and many magical methods are prompt at this point to aid the "fighter against death," who while maintaining his detached position can feed his physical vitality through a "pact" with "infernal" forces, from which he can effectively absorb heat and energy so as to get over the interruption. And this can be the beginning of serious deviations.

But there is the other way, the *solar* one, by which the "fighter against death" brings detachment to perfection by uniting with that force which is the true original essence of his spirit, which is the *purusha* correlating not with a particular and mental *prakṛti,* but with the entire *prakṛti,* which means more or less the whole manifested order. Then he can get over the neutral point, because a force comes to him from above that is capable of compensating for the imbalance, sustaining and animating his life, producing a profound transformation of his whole being. He who has experienced the danger of plunging into the darkness, from which dark heat and light can indeed be obtained, and has had the strength to resist the fascination of this heat and light that would propel him to Dionysian indulgence, and then become a continual necessity for his life and his zest for life, can truly comprehend what the solar direction is, the purushic direction, and seek to attain in it the authentic heat and the authentic life.

A further consideration may be added: if the provisional mental "I" of man detaches itself solely from the mental dynamic and tries to confront with its own resources the world of emotions, anguish, fear, desire, and the organic-instinctive attachments to physical life, it will very likely be overwhelmed or fooled. Only by connecting with a higher force, which no longer fights on the same level as one's adversary, can the disciple become the warrior capable of reducing the enemy to obedience. Here the isolation of the mental *purusha* is only the beginning. From a certain point of view, it is only a preparation. What is further needed is a "contact."

The deeper sense of the Catholic teaching is no different, namely that only through "grace" can one fight successfully against "sin" and "temptation." In Hindu traditions—some of them at least, that also appear in the *Bhagavad Gita*—there is the similar idea of the opportunity of integrating the merely cognitive life with *bhakti,* in *bhakti.* The term is commonly translated as "devotion," but it means rather a fervidly transcendent orientation of the soul toward the higher, since in India the theistic point of view has a very subordinate significance. *Bhakti* here means the force capable of carrying the disciple beyond that "neutral point" in which deviation and the danger of a titanic-Dionysian upheaval are almost inevitable. Where regular forms of initiation still exist, the ritual and hierarchical transmission of the "spiritual influences" integrates the results of the purely personal work of "separation." These influences serve precisely to vivify and transfigure the purushic nucleus that is already isolated, so as to facilitate the return to its primordial state, the realization of its true force and its true life. And this is the very point at which all dualism ceases, and in which one can develop in all its depth the work of true transmutation following the Royal and solar Art.

XI.2

The Ascetic, Fire, Rock, Space

From the *Milindapañha*

The Milindapañha *is an exposition of Buddhist doctrine given in the form of a conversation between the sage Nāgasena and King Milinda, who corresponds to the Greek historical king Menander, who had extended his realm to some regions of northern India in the second half of the second century BC. The passages translated here comprise chapter 3 of book VII (11–30).*[1]

I

"Venerable Nāgasena, those five qualities of fire which you say he [the ascetic] ought to take, which are they?"

"Just, O king, as fire burns grass, and sticks, and branches, and leaves; just so, O king, should the strenuous ascetic,[2] earnest in effort, burn out in the fire of wisdom all evil dispositions which feed on objects of thought, whether subjective or objective, whether desirable or the reverse. This, O king, is the first quality of fire he ought to have.[3]

---

1. [The present version is taken from *The Questions of King Milinda,* trans. T. W. Rhys Davids (Oxford: Clarendon, 1894), pt. II, bk. VII, chap. 3, §§11–15, 21–30; pp. 311–12, 314–17. In all likelihood, this also served as basis for the Italian translator. —*Trans.*]

2. [Following the Italian version, the word *bhikshu* whenever it occurs in Rhys Davids's translation is replaced by "ascetic." —*Trans.*]

3. It should be remembered that in Buddhism, as in the yoga of Patañjali, the task of the "ascetic" is to destroy, "burn up" all the roots, that is, the potential tendencies harbored

"And again, O king, as fire has no pity, neither mercy; just so, O king, should the strenuous ascetic, earnest in effort, show no pity, neither mercy, to any evil dispositions (*saṃskāra*). This, O king, is the second quality of fire he ought to have.

"And again, O king, as fire destroys cold; just so, O king, should the strenuous ascetic, earnest in effort, lighting up in his heart the burning fire of zeal, destroy all evil dispositions therein. This, O king, is the third quality of fire he ought to have.

"And again, O king, as fire, seeking no favor of any man, bearing no ill-will to any man, makes heat for all; just so, O king, should the strenuous ascetic, earnest in effort, dwell in spirit like the fire, fawning on none, bearing ill-will to none. This, O king, is the fourth quality of fire he ought to have.

"And again, O king, as fire dispels darkness, and makes the light appear; just so, O king, should the strenuous ascetic, earnest in effort, dispel the darkness of ignorance, and make the light of knowledge to appear. This is the fifth quality of fire he ought to have. For it was said, O king, by the Blessed One, the god over all gods, in his exhortation to Rāhula, his son: 'Practise thyself, Rāhula, in that meditation that acts like fire. Thereby shall no wrong dispositions, which have not yet arisen, arise within thee, nor shall they that have arisen bear sway over thy heart.'"

2

"Venerable Nāgasena, the five qualities of the rock that you say he ought to have, which are they?"

"Just, O king, as rock is firm, unshaken, immovable; just so, O king, should the strenuous ascetic, earnest in effort, never be excited by alluring things—forms, or sounds, or scents, or tastes, or touch—by veneration or contempt, by support or by neglect, by reverence or its absence,

_____

(*cont.*) in or invading the depth of the being, irrespective of their good or bad qualities. All that is considered in them is the force that tends to attach one to anything conditioned, and as such they are rooted out. *Saṃskāra* is one of the terms for these roots; in the East the teachings about them give enormous range and a complete systematization to what in Europe has been presented, and at the same time deformed, by "psychoanalytic" theories.

by honour or dishonour, by praise or blame, nor should he be offended by things that give offence, nor bewildered on occasions of bewilderment, neither should he quake nor tremble, but like a rock should he be firm. This, O king, is the first quality of the rock he ought to have. For it was said by the Blessed One, the god over all gods:

> 'The solid rock's not shaken by the wind,
> Just so the wise man falters not, nor shakes,
>   At praise or blame.'

"And again, O king, as a rock is firm, unmixed with extraneous things; just so, O king, should the strenuous ascetic, earnest in effort, be firm and independent, given to association with none. This, O king, is the second quality of the rock he ought to have. For it was said, O king, by the Blessed One, the god over all gods:

> 'The man who mixes not with householders,
> Nor with the homeless, but who wanders lone,
> Without a home, and touched by few desires,—
> That is the man I call a Brāhmana.'

"And again, O king, as on the rock no seed will take root; just so, O king, should the strenuous ascetic, earnest in effort, never permit evil dispositions to take root in his mind. This, O king, is the third quality of rock that he ought to have. For it was said, O king, by Subhūti, the Elder:

> 'When lustful thoughts arise within my heart,
> Examining myself, alone I beat them down.
> Thou who'rt by lust excited, who by things
> That give offence, allowest of offence,
> Feeling bewildered when strange things occur,
> Thou shouldst retire far from the lonely woods.
> For they're the dwelling-place of men made pure,
> Austere in life, free from the stains of sin.
> Defile not that pure place. Leave thou the woods.'

"And again, just as the rock rises aloft, just so should the strenuous ascetic, earnest in effort, rise aloft through knowledge. This is the fourth quality of the rock he ought to have. For it was said, O king, by the Blessed One, the god over all gods:

> 'When the wise man by earnestness has driven
> Vanity far away, the terraced heights
> Of wisdom doth he climb, and, free from care,
> Looks over the vain world, the careworn crowd—
> As he who standing on the mountain top
> Can watch his fellow-men still toiling on the plain.'

"And again, O king, just as the rock cannot be lifted up or bent down; just so, O king, should the strenuous ascetic, earnest in effort, be neither lifted up nor depressed. This, O king, is the fifth quality of the rock he ought to have. For it was said, O king, by the devout woman, Kulla Subhaddā, when she was exalting the recluses of her own sect:

> 'The world is lifted up by gain, depressed by loss.
> My ascetics remain alike in gain or loss.'

3

"Venerable Nāgasena, those five qualities of space which you say he ought to have, which are they?"

"Just, O king, as space is everywhere impossible to grasp; just so, O king, should it be impossible for the the strenuous ascetic, earnest in effort, to be anywhere taken hold of by evil dispositions. This, O king, is the first quality of space he ought to have.

"And again, O king, as space is the familiar resort of Rishis, and ascetics, and gods, and flocks of birds; just so, O king, should the strenuous ascetic, earnest in effort, make his mind wander easily over all things with the knowledge that each individual (samkhāra) is impermanent, born to sorrow, and without any abiding principle (any soul).

This, O king, is the second quality of space he ought to have.[4]

"And again, O king, as space inspires terror; just so, O king, should the strenuous ascetic, earnest in effort, train his mind to be in terror of rebirths in any kind of existence. To seek no happiness therein.[5] This, O king, is the third quality of space he ought to have.

"And again, O king, as space is infinite, boundless, immeasurable; just so, O king, should the righteousness of the strenuous ascetic, earnest in effort, know no limit, and his knowledge be beyond measure.[6] This, O king, is the fourth quality of space he ought to have.

"And again, O king, as space does not hang on to anything, does not cling to anything, does not rest on anything, is not stopped by anything; just so, O king, should the strenuous ascetic, earnest in effort, neither in any way depend on, nor cling to, nor rest on, nor be hindered by either the families that minister to him, or the pupils who resort to him, or the support he receives, or the dwelling he occupies, or any obstacles to the noble life,[7] or any requisites that he may want, or any kind of evil inclination. This, O king, is the fifth quality of space he

---

4. This refers to Buddhism's general idea about samsaric existence. With reference to everything that is generated (literally: composed, formed = *samkhāra*) and has a merely individual reality, it affirms the nonexistence of a substantial, immortal, and permanent principle (such as the Upanishadic *ātmā* is with regard to man) and the fluidity of every being, which, concretely, is composed merely of a current of associated states. That which in popular Buddhist teachings is called "suffering" in fact corresponds to a term better translated as "agitation" and "impermanence," a sense that was increasingly assumed in the doctrinal developments of Buddhist teaching. But beyond the samsaric states of existence there remains the immutable, called in that teaching by the well-known and much misunderstood term of *nirvāna*.

5. One must remember that, like any high initiation, Buddhism does not aim at the passage from one form of existence to another (a "rebirth"), even to what is symbolized by the "heavens" and "paradises," but aims at the unconditioned state, superior to the bonds of any manifested form.

6. This really means the knowledge to which the "measure" of the common intellect does not apply (*mens* and *mensuro*), namely spiritual knowledge.

7. [Rhys Davids has "obstacles to the religious life." The Italian reads "*ostacoli alla nobile vita,*" with the following footnote. —*Trans.*] The term "noble" corresponds in the text to *ārya*, or literally to "Aryan," a term whose meaning is more that of an interior race, embracing the ideas of nobility, rectitude, sacrality. Buddhism, which was created by a prince of the Aryan stock, continuously uses this term both as an adjective and as a noun.

ought to have. For it was said, O king, by the Blessed One, the god over all gods, in his exhortation to Rāhula, his son: 'Just, Rāhula, as space rests nowhere on anything, so shouldst thou practise theyself in that meditation that is like space. Thereby shall neither pleasant nor unpleasant sensations, as they severally arise, bear sway over thy heart.'"[8]

8. The symbol of space, as support for contemplation leading to realization, has acquired ever more importance in Mahayana Buddhism, so that it is often associated with the notion of the *śūnya*, that "void" which is an essential sign of the Perfected and the Incomprehensible: that to which it is said that "neither gods, nor men, nor demons know the way."

Spiritual Authority and
Temporal Power

One of René Guénon's works is dedicated to the problem of the relationship between spiritual authority and temporal power,[1] an important problem not only from the traditional but also the esoteric point of view. Since our ideas on the subject do not entirely agree with Guénon's, it seems good to explain the various reasons.

According to Guénon, every normal and traditional civilization is characterized by the primacy of spiritual authority over temporal power. As soon as temporal power emancipates itself, and especially when it claims to subjugate the spiritual authority for contingent and political goals, an involutive process begins, and the development of civilization slides steadily downward. Eventually, the representatives of temporal power can no longer maintain their position, causing a breakdown that leads to the world of materialistic and rebellious masses.

We largely agree with all that. The divergence of our point of view begins when the problems arise, first, of the basis for the spiritual authority, and second, of those who might legitimately represent it.

For Guénon, spiritual authority is tied to "knowledge," to "contemplation," and to the priestly caste, whereas temporal power is tied to

---

1. R. Guénon, *Autorité spirituelle et pouvoir temporel* (Paris: Vrin, 1929). A new edition appeared in 1950.

"action" and the warrior or regal caste. This is debatable. Let us state at the outset that our consideration—and Guénon's, too—is not restricted to more recent times. Obviously in recent times (in which we include the cycle of the great European dynasties) the warrior caste has been limited to exercising temporal power, restricted to military, political, administrative, and juridical functions, and having little sacred about it. But that seems to refer less to the warrior caste itself than to its degradation. In the same epoch, that which represents itself as the priestly caste, or rather as the clergy, shows just as much degeneration from what was originally the élite of the true hieratic representatives of spiritual authority.

For now, let us consider the basis of the latter. Guénon speaks of "those principles that are the eternal and immutable essences contained in the permanent actuality of the divine Intellect" (p. 22), principles that provide "knowledge par excellence" (p. 45) and constitute the fulcrum of the "traditional doctrine," of "orthodoxy," and of the inexorable authority of the traditional castes (p. 33). Rather than principles, we prefer to speak here of higher states of being that are to be realized. As we know, the esoteric concept of "tradition" refers to a certain stabilization of those states, brought about by a chain of qualified beings. Its natural consequences are the legacy of a knowledge that is not merely human, a certain status, and a certain immaterial influence. Now, understood in this more concrete sense, one cannot see why "tradition" should be the monopoly of the priestly castes. At the origins, in a whole series of cases it was the regal tradition that had this very significance, such that it could legitimately claim the supreme authority for itself. Fragments of this ancient regal world have come down even to our own times: we could mention, for example, the Japanese tradition of divine royalty.

As we have seen, Guénon clearly distinguishes "knowledge" from "action," attributing the former to the priestly caste, the latter to the warrior caste. But on a higher plane this is a relative distinction. Guénon himself has often emphasized that knowledge, in the metaphysical and esoteric sense, and realization (action) are inseparable. Thus, admitting that "action" is the special field of competence of the warrior caste, the possibility always remains of conceiving of it as the basis for a higher realization. We cannot see why Guénon, when dealing with the warrior caste, considers only the material kind of action, and that which serves only temporal interests and realizations. The celebration of warrior action contained in the *Bhagavad Gita,* for instance, opens very different perspectives: here action becomes the very path to "heaven" and to liberation. In truth, the way of that "which is only affirmed by itself, independently of any sensible support and works, as it were, invisibly" (p. 30) cannot be made the monopoly of the spiritual authority of the priestly type. Regal majesty, that blend of Olympian detachment and power that is characteristic of the true rulers, the irresistible force of command, the august and supranatural aura that surrounds the heroes and sovereigns of the traditional world—all that represents something equivalent, though realized above all on the basis of action and the nature of a *kshatriya,* a warrior. To limit oneself to considering the warrior or king who has descended to wielding only temporal power is as wrong as to consider the priest merely as the theologizing mediator of the divine, or the "carer of souls" as in devotional religion: a far different type from the true hieratic representative of spiritual authority.

Guénon emphasizes the fact that in the original state the two powers were not separate, but "contained in the common principle from which they emerged, and of which they represent two indivisible aspects, indissolubly bound in the unity of a synthesis that is both superior and anterior to their distinction" (p. 14). This is an important point. But once it is recognized, namely that the original type was simultaneously "regal" and "sacerdotal," and that these these two terms were only defined in a later period of secession, why should one of the functions be further from the origin than the other, and less able to serve as the basis for an eventual reintegration of the primordial state? We would go further still: it seems to us that the unique caste corresponding to that undivided power at the origins would have had more a regal than a priestly character. Guénon himself equates that state to the "autonomous Individuals" mentioned by Lao-Tze, the *svecchācārī,* a word in the Hindu tradition meaning "those who can do whatever they wish," and the beings in Islamic esotericism "who are a law unto themselves" (pp. 14–15). They are obviously the same as the Hermetic "immaterial race without a king," which has often been mentioned in these pages. One can hardly deny that such a type would have had qualities that are more "regal" than "priestly."

Moreover, among all peoples the most recurrent term for the divinity itself is the regal one of "Lord." Guénon himself uses the term *King of the World*" to designate the supreme center of the primordial spiritual authority, and emphasizes (p. 137) the relationship between the metaphysical concept of the "world axis" and the symbolism of the *scepter,* emblem of regal dignity. We can juxtapose the Hermetic affirmation: "After God, we will honor those who offer us his image and wield the scepter . . . the statues of whom are beacons of peace in the storm,"[2] with the Upanishadic teaching, according to which the Brahman "created a higher and more perfect form than himself, the warrior nobility, namely the warrior gods," to which it adds "There is none superior to the warrior nobility, and that is the reason that the priest humbly venerates the warrior when the consecration of a king takes place."[3] Moreover, in China no priestly caste existed: the "mandate of Heaven" was assumed directly by the emperor, whose function was enhanced with a openly magical significance: his conduct was thought to influence even the cosmic forces. At the center of ancient Egypt we again find a regal type, in a tradition that simulaneously has an initiatic character; a priestly dynasty did not form until a later period, at Thebes. The first kings of Rome (and later the emperors) simultaneously held the office of pontifex, and it was they who performed the *sacra* (rites). Up to the Middle Ages what we might call the "regal mystery" was preserved; for example, in the allusions to the enigmatic "royal religion of Melchizedek," while various orders of chivalry, especially the Templars, sought to integrate the warrior type with an ascetic, priestlike, and sometimes even initiatic dignity.

We should not forget that wherever "priesthood" is mentioned in reference to the origins, it risks a confusion of language and the diffusion of a pernicious error, because the type in question has very

---

2. *Corpus Hermeticum,* XVIII, 15.
3. *Bṛhadāraṇyaka Upanishad,* I, vi, 11.

different traits from those that everyone thinks of today, when priests or clergy are mentioned. Let us take only the example of the Brahmin, the "sacerdotal" prototype of the ancient Indo-Aryan civilization: he appears more with the characteristics of a "magus" in the higher sense. He is the lord of the *brahman,* which was originally understood not in Vedantic terms but as a pure magical force. He is the holder of formulas and rituals, able to act even on the highest divinities. This is the field in which his "wisdom" is essentially defined. But the "magical" element, through its relation to the power of command and a virile attitude, is much closer to the warrior spirit than to the priestly in the current sense.

We cannot see how Guénon can state, as a principle, that regal initiation corresponds to the "physical" and priestly initiation to the "metaphysical," or the former to the "Lesser Mysteries" and the latter to the "Greater Mysteries" (p. 40). On the contrary, it is documented that in the Eleusinian Mysteries, for instance, it was thought that initiation conferred on the king a dignity superior to that of the priests or sages.[4] The Hellenic archon, like the Roman emperor later, was assimilated to Zeus and sometimes to Heracles as "Olympian" hero.[5] Identical views figure in Mithraism, another example of an initiation favoring the warrior element. Thus, for royalty the initiatic point of reference, ritual or symbolic, was not the "physical" (i.e., the "natural") order, but the "metaphysical," the "supraworldly." Regal majesty always served as an image of that of the "King of Heaven."

The problem under discussion is not of merely speculative or historical interest, but is also important from the point of view of a traditional reconstruction: that much is evident to whoever relates it to the other problem, that of East and West. The general trend of the West is far more "active" than "contemplative," and its predominant ideal is the "warrior," *kshatriya* (in the fullest possible extent of the term), rather than the "priest." These things are obvious, and already empha-

---

4. V. Magnien, *Les mystères d'Eleusis* (Paris, 1929), 193–94.
5. Magnien, *Les mystères d'Eleusis,* 195, and G. Costa, *Giove ed Ercole* (Contributi allo studio della religione romana dell'Impero; Rome, 1919).

sized in more than one essay of the present collection. Moreover, we do not believe that this characteristic of the West is explicable by a degenerative process: we already find it, in fact, in the most ancient Western traditions. Nor has it failed to influence the esoteric domain, too. To take a single example: while Hermetism is one of the principal Western initiatic traditions, we should note that while the Hermetic art is often called sacred, hieratic, or "divine," its most frequent designation is that of *Ars Regia,* the "Royal Art." There are also some significant variations in the symbolism of Western esoteric doctrine. Two examples: in the hierarchy of elements in the East one usually finds Fire first, then Air; but in the West, first the Air and then (in the sense of a higher dignity) the Fire. In the East, the color white corresponds to *sattva,* the highest of the three *gunas,* while the lower *guna* of *rajas* is red; also "knowledge" is very often symbolized by the white lunar light. The whole of the Western Hermetic tradition, and with it more than one school of magic, concurs in a reversed arrangement: the *albedo* or white regimen, always placed under the feminine, lunar sign, is an inferior degree to the *rubedo* regimen, the red, whose symbol is the *royal* purple and the element of Fire. These are telling symptoms that speak of more than a casual variation of symbolic expressions: rather, they display a specific form of traditional instruction congenial to a "warrior" nature.

To underrate this arrangement by way of the thesis that the supreme authority can only be legitimately held by the priestly caste is not only unjustified but also dangerous, if one does not want to cause misunderstandings and if one considers the practical consequences. In the West, this would mean reinforcing the "Guelph" faction and flattering it with the pretense that the Christian or Catholic clergy embodies the same dignity as Guénon refers to when he speaks of the "sacerdotal caste": namely that it is right in claiming supreme spiritual authority in the Western world. This is in no way the case. One of the basic causes of Western civilization's distress is the fact that a world essentially composed of *kshatriya,* warriors, has for centuries lacked a fitting "soul." The spiritual authority of the religion that has come to predominate in the West is thoroughly "priestly" in tone, so as to cause an unhealthy dualism, or else compromises that are anything but constructive. The one and only spiritual authority that the West can obey without violence and denaturation is that which takes shape on the basis and in the framework of a *kshatriya* tradition. But we do not want to repeat things already said.

Instead, something should be said about the problem of decadence. Guénon seems to see its cause in the revolt of the warrior caste against the priestly caste. The warrior caste, "after having originally been subject to the spiritual authority, rebelled against it, declaring itself independent, or even tried to subordinate that authority to itself, which it had originally always acknowledged as the foundation of its power" (p. 29).[6] If Guénon had simply said that decadence began with the revolt of the political power against the spiritual authority, he would have been right. But by expressing himself thus and involving the two castes, his point is contestable. A thesis of this kind in fact presupposes a hierarchical arrangement like that of the Catholic (and, what is more, Guelph) Middle Ages; or, with due reservations, of Brahmanic India in a period which, besides, was in no way that of the origins. But there have been civilizations, indisputably traditional, whose hierarchical structure was different and whose principle of decadence was equally different. For example, how could one apply this thesis to ancient China, which, as we have said, had a "celestial" royalty, not subordinate to a priestly caste, or to the ancient Nordic peoples, whose situation was analogous and whose king was legitimized simply through his quality of being of the blood of the "Ases"? In other cases we have the opposite; there are cases in which the setting up of a priestly caste against sacred royalty marked the beginning of a subversion and of decadence. Such was the case, for example, in ancient Egypt and, to an extent, in ancient Persia. For our part, we prefer to generalize by saying that in a whole cycle of civilization derived from the Hyperborean and distinguished by the polar symbol, the takeover of a "priestly" spirituality represented a disintegra-

---

6. [The subject of this quotation, in Guénon's original, is not the "warrior caste" but "the warriors." —*Trans.*]

tion and the effect of outside influences, linked to the cycle of the Demetric-matriarchal civilizations of the South.[7]

Our thesis is thus that the primacy or predominance of a warrior or regal tradition over a clergy or a priesthood, like the primacy of action over knowledge, does not by itself constitute any lowering of level or involution. That comes from the loss of contact with metaphysical reality, whether that loss occurs when the sacral and initiatic concept of regality materializes into a merely temporal and political function; or else when the original priestly function degenerates into ecclesiastical and clerical survivals, opaque dogmatic forms, and relationships of simple devotional religiosity.

In one form or another, decadence has for some time been at work in the Western world. The first condition for an effective reaction would be to reestablish contacts with metaphysical reality. But barring some unpredictable general mutation, that seems more problematic than ever.

---

7. This thesis has been developed and documented in Julius Evola, *Rivolta contro il Mondo moderno*, 3rd ed. (Rome: Edizioni Mediterranee, 1969), part II. [See Evola's *Revolt against the Modern World*, trans. Guido Stucco (Rochester, Vt.: Inner Traditions, 1995). —*Trans.*]

About Drugs

Since in volume II of Introduction to Magic *(pp. 146–52) there was a discussion of what alchemical Hermetism calls the "corrosive waters," we think it useful to publish the confidential instructions about a higher use of drugs from a group with which we have been in touch, for its many points of contact and certain details. The reader will not fail to recognize the absolute difference of the experiences in question, and of their orientation, from the profane use of drugs that is extremely widespread among the younger generation, and can only have the effects of degradation and self-destruction.*[1]

For any kind of drug, including simple stimulants, when used not for profane but for higher purposes, the first thing to consider is the so-called *personal toxic equation.*

This has been defined as "the functional psychophysical reaction to a given substance by a given individual, which occurs differently than in other individuals, not only in quantity but also in quality."

The deep cause of this difference has remained unknown. Toxicological researches find the mode of action of drugs and stupefacients undefinable as regards their effects, because although there are chemical reactions at work, the mechanism of how all these substances act remains unclear.

Thus, we should accept that it is essentially a matter of *stimuli,*

---

1. [This essay was added to the 1971 edition of *Introduzione alla Magia. —Trans.*]

which can affect quite diverse levels of the being, causing reactions that depend on the structure of those levels in the individual concerned.

• • •

To the extent that the individual is able to act on these levels, that is, to predispose them in one direction or another or to direct the stimulus to one level or another, the personal toxic equation will become *variable.* One can then expect either a special type of effects *that do not happen at all to others,* or effects that differ from what some drug or other would produce in the same individual, if he approached these experiences passively.

The above should be seen as the fundamental principle of any non-profane use of drugs.

In such use, one must therefore consider:

1. The natural predisposition of the individual;
2. The preparation, which creates a very specific orientation, which in turn will condition the direction of efficacy of the substances used and the course of the experiences;
3. The *channel* constituted by the individual's adherence to a chain or tradition, an adherence that can provoke the engagement of a specific psychic current, and also experiences of a higher order, in the case of drugs whose nature, or high dosage, or a special kind of usage amplifies the contents and reactions of consciousness and of the individual subconscious (see fascicle B).[2]

• • •

Before going into details, we must keep in mind the current classification of drugs as:

1. Excitants,
2. Euphoriants,

---

2. [This parenthesis, *"vedi fascicolo B,"* presumably refers to a section of the "confidential instructions" from which this excerpt is taken. —*Trans.*]

3. Inebriants,
4. Hallucinogens,
5. Narcotics.

In the West, the best-known mild *excitants* are coffee and tea. Obviously, their use is of no interest to their habitual consumers.

If one is not used to them, and therefore able to notice a distinct effect, it is harmless but useful for lucid mental concentration.

Tobacco belongs among the excitants. Here we must repeat what we have already said: that habit in profane life paralyzes usefulness. However, the occasional use of strong and unadulterated tobacco (like Brazilian or Havana cigars), if one can stand it, may bring about a state of active inebriation in which one maintains all one's intellectual and volitive faculties.

Among the natives of America, highly concentrated extracts of tobacco, taken fasting, were and are used for initiatic purposes and as the preparation for visions by neophytes during their mountain retreats. But we know little more than this vague information.

The *euphoriants* carry the action of the excitants further, without yet causing particular changes of state. Among these we can count sipamine, pervitin, aktedron, and similar preparations.[3] Which of these can produce a truly euphoric state depends on the personal toxic equation. Its positive effects may be a higher lucid self-presence and a dynamization of the psychic and even intellectual faculties.

The disciple should not let these positive effects go to waste by using them for common purposes.

When the substance does not correspond to the personal toxic equation, that is, it does not suit his own constitution, the euphoric effect is minimal and increases the negative consequence (which one always has to expect as a repercussion, even in positive cases): the inability to sleep during the twenty-four hours following the experience.

---

3. [According to the French translator (*Ur & Krur* [Milan: Archè, 1985], 227n.), these are the names of euphoriant products in use in Italy from the 1950s to the 1960s. —*Trans.*]

Already with the category of euphoriants one has to be on one's guard, because there is the possibility of the *deviation* of the experience, which happens to a greater degree in the use of veritable drugs, the stupefacients and hallucinogens.

The danger of a euphoric state is that it takes over the *sensorial body* by arousing pleasure, a diffuse and voluptuous feeling that colors all sensation.

One finds this danger above all in the use of morphine, cocaine, and heroin, substances that can still be classified as euphoriants if not taken at high dosage.

In mentioning this danger, we are entering *the region of what depends on the particular attitude of the subject, and on his ability to control and direct the whole experience.*

He has, in fact, the opportunity—if he has the habit of subtle self-control—of *preventing* the action of the drug from essentially or exclusively affecting the *sensorial body* and being reduced to the euphoria of pleasure.

It is impossible to draw a firm line of separation between euphoriants and *inebriants*. Ancient traditional teachings considered many forms of inebriation, both sacred and profane.

The truth is that there are no sacred inebriations as opposed to profane ones: an inebriation is "sacred" or "profane" according to how the disciple accepts and experiences it, and according to the plane on which he allows it to act.

However, it seems that the different constitution of modern man excludes those forms of inebriation able to lead to ecstasy, as were employed in antiquity and in the "orgies" of the Mysteries. These always allude to inebriations caused by substances and liquors.

The two last categories of drugs are the *hallucinogens* and the *narcotics*. They have in common the property of interrupting the normal waking state. With *narcotics,* among which we can include anesthetics, this interruption may be a pure and simple loss of consciousness, producing a deep and lethargic sleep. Otherwise the resultant state is the liberation of fantasy from the physical senses, on the same plane as everything that happens in dreams.

Drugs in the true sense have as their chief characteristic that of hallucinogens; but one can add a parallel euphoric effect, with the predominant and dangerous variation of the feeling already mentioned, that of pleasure and even beatitude.

This is especially the case with cannabis extracts, the active principle of nightshades, opium, and hashish. But in these cases, too, one finds subjects reacting in the most diverse ways, which it is impossible to predict or explain in a satisfactory way.

One of these drugs is *peyote,* which has also been used by Native Americans for magical purposes, because it is thought to bring one into contact with divinity or the gods. It is from this that the *anhalonium lewini* has recently been extracted, of which Aleister Crowley made much use.

The habitual effects (normal in the common man) are described as "a special awakening of pleasure of a particular quality, together with the perception of sensible phantasms, or the highest concentration of the inner life in its purest state. This may have extraordinary aspects, superior to reality and never before imagined, making the subject believe that he is transported to a different and new world of the senses and the spirit."

The above description shows the two possible facets of the experience. The same kind of effects are produced by the *mescal,* also of American origin, from which *mescaline* is made pharmaceutically and commercially. The effects reported include visions, hallucinations, and abnormal bodily sensations, though consciousness remains clear and active, and the activity of thought proceeds in the normal way.

Controlled experiments have also been made with mescaline, in which the subject can stay in contact and communicate with others during the experience.

This opens up possibilities, so long as a Master is present.

But he would still need to know about the dosage of the drug. It is not easy to find without medical prescriptions.

Besides, for mescalin, and for all other drugs of that sort, we must point out that in practice it is almost impossible to find them directly prepared from the sources, which are plants. One can only find synthetic chemical preparations, in which various subtle elements of the drug are destroyed and do not act in the way that is of interest to us.

In the case of *mescal,* the experience goes as follows:

First one feels abnormal bodily sensations: great lightness or heaviness, the feeling of flying or plunging down.

Then one has visual phenomena, with geometric figures predominating.

Later on, images and panoramas appear, usually in fantastic colors.

All these phases should be observed and put behind one. There follows a phase of symbolic visions, full of evident or hidden meaning. What we will say later on concerning the ultimate effects of ether applies to this state. But most people lose consciousness before reaching this final stage, which is the essential one for spiritual purposes.

The disciple must be absolutely dissuaded from using drugs like opium or hashish, which have only a hallucinogenic effect, for initiatic purposes. The effect of dynamization of the fantasy is so direct and violent that the spirit falls into a passive state (intentionally or, worse, unintentionally), becoming the mere spectator of a phantasmagoria.

For the drugs that act thus, the spiritual peril consists in the deviation we have mentioned: the vampiric activation of the *sensorial body.* If one does not have a highly developed ascetic and initiatic preparation that has been severely confirmed (tested), it is difficult for the spirit to resist the temptation of giving in, identifying and immersing itself in the sensations of ecstatic and beatific pleasure.

From our point of view, this must be considered as a regressive and purely dissolvent state, leading to a spiritual level even lower than that of the profane.

• • •

The danger just mentioned is less in the use of *narcotics* in the proper sense, because they generally do not cause such sensations.

Firstly, they can cause strong reactions of repulsion, and very unpleasant organic effects.

However, the ability to master these reactions and overcome these states already guarantees there is a force present in the subject that can be trusted to produce a positive and not a deviant course of the experience.

The main difficulty in using narcotics is naturally that of maintaining consciousness.

We should mention the same kind of difficulty in the use of the *anhalonium lewini* and of *mescal* (or mescaline). In fact, we know that few succeed in reaching the state in which initiatically significant experiences occur, coming after the abnormal physical sensations, the visions, hallucinations, and so on. Consciousness is almost always lost before getting so far. Communication is also interrupted with any others who are present.

In the case of *chloroform*, this difficulty is practically insuperable for most people. It is also very difficult to administer to oneself. In both cases this is due to the fact that its action is not gradual and hard to control.

For individual experiences, it is better to use *ether.* The substance is easily obtained. It is advisable to use the refined quality that is used not for simple anesthesis but for narcosis in surgery.

The technique of using it is progressive, and one can regulate it by oneself.

The best time is the evening, long enough after eating for digestion to be finished, and in bed.

The first phase, in a first experimental period, is to inhale the ether from the bottle slowly and deeply through one nostril, holding the other nostril closed with a finger and exhaling through the mouth.

The second phase, in a second experimental period, is to inhale the ether slowly and deeply through the mouth and exhale through the nose.

From the physical point of view, one needs to have control of one's organism, because very often, when starting out, in most people it produces sudden and violent symptoms of nausea and vomiting.

It is important to stay absolutely still, because any movement provokes retching. These spasms can and should be suppressed as they arise. Later they will cease to occur, unless the subject is absolutely refractory to the substance. In that case one must give up ether.

One has to expect, in the first attempts, that at a certain moment one will lose consciousness and fall asleep. Little by little one gains the ability to maintain consciousness for a longer time.

Internal conditions: One needs to possess a particular strength of concentration, attention, and vigilance over the sensations, besides an *absolutely active attitude.*

The latter requisite is the key to any initiatic progress during the experience, avoiding the risks of its deviation and, in general, of enslavement to the drug.

The active attitude is like that of someone who is ready and expecting to make a leap.

Therefore, one should not just wait for the sensations and the change of consciousness to happen, but like a spider waiting at the center of its web, one must suddenly grab it and make a corresponding *act of one's own consciousness.*

Second, the active attitude means not letting oneself be surprised and overcome by the sensations, however intense, unexpected, seductive, and marvelous they may be. As soon as they occur and open up, *one must unite a force of one's own to them.*

For example, if the sensation is of force 5, by the addition of the I (which, however, must not alter or interrupt it) the charge should be, let us say, force 7.[4] One will thus have an advantage of 2 over the stimulus.

This is the first and indispensable condition for not passing under the regime of passive sensations, in which only the *sensorial body* is activated, with regression of the will, as happens in the normal course of action of drugs on the profane.

Second, it is also the necessary condition for keeping one's *independence from the drug.*

---

4. [The Italian reads "*la carica non dovrà essere, diciamo, sette*" ("The charge should not be, let us say, seven.") I omit the negative, as does the French edition, which reads "*l'apport du Moi . . . devra être, disons, de force 7.*" —*Trans.*]

It has been verified that when the disciple has really followed this line, he has not become the slave of the substance. Because he is only seeking a stimulus, while the chief thing is the exercise of his will, he can also do without it at any moment, avoiding the danger of addiction and other negative consequences. Thus, it will always be he who decides when he will use the substance and when he will not.

Keep firmly in mind the danger, if one does not hold to these principles. *We cannot stress this enough.*

The first effect of experiments with *ether* (and similar substances, as well as hallucinogens) is an *opening of sensitivity and synesthesia,* a sense of ecstatic lightness and expansion, and a special resonant quality united to one's perceptions (given that one remains for a good while in contact with the external world).

One passes on to an internal consciousness in which the mental processes are galvanized.

Then the mental processes are neutralized, they become *discontinuous,* and thoughts, ideas, or images appear that usually have an intensity all their own.

One must stay very attentive, in the sense of maintaining inner neutrality or intellectual impassivity in the face of these thoughts, because they may present a false appearance of evidence and truth. In fact, this has nothing to do with their contents, but depends exclusively on the general state in which one finds oneself when they appear to the mind.

It is like a color that can be added to anything.

Going beyond this phase one may also experience hallucinations of sight or sound (images or voices), depending on one's predisposition. These too have an accidental and secondary quality. They have no spiritual significance.

But there are some who stop there.

The next phase is a higher, ecstatic freedom, devoid of psychic contents. It corresponds to the common state of deep sleep.

The point of transition is often marked by a feeling of terror or anguish. One believes that to take one step further will lead to death.

Images and voices may also reinforce this sensation. One must be bold and absolutely want to go ahead, "come what may."

If consciousness holds firm up to this state (after the death point), this is the state in which phenomena of initiatic importance may occur, if the experiencer has the *exorcizing circle of protection*, bestowed by the chain, or through an innate or acquired dignity.

One must be aware that the state now described is one of *psychic void*. The void attracts forces, influences, "archetypes" from the unconscious and the intermediary realm, not material but not divine.

It is already a valid guarantee if consciousness is maintained, if consciousness of the I is preserved up to this state and not dissolved; that means that at least one of the three protective conditions is present. Then the "I" principle can have an exorcizing power by the sole virtue of its presence.

But the active state should be maintained, not only in the sense of self-presence and courageous affirmation but also as a *faculty of invocation:* orienting itself to the higher, profoundly desiring transfiguration.

In this state, the negative result (due to the lack of the protective esoteric circle with its exorcizing virtue) is a visionary phantasmagoria that comes with all the theosophical trimmings. In the positive result the essential realization should be *the initiatic disclosure of the I,* the experience of the second birth.

Due to the extreme variance of individual dispositions, we cannot describe for outsiders the general schemes of all that can be experienced, and all that is possible in principle, in this state.

There can be no guide in these experiences because, unlike those of *mescal* or *anhalonium,* one cannot have a Master by one's side, or an assistant with whom one remains in contact. Each one has to find the path and organize the experience for himself, following his own intuitions and with his own responsibility, through repeated attempts.

We come now to consider the use of symbols. On the way to this state of higher freedom, the *projection* of a symbol may be a support. The symbol can also serve as basis for the *initiatic disclosure of the consciousness of the I,* if one is chosen that can serve this function.

The tradition to which the disciple belongs through regular

adherence, or the direction seriously cultivated along an individual path based on elective affinity, properly verified, will indicate case by case what symbol lends itself to this function.

Moreover, the state of higher freedom is generally able to yield *the illuminative or inspired disclosure of the content of any symbol whatever,* whether graphic (visual), verbal, or conceptual: ideograms and pentacles.

That means that one who has adequately mastered this state and, while in it, projects a given symbol (not of course arbitrary, but one of the true symbols of the sacred initiatic traditions or of our chain), may receive the revelation of its hidden synthesizing and intuitive meaning, in an act of the intellectual light, beyond any discursive, conceptual, and interpretative element.

In this dimension the symbols are metaphysical realities. They therefore have both a cognitive and a magical content.

Like the experiences of initiation and of theurgy, these states of consciousness, artificially produced, may also have a power of evocation.

One can try thereby to enter into contact with the entities such as are described in the Delta fascicle[5] on the theurgy of the chain.

The individual who operates alone, even if protected by his spiritual orientation and by the power of the chain, should not venture lightly into this domain, because he can never be certain that his magical circle does not have gaps of lesser resistance.

Thus, the Masters exhort us to follow only the quest of the intellectual light and of the initiatic disclosure of the I, when using drugs of the narcotic and hallucinogenic types.

Keep in mind that all the conditions indicated for the spiritual attitude (activity, utterly lucid vigilance, active conversion of the contents of sensation, etc.) also hold good for the non-profane use of substances of other types, like inebriants, whose action does not go as far as the detachment of consciousness.

In the use of ether, once a certain point is reached (whether satisfying or still unsatisfying), one will decide to stop there. This decision, which

---

5. [See note 3 above. —*Trans.*]

revokes the decree of conscious self-awareness, suffices for an extremely deep, dreamless sleep to immediately ensue. It is a beneficial sleep.

• • •

Repercussions: We repeat that one must be very careful not to develop a habit with the use of this or any other drug.

To obtain their effects, and simply for training oneself and getting over the initial difficulties, it is natural to spend a period of assiduous use. But these will always be specific periods that one will decide on now and again, allowing intervals of time to pass between them.

However little one allows oneself a margin of passive absorption of ecstatic states on the part of the *sensorial body,* in the case of even a partial habituation to the drug, the repercussion will be a state or feeling of alienation from the world, and an almost physical disgust for ordinary life. This is why there are frequent cases of suicide among profane ether addicts.

In the field of *positive* repercussions: the morning and the day after a session one may feel a sort of animation and inspired openness of outward experiences; a deep and evident significance may be directly perceived in things, people, landscapes, or natural phenomena; their true being will reveal itself.

To obtain perceptions of this kind, which are very easily suffocated by the ordinary kind of sensation, one must stay open in spirit and isolated, without directly relating to others.

Especially during the first experiments, it is best to spend the chosen period in the countryside, hardly seeing anyone, speaking as little as possible, avoiding reading and not applying one's thinking powers. Only when the subtle sensitivity has been reinforced can the benefits described (fringes of repercussion) also be obtained, somewhat more weakly, in city life.

Little by little these fade away, and then the danger arises again of resorting to drugs to recapture them.

• • •

The disciple must never forget that the object of these instructions is always a *"corrosive water."*

We mean by this that an indispensible requirement is the presence of an essential inner nucleus, which will not let itself be submerged (thus avoiding addiction) and is capable of keeping itself intact.

This does not prevent the fact that the use of all these substances (unlike the simple excitants) has as its inevitable consequence a *disaggregation in regard to the global psychic complex*. That nucleus alone is unharmed.

In other words, the effect is the opposite of what may be attained by the path of increasing integration of all the subtle, psychic, and psychophysical principles around the nucleus of the I. *Everything that may have been achieved in that direction will be lost and destroyed by using drugs.*

The disciple must therefore reflect, and consider that if he has decided on the use of the technique of drugs for serious motives, he must expect that for months or even years there will be *negative conditions* for all that he might realize by following the other path (that of psychophysical integration). And he will have to wait patiently before he can find himself at the starting point again.

The other possibility is to follow exclusively the technique of the corrosive waters, choosing to make it the axis of his own path and of his whole life. This is such a risky matter that it can only concern an individual with a qualification, a constitution, and a magical system of protection that are *more than exceptional.*

XI.5

Various Commentaries

SEEING WITHOUT WANTING TO SEE

The psychic habit created by man in the constant and exclusive use of his physical senses is the greatest obstacle to perception of a higher order. This habit forms the instinctive tendency to reduce everything to those sense reactions, which interrupt the process by their intervention and interference. The effect of the initial practices may be to present sensations and visions that we unknowingly exclude from consciousness, because our eyes immediately look elsewhere, and our attitude is faulty.

Take the special case of visions. Anyone who has advanced in initiatic practice knows how often, in phases of "silence" and isolation of the I, and sometimes even in the waking state, there are manifestations such as "presentiments" of luminous sensations, colors, and in some cases of "figures." For the beginner, this is what happens in most cases: he instinctively interrupts the inner state in which that hint of experience occurs, and reattaches himself to "earth." As soon as this "something" is noticed, an effort is made to seize the experience, to define and appropriate it, to *see* it—but this effort is channeled along ordinary visual perception. Thus, we unintentionally resort to the physical organ, the eye, as if it were a matter of staring harder to catch a fleeting sensation of material light. With the effort of "seeing," such a reaction leads back to the physical body, so that the gap closes and the possibility that arose comes to nothing.

It is not easy to overcome this deviating instinct, for the very reason that it is an instinct, an automatism, and a rapid subconscious motor reflex of the animal being. In its depths two roots of the feral life are active, even if only in subtle form: fear, and the instinct of appropriation.

One needs to be able to make one's spirit stay *immobile,* excluding the impulse to "grasp" the sensation, which only drives it away. In this situation one must be able to evoke a state *like that of a dreamer,* with neither desire nor expectation of the perception.

Something similar can be said about certain experiences of an intuitive character. The habit of *thinking* neutralizes them. An instinct of the same sort refers us to the brain, and a rational process intercepts and eliminates the act of higher intellection, whose speed and winged subtlety then pass without trace among the slow and dense forms of human cerebration.

WAYS TO THE "VOID"

It is difficult to achieve the state of mental "void" and at the same time maintain the condition of clear and active consciousness (as is required for our work), if one does not use—even if only provisionally and as aids—supports that substitute for what is offered by the body with its various faculties, which are the very foundation of consciousness and of the sense of "I" for the ordinary man.

These aids are the *symbols,* abstract forms that provide points of support for the effort of concentration, while not evoking any representation that would bring one back to those psychophysical determinisms that are to be neutralized by the condition of the "void."

Generally, it is only after having relied on the "body" of a symbol that the pure mental force can concentrate on itself alone and become truly free. It is hard for someone who aims directly at the "void" not to enter a state of diminished consciousness, or at least of the sense of the "I," because feeling himself without any formal foothold is not part of his habitual experience. There is a basic opposition between these two binomials: *consciousness-form* and *formless-unconsciousness.* It takes long and patient work to overcome it, in which the use of subtle and abstract forms, such as symbols, is of capital importance.

But for the symbols to be able to act as ways of awakening and communication, a further condition is needed: the capacity of *love*. This is not easy to explain: what could it mean to "love" a symbol? Yet it is simply comparable to the process of transmitting a living fire of the soul to a person, until it touches her, enwraps her, and in turn generates a feeling and a motion of the soul.

Therefore, one needs to form and *fabricate* a soul for the symbol with one's own soul and one's own warmth (one of the meanings of the mysterious "cooking" of the alchemists), and when the creature is complete, when the symbol is alive and not merely "represented"—it is then that a change of state may manifest: *another* force appears, which you feel is not yours and which adds to yours and bears it in the *right* direction, accelerating the rhythms up to a state of light and realization.

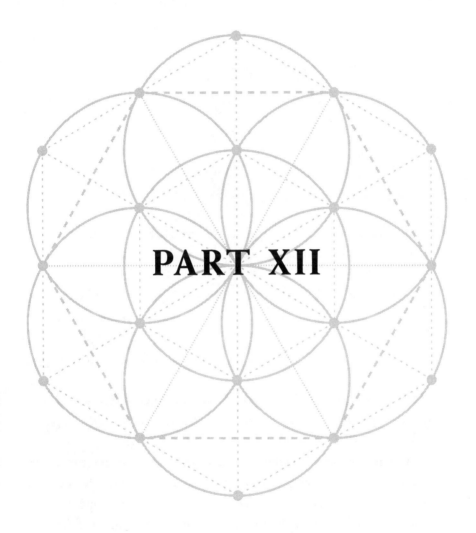

PART XII

XII.1

The "Great Sign"

On Stage and in the Wings[1]

At the end of 1913, signs began to appear that something *new* was summoning the forces of the Italic tradition. These signs were directly perceived by us.

In our "study," without anyone ever knowing how it could have got there, we found a sheet of paper. On it was sketched a route, a direction, a place. A route beyond modern Rome; a place where the presence of the ancient city survived, both in its name and in its silent and august remains.

Later indications received through one who then served us as intermediary between the bodiless and the embodied, confirmed the place, specified a mission, a date, and a person entrusted with it.

It was in the period sacred to the force that *raises* the sun in its annual course, after having touched the magical house of the Ram: in the period of the *Natalis Solis invicti* (birthday of the unconquered sun) and in a night of menacing and rainy weather. The route was followed. The place was found.

The fact that nobody noticed the unusual nocturnal expedition;

---

1. Narrative sent to us in 1929, which is published here simply as a document. [This enigmatic contribution is the subject of a recent book: Cristian Guzzo, *La Grande Orma: Anatomia di un mito* (Rome: Progetto Ouroboros, 2019). —*Trans.*]

that the person who guided us recalled nothing afterward; that no meeting occurred, and then that the grille of the archaic tomb was open and the guard absent—all that was naturally willed by "chance." A little scraping revealed a cavity in the wall. Inside there was a longish object.

Long hours were needed to remove the outer wrapping, resembling bitumen, hardened by centuries, which at last revealed what it had protected: a band and a scepter. On the band were written the signs of a ritual.

And the ritual was performed month after month, every night, without fail. And with astonishment we felt the coming of forces of war and forces of victory; and we saw shining in its light the ancient and august figures of the "Heroes" of the Roman race; and a "sign that cannot fail" was sealed by the bridge of solid stone that unknown men built for them in the deep silence of the night, day after day.

The horrendous war that broke out in 1914, unexpected by any others—we foresaw it. We knew its outcome. Both were seen in the place where things are before they become real. And we saw the potent act that an occult force willed from the mystery of a Roman tomb; and we possessed, and still possess, the brief regal symbol that would hermetically open to it the ways of the world of men.

• • •

1917. Various events. Then the collapse. Caporetto.[2]

A dawn. In the limpid Roman sky, above the sacred Capitoline Hill, the vision of an Eagle; and then, carried by its triumphant flight, two coruscating warrior figures: the Dioscuri.

A sense of greatness, of resurrection, of light.

In the midst of devastation by the tragic news of the Great War, this apparition gave us the hoped-for word: a triumphal announcement was already inscribed on the Italic calendar.

• • •

---

2. [Defeat of the Italian forces by the Austrians. —*Trans.*]

Later, in 1919. It "chanced" that the same forces, using the same person, communicated to him who now heads the Government—at the time, director of a Milanese newspaper—the announcement: *You will be Consul of Italy.*" It was likewise "chance" that the ritual form of augury was transmitted to him—the same as on the pontifical key: *"Quod bonum faustumque sit"* (May it be good and fortunate).

Later. After the March on Rome. An insignificant fact, an even more insignificant occasion. Among those who paid homage to the Head of Government, a person clothed in red came forward and handed him a Fasces. *The same forces willed that:* and they willed the exact number of rods, the way of cutting them, and the ritual binding of the red ribbon; and they also willed—once again—the "chance" that the ax for this Fasces should have been an archaic Etruscan ax, to which equally mysterious ways led us.[3]

• • •

Now a grand monument is being erected, in whose central niche will be placed the statue of archaic Rome. May this symbol return to life, in all its power! May its light blaze out again!

In a nearby street, a central one of the old city, which in the time of the Caesars corresponded to the place of the cult of Isis (and remains of Egyptian obelisks were found there), there stands a strange little edifice. All that interests us about it is this: as the adamantine certainty of resurgent Roman fortune, a sign was inserted and remains to this day: a sign that is at the same time a Hermetic symbol: *the crowned Phoenix arising from the flames.* Around the sign are these letters:

R. R. R.

I. A. T. C. P.

---

3. The fact was reported in a communication that can be found, for example, in the *Piccolo* of Rome, May 24, 1923, where one may read in detail about the fasces that was presented: "The bronze ax came from a two-thousand-year-old Etruscan tomb and has the sacred shape . . . Some similar examples are preserved in the Kircherian Museum. The *twelve* rods of birch, following the ritual prescription, are tied with bands of red leather, which make a loop at the top for suspending the fasces, as in the relief sculpture on the stairway of the Palazzo dei Conservatori on the Capitoline Hill.

EA

Esotericism, the Unconscious, Psychoanalysis

There is much talk these days about so-called psychoanalysis and its theories of the unconscious and the subconscious. All that, as regards its own field, has very little interest from our point of view. Originally it dealt with notions and theories shaped by neurologists and psychiatrists for the study and cure of their patients. But soon the tendency asserted itself (already started by Théodule Ribot) of claiming to shed light on the normal by way of the abnormal and the psychotic. Psychoanalysis then abandoned the therapeutic field in which it had been born, and where it may sometimes have been quite valid, and went on to a general interpretation of man and his psychic, moral, and spiritual life. Even after these developments, the phenomenon would not have been worth much attention: it would serve as one of many signs of the times, that is, of the current intellectual disorder. But recently it has gone further still: a spiritualizing variety of psychoanalysis has appeared, applying itself to things of the initiatic and esoteric order, with the pretension of introducing the "scientific" point of view to them and shedding a light that never existed before.

We are not sure whether to call such a pretension more grotesque or more infantile. But there it is: a species of academic freemasonry has now assigned itself the monopoly of the science, decreeing that any knowledge other than its own is inconceivable, and the common public lets itself be hoodwinked. In fact, all that it has managed to learn or admit in this field are the most elementary notions that the traditional sciences have known for centuries, even for millennia. How pitiful are those who need the "confirmation" and "discoveries" of these last-minute epigones to accept views that have been established for ages in a doctrinal system on very different foundations! They should be laughing off the "scientific" presumption of these latecomers who, lacking any true principle, set up suggestive and muddled, if not aberrant, theories, pretending to know more than any of their predecessors, who should have been their schoolmasters.

Back to the starting point: since there is so much talk about this, we will address some fundamental points concerning the subconscious. Then we will show in more detail what this current of psychoanalysis really is, which more than any other presumes to bring the "light of science" into the very world of esotericism and spirituality.

I. NATURE OF THE SUBCONSCIOUS

That not all of psychic life is illuminated by distinct consciousness; that consciousness admits degrees and zones of more or less deep shadow: these certainly did not wait till our day to be "discovered." But the misunderstanding arose as soon as the term *unconscious* was used and the attempt was made to distinguish between conscious and unconscious. The latter term should only be used to refer to contents of the soul, psychic processes and forces that are *absolutely* foreign to consciousness and in no case able to become conscious. The so-called "unconscious" can only correspond to forms of a *different* consciousness, more or less excluded from that of the individual I, or to contents already known that have become potentialities of consciousness. To talk of a "psychic unconscious" is nonsense, because the completely unconscious ceases to be psychic and becomes a simple synonym for matter, for the not-I. No less absurd and perverse is giving the "unconscious" a sort of personality, making it an autonomous entity vis-à-vis the conscious I, so as to splinter or compromise the fundamental unity of the being. Thus, one should only speak of "unconscious" in a relative sense; if a term has to be used it should be *subconscious*.

Given that, we will indicate the principal zones to be distinguished in the subconscious.

The shallowest layer consists of the individual subconscious in a strict sense, corresponding to the psychic contents of ordinary life that were once conscious and have since passed into the shadows, either naturally over time or through various individual actions of exclusion or removal. The world of memory is the most typical example. Things experienced or known and then "forgotten" have become subconscious: they have become psychic potentialities. We know that they can emerge suddenly and inexplicably. We also know that in special moments, like deathly peril, the recall of one's whole life can unfold, even in tiny details that one thought were forever obliterated.

Second, we should consider the zone of the historical and collective subconscious, concerning ideas and influences that, while forming part of the individual's life, derive from his belonging to a given community or race, regarding its present and also its past (the collective-ancestral and "historical" subconscious).

The third and deeper zone is the organic or phyletic subconscious, corresponding to those forces and impulses that are more or less common to all of humankind, referring to man as a general biological being beyond the differences of races and historical groups.

However, beside these three aspects the subconscious has others that evade profane research, because they belong to experiences and lines of heredity that are not materially identifiable. For example, the Eastern concept of *saṃskāra* refers to subconscious images and tendencies in the individual's soul that derive from other existences and other states of being. From the esoteric point of view, it is in forces of this kind that one finds the original cause of the I's having a given tangible heredity and a given current of individual experience. To offer an example, the analysis of a certain individual trait may lead to an element of the historical-collective subconscious and of the biological heredity. But if one wants to go on to explain this element, namely the ultimate reason for its presence in the psychic life of this individual, analysis has to take another track, and seek the answer in none other than the notion of *saṃskāra*.

Up to this point we are in the domain of the subconscious that can rightly be called samsaric, because it is attached to the current of becoming, whether individual or collective. Beyond that there is a subconscious that might be called cosmic-metaphysical, whose meaning may be given as follows. The esoteric doctrine of correspondence between the macrocosm and the microcosm, between that which is above and that which is below, that which is external and that which is internal, postulates the presence in man of the powers and principles that, in a wider sense, reside at the basis of manifestation. Between what they are in themselves and how they appear and act in man there is only a difference of modality and degree of consciousness. Thence comes the idea of a subconscious of the I that contains these presences and actually constitutes the differential between his finite consciousness and that of the supraindividual, transcendent I (the *ātmā* of Hindu metaphysics). Esoterically, man's experience of the body concretizes this differential, this subconscious zone that contains forces and modes of being falling outside a given individual consciousness, yet being an integral part of the I. Where this subconscious becomes transparent, certain limits and conditions of the individual fall away of themselves, beginning with the condition of space and consequently the limit between one I and another, and between the I and the not-I.

In short, this is the image one should form of the subconscious and its zones. As for the relations between conscious and unconscious, the correct principle is that consciousness can only come from consciousness, and the subconscious is always a silencing, neutralizing, obfuscation, or limitation of the conscious. It is the form taken by contents that originally belonged to the sphere of consciousness in general, whether individual, supraindividual, samsaric, or transcendental.

2. FREUDIAN PSYCHOANALYSIS

Coming now to the sort of psychoanalysis that is considered "orthodox"—in other words, that which follows the theories of Sigmund Freud—we will be very brief. Its chief characteristic is to make the subconscious (which it identifies with the unconscious) the essential part of the I, attributing to it every motive force of the personality and of conscious life. Obviously, this can only be the case in a completely degraded human type. As for the content of this subconscious, it is well known that for Freud it was almost exclusively sexual, involving "repressed" sexual impulses that are not recognized and accepted but inhibited by waking consciousness; impulses that in the form of "complexes" exert a more or less pathogenic action on the psychic life.

We do not need to describe the level to which views of this sort lead. The only thing to retain is the Freudian concept of the *libido,* which does not simply mean sex in general, but finds its most typical expression in sex and sexual pleasure. Libido is the pleasure of any identification, any contact, even if the object has no direct relation to a woman, but is a thing, an image, an idea, a sensation. For Freud, the subconscious feeds on libido. Putting this concept in its proper place, it corresponds to the esoteric notion of the "trunk of desire" that makes up the substratum of samsaric existence and of all the states in which an ordinary being's experience usually unfolds, unless the transformation of spiritual awakening intervenes. However, for all its claim to universality, the Freudian libido almost always gravitates around the plain fact of sex. The reference points for it and for the complexes deriving from it are the eroticism that is supposed to develop in infancy, and has an ancestral and collective origin going back to the life of savages, which is supposed to be at a similar infantile stage, and likewise essentially determined by sexual matters.[1] That is what Freudianism reduces the subconscious to. In practice, the suppression of inhibitions and "repressions," the recognition of this subconscious's impulses in order to allow them a direct or indirect satisfaction (through surrogates, transpositions, etc.) and give the libido a means to discharge itself—such is the "morality" that Freudianism has deduced from a method which, at best, can only be approved of as therapy in the case of the split and prostrated personality of certain hysterics and sexual psychopaths.

---

1. Here we can disregard a second main source that Freud went on to recognize beside the libido: the impulse toward death or destruction (*Todestrieb*). Moreover, there is another type of psychoanalysis (e.g., that of Wilhelm Reich) that has deduced it from the first, from repression of the libido.

3. JUNG'S COLLECTIVE UNCONSCIOUS

We now move on to the spiritualizing psychoanalysis whose chief exponent is the Swiss psychiatrist C. G. Jung. He has resolutely invaded the domain of myth, symbol, mysticism, and esotericism, and since his views are not so trivial as in Freudianism, some "spiritual" people have taken them seriously, to the point of supposing that they validate through the "scientific" point of view of modern psychology the views and teachings of ancient and Eastern wisdom. In reality, Jung's interpretations turn out to be a distortion and a degradation, and it is truly with deep displeasure that one sees this psychiatrist multiplying his writings and gaining a large audience. Not content with getting his hands on an esoteric Taoist text, *The Secret of the Golden Flower,* and commenting on the *Tibetan Book of the Dead,* Jung has joined a modern scholar of mythology, Karl Kerényi, who is not unqualified but has incomprehensibly entrusted him with the "scientific" interpretation of various classical myths. Finally, Jung has published a voluminous work on alchemy and another dedicated to the theories of Paracelsus, not to mention the works in which he has expounded the principles of his own psychoanalytic theory.

This theory, for all its surface improvements, is no different from Freud's in the points that are essential to us, namely the relation between conscious and unconscious. No less than Freud, Jung holds that the fundamental force of the human psyche is made from an unconscious that is radically so, which has never been conscious and cannot be resolved into consciousness.[2] This unconscious takes on the traits of an autonomous entity, collective in character,[3] which transcends the individual: it is a totality of which the conscious person is merely an arbitrary sub-

---

2. C. G. Jung and C. Kerényi, *Essays on a Science of Mythology,* trans. R. F. C. Hull (New York: Pantheon Books, 1949), 104: "[the archetypes] do not refer to anything that is or has been conscious, but to something *essentially unconscious.*" Italics original.
3. C. G. Jung, *Psychology and Alchemy,* trans. R. F. C. Hull, 2nd ed. (Princeton: Princeton University Press, 1968), 50: "to begin with, [modern man] can only understand the unconscious as an inessential and unreal appendage of the conscious mind, and not a special sphere of experience with laws of its own."

division. On the one hand, Jung insists on the impenetrability of this unconscious.[4] On the other hand, though he claims to be doing only science and psychology and keeping away from metaphysics, he takes the unconscious to be a species of mystical entity, more or less identified with "Life," with the "Irrational," with the "Dionysian" depths of existence as opposed to its clear, intellectual, and volitive side. In both cases there are references to a reality bound not only to the primitive ancestral soul (falsely called "archaic"), but also to the animal and biological heredity and to materiality.[5] With this we find ourselves on the same plane as evolutionism, for this unconscious does in fact appear more or less as a superstitious personification of the vital, irrational, and atavistic substratum of the human being, thus to the lowest and nature-bound level of the general subconscious, for all that Jung wants to put into it, as we shall see. He unhesitatingly holds that the conscious derives from the unconscious—which even for the most elementary philosophy is utter nonsense. For him it is an "arrogant claim" that consciousness comprises the whole soul, and an illusion to believe that consciousness arises of itself.[6]

Like Freud, Jung sees in the unconscious the very source of libido,

---

4. C. G. Jung, *Two Essays on Analytical Psychology,* trans. R. F. C. Hull, 2nd ed. (New York: Pantheon Books, 1966), 177: "'No mortal mind can plumb the depths of nature'— not even the depths of the unconscious."

5. Jung and Kerényi, *Essays on a Science of Mythology,* 127: "The deeper 'layers' of the psyche . . . become increasingly collective until they are universalized and extinguished in the body's materiality, i.e., in the chemical bodies." *Psychology and Alchemy,* 134: "The symbolism of the rites of renewal, if taken seriously, points far beyond the merely archaic and infantile to man's innate psychic disposition, which is the result and deposit of all ancestral life *right down to the animal level*" [italics by Ea. —*Trans.*]. *The Secret of the Golden Flower,* translated from Chinese into German by Richard Wilhelm, subsequently translated from German by Cary F. Baynes, with commentary by C. G. Jung (London: Routledge & Kegan Paul, 1962), 87: "[T]he fact of the collective unconscious is simply the psychic expression of the identity of brain-structure irrespective of all racial differences."

6. *Psychology and Alchemy,* 481, 433. *The Secret of the Golden Flower:* "Indubitably (!) consciousness originally proceeds from the unconscious." [Sourced to the German edition, p. 16, but not found on the equivalent page of the English edition. Possibly a paraphrase based on p. 87 of the latter. —*Trans.*]

from which the psychic elements flow into us, and says: "Nobody, of his own free will, can strip the unconscious of its effective power."[7] The only difference from Freud is that Jung mythicizes: he conceives of the libido also as *mana,* as the fascinating force that savages believe to fill certain objects. In every case, the soul is supposed to have its roots in this collective substratum and to draw all its life and every motor impulse from it. Hence the natural consequence that "the psyche is an irrational datum and cannot, in accordance with the old picture, be equated with a more or less divine Reason."[8] Is this not enough to confirm the level at which all this psychiatrist's thinking stands?

We move on to consider the possible relationships between the I[9] and the unconscious. Jung's whole work, like that of psychoanalysts in general, is marked by a polemical hostility to the personal consciousness. They suppose that it has no reality in itself, though it presumes to cut itself off from the unconscious, from "Life"; it denies the unconscious, refuses its demands, and thinks it can wield a dictatorship on the basis of the purely intellectual and volitive faculties, suffocating the instincts and feelings. But this is an impossible task: the unconscious is ever present and has its revenge on this type of person: it asserts itself in every case, pressing in various guises on consciousness and upsetting its illusory balance with irruptions and conflicts that can end up as neuroses, hysteria, and even insanity.

With such notions Jung more or less adopts the general views of psychoanalysis and of those irrationalists who, like Ludwig Klages, accuse the usurping and destructive "spirit" as the enemy of "life," and have attacked the crystalline ideal of consciousness.[10] In the last analysis this current can be traced back to Rousseau, because it is essentially a

---

7. Jung, *Two Essays,* 167.

8. Jung, *Two Essays,* 124.

9. [In both Italian and English psychological literature, Jung's *ich* is usually translated as "ego." However, as the present essay continues to use "l'Io," this is rendered consistently as "the I." —*Trans.*]

10. *Psychology and Alchemy,* 159: "The unconscious is . . . the painful lie given to all idealistic pronouncements, the earthliness that clings to our human nature and sadly clouds the crystal clarity we long for."

revindication of nature and instinct as the presumed basis of the healthy life, as opposed to the artificial and deviant life shaped by civilization. Thus, Jung declares that our whole spiritual life suffers from "violent repression of the instincts which hysterically exaggerates and poisons our spirituality."[11] He blames "a morality that destroys the human being" and urges us to "follow the law of the earth," to "live and recognize the instincts,"[12] as the premise for the development of the "Self," of which more below. But in this regard, Jung's original contribution consists of the theory of the so-called *archetypes*.

4. THE ARCHETYPES

The archetypes correspond to fundamental forces of the collective unconscious, hence also of the deep layers of the soul. They are elementary, psychic-vital energies ever present and organically united to the I, which is rooted in them.[13] And here comes the insertion, or, better, the irruption into the world of myth and symbol. As said above, the tendencies of the unconscious, though unknown, manifest in spite of all; but while the state of division persists, they manifest in *projections,* in fantastic images or images that superimpose themselves on reality, charging the things or persons in it with the fascinating and "libidinous" quality that belongs to the basal energy of the unconscious. Hence the theory of symbols and figures, variegated yet constant and, as Jung says, universal, corresponding to such projections. Given these assumptions, such manifestation of the archetypes would mainly happen in states of reduced or weakened consciousness. Thus, Jung started out with the material of dreams and the fantasies of psychotic and hysterical subjects (delirium, hallucinations, visions). He thought that this proved that the recurrent images had nothing individual or arbitrary about them, but had an atavistic and typical character and an exact correspondence

---

11. *The Secret of the Golden Flower,* 126.
12. *The Secret of the Golden Flower,* 89. [Only the first of the three expressions is found at the cited location. —*Trans.*]
13. Jung, *Two Essays,* 212–21 [but not evident there. —*Trans.*].

with myths, fairy tales, and popular and traditional symbolisms. All of that was supposed to contain "original revelations of the preconscious psyche, involuntary statements about unconscious psychic happenings."[14] Even the world of religion was understood in this sense, as "a vital link with psychic processes independent of and beyond consciousness, in the dark hinterland of the psyche."[15] As if that were not enough, Jung asserted that the figures that his patients saw, dreamed, drew, and even danced corresponded to certain esoteric symbols. Thus, he started talking about "European *mandalas*," seeing in figures that serve in esotericism for contemplation and evocation just so many manifestations of the archetypes of the collective unconscious, exactly like those produced in states of diminished or morbid consciousness. The more the field of the conscious principle is barred, the more the unconscious forces and their images appear as if they exist outside the individual, even as spirits and magic powers. There are cases in which the manifestation of the archetype has an obsessive character. The conscious personality that cannot discern its nature can be overwhelmed and lose its equilibrium. Then the archetype takes possession of the soul. Jung sometimes goes so far as to consider the archetypes, the contents of the unconscious, as "psychic entities," "numina" fearful to behold,[16] and writes: "to let the unconscious go its own way and to experience it as a reality is something that exceeds the courage and capacity of the average European. He prefers simply not to understand this problem. For the spiritually weak-kneed this is the better course, since the thing is not without its dangers."[17]

However, all that the archetypes want in ordinary life is for the conscious person to recognize the vital unconscious, accept its contents, and, incorporating them in its individual life, "integrate" itself with them. Jung calls this development the *individuation process*. The final stage would be the "integral personality" that includes both con-

---

14. Jung and Kerényi, *Essays on a Science of Mythology*, 101.
15. Jung and Kerényi, *Essays on a Science of Mythology*, 102.
16. Jung, *Psychology and Alchemy*, 183.
17. Jung, *Psychology and Alchemy*, 52.

scious and unconscious and is called the "Self" (*das Selbst*). Jung has no doubt that all mystical and initiatic developments are only more or less confused forms of the "individuation process" (because "scientific clarity," understanding in terms of positive psychology and not cloudy metaphysics, only arrived with his psychoanalysis). For example, all the alchemical procedures with their Hermetic symbols are taken as images of this process, not recognized at their proper level but projected onto material substances and onto the myth of an absurd work of chemical transmutation.[18] The same is said of the initiatic processes treated in the Taoist mystery of the "Golden Flower." In general, figures like those of the Buddha or Christ are nothing but "projections" of the unconscious, and specifically of the archetype of the "Self," the endpoint to which the process of individuation leads.[19] Nonetheless, the basic principle of psychoanalysis is that until the archetype presents itself in "projections," that is, in images or external representations, it remains unconscious and its real contents are inactive, as is the force that, through it, wants to be recognized by the conscious personality in order to transform it. Then the "images" are accepted and "realized." One should become conscious of them by letting them possess one, accepting the solicitation that they embody, which only then ceases to act as an autonomous unconscious complex. This is the criterion by which Jungian psychiatry pretends to evaluate, in terms of life and true consciousness, the dogmas, divine figures, and symbols of religions. It presents itself as a sort of psychologistic esotericism (if you will pardon the expression) even regarding initiatic traditions, as it discovers everywhere alleged "archetypes," symbols, and phases of the "individuation process."

Before saying more about this process, let us bring a little order into this impossible mess of ideas. First, we will trace a firm line of

---

18. Jung, *Psychology and Alchemy*, 34. Jung does not doubt for a moment that when the alchemical work referred to real bodies and procedures, it led nowhere and was finally supplanted by modern chemistry; see *Psychology and Alchemy*, 37. On p. 239 he writes: "it is certain beyond all doubt (!) that no real tincture or artificial gold was ever produced during the many centuries of earnest endeavour," the whole attempt having been "portentously futile."

19. Jung, *Psychology and Alchemy*, 18.

demarcation. The whole world of an I that is divided and sick, in the grip of its "complexes," its instincts, and the collective unconscious, has no relation whatever to the plane of mythology, traditional symbols, the processes of supranormal realization, nor even that of religion. Psychiatrists like Freud or Adler are much more acceptable than Jung, because they deal essentially with empirical cases that may well be real, with repressed sexual impulses and the like, keeping to a naturalistic and commonplace plane. And though Freud, and even more his disciples like Silberer (who found such equilibrium in psychoanalysis that he ended in suicide), touched on the world of symbols, the aberrant quality of their sexual interpretations leaps to the eye of any normal person, precisely because these interpretations do not cloud the issue and remain visibly in the world of neuropaths, savages, and beings in whom the libido really is the chief motive of all their psychic life. Jung, however, while essentially staying on the same plane—since, as we have seen, his unconscious is simply the subpersonal, vital, and even partly biological substratum of the collective life—brings in "spiritual" elements of every sort, exacerbating the confusion and providing a new opportunity and a more subtle method of reducing the higher to the lower.

As for the "archetypes," in the great majority of cases one should consider as totally accidental and irrelevant any correspondence between traditional symbols and myths and motives occuring in dreams, visions, or the delusions of psychopaths. As for the "archaic" heredity, here too Jung has no idea what is in question and no capacity for discrimination. True, such heredity can be made from irrational and vital impulses, but the symbols and myths in question have very little to do with that sphere. They do not figure in primitive life as "projections" from the unconscious psyche, but only as degraded remnants and twilight or nocturnal echoes of realities of quite another plane: it is only as residues that they appear as centers of crystallization for irrational forces. Psychoanalytic interpretation casually puts on the same level the reports of ethnologists, which concern the primitive psyche, and what belongs to the great spiritual traditions; we have seen that even in religious dogmas Jung sees only the effects of processes of the unconscious psyche. This is pure nonsense. Everything to do with traditional symbols and myths originally belonged to a plane of *supraconsciousness,* referring not to the vital, collective, and irrational substratum, but to metaphysical reality: to what the ancients called the "world above," and with precise reference to its luminous and "Olympian" nature, the "intelligible world," κόσμος νοητός. The ancients' plain opposition between this world and the "demonic" or "infernal" world should have taught Jung something!

In any case, if the whole of psychoanalytic theory is really pure psychologism, with the "archetypes" one is only dealing with varieties of human psychology, individual or collective as the case may be. What we have called the "metaphysical subconscious" does not enter into it, while the true character of the archetypes, if they refer to traditional symbols, is a metaphysical and nonhuman one, just as their origin is nonhuman. They are *signatures* of the integral being of man, which as such reflects the powers of the cosmos and of the "world above."

It is evident that "integration" as Jung understands it on the basis of *his* archetypes, is nothing but a caricature of the process of initiatic integration. The difference can be put in a few clear words: the entire psychoanalytic procedure is valid, *in the most favorable hypothesis,* for restoring a split and neuropathic human type to normality and health; the initiatic process, instead, starts from a normal and sane human type, to lead him beyond the human condition. It has as its point of departure what for psychoanalysis is the point of arrival, and a hard enough goal to attain, given the "subjects" with which it deals.

5. JUNG'S "MORALITY"

A particularly outlandish point in Jung is his attribution of a sort of compulsory character to the "individuation process." Certainly, one can imagine the libido and the unconscious, collective complexes impinging on the psychic life of certain human types, and prevailing in one way or another, whether or not the conscious I wills it. But it is absurd to think of the processes as passive and unconscious when the realization of the "integral personality" is in question, which is strictly equivalent to superseding human nature with suprahuman nature.

A realization of this kind, linked not to the unconscious but to a highly potentized consciousness, cannot possibly relate to what Jung calls the "Self." First of all, the practical direction of any initiatic discipline and high ascesis is the diametrical opposite of the psychoanalytic method. On the one hand, the latter is intended to favor reduced states of consciousness that allow the unconscious contents the greatest freedom to flower in images, visions, or associations. Such states remove the inhibition with which individual consciousness opposes the unconscious, because it finds most of its contents disagreeable and disturbing. This is essentially the method that Jung calls "active imagination," though we may well ask why "active," when in Jung's own words it "is based on a deliberate reduction of consciousness"![20] On the other hand we must consider the general psychoanalytic morality that exhorts one to abandon oneself to "Life," and "accept the law of the Earth," taking on all the demands of the emotional, instinctive, and obscure part of one's own soul. It does not take special erudition to know that any introductory discipline for higher realization is based, instead, on an extreme potentialization of consciousness, a detachment from the instinctive life and a complete mastery of it. It takes a Jungian incomprehension to suppose that this relaxation and capitulation of the conscious personality, which are the essence of his method, could have anything to do with the notion of the Tao, for example, which is explicitly identified with the "Way of Heaven" and refers to a transcendent spontaneity. Thus, in the Taoist text that he claims to "illuminate" psychoanalytically, Jung treats as nonexistent the precise injunction to "concentration," to submission to the "celestial heart" of the "inferior heart" tied to the world and to desires, like a rebel general who must be brought back to obedience to his rightful sovereign; to the domination and "distillation" of the obscure and feminine part of the soul, to transform it into

---

20. Jung and Kerényi, *Essays on a Science of Mythology*, 228: "active imagination" is a "method . . . of introspection, namely the observation of the stream of interior images: one concentrates one's attention on some impressive but unintelligible dream-image, or on a spontaneous visual impression, and observes the changes taking place in it." "Under these conditions, long and often very dramatic series of fantasies ensue," also visions, inner dialogues, and so forth. "[I]n the not infrequent case of latent schizophrenia the method may . . . prove extremely dangerous."

pure *yang* (the masculine principle).[21] Holding on to one's own desires, neglecting the "fixation of the light," leads not to "the repose and void in the heart" and the Tao, but along the "downward path."[22] In reality, the sense of expansion that a split or rigidified individual feels if he ceases to resist, if he "opens up" and abandons himself—that a more or less neuropathic type feels when he succeeds in accommodating his personal problems with his instincts, his unconfessed thoughts, and the unconscious part of his soul—all this Jung mistakes for the sentiment of detachment and liberation found in states of high ascesis or pure initiatic intellectuality. Continuing with reference to Taoism, Jung wants to appropriate the formula of "return to the origins" as if the presuppositions were the same. According to every traditional view, the origin of the conscious principle is a luminous force from above; according to Jung, it is the irrational collective unconscious, by definition impenetrable. It is easy to see what the "return to the origins" can signify in this second context: not integration and "individuation," but regression.

6. THE "INDIVIDUATION PROCESS"

Let us take the trouble to look more closely into how the "individuation process" unfolds. It is a matter of gathering, recognizing, and "realizing" a series of archetypes presented in dream and similar states, either spontaneously or with help. The first seems to be that of the *Child,* who represents "the preconscious childhood aspect of the collective soul"[23] and whose unconscious content is the impulse to reestablish contact with that state. Next comes the archetype of the *Woman.* Here we meet the

---

21. *The Secret of the Golden Flower.* [Sourced to the German edition, "pp. 123ff." The actual words are not found in the English edition; the closest expressions are on 54–55, 64–65. —*Trans.*]

22. The reader may refer to the interpretation of this same Taoist text in *Introduction to Magic,* vol. II, 379–94, where among other things it is mentioned that the psychoanalytical method of "active imagination" corresponds to conditions against which the text explicitly warns, because they lead to the "ten thousand ensnarements" and the "world of the demons."

23. Jung and Kerényi, *Essays on a Science of Mythology,* 134. [What appears to be the corresponding phrase in the English edition reads "the pre-conscious and the post-conscious nature of man." —*Trans.*]

theory of the anima[24] juxtaposed to the animus. In a man, the conscious principle or personal I takes on virile traits, ignoring, repressing, or tyrannizing the feminine aspect of his own being, which is precisely the soul (*anima* in Latin) linked to the unconscious and emotional forces of the deepest psychic layers. But this inhibited part of the personal consciousness wants to be of equal value, and in various ways compensates or confronts the one-sidedness of the animus or masculine I. Such is the action of the archetype of the "Woman," a hereditary image that is "projected" in various forms: now identified with the figure of the mother or sister, now with the beloved lady, but always saturating the real being with an enchanting force or *mana,* belonging to the unconscious ancestral archetype.[25] Naturally, in mythology, dreams, and legends the figures of Goddesses, Divine Mothers, the Virgin, "She who must be obeyed," and so on, refer to this process of irruption from the unconscious. Likewise, in symbols and traditional figures of the androgynous type, what wishes to affirm itself unconsciously is the image of the fusion of animus with anima, of the masculine part of one's being with the unconscious feminine and irrational part. According to Jung, this is what the *Mysterium coniunctionis* (mystery of conjunction) spoken of in esotericism and Hermetism is positively reduced to.

But this subterranean part, this anima, while it keeps its autonomous, antithetical character, also has the archetypal symbols of a demon, a hostile and fearful force, Dragon, Serpent, and so forth. Here begins a new stage of the "individuation process," which may be a phase of crisis.[26] But once the anima is recognized and accepted, the archetype loses its character as an autonomous complex, the corresponding images

---

24. [Throughout this work, the Italian *anima* is translated as "soul." However, when the author italicizes the word to distinguish it as a Jungian term, I use the English equivalent of "anima." —*Trans.*]

25. Jung, *Two Essays,* 188–98.

26. Jung, *Two Essays,* 161. A breakdown of normal equilibrium and a "renunciation of one's dearest illusions" may be necessary for consciousness to be able to grasp and absorb the contents produced by the unconscious, and reach a new equilibrium. *Two Essays,* 163: The collapse of the persona "always feels like the end of the world, as though everything had tumbled back into original chaos." Naturally it is on this basis that Jung believes he can interpret the symbols of initiatic death, dissolution and renovation, and so forth.

are depotentized, lose their *mana* and their enchanting power. The obsession they exercise ceases and the conscious principle then realizes the figure of him who has vanquished the demon. But there is no more to that than the effect of a new archetype erupting, the so-called *mana-personality*. This is an atavistic, archaic, and collective image such as the Man-God, the Hero, the Magus, the Saint, the divine Chief, the "man of power." It is also connected to the "father complex" as imagined in Freudian psychoanalysis. So, a new obsession starts. "[T]he 'magician' [i.e., the contents of the new archetype] could take possession of the ego only because the ego dreamed of victory over the anima. That dream was an encroachment, and every encroachment of the ego is followed by an encroachment from the unconscious."[27] But if instead the I gives up its pretense to victory, the power of the father complex also ceases automatically, like that of the mother (the "Woman" archetype). By recognizing the archaic content, the "mana-personality" that had one in its power dissolves and one returns to oneself.[28]

The final archetype is the one that expresses the "Self," already mentioned. The desire for God, the impulse to divinification and all the divine and superhuman figures of religion proceed from the power of this ultimate archetype, and should be explained by the relevant process of the collective unconscious. The various symbols characterized by the "center," the "European mandalas" and suchlike signs in dreams and visions, have the same significance. However, the substance of this final archetype, once revealed by psychoanalysis and no longer seen in "projections," is as confused as one can possibly imagine. Jung speaks here of a state in which the center of personality no longer coincides with the I, "and instead is located in a hypothetical point between the conscious and the unconscious."[29] The Self (*Selbst*) is described as "something irrational, an indefinable existent, to which the ego is neither opposed nor subjected, but merely attached, and about which it revolves . . . a transcendental postulate which, although justifiable psychologically,

---

27. Jung, *Two Essays*, 229.
28. Jung, *Two Essays*, 237.
29. *The Secret of the Golden Flower*, 124; Jung, *Two Essays*, 221.

does not allow of scientific proof."[30] And this despite the fact that the unconscious, to which one has been opened, is supposed to be henceforth integrated into consciousness. "The Self," says Jung, "has as little to do with the I as the sun with the earth." At this point "the individuated I feels itself as the object of an unknown and superior subject," a feeling that Jung believes can actually be related to the words of Saint Paul: "Not I live, but Christ lives in me"—only that the "Christ," the "God in us," would be the collective unconscious with everything it contains, deducible in its universality (as we have seen) from the "identity of the structure of the human brain"![31] At any rate, the "Self" remains and will always remain a unity and an entity supraordinate to the conscious I.[32] This situation is considered as "the ultimate stage to which psychological observation can reach," and at the same time the conclusion of the whole "individuation process."

This is certainly not the place for a criticism of this ballet of more or less pathological images that Jung offers as the key to understanding mystical and initiatic experience, if only because some of the figures and themes would appear as the most banal and disorderly collection of dreams, deliriums, and digressions. To tell the truth, with a little optimism and ingenuity one can draw all one wants from material of this sort and "discover" the phases of the "individuation process" everywhere, on the pretext that images of it appear, no matter how banal.

Nonetheless, there is one significant point regarding the strange theory of the "mana-personality." Jung indicates that in the ideal of the virile personality, master of the irrational part of his own being and endowed with nonhuman powers, he sees nothing but the expression of a pathological form, due to the revival and irruption of a primitive and ancestral "archetype," more or less like the Freudian theory of the "superego," which is also attributed to a form of "autistic" hysteria.

The mystical finale may go beyond the level of the sensations of

---

30. Jung, *Two Essays*, 240. [Evola renders the last phrase as "an unknowable being that surpasses our faculty of comprehension." —*Trans.*]

31. *The Secret of the Golden Flower*, 132.

32. Jung, *Two Essays*, 177.

sufferers finally freed from their troubles, but there cannot be the least analogy with anything concerning metaphysical and initiatic realizations: these are well known to have the characteristics of *identity* and *centrality*. Instead, at the end of what should have been a process of integration, dualism remains: the I gravitates around an unknowable "something" that is supraordinate to it, in the relation of subject to its object. All in all, haven't we gone back to the starting point, except that all the resistances and inhibitions have been abolished?

Jung's references to Eastern metaphysics, Hindu or Taoist, are truly absurd. The *ātmā* or Tao as a principle that stands beyond every pair of contraries—thus also beyond the conscious as a finite consciousness, and that which falls outside it—has not the slightest resemblance to the Self as thought up by Jung. The former always remains transcendent experience and light, not the oscillating of the I between conscious and unconscious: an unconscious that, as we know, remains impenetrable and supraordinate to the I even at the final stage.

We can say in general that Jung does not offer a "psychological interpretation" of metaphysics, but stays in a domain that from beginning to end is merely psychology, and even when the "collective" is concerned does not cease to be simply human. The *ātmā* of Hinduism is one with Brahman, the principle and basis of all manifestation, just as the Tao in the Far Eastern tradition is conceived of as the supreme reality, from which both Heaven and Earth derive their being. Everything referring to it, therefore, has a character that is not "psychological" but that of transcendent experience. Jung, since he cannot avoid taking account of it, tries to get out of it by saying that "it would do a great injury" to such metaphysical teachings if one were to take them literally, and if one saw the Easterners as anything other than "psychologists expressing themselves through symbols." And he adds: "If it were really metaphysics that they mean, it would be useless to try to understand them."[33] And in fact Jung has not understood anything, and has been handling things with which he should never have concerned himself.

We might also mention here that the process of "projection" is well

---

33. *The Secret of the Golden Flower,* 129.

known in esoteric and especially magical traditions, in the specific sense of the appearance in images or visions of psychic contents and forces and principles that, in the last analysis, are always part of the I's nature, even if not immediately recognized as such. Jung could have realized this when dealing with the *Tibetan Book of the Dead*. He could have seen from this text (even if it did not need a psychoanalyst to formulate it) the eminently initiatic principle of *killing* the projections upon recognizing them and realizing their content. So there is nothing new there for us. The fact remains that for Jung and psychoanalysts in general the subconscious is a sack into which one indiscriminately stuffs all sorts of things, from the lowly contents of the biological and collective subconscious up to what may relate to a real and true supraconscious. And because the psychoanalytic method is the most primitive imaginable, consisting of "opening" and looking inside—the result is naturally a witches' sabbath, a confused and chaotic regurgitation that no psychoanalytic effort can put to rights. Things are different on the initiatic path, for reasons already given, thanks to the preliminary disciplines aimed at neutralizing the "infernal" regions of the subconscious, and preventing their detritus from diverting, obscuring, or tainting the manifestation and conscious realization of supraindividual and suprahuman contents.

As for the advisability of not inhibiting this or that instinct—in the lowest sense of the word, as in the sphere of moralism and virtue—because it could cause poisoning or deviation in the life of the soul, that is a "private" matter which, in any case, concerns elementary levels and has nothing to do with the tasks and experiences of high ascesis. One can allow recognition of the "laws of the earth" in the sense of the healthy equilibrium of the classical ideal, and one may consider some forms of Christian asceticism as pathological, obsessed with carnal and sexual matters. But it is a very different matter to proclaim a religion of the irrational and unconscious part of one's own being, and to reduce the I to something with no life of its own that gravitates around it and is supposed to recognize it as its native soil. At any rate, in this particular point the psychic hygiene of the divided men of this civilization is one thing, the order of spiritual values another, whereas psychoanalysis obviously confuses them and does not hesitate to subordinate the latter to the former—to "hygiene" and to eliminating "disturbances" in individuals who for that very reason are unqualified for anything else.

It follows from its own premises that the whole imaginary "individuation process" cannot have anything but a psychological significance. What else could one expect to get from a method that consists of nothing but observing dreams and fantasies, or provoking them deliberately through states of reduced consciousness, then blathering about them, not so much because one lacks principles as because one has the wrong ones? The psychoanalytic way and the initiatic way of exploring the deep layers of the I are as far apart as heaven from earth. We will repeat that the latter has nothing to do with a psychotherapeutic process, because it starts out with a sane and normal person, in good order as to the forces on which the sense of his I rests, in the human state of existence. Second, the true goal of the initiatic path is the realization as *supraconscious* of what is called the cosmic-metaphysical subconscious. To achieve it, we have said that rather than opening oneself to the atavastic, collective unconscious, one must free oneself from it and neutralize it, because it is the very "guardian of the threshold," the force that blocks the vision, prevents awakening and the participation in that higher world, to which the true notion of archetype refers. Meanwhile dreams, fantasies, delirious images, subjective or collective imaginations should be taken for what they are: a sphere lacking any higher significance and hence no secret to anybody.

Once all this is recognized, the scope of Jung's theories is sufficiently clear and the conclusion obvious. Anyone today who thinks that such psychoanalysis can provide any "scientific" interpretation of initiatic concepts or any spiritual processes whatever needs to be convinced that he has not even begun to understand these and is totally "off track."

Jung has written: "Modern man must therefore consider himself fortunate not to have come up against Eastern ideas until his own spiritual impoverishment was so far gone that he did not even notice what he was coming up against. He can now deal with the East on the quite adequate and therefore innocuous level of the intellect, or else leave the whole matter to Sanskrit specialists."[34] This is exactly what we would say about Jung himself, but in a wider sense: it is fortunate that this psychiatrist understood nothing, and could only see extensions of pathological experiences and psychotherapies whenever he came upon the vestiges of Wisdom and the Art.

---

34. *Psychology and Alchemy,* 355.

ANAGARIKA GOVINDA

The Double Mask

He had a dream – you ask "who?"
It doesn't matter – someone.
Perhaps it was you – one day you dreamed this dream.
He stood on a sacred hill – crowned by a temple,
And looked down, toward the plain – and saw people
Coming up – in a long, winding procession.
They wore fluttering garments – and bore strange masks
On reaching the summit – they bowed toward the
*   sanctuary,*
After having worshiped in silence – they went to the
*   opposite part.*
It was then that he noticed – that they were wearing
*   two masks,*
Whereby it seemed – that they were withdrawing
With the face turned to the sanctuary.
The air was full of incense – when he entered the
*   Temple.*
Having crossed three atria – the atrium of Devotion
At whose center burned the sacred flame;
The atrium of Just Conduct – which contained the tables
*   of the Law*
And the atrium of Meditation – where the fountain of
*   clear knowledge*

Quenches the seeker's thirst – he finally reached the
  Holy of Holies:
And suddenly found himself – between the images of
  two divinities.
Not being able to bow towards one – without turning
  his back on the other
He left in confusion.
While he was retracing his steps – a priest approached
  him
Who had in his hands two masks – and told him to put
  them on.
He did so – and when he reentered
The Holy of Holies – it was empty.

Magical Perspectives,
According to Aleister Crowley

In the English magical theater of today, Aleister Crowley is a leading player. In the common view he belongs to the "blackest" and even satanic side, an appearance that he himself fostered by calling himself "The Great Beast 666." But in reality, this was largely a front: the fact is simply that Crowley followed the "Left-Hand Path," for which he was extraordinarily qualified. His life was many-sided and complex: he was a poet, a painter, a student of natural sciences, an explorer, an alpinist (including two climbs in the Himalayas); he was in contact with secret organizations of every kind, and it is also said that he had an occult part in some recent political movements. He practiced ceremonial and evocatory magic, and by that very method, in Cairo, he is said to have transmitted from an entity called Aiwass a sort of revelation, or a new law, which he christened the "Law of Thelema" and made himself its preacher. Its cornerstones are the two maxims: "Every man is a star," and "Do what you will: that shall be thy supreme law."[1] By thus formulating the second maxim, Crowley, as was his wont, wanted to *épater le bourgeois* (shock the bourgeois), because the real meaning of it is not to indulge in unbridled license, but to exclude

---

1. [I translate these maxims literally from the Italian. Crowley's own wording was: "Every man and every woman is a star," and "Do what thou wilt shall be the whole of the law." —*Trans.*]

any external and extraneous law in favor of that deeper will, on the basis of which every man appears as the manifestation of a force from above (of a "star"). In practice, Crowley's magic was similar to the tantric type: sexual magic and the use of drugs played a large part in it. It is said that several of his disciples ended in insanity or suicide (the two possibilities that always haunt the "direct path"); but he himself died in 1947 at the age of seventy-two, in full possession of his faculties.

The passages that we reproduce here belong to the *Liber Aleph, the Book of Wisdom or Folly,* which at present (1953) exists only in manuscript.[2] Despite a certain syncretism and a somewhat extravagant style, the reader will easily find elements here of the traditional magical discipline. The few notes are by the translator.[3]

DE ARTE MENTIS COLLIGENDAE
(ON THE ART OF COLLECTING THE MIND)

1. Mathematica (Mathematics) [Aτ, 47][4]

Now, concerning the first Foundation of thy Mind I will say somewhat. Thou shalt study with Diligence in the Mathematics, because thereby shall be revealed unto thee the Laws of thine own Reason and the Limitations thereof. This Science manifesteth unto thee thy true Nature in respect of the Machinery whereby it worketh, and showeth in pure Nakedness, without Clothing of Personality or Desire, the Anatomy of thy conscious Self. Furthermore, by this thou mayst understand the Essence of the Relation between all Things, and the Nature of Necessity, and come to the Knowledge of Form. For this Mathematics is as it were the last Veil before the Image of Truth, so that there is no Way better than our Holy Qabalah, which analyseth all Things soever,

---

2. [*Liber Aleph* appears to have been written around 1918 and first published in 1962 by Thelema Publishing Co., West Point, California. These excerpts follow the second edition, edited by Hymenaeus Beta (York Beach, Me.: Weiser, 1991). —*Trans.*]

3. [I.e., the translator of Crowley's English into Italian, presumably Evola himself. —*Trans.*]

4. [Crowley's text is numbered with Greek letters (including the archaic letters ϙ Koppa and ϝ Digamma), given here in brackets with the regular numbering. —*Trans.*]

and reduceth them to pure Number; and thus their Natures being no longer coloured and confused, they may be regulated and formulated in Simplicity by the Operation of Pure Reason, to thy great Comfort in the Work of our Transcendental Art, whereby the Many become One.

2. Classica (Classics) [Aυ, 48]

My son, neglect not in any wise the Study of the Writings of Antiquity, and that in the original Language. For by this thou shalt discover the History of the Structure of thy Mind, that is, its Nature regarded as the last term in a Sequence of Causes and Effects. For thy Mind hath been built up of these Elements, so that in these Books thou mayst bring into the Light thine own subconscious Memories. And thy Memory is as it were the Mortar in the House of thy Mind, without which is no Cohesion or Individuality possible, so that the Lack thereof is called Dementia. And these Books have lived long and become famous because they are the Fruits of ancient Trees whereof thou art directly the Heir, wherefore (say I) they are more truly germane to thine own Nature than Books of Collateral Offshoots, though such were in themselves better and wiser. Yea, o my Son, in these Writings thou mayst study to come to the true Comprehension of thine own Nature, and that of the whole Universe, in the Dimension of Time, even as the Mathematic declareth it in that of Space: that is, of Extension. Moreover, by this Study shall the Child comprehend the Foundation of Manners: the which, as sayeth one of the Sons of Wisdom, maketh Man.

3. Scientifica (Science) [Aφ, 49]

Since Time and Space are the Conditions of Mind, these two Studies are fundamental. Yet there remaineth Causality, which is the Root of the Actions and Reactions of Nature. This also shalt thou seek ardently, that thou mayst comprehend the Variety of the Universe, its Harmony and its Beauty, with the Knowledge of that which compelleth it. Yet this is not equal to the former two in Power to reveal thee to thy Self; and its first Use is to instruct thee in the true Method of Advancement in Knowledge, which is, fundamentally, the Observation of the Like and the Unlike. Also, it shall arouse in thee the Ecstasy of Wonder; and it shall bring thee to a proper Understanding of Art Magick. For our Magick is but one of the powers that lie within us undeveloped and unanalysed; and it is by the Method of Science that it must be made clear, and available to the Use of Man. Is not this a Gift beyond Price, the Fruit of a Tree not only of knowledge but of Life? For there is that in Man which is God, and there is that also which is Dust; and by our Magick we shall make these twain one Flesh, to the Obtaining of the Empery of the Universe.

DE VIRTUTE AUDENDI
(ON THE VIRTUE OF DARING) [Aσ, 46]

Yet this I charge thee with my Might: Live Dangerously. Was not this the Word of thine Uncle Friedrich Nietzsche?[5] Thy meanest Foe is the Inertia of the Mind. Men do hate most those things which touch them closely, and they fear Light, and persecute the Torchbearers. Do thou therefore analyse most fully all those Ideas which Men avoid; for the Truth shall dissolve Fear. Rightly indeed Men say that the Unknown is terrible; but wrongly do they fear lest it become the Known. Moreover, do thou all Acts of which the common Sort beware, save where thou hast already full knowledge, that thou mayest learn Use and Control, not falling into Abuse and Slavery. For the Coward and the Foolhardy shall not live out their Days. Every Thing has its right Use; and thou art great as thou hast Use of Things. This is the Mystery of all Art Magick, and thine Hold upon the Universe. Yet if thou must err, being human, err by excess of courage rather than of Caution, for it is the Foundation of the Honour of Man that he dareth greatly. What sayth Quintus Horatius Flaccus in the third Ode of his First Book? Die thou standing!

DE CLAVICULA SOMNIORUM
(OF THE KEY OF DREAMS) [π, 17]

And now concerning Meditation let me disclose unto thee more fully the Mystery of the Key of Dreams and Phantasies. Learn first that as

---

5. [Sentence omitted in the Italian. —*Trans.*]

the Thought of the Mind standeth before the Soul and hindereth its Manifestation in consciousness, so also the gross physical Will is the Creator of the Dreams of common Men. And as in Meditation thou doest destroy every Thought by mating it with its Opposite, so must thou cleanse thyself by a full and perfect Satisfaction of that bodily will in the Way of Chastity and Holiness which has been revealed unto thee in thine Initiation. This inner Silence of the Body being attained, it may be that the true Will may speak in True Dreams; for it is written that He giveth unto His Beloved in Sleep. Prepare thyself therefore in this Way, as a good Knight should do.

DE SOMNO LUCIDO
(ON LUCID SLEEP) [ϙ, 18]

Now know this also, that at the End of that secret Way lieth a Garden wherein is a Rest House prepared for thee. For to him whose physical Needs (of whatever Kind) are not truly satisfied cometh a Lunar or physical Sleep appointed to refresh and recreate by Cleansing and Repose; but on him that is bodily pure the Lord bestoweth a solar or lucid Sleep, wherein move Images of pure Light fashioned by the True Will. And this is called by the Qabalists the Sleep of Shiloam, and of this doeth also Porphyry make mention, and Cicero, with many other Wise Men of Old Time. Compare, o my Son, with this Doctrine that which was taught thee in the Sanctuary of the Gnosis concerning the Death of the Righteous; and learn moreover that these are but particular Cases of an Universal Formula.

DE VIA INERTIAE
(ON THE WAY OF INERTIA) [Aγ, 29]

Of the Way of the Tao I have already written to thee, o my Son, but I further instruct thee in this Doctrine of doing Everything by doing Nothing. I will first have thee to understand that the Universe being as above said an Expression of Zero under the Figure of the Dyad, its Tendency is continually to release itself from that strain by the Marriage of Opposites whenever they are brought into Contact. Thus thy true Nature is a Will to Zero, or an Inertia, or Doing Nothing; and the Way of Doing Nothing is to oppose no Obstacle to the free Function of that true Nature. Consider the Electrical Charge of a Cloud, whose Will is to discharge itself in Earth, and so release the Strain of its Potential. Do this by free Conduction, there is Silence and Darkness; oppose it, there is Heat and Light, and the Rending asunder of that which will not permit free Passage to the Current.

DE VIA LIBERTATIS
(ON THE WAY OF LIBERTY) [Aδ, 30]

Do not think then that by Non-action thou dost follow the Way of the Tao, for thy Nature is Action, and by hindering the Discharge of thy Potential thou doest perpetuate and aggravate the Stress. If thou ease not Nature, she will bring thee to Dis-ease. Free therefore every Function of thy Body and of every other Part of thee according to its True Will. This also is most necessary, that thou discover that true Will in every Case, for thou art born into Dis-ease; where are many false and perverted Wills, monstrous Growths, Parasites, Vermin are they, adherent to thee by Vice of Heredity, or of Environment or of evil Training. And of all these Things the subtlest and most terrible, Enemies without Pity, destructive to thy will, and a Menace and Tyranny even to thy Self, are the Ideals and Standards of the Slave-Gods, false Religion, false Ethics, even false Science.

DE MOTU VITAE
(ON THE MOTION OF LIFE) [σ, 20]

Learn then, o my Son, that all Phenomena are the Effect of Conflict, even as the Universe itself is a Nothing expressed as the Difference of two Equalities, or, an thou wilt, as the Divorce of Nuit and Hadit.[6] So

---

6. Nuith and Hadith, in the terminology used by Crowley with a certain reference to the ancient Egyptian tradition, are the cosmic Feminine and Masculine; they are the Dyad, and above them is the "null" or Zero, equivalent to the "void" (śūnya) of Mahayanic Buddhism.

therefore every Marriage dissolveth a more material, and createth a less material Complex; and this is our Way of Love, rising ever from Ecstasy to Ecstasy. So then all high Violence, that is to say, all Consciousness, is the spiritual Orgasm of a Passion between two lower and grosser Opposites.[7] Thus Light and Heat result from the Marriage of Hydrogen and Oxygen; Love from that of Man and Woman, Dhyana or Ecstasy from that of the Ego and the non-Ego.

But be thou well grounded in this Thesis corollary, that one or two such Marriages do but destroy for a Time the Exacerbation of any Complex; to deracinate such is a Work of long Habit and deep Search in Darkness for the Germ thereof. But this once accomplished, that particular Complex is destroyed, or sublimated for ever.

DE MORBIS SANGUINIS
(ON DISEASES OF THE BLOOD) [τ, 21]

Now then understand that all Opposition to the Way of Nature createth Violence. If thine excretory System do its Function not at its fullest, there come Poisons in the Blood, and the Consciousness is modified by the Conflicts or Marriages between the Elements heterogeneous. Thus if the Liver be not efficient, we have Melancholy; if the Kidneys, Coma; if the Testes or Ovaries, loss of Personality itself. Also, an we poison the Blood directly with Belladonna, we have Delirium vehement and furious; with Hashish, Visions phantastic and enormous; with Anhalonium, Ecstasy of Colour and whatnot; with divers Germs of Disease, Disturbances of Consciousness varying with the Nature of the Germ. Also, with Ether, we gain the Power of analysing the Consciousness into its Planes and even of discovering the hidden Will and Judgment upon any Question; and so for many others.

But all these are, in our mystical Sense, Poisons; that is, we take two Things diverse and opposite, binding them together so that they are

---

7. [The Italian reads *una passione fra due opposti, fra un principio debole e un principio forte*: "a passion between two opposites, a weak principle and a strong principle." —*Trans.*]

compelled to unite; *and the Orgasm of each Marriage is an Ecstasy, the lower dissolving in the higher.*[8]

DE SAPIENTIA IN RE SEXUALI
(ON WISDOM IN SEXUAL MATTERS) [Aϙ, 44]

Consider Love. Here is a Force destructive and corrupting whereby many Men have been lost. Yet without Love Man were not Man.[9] Therefore thine Uncle Richard Wagner made of our Doctrine a musical Fable, wherein we see Amfortas, who yielded himself to Seduction, wounded beyond Healing; Klingsor, who withdrew himself from a like Danger, cast out for ever from the Mountain of Salvation; and Parsifal, who yielded not, able to exercise the true Power of Love, and thereby to perform the Miracle of Redemption. Of this also have I myself written in my Poema called *Adonis*. It is the same with Food and Drink, with Exercise, with Learning itself; the Problem is ever to bring the Appetite into right Relation with the Will. Thus thou mayst fast or feast; there is no Rule, but that of Balance. And this Doctrine is of general Acceptation among the better sort of Men; therefore on thee will I rather impress more carefully the other Part of my Wisdom, namely, the Necessity of extending constantly thy Nature to new Mates upon every Plane of Being, so that thou mayst become the perfect Microcosm, an Image without Flaw of all that is.

DE CURSU AMORIS
(ON THE WAY OF LOVE) [ʋ, 22]

I continue then, o my Son, and reiterate that this Formula is general to all Nature. And thou wilt note that by repeated Marriage cometh Toleration, so that Ecstasy appeareth no more. Thus his half grain of Morphia, which at first opened the Gates of Heaven, is nothing worth to the Self-poisoner after a Year of daily Practice. So too the Lover fin-

---

8. Our italics: this phrase comprises the key of the magic of poisons, or "corrosive waters."
9. [The Italian omits the passage from here through "Poema called Adonis." —*Trans.*]

deth no more Joy in Union with his Mistress, so soon as the original Attraction between them is satisfied by repeated Conjunctions. For this Attraction is an Antagonism; and the greater the Antinomy, the more fierce the Puissance of the Magnetism, and the Quantity of Energy disengaged by the Coition. Thus in the Union of Similars, as of Halogens with each other, is no strong Passion or explosive Force; and the Love between two Persons of like Character and Taste is placid and without Transmutation to higher Planes.

DE NUPTIIS MYSTICIS
(ON THE MYSTIC MARRIAGE) [φ, 23]

O my Son, how wonderful is the Wisdom of this Law of Love! How vast are the Oceans of uncharted Joy that lie before the Keel of thy Ship! Yet know this, that every Opposition is in its Nature named Sorrow, and the Joy lieth in the Destruction of the Dyad. Therefore, must thou seek ever those Things which are to thee poisonous, and that in the highest Degree, and make them thine by Love. That which repels, that which disgusts, must thou assimilate in this Way of Wholeness. Yet rest not in the Joy of the Destruction of each complex in thy Nature, but press on to that ultimate Marriage with the Universe whose Consummation shall destroy thee utterly, leaving only that Nothingness which was before the Beginning.

So then the Life of Non-action is not for thee; the Withdrawal from Activity is not the Way of the Tao; but rather the Intensification and making universal every Unit of thine Energy on every Plane.

ULTIMA THESIS DE AMORE
(FINAL THESIS ON LOVE) [ϝ, 6]

Therefore, o my Son, be thou wary, not bowing before the false Idols and ideals, yet not flaming forth in Fury against them, unless that be thy Will.

But in this Matter be prudent and be silent, discerning subtly and with Acumen the Nature of the Will within thee; so that thou mistake not Fear for Chastity, or Anger for Courage. And since the Fetters are old and heavy, and thy Limbs withered and distorted by reason of their Compulsion, do thou, having broken them, walk gently for a little while, until the ancient Elasticity return, so that thou mayst walk, run, and leap naturally and with Rejoicing. Also, since these Fetters are as a Bond almost universal, be instant to declare the Law of Liberty, and the full Knowledge of all Truth that appertaineth to this Matter;[10] for if in this only thou overcome, then shall all Earth be free, taking its Pleasure in Sunlight without Fear or Phrenzy. Amen.

DE TAURO
(ON THE BULL) [Eφ, 153]

Concerning the Bull, this is thy Will, constant and unwearied, whose Letter is Vau, which is Six, the Number of the Sun. He is therefore the Force and the Substance of thy Being; but, besides this, he is the Hierophant in the Taro,[11] as if this were said: that thy Will leadeth thee unto the Shrine of Light. And in the Rites of Mithras the Bull is slain, and his Blood poured upon the Initiate, to endow him with that Will and that Power of Work. Also in the land of Hind is the Bull sacred to Shiva, that is God among that Folk, and is unto them the Destroyer of all Things [that be opposed to Him[12]]. And this God is also the Phallus, for this Will operateth through Love, even as it is written in our Own Law. Yet again, Apis the Bull of Khem hath Kephra the Beetle upon His tongue, which signifieth that it is by this Will, and by this Work, that the Sun cometh unto Dawn from Midnight. All these Symbols are most similar in their Nature, save as the Slaves of the Slave-gods have read their own Formula into the Simplicity of Truth. For there is naught so plain that Ignorance and Malice may not confuse and misinterpret it, even as the Bat is dazzled and bewildered by the Light of the

---

10. [The Italian version of this section concludes here. —*Trans.*]

11. [The Italian has *Toro*, bull, rather than Taro = Tarot. —*Trans.*]

12. [Phrase absent from the second edition of *Liber Aleph,* but present in the first and in the Italian. —*Trans.*]

Sun. See then that thou understand this Bull in Terms of the Law of this our Æon of Life.

DE LEONE (ON THE LION) [Eχ, 154]

Of this Lion, o my Son, be it said that this is the Courage of thy Manhood, leaping upon all Things, and seizing them for thy Prey. His letter is Teth, whose Implication is a Serpent, and the Number thereof Nine, whereof is Aub, the secret Fire of Obeah. Also Nine is of Jesod, uniting Change with Stability. But in *The Book of Thoth* He is the Atu called Strength, whose Number is ELEVEN[13] which is Aud, the Light Odic of Magick. And therein is figured the Lion, even THE BEAST and Our Lady BABALON astride of Him, that with her Thighs She may strangle Him.[14] Here I would have thee to mark well how these our Symbols are cognate, and flow forth the one into the other, because each Soul partaketh in proper Measure of the Mystery of Holiness, and is kin with his Fellow. But now let me shew how this Lion of Courage is more especially the Light in thee, as Leo is the House of the Sun that is the Father of Light. And it is thus: that thy Light, conscious of itself, is the Source and Instigator of thy Will, enforcing it to spring forth and conquer. Therefore also is his Nature strong with Hardihood and Lust of Battle, else shouldst thou fear that which is unlike thee, and avoid it, so that thy Separateness should increase upon thee. For this Cause he that is defective in Courage becometh a Black Brother, and To Dare is the Crown of all thy Virtue, the Root of the Tree of true Magick.

ALTERA DE LEONE (FURTHER ON THE LION) [Eψ, 155]

Lo! In the First of thine Initiations, when First the Hoodwink was uplifted from before thine Eyes, thou wast brought unto the Throne

---

13. [The Italian text has *dodici* (twelve) here. —*Trans.*]

14. [From "astride" to the end of the sentence, the Italian text substitutes *con le mani sulla sua bocca, per dominarlo* (with her hands on his mouth to dominate him). —*Trans.*]

of Horus, the Lord of the Lion, and by Him enheartened against Fear. Moreover, in Minutum Mundum, the Map of the Universe, it is the Path of the Lion that bindeth the two Highest Faculties of thy Mind. Again, it is Mau, the Sun at Brightness of High Noon, that is called the Lion, very lordly, in our Holy Invocation. Sekhet our Lady is figured as a Lioness, for that She is that Lust of Nuit toward Hadit which is the Fierceness of the Night of the Stars, and their Necessity; whence also is She true Symbol of thine own Hunger of Attainment, the Passion of thy Light to dare all for its Fulfilling. It is then the Possession of this Quality which determineth thy Manhood; for without it thou art not impelled to Magick, and thy Will is but the Slave's Endurance and Patience under the Lash. For this Cause, the Bull being of Osiris, was it necessary for the Masters of the Æons to incarnate me[15] as (more especially) a Lion, and my Word is first of all a Word of Enlightenment and of Emancipation of the Will, giving to every Man a Spring within Himself to determine His Will, that he may do that Will, and no more another's. Arise therefore, o my Son, arm thyself, haste to the Battle!

DE VIRO (ON THE MAN) [Eω, 156]

Learn now that this Lion is a natural Quality in Man, and secret, so that he is not ware thereof, except he be Adept. Therefore is it necessary for thee also To Know, by the Head of thy Sphinx. This then is thy Liberty, that the Impulse of the Lion should become conscious by means of the Man; for without this thou art but an Automaton. This Man moreover maketh thee to understand and to adjust thyself with thine Environment, else, being devoid of Judgment, thou goest blindly upon an Headlong Path. For every Star in his Orbit holdeth not his Way obstinately, but is sensitive to every other Star, and his true Nature is to do this. O Son, how many are they whom I have seen persisting in a fatal Course, in Sway of the Belief that their dead Rigidity was Exercise of Will. And the Letter of the Man is Tzaddi, whose Number

---

15. [The Italian text has *necessario presentarlo più specialmente nell'incarnazione*, i.e., "to incarnate it" or "him," rather than "me." —*Trans.*]

is Ninety, which is Maim,[16] the Water that conformeth itself perfectly with its Vessel, that seeketh constantly its Level, that penetrateth and dissolveth Earth, that resisteth Pressure maugre its Adaptability, that being heated is the Force to drive great Engines, and being frozen breaketh the Mountains in Pieces. O my Son, seek well To Know!

---

16. [The Italian text omits the previous three words. —*Trans.*]

Envoi

Now that the task that the Ur Group set itself in organizing this collection of essays is virtually done, it is time to say a few words of farewell to those who have followed us up to now.

We have been addressing the few whom a higher vocation renders unsatisfied by the values and accomplishments of ordinary human life, in order to give them a sense of the paths, the truths, and the horizons of what is called the initiatic or the secret tradition. We have precisely drawn the frontier that separates these disciplines from the "spiritualist" and occultist forms, sources of mystification and often run by charlatans, which currently enjoy an epidemic of diffusion among a mindless and dilettantish public. We have explained what should be thought of psychoanalysis and metapsychology, recent concoctions that have made such an impression on provincials of the spirit. At the same time we have denounced all confusion of initiatic reality with the fields of competence of profane science, and with the world of mysticism, morality, and religion. Consequently, our main concern has been to give out a body of teachings relating above all to practice and to realization, corroborating them with accounts of real, lived experiences, as well as traditional texts and references, varied but always converging in a single direction. Compared to other attitudes even within the initiatic domain, this is a direction that gives special importance to concepts of freedom, of power, and of spiritual virility.

In the three volumes of these essays we have communicated whatever we could, following the task mentioned. We have not set up any "occult" scenery, and have spoken with sufficient clarity not to deceive anyone with sensational promises or with the mysterious ceremonial that seems obligatory to many who are hawking the by-products of esotericism and yoga today. As for what we have offered, each will use it as he thinks best, and according to his qualification and interest. Enough reference points have been given to the discerning reader for going a good distance on his own, in study or in practice; and with a certain variety, intended to suit individual inclinations. If anyone wants to know more, it would be difficult to find it in any written exposition.

In the practical domain, we have often mentioned that the conditions of the present epoch, whether collective or for the individual, are more unfavorable than ever for a transcendent development of the I, and that each one is left more or less to himself, at least for a good way on the path. He will soon be discouraged if not endowed with a calm firmness and a subtle energy; if he seeks confirmations and results that are direct and tangible; or if, insufficiently serious about his vocation, he creates illusions. On the other hand, it is certain that one who has had the sense of transcendent reality, even if only for a glimpse, can never efface it. "The Dragon's bite never scars over." Something will have taken form in his soul that will subsist, even without his being distinctly conscious of it and despite all upsets, from which he will always be able to draw strength to wait, to persist, to resume, to dare.

Another source of perseverance can be the idea that, however vast the distance, one is known and awaited by those on the other shore. Just as some sounds from the valley travel with strange clarity to the mountain peaks, every right intention is perceived. From the second manifesto of the Rosicrucians comes the idea that "thoughts, joined to the real will of the reader, are capable of making us known to him and him to us."[17] The same text also speaks of belonging to an initiatic chain, which has nothing to do with joining visible and named organizations or "societies"; it is not granted by ceremonies, but *in fact,* even without

---

17. [A paraphrase from Chapter 6 of the *Confessio Fraternitatis R.C. ad eruditos Europae,* 1615. —*Trans.*]

knowing it, when the right will is present and one is on the way of right realization.

Another point also needs emphasis under today's conditions, when sects are proliferating and a herd instinct is asserting itself everywhere. One should mistrust everything that has any exterior character, and all who pretend to be able to provide what only an exceptional internal action can achieve, thanks to the fire of consciousness and of concentration. In all cases you should be sincere—to the point of being pitiless—in examining what you really want: because otherwise, if there is an inner untruthfulness, right action is not possible. But if you are truly aiming at initiatic-magical realization, remember unfeignedly the ancient saying: the way to it is like "walking on the edge of a sword." That is why it may be better to give up an enterprise that exceeds your own strength than to play with vain substitutes.

At the end of our task, it has been necessary to repeat all this frankly. It is not our business to try to satisfy anyone's weakness or illusions. We have not been talking to infants, but to mature and serious people. Now that we have cleared the ground sufficiently and, we hope, contributed a necessary work of clarification, it remains for each one, once he has taken due measure of himself, to make appropriate use of what has been expounded up to now. And may such use be auspicious to him: that is our best wish—from the *Gruppo di Ur.*

Index

Page numbers in *italics* refer to illustrations.

BOOKS OF RELATED INTEREST

Introduction to Magic, Volume I
Rituals and Practical Techniques for the Magus
by Julius Evola and The UR Group

Introduction to Magic, Volume II
The Path of Initiatic Wisdom
by Julius Evola and The UR Group

Revolt Against the Modern World
Politics, Religion, and Social Order in the Kali Yuga
by Julius Evola

Ride the Tiger
A Survival Manual for the Aristocrats of the Soul
by Julius Evola

Men Among the Ruins
Post-War Reflections of a Radical Traditionalist
by Julius Evola

The Hermetic Tradition
Symbols and Teachings of the Royal Art
by Julius Evola

The Doctrine of Awakening
The Attainment of Self-Mastery According to
the Earliest Buddhist Texts
by Julius Evola

Julius Evola
The Philosopher and Magician in War: 1943–1945
by Gianfranco de Turris

INNER TRADITIONS • BEAR & COMPANY
P.O. Box 388
Rochester, VT 05767
1-800-246-8648
www.InnerTraditions.com

Or contact your local bookseller